George Gale

Upper Mississippi

Or, historical sketches of the mound-builders, the Indian tribes and the progress of civilization in the North-west, from A.D. 1600 to the present time

George Gale

Upper Mississippi
Or, historical sketches of the mound-builders, the Indian tribes and the progress of civilization in the North-west, from A.D. 1600 to the present time

ISBN/EAN: 9783337096939

Printed in Europe, USA, Canada, Australia, Japan

Cover: Foto ©ninafisch / pixelio.de

More available books at **www.hansebooks.com**

UPPER MISSISSIPPI:

OR,

HISTORICAL SKETCHES

OF

THE MOUND-BUILDERS, THE INDIAN TRIBES,

AND THE

PROGRESS OF CIVILIZATION

IN THE

NORTH-WEST;

FROM A.D. 1600 TO THE PRESENT TIME.

BY GEORGE GALE.

CHICAGO:
CLARKE AND COMPANY.
NEW YORK:
OAKLEY AND MASON.
1867.

Entered according to Act of Congress, in the year 1867,
BY GEORGE GALE,
In the Clerk's Office of the District Court for the Northern District of Illinois.

WESTERN
BOOK MANUFACTURING CO.,
CHICAGO.

PREFACE.

THAT portion of the United States to which the following pages are chiefly devoted, was known to the old French traders and settlers as "upper Louisiana," and included the country above the mouth of the Ohio river. That region is now generally called in the West by the name of the "upper Mississippi." The inhabitants of our Atlantic States generally spoke of this territory as "the country north-west of the Ohio river," which name they finally abbreviated to the "North-west;" and were understood by that name to include all the country in the United States extending west from the foot of Lake Erie and the Ohio river to the Rocky mountains.

This region was first explored and occupied by French traders and Catholic missionaries from Canada, and was but little known to the English until after the surrender of Canada in 1760, by which the English became possessed of the French trading-posts; but the Pontiac war, which soon followed, implicated many of the French traders and missionaries in the conspiracy against the English, and led to their expulsion from the country; and the long wars which followed soon after in Europe had the effect to lock up the early authentic history of the North-west in the archives of the French government. Many of these documents, however, have lately been copied, by the permission of the French officials, and published by the authority of the legislatures of New York and some other States; and valuable information touching this history has thus lately been brought to the knowlege of our inhabitants. But as this mass of facts, together with the explorations of the early French travelers and missionaries, are not collated and condensed so as to be of value to the mass of the people, the writer has attentively examined these volumes, with the American histories, and the laws and documents of the United States and of the several States, and thus collected the leading incidents in the history of the north-west; to which he has added his own knowledge of events derived from a residence in the country of over twenty-six years.

In handling this mass of facts, the writer has endeavored to group together the kindred subjects for perspicuity, and by condensation to bring them into as small a compass as practicable, leaving mainly to the reader to make his own speculations on the motives of the actors, and draw his own philosophical conclusions. In this manner he has attempted to bring to light the extinct race of people called the "Mound-Builders," locate the north-western Indian tribes, and trace their wars with each other, and their connection with the "French and Indian" wars of the colonies, and their wars against the United States; marking their emigrations, and detailing the efforts of the whites to Christianize and civilize them; follow the tides of white emigrations, noting the organization of territorial and State governments, and other institutions; describe the physical character of the Mississippi, and the great lakes, and giving the progress of their navigation and commerce; mark the building of canals, railroads, telegraphs, and other works of internal improvement; and give statistics of the general advancement of civilization.

While the writer has not taken the space for the citation of authorities, he has made a special effort to gather the data from the most original and authentic sources.

It is not supposed that a work of this kind will be likely to beguile the devotee of pleasure; but the writer believes that it will be found acceptable and useful, not only to the student of history, but the statesman and merchant, and a welcome companion in all private libraries. With this hope it is presented to the public by

THE AUTHOR.

GALESVILLE, *Wisconsin, September*, 1867.

CONTENTS.

CHAPTER I.
The Mound-Builders 11

CHAPTER II.
The Indian Tribes, from their discovery to 1755 . . . 41

CHAPTER III.
The Indian Tribes, from 1755 to the close of the Pontiac war in 1764 68

CHAPTER IV.
The Indian Tribes, from 1764 to the close of the war with Great Britain in 1815 91

CHAPTER V.
The Catholic Missions 114

CHAPTER VI.
The Protestant Missions 135

CHAPTER VII.
The Iroquois, Hurons, Delawares, and Mohegans . . . 159

CHAPTER VIII.

The Illinois Confederacy 172

CHAPTER IX.

The Winnebago Confederacy 182

CHAPTER X.

The Winnebago Confederacy (concluded) 194

CHAPTER XI.

Dakota, or Sioux Confederacy 224

CHAPTER XII.

The Sioux Massacre 245

CHAPTER XIII.

The Chippeway Confederacy 265

CHAPTER XIV.

The Sacs, Foxes, and Potowatomies; and a table of the population of all the tribes in the United States in 1866 . . 291

CHAPTER XV.

The States of Ohio, Indiana, Illinois, and Michigan . . 320

CHAPTER XVI.

The State of Wisconsin 340

CHAPTER XVII.

The States of Missouri, Iowa, Minnesota, Kansas, and Nebraska; and territories of Dakota, Colorado, and Montana, 367

CHAPTER XVIII.

The Mississippi, and its Navigation 388

CHAPTER XIX.

The Great Lakes, and their Navigation 415

CHAPTER XX.

Canals, Railroads, Telegraph Lines, and Commerce . . 433

CONCLUSION 449

THE UPPER MISSISSIPPI.

CHAPTER I.

THE MOUND-BUILDERS.

A POET has mournfully declared that "Greece lies slumbering in the tomb;" but, from the perpetuity of her works of art, the imagination still hears the voice of Pythagoras, the founder of Philosophy, arguing his various speculative theories; Herodotus discoursing on the history of Egypt and surrounding nations; Xenophon detailing the exploits of Cyrus and the "ten thousand Greeks;" Plato preaching of the "transmigration of souls;" while Socrates proclaims the soul's immortality; and Homer sings of the beauty of Helen, and of the bravery of Hector and of Achilles.

But to us of the New World, there is a "Greece" that, literally, "slumbers in the tomb." A nation or people, which for centuries occupied a territory nearly as large as all Europe, and had a population which probably numbered its millions, have left the graves of their fathers and the temples of their gods so unceremoniously, that their very name has disappeared with them; and we only know of their existence by their decayed walls and tumuli, and by their bones, exhibiting the human form, although in a far-gone state of decay. No written language, or hieroglyphic, tells us the thoughts of their philosophers, the philippics of their orators, the heroic exploits of their warriors, nor of the beauty or chastity of their Helens. The rude tempests of ages have swept over their country, unmindful of their former power, while the dusky savage pursues the chase and the war-path, heedless of the sanctity of the ground on which he treads.

To this lost people the antiquarian has applied the name of "The Mound-Builders," as descriptive of an unknown people. It is proposed in this chapter to overhaul the relics of the Mound-Builders, and present to the reader the facts, with observations and deductions, relating to this interesting and ancient race of people.

In calculating the extent of the territory of the Mound-Builders, we assume that all the territory in the region round about the clusters of mounds, was the territory of this people, without hazarding an opinion that their territory extended any further. They may have occupied extensive regions of country where they did not choose to make monuments, and there may be extensive regions where these monuments exist, but we have as yet no trace or record of them.

It is possible that they may have had the same customs of the modern Indian tribes, of carrying their dead to certain general localities for interment. The *Dakotas*, at the time of the visit of Captain Carver to that tribe, in 1766, had a common burying ground a short distance above St. Paul, Minnesota; and at a later day, one instance, at least, is known of a Dakota squaw carrying on her back, in a blanket, her deceased husband from Lake Pepin to St. Paul, a distance of nearly one hundred miles. The same custom was prevalent two hundred years since, according to the Jesuit missionaries, from the Chippewas of Lake Superior to the Abenakis of the Penobscot in Maine.

So far as explorations now extend, the chief territory of the Mound-Builders is the Mississippi Valley, including the territory along the Atlantic and Gulf, from North Carolina to Texas; and along the southern shores of the great lakes, from the St. Lawrence river, to the Fond du Lac of Lake Superior. As these mounds have been found quite numerous at the Bute Prairies, in Oregon, and along the Gila and

Colorado rivers of California, we may with safety claim nearly the whole of the United States and her territories as within their jurisdiction. This gave them as fine and rich a country of its extent, as the world can produce.

The chief capital, or seat of this magnificent empire, was probably along the valley of the Ohio river, in the State of Ohio, judging from the elaborate extent of their works in that region. They, like the Iroquois, probably called that river the Ohio, or *Beautiful* river.

One of the first points for our consideration, in examining into the condition of an unknown people, is to ascertain their intellectual capacity. Fortunately for us, on this point, Dr. Morton, of Philadelphia, has devoted considerable attention, and, in his "Crania Americana," has given a number of specimens of skulls taken from the mounds, to which the writer, in the following table, has added a skull taken from a mound in Racine, Wisconsin, as given by Mr. Lapham:

Table of Cranial Development.

	Grave Creek.	Tenn.	Racine.	Sciota.
Longitudinal diameter	6.6 in.	6.6 in.	6.8 in.	6.5 in.
Inter-parietal	6.	5.6	5.3	6.
Vertical	5 deg.	5.6		6.2
Frontal		4.1		4.5
Inter-mastoid arch		15.2		16.
" line		4.4		4.5
Occipito-frontal arch		14.	13.8	13.8
Horizontal periphery		19.5		19.8
Facial angle	78 deg.	80 deg.	76 deg.	81 deg.
Internal capacity		80 inch.		90 inch.

According to Dr. Morton, the mean internal capacity of the skulls of the different races of people are as follows: Ethiopian, 78 cubic inches; Malay, 81; American Indians, 82; Mongolians, 83; Mound-Builders, 85; and Caucasian, 87.

Dr. Morton, from his investigations, came to the conclusion that there is a great similarity in the *cranial* development of the Mound-Builders, the Mexicans, Peruvians, and all the modern tribes of Indians, and that they all differ materially from the races on the eastern continent.

As no mummy of the Mound-Builder has been found in full, we have no positive information of the form or appearance of the face and body. The *crania* gives a moderate intellectual development; the teeth and jaw-bones show only a fullness about the mouth: the pipe sculptures represent the usual varieties of countenances, with rather a fullness of face, and, occasionally, the Roman nose; while the bones of the body indicate, says Messrs. Squier and Davis, "a massiveness, and seem to have been less projecting than those pertaining to the skeletons of a later day."

From a man-shaped mound opened at Galesville, Wisconsin, in 1860, by Drs. Young and Johnson, and the writer, there were obtained pieces of the crushed skull, upper jaw and teeth, the left side of the lower jaw and teeth, both thigh bones entire, one shin bone, and many others of less importance.

The thigh bones were eighteen and three-fourths inches in length, and three and three-eighths inches in their smallest circumference; and the shin bone was fourteen inches in length, and three and one-fourth inches in smallest circumference. From these measurements they inferred that the man was about five feet and ten inches in height, and strongly built; and from the decayed condition of some of the teeth, perhaps from fifty to sixty years of age at the time of his decease. His skull varied from three-sixteenths to one-fourth inch in thickness; his jaws were round and full, but not distorted; and his teeth were of the usual number and variety of the white race. These bones are now preserved in the museum of the "Upper Mississippi Historical Society" at Galesville.

That the Mound-Builders were very numerous, can not admit of a doubt, from the great extent of their territory and the magnitude of their earth-works. In the State of

Ohio alone, it has been estimated that there are 10,000 mounds and 1,500 inclosures. At Bute Prairies, in Oregon, according to the narrative of the "United States Exploring Expedition," there are "many thousands in number."

According to the surveys in Wisconsin, there have been examined about 100 near Racine, 100 near Milwaukee, about 100 near Big Bend on the lower Fox river, about 100 at Waukesha, about 100 near Fort Atkinson, 100 near Summit, 200 near Madison, 100 near Horricon, 100 near Mayville, 100 near Bartlett's landing in Vernon county, 100 at Prairie du Chien, 200 in La Crosse valley, and large numbers in the region of the Blue Mounds, along the Wisconsin river, the Fox river of Green bay, and Lake Winnebago. They have been noticed along most of the creeks and rivers of the State, and new investigations are continually bringing them to light. The writer has also noticed nearly 500 in the southern part of the county of Trempealeau, which are of greater variety than in any other one locality in the State. It is safe to say, that probably 10,000 mounds have already been noticed in Wisconsin.

Mr. Lapham, in his "Antiquities of Wisconsin," page 79, remarks that "it is believed that no works of any considerable extent exist above this point (La Crosse) on the Mississippi." As large numbers of these works exist at the first village above La Crosse, called La Crescent, in Minnesota, only three miles from La Crosse, and in the county of Trempealeau, twenty miles above, in Wisconsin, we are strongly cautioned against harboring the idea that all the works of the Mound-Builders have already been discovered. It is probable that nearly all the States and territories included within the empire of the Mound-Builders, on full examination, will be found to contain as many works of this people as the States of Ohio and Wisconsin.

Many of these works are of gigantic proportions. The mound near Miamisburgh, Montgomery county, Ohio, contains 311,353 cubic feet; one at the mouth of Grave creek,

Virginia, is 70 feet high and 1,000 feet in circumference; one at Cahokia, Illinois, is 90 feet high and over 2,000 feet in circumference, containing over twenty million cubic feet of earth; while the mound at Selserstown, Mississippi, covers an area of six acres.

The embankment inclosures are also of great extent, and some times include four hundred acres of ground. One near the Miami river has upwards of four miles of embankments, and only incloses about one hundred acres. The group of works at the mouth of the Sciota river has an aggregate of at least twenty miles of embankments, but only incloses about two hundred acres.

In estimating population from the number of earth-works for graves, we may be justified in calculating that monuments were only erected to the men who had distinguished themselves among their fellows; for such have been the customs of the world.

In the *Æneid*, VI., 232, it is said of the tomb of the Trojan Hector:

"On it Æneas piously heaped
A mighty mound sepulchral. The oar, the trumpet,
Arms of the man, the airy summit crowned."

The dying Anglo-Saxon poet, Beowulf, enjoins his friends to

"Command the famous in war
To make a mound,
Bright after the funereal fire,
Upon the nose of the promontory,
Which shall, for a memorial
To my people,
Rise high aloft
On Heonesness;
That the sea-sailors
May afterwards call it
Beowulf's barrow,
When the Brentings
Over the darkness of the floods
Shall sail afar."—*Beowulf*, V. 5599.

Even our modern Indians occasionally throw together piles of stones over some of their distinguished men; two such piles having been observed back of Red Wing, Minnesota; but probably fifty such piles do not exist in the Mississippi valley.

We must further take under consideration the fact, that the Mound-Builders had but few of the aids of civilization for such works, and must have appropriated a large amount of time to prepare their food and clothing, and to seasons of relaxation and merriment. We must, also, make allowance for the sick and indolent, the soldiers, merchants, mechanics, priests, and officials, according to the regulations of semi-barbarous nations.

From these data, may we not safely estimate that the Mound-Builders, in the height of their glory, had as great a population within their territory as existed in the same territory of the white population in 1850.

By referring to the census of that year, we find accredited to the

Mississippi valley	8,641,754
Pacific slope	117,271
Gulf	1,702,992
Great Lakes, say	1,537,983
Total,	12,000,000

It might be urged against this estimate, that we, in 1850, had more populous cities within the territory than the Mound-Builders; but that excess might be balanced by the large number of Mound-Builders between the Mississippi and the Pacific, where, in 1850, the white population was comparatively sparse.

Involved with the question of population, is the fact, were the Mound-Builders an agricultural people? On this subject, Mr. Gallatin, of New York, in speaking of the mound at Grave creek, remarked:

"It indicates not only a dense agricultural population, but

also a state of society essentially different from that of the modern race of Indians north of the tropic.

"There is not, and there was not in the sixteenth century, a single tribe of Indians (north of the semi-civilized nations) between the Atlantic and the Pacific, which had means of subsistence sufficient to enable them to apply, for such purposes, the unproductive labor necessary for the work; nor was there any in such a social state as to compel the labor of the people to be thus applied."

Egypt is celebrated for her pyramids; but she was also equally celebrated for her dense population, and the extent of her granaries. The nomadic tribes of the old world have never been celebrated for elaborate monuments, and have never lived in walled cities; while all the nations of the East which dwelt in inclosed cities and built elaborate works, were agriculturalists.

The fact that the Mound-Builders built such extensive earth-works, is quite conclusive evidence that they were not only familiar with digging the earth, but that this was their principal employment.

They were evidently great smokers; and if they smoked tobacco, they probably procured it by cultivation as did the modern Indians, who not only cultivated tobacco, but also corn, peas, beans, gourds, and melons, when they were first discovered by the Europeans.

Our *O-chunk-o-raws*, of Wisconsin, who, in 1639, were said to be "sedentary and very numerous," when first visited by missionaries in 1669, and by Captain Carver in 1766, were cultivating tobacco and the other articles heretofore enumerated. Indeed, the Indian *caches*, or deposits of corn, are said to have saved our Pilgrim Fathers from starvation the first winter that they inhabited the bleak New England coast.

Another evidence that the old Mound-Builders cultivated the soil, is derived from the fact that their mound villages are found located near or upon the richest tables of land in the country, and near a permanent supply of good water. A large proportion of the villages and cities of the Mississippi valley now occupy the sites of ancient mound cities.

When this ancient population learned agriculture, becomes a very interesting question, in view of the fact that when this country was discovered by Europeans, none of the *cereals*, such as millet, rice, rye, wheat, barley and oats, so common on the eastern continent, were known in America; while the corn, potatoes and tobacco of America were equally unknown in Europe, Asia, and Africa. This fact, alone, not only argues the great antiquity of the people in America, but, in a measure, destroys the hypothesis that the Mound-Builders, or the present race of Indians, were the " lost ten tribes of Israel," the castaway Phœnicians, or the piratical Normans.

It may not be surprising to us, that some of the customs of either the Mound-Builders, or the modern tribes of Indians, may be similar to some of the customs of the eastern continent, when we take under consideration the fact of the common origin of the human race, and the identity of the human form and intellect; but it would surprise us that even a semi-educated and semi-civilized people should relapse so completely into barbarism as to leave neither written manuscript, hieroglyphic, nor sculptured cornice. If the American races ever had an ancestry on the eastern continent, it is probable that it was anterior to *Confucius* of the Chinese, the *Vedas* of the Hindoos, the Hieroglyphics of the Egyptians, and the Pentateuch of the Hebrews.

The Mound-Builders were evidently somewhat acquainted with commerce, judging from the articles found in the mounds. In Ohio we find pearls, sharks' teeth, and marine shells from the Gulf and the Atlantic ocean, obsidian from Mexico and the Rocky Mountains, native copper and silver from Lake Superior, lead from Wisconsin, Illinois, Iowa and Missouri, and syenite and greenstone from northern Wisconsin, Alleghany and Rocky Mountains.

Their system of traveling for the purposes of commerce, was probably the same as that of the modern Indians — by canoes along the navigable rivers. Since this country has become known to the whites, trading fleets of several hundred canoes have visited Quebec from the head of Lake Superior and from Green Bay; while war parties of the Sioux of Mille Lac, have passed two thousand miles down the Mississippi, and war parties of the Five Nations, of New York, have carried their victorious arms to Mackinaw and Lake Superior, and by way of the Ohio river to two hundred miles west of the Mississippi.

To what extent the Mound-Builders may have trafficked in corn, tobacco, skins, and clothing, we have no means of judging. Nor have we any means of judging of the kind of habitation which sheltered the family from the winter's cold. It was evidently neither stone, brick or dirt, as no remains of such dwellings can be found. They must have lived either in tents or wooden tenements, all vestiges of which have long since disappeared.

But while they paid but little attention to their houses, it was not uncommon for them to surround what is supposed to have been the site of their villages with an earth embankment, about equivalent to our ditch fences. These were often built with three sides only — the fourth side being a steep bank of a creek or river. Another style was to run a straight embankment across a promontory of some high table land. A third style was to make double or triple embankments, one within the other. The height of these embankments, and their location, forbid the idea that they were designed as fortifications; and while they might have been sacred inclosures, it is far more probable that they were designed solely as fences to protect themselves either from their herds, or from the droves of buffalo which inhabited the Mississippi valley. When the first hunter was going down the Wisconsin river to settle at Prairie du Chien, in about 1727, he was obliged to stop his canoe several hours to allow a drove of buffalo to ford that river. In some instances, in Ohio, these inclosures have graded ways, embanked on each side, running to the water.

In the manufacture of arrow-points, stone axes, spearheads, and some implements of copper, the Mound-Builders did not much excel the modern races of Indians, but they carried the art of the sculpture of pipes to a high degree of perfection. These pipe sculptures are imitations of most of the common birds and animals known to the white pioneers of North America; also, of the human face and head. They displayed a fine, modest, pure taste, and close observation to natural positions, thereby indicating a people considerably advanced in civilization — the savage tastes delighting in monstrosities and caricatures, instead of faithful copies of the original.

The Mound-Builders were evidently great smokers, and probably believed, with the modern tribes, that tobacco was a gift of the Great Spirit, by the use of which they might receive inspirations from the Deity. It is a remarkable fact, that all modern tribes of Indians of North America still hold the pipe as a sacred emblem of peace; and when it is presented by one party, the fiercest battle must cease until the council can be held, and the propositions considered and determined.

When Father Marquette first explored the Mississippi from Prairie du Chien to Louisiana in 1673, this sacred emblem was at once recognized by every savage nation that inhabited its banks or propelled the canoe along its turbid waters. These pipes of the Mound-Builders were not made of the friable pipe-stone of Minnesota (that locality evidently then being unknown), but mostly of a very fine porphyry of many shades of color. Some varieties are of a greenish brown base, with fine white and black granules; others of a light brown base, with white, purple, and violet-tinged specks; but most are red, with white and purplish grains. Some very much resemble the modern Indian pipe-stone in color, but greatly exceed it in hardness.

As the Mound-Builders evidently were not worshipers of idols, they have left us no sculptures of idol deities, or of the full form of man.

It is claimed for the Egyptians, that they became the fathers of geometry from the necessity of dividing out to the tillers of the soil the overflowed bottoms of the Nile; but the Mound-Builders have exhibited the most exact geometrical skill in many of their embankments and inclosures, without any such necessity. This point was tested by actual survey, among others, of the two circle, and one square, inclosure at Liberty township, Ross county, Ohio. One of these circles was 800 feet in diameter, and the other 1,700 feet, while the square was exactly 1,080 feet on each side. Pythagoras himself could not have struck those circles nor made that square, without an actual measurement on geometrical principles. The same scientific accuracy runs through nearly all their earth-works. At Seal township, in Pike county, Ohio, there is an accurate ellipse, and a circle with a square embankment inside, the corners touching the circle. At Brush creek, Kentucky, there is an hexagonal inclosure precisely fifty feet on each of the six sides. The same artistic merit, however, has not been displayed in their animal effigies; but their similarity may have been somewhat disfigured by the washing of rains for a thousand years.

In fortifications for defense, the Mound-Builders have exhibited a very respectable degree of military art. In the first place, they have judiciously selected commanding positions, naturally strong, and easily rendered comparatively impregnable to the ancient warlike implements. In the second place, they never failed to include within their fortifications a good supply of water, and never allowed the contingency to exist that such supply might be cut off by an enemy. This precaution might well have been followed by some of the officers in the great rebellion, particularly by Colonel Mulligan, at Lexington, Missouri. In the third place, all the accessible points were strongly fortified with stone walls or embankments, or both; and the gateways or sally-ports were much stronger and more intricate than those of modern warfare. These walled inclosures were often of considerable extent. The one near Brownsville, Ross county, Ohio, incloses one hundred and forty acres, with a wall and embankment over two and a quarter miles in length; and "Fort Ancient," in Warren county, Ohio, has a wall and embankment between four and five miles long, and in some places twenty feet high.

The Chillicothe and Cincinnati region of Ohio seems to have been the last great stronghold of the Mound-Builders, as it is in this region that the most important fortifications were made.

Wisconsin can scarcely dignify any of her old earth-works into fortifications. The most important in this State is Aztalan. This is a three-sided inclosure, with the open side on the bank of the west branch of Rock river, with a steep declivity of only fifteen feet to the water. The north bank is 631 feet long; the west, 1,419 feet; and the south, 700 feet; — the three banks, with that of the creek, inclosing seventeen and two-third acres. The walls are about twenty-two feet wide on the ground, and vary from one to five feet in height. Allow for the action of the rains upon an earth wall for several centuries, and we conclude that it originally might have been from four to eight feet high, — a respectable fence, but a poor protection against an assaulting enemy.

But what destroys the probability that the Aztalan works were a fort, is the fact that it was commanded by a ridge on the west side, and the bank on the opposite side of the creek, — both within an arrow-shot of the inclosure.

The Mound-Builders were evidently not a warlike people, as we find no instruments for aggressive movements, except the ordinary spear, ax, knife, and arrow, which might only have been used for hunting purposes.

It is customary to divide the different ages of Europe into the Stone age, the Copper or Bronze age, and the Iron age. The oldest, of course, was the Stone age, or the age in which the ancients used only stone knives, axes, arrows, etc. This division is said to be finely illustrated at an old crossing or ford of a river in Ireland, where a good many battles had been fought among the ancient natives. On digging into the bank of the river, numerous war instruments of iron were found; on continuing down they found a strata containing instruments of copper; and still deeper they reached the strata where the instruments of war were of stone. These deposits had been covered up from time to time by the river overflowing its banks, and leaving deposits of sand, gravel, and clay, over the carnage of war. As the Mound-Builders had no instruments of iron, and but few hammered out of native copper, we conclude that they had made but little progress in the Copper age, and had not learned the art of smelting the ore.

The most important localities where flint rock was found, both by the Mound-Builders and modern Indians, for the manufacture of arrow points, spear heads, etc., in the Mississippi valley, were "Flint Ridge," in the counties of Muskingham and Licking, Ohio, and "Flint Bluffs," or "Silver Bluffs," in the western part of Jackson county, Wisconsin. About the hills in all these localities, countless numbers of pits, from two to fourteen feet deep, have been dug, from which the stone has been taken for manufacture. but all of their instruments were not made of flint. There have been found in the mounds of Ohio and further south, articles worked with skill from limpid crystals of quartz, manganesian garnet, and obsidian.

Messrs. Squier and Davis, in their account of the Ancient Monuments of Ohio, state that "The copper and silver found in the mounds were doubtless obtained in their native state, and afterwards worked without the intervention of fire. The locality from which they were derived, seems pretty clearly indicated by the peculiar mechanico-chemical combination existing in some specimens between the silver and copper, which combination characterizes only the native masses of Lake Superior."

That they may have obtained the metal at that locality is very probable, as they left mounds on the bank of the Ontonagon river, a very important locality of native copper. Occasional specimens of native copper, however, are found in the drift through Wisconsin and Illinois; but they are supposed to have come from Lake Superior.

The Mound-Builders are supposed to have been very religious, as well as very superstitious; but what their religion or superstitions were, we do not know. It is impossible at this day to determine the forms of their religion; but it is almost certain that it was not Christian, Hebrew, or Pagan. There is, however, a striking similarity between their religion and that of the modern Indians, and the religion of the ancient Magi of Persia, before the days of Zoroaster.

The Magi worshiped fire, and believed in a good **and** a bad Spirit, and performed their worship on the tops of hills and in the open air. They also worshiped the sun, and the natural objects on the earth. After the death of Cambyses they usurped the Government, but were overthrown, and many of the leaders in the rebellion slain. Many of them might have emigrated to America. But standing out against this hypothesis, is the fact that they would probably have brought with them some of the civilization of Persia and Media; whereas, nothing has ever been found in this country. Every hypothesis of an Asiatic emigration within the last three thousand years, must answer the question, " Where are the letters and the productions of art of Asia at that period?"

The first class of mounds which writers at this day have

selected as of sacred origin, are the elevated squares or truncated pyramids of earth. Several of these occur in an inclosure at Marietta, Ohio. The largest one is one hundred and eighty-eight feet long by one hundred and thirty-two feet wide, and ten feet high. Midway upon each of its four sides are graded ascents, twenty-five feet wide and sixty feet long, in a right line from the mound. These graded ascents were evidently designed to render the mounds easy of ascent by processions of the people. Some of this class have but one graded ascent, like the great mound at Cahokie, Illinois, which is seven hundred feet long by five hundred feet wide at the base, and ninety feet high, with a graded ascent at one end only. The top of the mound has a first and second table. The lowest table on the top is one hundred and sixty feet wide, and three hundred and fifty feet long; while the summit or top had a flat table of two hundred feet wide by four hundred and fifty feet long. The whole mound is estimated as containing twenty millions cubic feet of earth. The monks of the order of La Trappe have for some time occupied the top of the mound with their house and garden.

In Wisconsin, this class of mounds are much less in size, and have only been noticed at three localities: viz., at Aztalan, Ontonagon river, and at Trempealeau village. At Aztalan there are three of this class, one of which is sixty by sixty-five feet level area on the top, with an indistinct graded way at the south-east corner. The other two are a little less in area. The mound at Trempealeau is about seven feet high, with a level surface at the top about twenty-five by fifty feet, with graded ways from each of the four sides about twenty-five feet long, with the full width of the sides. Others may yet be discovered.

In a circular truncated mound at Portsmouth, Ohio, there is a graded way, or terrace, running horizontally round the mound, with a spiral pathway from the terrace to the summit. Near the town of Franklin, Tennessee, is a circular

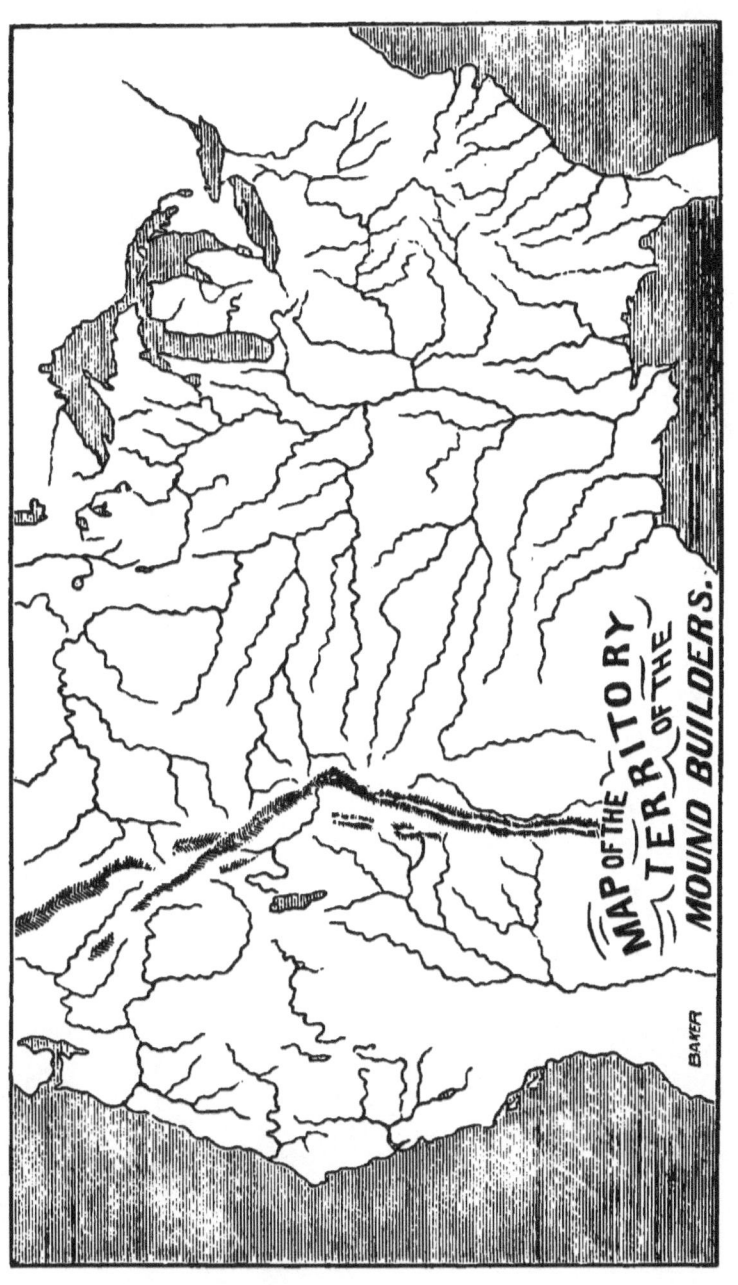

truncated mound, fifteen feet high, with a graded way to the ground only on one side. Several of this kind are found in the southern States. Another remarkable mound of this class, near Lovedale, Kentucky, is octagonal in form, each side measuring 150 feet long, with three graded ways to the surrounding soil. Nearly opposite the head of Blannerhassett's island, in Virginia, is a diamond-shaped, truncated pyramid, surrounded by a ditch and embankment in the form of the ellipse.

The truncated mounds are very sparse in the north, but become more numerous as we approach the Gulf of Mexico. At Aztalan, Marietta, and some other places, they are within inclosures, but at others they are not. This class of mounds, on examination, have yielded no evidence that they were burial mounds, but have been regarded as the site for temples devoted to the worship of the sun, or some other imaginary deity; or, in the opinion of some, as the trocallis of the city of Mexico for bloody sacrifices.

Another very important class of mounds, inclosing supposed altars, are found in many parts of the west. The altar is generally made of clay, but instances occur of stone. They are round, elliptical, square, or parallelograms, and from two to fifty feet across, although generally from five to eight feet. They are built on the ground, from ten to twenty inches high, with a concave or hollow on the top like a bowl, and the clay is burned very hard and deep. When found, the altar generally contains ashes, calcined bones, fragments of pottery, calcined stone arrow-heads, and sometimes discs of copper. Over the whole is raised a large mound, with alternating strata of sand and common earth. After the altar was constructed, it is supposed that human bodies were placed thereon and burned with an intense heat, after which the mound is raised over the whole. We have no means of judging whether the human bodies were placed on the altar when alive or dead, but may we not infer that the cavity in the altar was to hold the blood, while the calcined arrow-heads were originally the arrows shot to take the life of the victims? In a mound of this class, at Mound City, Ohio, were found, intermixed with much ashes, nearly 200 pipes carved in stone, many pearls and shell beads, numerous discs, tubes, etc., of copper, and a number of ornaments of copper, covered with silver. The pipes were much broken, and portions of the copper melted with the intense heat.

Another mound in Mound City, yielded nothing but a large number of plates of mica. Another yielded bones with ten bracelets, which had evidently been worn as ornaments on the arms. Another mound had no regular altar, but contained more than 2,000 discs of horn-stone or flint, each about six inches long, four wide, and about three-fourths of an inch thick. They were evidently buried, either to secrete them from enemies, or as a magazine for future use, or for superstitious purposes; or possibly to improve their quality with a view of manufacturing them into spear and arrow-heads. Some of these altars show signs of having been used for a considerable period before they were covered with earth.

That these mounds were not always burial places, is evident from the fact that many of them contain no signs of human bones. The Mexicans are said to have sought for burial places near some altar, or temple, or sacred place where sacrifices were made. Among them, burial by fire was often practiced.

In Wisconsin, the writer is not advised that any of the altars formed like those of Ohio have yet been found, but burnt clay and charred human bones are common. Mr. Lapham opened a mound at Aztalan that indicated a series of burnings of clay and bones, as though it had been the practice to cover each burning with a thin strata of earth, and had so continued until the mound reached its present height.

Another class of mounds, which is by far the most

numerous in the United States and territories, is the conical mounds. These occur, not only within and about the inclosures of Ohio and other States of the Mississippi valley, but in many places, including Minnesota and Oregon, where inclosures are not common. They are generally from eight to fifty feet in diameter, and from one to twenty feet in height, and occasionally of much larger dimensions. Some of these conical mounds are found to inclose altars, but are regarded generally as simple burial mounds.

Many of these contain ashes, coals, and charred bones, which indicate that it was a common practice to burn the bodies on the surface of the ground without the erection of an altar. Others, and by far the greater number, contain either bones in a far-gone state of decay, or more generally the ashy appearance or deposit of bones already decayed. These conical mounds occasionally contain arrow and spear heads, and pottery, but more generally are entirely destitute of articles manufactured. The state of preservation of the bones in the mounds, depends mainly on the amount of clay used in the construction of the mounds — a compact clay preserving them for a long period, while in a loose, porous soil, they decay in a short time.

Another very important class of mounds are called " animal mounds," or " effigies of animals," the chief locality of which, according to present discoveries, is Wisconsin, although a few of marked character have been noticed in Ohio and Michigan.

One of the most important of this class in Ohio, is "The Serpent," in Adams county. It is on a point of a ridge at " Three Forks," on Brush creek, 150 feet above the creek. " The Serpent's " head is near the point of the ridge, and extends in graceful undulations and curves along the summit of the ridge for 700 feet, terminating with a triple coil of the tail, the extreme length being about 1,000 feet. The mouth is open, evidently attempting to swallow an egg, or oval figure, within its distended jaws. The egg, or oval figure, is an embankment four feet high, 160 feet long, and eighty feet in its greatest diameter. The embankment representing the serpent is five feet high and thirty feet wide at its base, near the center, and diminishes a trifle towards its head and tail.

"The Serpent" entered into the religious superstitions of nearly all the old nations of Europe, Asia, and Africa. The *Vedas* of the Hindoo represents that the earth is placed on an enormous snake with 100 heads, and that when the snake shakes one of its heads it produces an earthquake. The great temple of Abury, in England, was built in the form of a serpent by the ancient Celts. The snake also entered into the religious ceremonies of the Mexicans. Even the modern Winnebagoes and Dakotas apply to the snake the word *Wakon*, or Spirit, and hold it sacred.

"The Alligator," in Licking county, Ohio, near Granville, is another interesting effigy. Its extreme length is two hundred and fifty feet; the breadth of the body, forty feet; the length of its legs, each, thirty-six feet; and its height from four to six feet. At the right of the effigy is a circular elevation, covered with stones much burned, with a graded way ten feet wide, from the body to the supposed altar of stones. Excavations have been made in the "Alligator," but nothing has been discovered, except stones and a fine clay used in building the effigy. The ancient Egyptians held the alligator as sacred.

The effigies of men, animals, and inanimate things, are very numerous throughout Wisconsin. The men mounds are sometimes with legs, but more numerously without them.

Of the former class, effigies have been noticed at Milwaukee, Waukesha, Ripley lake, Sec. 26 T. 12 R. 16 E, Utica, Sec. 35 T. 9 R. 4, One-Mile creek (Adams county,) Mauston, and at Galesville. Effigies of men with legs occur at Sec. 19 T. 9 R. 6 E., Honey Creek mills, Sec. 9 T. 16 R. 2 W., seven miles E., Blue mounds, Muscoda, and Sec.

35 T. 9 R. 1 W. These latter mounds are represented with legs down about to the knees.

Mr. Wm. H. Canfield, near Baraboo, in Sauk county, Wisconsin, has surveyed a mound at that place of an effigy of a full-length man, the first one yet discovered. The whole figure is two hundred and fourteen feet in length; the head thirty feet long, the body one hundred, and the legs eighty-four. The top of the head is nearly crescent shaped, giving the effigy a ghostly and unnatural appearance. Some of the other effigies represent the head as split open on top, each half of which has fallen part way to the shoulders. All of these effigies of men are evidently designed to represent some spiritual existences, taught by their religious superstitions.

Another class of mounds are the effigies of birds. These are mainly distinguished from the man-shaped mounds by the representation of a bill to the head; the body and wings corresponding with the body and arms of the man. These bird-shaped mounds occur at Waukesha, Honey creek, Sec. 3 T. 10 R. 7 E., Sec. 5 T. 10 R. 7 E., Sec. 6 T. 8 R. 5 W., English Prairie, in Iowa county, and Sec. 16 T. 8 R. 1 W. They are only about as numerous as the man-shaped mounds. There is no attempt in these effigies to represent any particular species of the bird that we can recognize, although they differ in their outlines, and in the imagination of the Mound-Builders they may have represented different birds.

Another quite numerous class are what Mr. Lapham denominates the "Turtle Mounds," which occur very numerously in the south-eastern part of Wisconsin. One figured by him at Waukesha has an extreme length of one hundred and seventy-six feet, of which one hundred and thirty feet belongs to the tail. If turtles in the days of the Mound-Builders had tails of this capacity, they must have wonderfully deteriorated in their tailships at the present day. It might have been intended to represent the lizard, but it comes much nearer the tadpole or polliwog, at that state of its existence when it begins to develop the feet. The peculiar development of the tadpole might well have attracted the attention of these superstitious people.

Well delineated turtles of the modern day are represented by mounds south-west of Galesville, in which the tail is represented as not much larger than the head and neck. These turtle mounds are about thirty-six feet long from the end of the nose to the end of the tail, and twenty-seven feet between the fore feet.

Near these turtle mounds is an effigy of a frog, nine yards long; nine yards between the ends of the fore feet, and eleven yards between the ends of the hind feet. He was probably of the bull-frog species. But the animal effigies are too numerous for the writer's limits to describe, and he will only remark, that at Galesville there are effigies of man, and of the frog, turtle, deer, bear, and perhaps the buffalo, the most numerous of which are the deer. Near Honey creek, in Sec. 19 T. 9 R. 6, are the bear and buffalo; at Mayville, the fox and beaver; at Horricon, the otter; at Ripley lake, the serpent. At these places and many others there are a great variety of effigies, probably intended to represent the different kinds of animals known to the Mound-Builders; many of which, however, may have been entirely imaginary, but among which the worm is conspicuous.

What object the Mound-Builders had in the laborious erection of these numerous effigies, of course we can only conjecture. Some have supposed that they were intended to represent the *totem* or town to which the deceased belonged, since many of the tribes of the present day use the pictures of animals to represent the tribe, as the English use the coat of arms to represent the family. This is based on two suppositions, entirely without evidence: first, that the Mound-Builders used *totems*, like the modern Indians; and, secondly, that, unlike the modern Indians, they raised mounds to represent their *totems*.

The second suggestion is, that they had names like the modern Indians; as, Black Hawk, White Bear, Buffalo, etc., and that their burial mounds were in imitation of the animal whose name they bore. But those suggestions are not only based on two suppositions, like the previous, without evidence, but ignore the fact that many modern Indians have names that can not be represented by an animal; such as, *Sleepy Eyes, Whirling Thunder, Hole-in-the-Day, Clear Sky, Screamer,* etc. According to that, such chiefs must go without honor to the next world; or, like the poisoned sailor, he must be buried without a funeral, because the church had no prayers for such a case of death.

May we not with far more probability infer, that these animal effigies were connected with the religious superstitions of the race, and that, as most heathen nations believe in the transmigration of souls to animals, these effigies may have been designed to perpetuate the name of the animal that the priest or relatives had directed the departed soul to enter. The doctrine of the transmigration of souls was, among many others, taught by Pythagoras and Plato, and has been illustrated by the poet Dryden in the following:

"In life's next scene of *transmigration* be,
Some bear or lion is reserved for thee."

Thus, the reader's attention has been called to some of the principal facts connected with the life and death of the Mound-Builders; but volumes will not exhaust the subject, nor generations perfect their history. Much will yet be learned, as new discoveries are made, and the mounds further examined in the progress of civilization.

By evidence satisfactory to the human mind, we know that they lived in great numbers throughout a vast region, labored, sported, loved, were given in marriage, begat children, nurtured them with parental care, worshiped, and died, and that their friends built monuments to their memory.

To the infidel, alas! this is all there is of man, but to the Christian there yet remains the Upper Sanctuary, the glories of which are not modified by the sorrows of humanity, and where the intellectual soul will grow in knowledge, as the child does in stature.

The origin of the Mound-Builders can only be the subject of speculation. Dr. Morton says, "That the study of *physical conformation alone*, excludes every branch of the Caucasian race from any obvious participation in the peopling of this continent;" but Dr. Morton goes farther, and declares, "that the organic characters of the people themselves, through all the endless ramifications of tribes or nations, prove them to belong to one and the same race, and that this race is distinct from all others." This conclusion is reached by the doctor in the examination of the skulls from different parts of the world, and is very sweeping, when we take under consideration the fact that no two skulls ever examined, agreed with each other in every particular.

But the arguments of Dr. Morton at least tend to show the great antiquity of the American race; and with the fact that neither the Mound-Builders nor the present Indian race have had the religious ceremonies of any of the Asiatics, Europeans, or Africans, to our knowledge, nor an acquaintance with any written language, we may well infer that they did not have their origin from the eastern continent since the knowledge of letters, or since the present religious ceremonies were established. Another similar argument exists in the want of identity of their language with that of any of the known languages of the eastern continent.

The age of trees growing on the mounds has been examined, and nearly 1,000 years into antiquity have been reached; but the mounds, or at least some of them, were then standing.

The time at which the Mound-Builders abandoned this country, or were exterminated by war, is entirely lost, and gone beyond our reach.

It is conceded that the modern Indian tribes have no traditions of the Mound-Builders or of the mounds. It is true that David Cusic, an educated Tuscarora, in 1825, compiled the traditions of the Iroquois, or six nations, in which he claimed that the Iroquois had fought an ancient people, probably the Mound-Builders, for several hundred years, and finally exterminated them. Mr. Galletin, however, not only pronounces the tradition fabulous, but a closer investigation into the tradition proves that it more probably relates to the *Kah-Kwah*, or Eries, which they conquered in 1655.

The Delawares had also, in 1819, come in for ancient fame; and as related to Mr. Heckewelder, their Moravian missionary, had a tradition claiming that when the Delawares removed east of the Mississippi, they found a people who called themselves the *Allegewi*, and who had fortifications which were of gigantic height. The Delawares called to their aid the Iroquois, who, they said, then lived on the Mississippi, and after a long war, conquered and drove the Allegewi down the Mississippi. General Cass, who was personally acquainted with the missionary, at once classed the tradition as a humbug, got up to excite the gullibility of their missionary, a business in which the Indians are known to be adepts. In this class may be placed the tradition by "*De-coo-dah*," of the Winnebagoes, as related by Mr. William Pidgeon.

This tradition is, in effect, denied by the Iroquois, as they claim that they were created in New York, and never lived on the Mississippi, and have no tradition of any league with the Delawares. The latter tribe may have assisted the Iroquois in driving the Akansea down the Mississippi about 1661.

The traditions of the *Aztecs*, the ancient people of Mexico, are supposed to give some light on the question of "What became of the Mound-Builders?" By those traditions they claim, that about 1160, they left their town in the north, called *Aztalan*, or place near the large water, and journeyed south for one hundred and sixty-five years, when they descried "an eagle grasping in its claws a writhing serpent, and resting on a cactus which sprung from a rock in the Lake Tescoco." "This had been designated by the *Aztec* oracles as the spot where the tribe should settle." This was the foundation of the city of Mexico.

Mr. Humboldt, who examined critically the traditions of the Mexicans, has declared that none of their traditions, running back 100 years before their conquest by the Spanish in 1520, are entitled to serious consideration. The same may be said of Indian traditions generally. Mr. Bartlett, who was at the head of the United States boundary commission, and gave much attention to the subject, says: "I have been unable to learn from what source the prevailing idea has arisen, of the migration of the Aztecs from the north into the valley of Mexico. The traditions which gave rise to this notion are extremely vague, and were not seriously entertained until Torquemada, Borturini, and Clavigero, gave them currency. But they must now give way to the more reliable results of linguistic comparison. No analogy has yet been traced between the language of the old Mexicans and any tribe at the north in the district from which they are supposed to have come; nor in any relics, ornaments, or works of art, do we observe a resemblance between them."

We notice among the speculations of infidel minds, a great readiness to turn these doubtful questions into positive arguments against the scriptural origin of mankind; but they appear to ignore the fact that, throughout the whole world, man has the same general form of body, organs of speech, and identity of mind, and however much either may be modified by education or locality, no nation has been found lacking any one of these prerequisites of man. While the African may have a head, and the Esquimaux a body, below the average size, we should remember that as great a difference often occurs in a single family; and he who argues that man originated from the monkey, only thereby makes a monkey of himself. The identity of the present Indians of the north-west with the inhabitants of eastern Asia, has been strongly urged to the writer by an eminent Presbyterian divine who has spent several years as a missionary in China, and among the Chinese in California.

Independent of tradition or of language, there is a strong impression on the minds of antiquarian travelers, of the identity of the Mexicans with the Mound-Builders, created by the supposed similarity of their customs and worship; and this impression is increased by the belief that the conquering nations were from the north-west, and that the fugitives naturally would have retreated south. Upon that hypothesis, it is a strong supposition that the Mobilian race along the Gulf of Mexico were the conquerors; and, as they must have incorporated some of the Mound-Builders into their nations, it might be expected that they would retain some of their civilization. This would, in part, account for a higher civilization, which in fact did exist in that warlike race, when visited by De Soto in 1540. But a doubt is raised to the whole of that hypothesis, as the center of the Mound-Builders' territory was held by the Winnebago Confederacy when first known to the whites, which Confederacy extended from Lake Superior to Arkansas river, and occupied the lower Ohio and Missouri rivers, and the territory west nearly to New Mexico; and if the Mobilians conquered the Mound-Builders, they were in turn driven south by the Winnebago Confederacy. In looking further, we find the latter Confederacy again being pressed south by the Dakotas, who extended from Lake Superior to the Rocky Mountains. Beyond all these, come the great Algonquin nations, extending from the Atlantic to the Rocky Mountains, and north to the frozen ocean, including the Esquimaux, and were probably as ancient a people on the continent as the Mound-Builders themselves. This antiquity of the Algonquin nations not only make them cotemporary with the

Mound-Builders, but will account for the non-discovery of mounds in the north, except along the south edge of their territory.

But there is even a possibility that the Mound-Builders were converted to a new religion, as was the Pagan Roman Empire in the days of Constantine, and thereby not only abandoned their superstitions of building tumuli, but became more nomadic and warlike. At some time a similar change must have occurred on the eastern continent, for they, too, have their tumuli at places, from England to the Indian ocean; but why the custom was abandoned, belongs to the unlettered ages of their people. Had there been a change of religion, a period of less than 1,000 years would probably have erased from their traditions every trace of the old superstition. But these speculations are all unsatisfactory, and we can only conclude that Deity filled, with that populous nation, some important *niche* in the great temple of humanity.

CHAPTER II.

THE INDIAN TRIBES, FROM THEIR DISCOVERY TO 1755.

PASSING from the Mound-Builders across an indefinite period, variously estimated at from 500 to 2,000 years, to the time when America became known to the Europeans, we find the whole continent peopled with numerous tribes, speaking different languages, but identical in complexion and physical construction, although evidently less civilized, and more warlike than their predecessors, the Mound-Builders.

The uniformity in the physical appearance of the present race will convey the idea that they are the legitimate descendants of the Mound-Builders; but this hypothesis is nearly destroyed by the radical difference in many of the tribal languages, and the total absence of the custom of building mounds. Although less civilized than the Mound-Builders, yet they were not totally deficient in this particular, but still understood the art of building fortifications, the cultivation of corn, tobacco, beans, peas and pumpkins, and the construction of stone knives, axes, arrow and spear-heads, and bows, arrows and spears; and were experts in hunting, fishing, and war. They even possessed considerable judgment in medicine, government, and hieroglyphical writing. Indeed, they were but little below the Celts of the British islands at the time of the invasion by Julius Cæsar, and nearly resembled, in their warlike customs, particularly in taking scalps, the ancient Scythians of European

Turkey. Following the explorations from Columbus, and including the first settlements of the Atlantic coast in North America, by the French, English, Dutch and Spanish, we gather the data that at that period the people of the region of country north of the Gulf of Mexico and east of the Rocky Mountains, may be classified by their languages nearly as follows:

1. The Algonquin, or Ojibwa Confederacy, occupied all the country to the frozen regions north of a line commencing near Cape Fear on the Atlantic, thence extending westerly to the mouth of the Illinois river, thence along that river, and by way of Lake Michigan, Falls of St. Mary, Lake Superior, and rivers and portages to the Lake of the Woods, and thence westerly to the Rocky mountains.

2. The Mobilian, or Cherokee Confederacy, occupying the country south of the line running westerly from Cape Fear to the north line of Tennessee, thence west to the Mississippi, thence by the Mississippi, Arkansas and Canadian rivers, to the Rocky mountains.

3. The O-chunk-o-raw, or Winnebago Confederacy, extending from Lake Superior to the Arkansas river, including the Wisconsin river and lower Ohio, and extending west to the Rocky mountains.

4. The Dakota, or Sioux Confederacy, extending west to the Rocky mountains from a line running from Kewenaw bay to the north-eastern corner of the present State of Iowa.

These lines between the different Confederacies must be understood as only approximating to correctness, as Indian boundaries were never well defined.

Nearly in this position, the Europeans found the territory of the Mound-Builders east of the Rocky mountains divided among four great Confederacies, all speaking radically different languages, but otherwise differing but little in manners, customs, religion, complexion, or physical construction; and all, like the Mound-Builders, but unlike the Europeans, used the pipe and tobacco. From whence came these Aborigines, has been the constant speculation of our ancestors in America; but every theory has failed before the light of investigation, and we only know that they have long resided in this country, and have a slight resemblance to the north-eastern Asiatics.

These confederacies were not generally confederacies of government, for they were divided up into a multitude of independent bands or tribes, often with no traditions of relationship, and in open war with each other, and even unable to speak each other's dialects of the same language. As the Indians had no written language, these dialects were rapidly formed in independent bands, and the obscurity of the dialect was in the ratio of the time that any particular band had been separated from the parent tribe. The same change, but with far less rapidity, exists in written languages, and the Greek of Athens and the Latin of Rome to-day, would have been barbarian to Demosthenes and Cicero.

The prominent tribes of the Algonquin Confederacy, which became distinguished in the early annals of New York, New England, and Canada, were the Mohegans of Massachusetts, Abenakis of Maine, Iroquois of New York, Delawares of Pennsylvania, Algonquins of Quebec, Hurons from Montreal to Lake Huron, Ottawas of the Georgian bay, Mascotens of Detroit, Miamies of the Wabash, Sacs and Foxes and Pottowatomies of Saginaw bay and Lake Michigan, Chippeways of the Falls of St. Mary, and Christinaux of Hudson's bay.

When the navigator, Samuel Champlain, founded Quebec in 1608, he ascertained that the Algonquin tribe at Quebec was at war with the tribes of New York; and believing that it was necessary to live in harmony with his immediate neighbors, entered into an alliance with them, offensive and defensive. Pursuant to such alliance, he led a war party of the Algonquins against the Iroquois in July, 1809, and on the 30th of the same month attacked a war party of 200

Iroquois at a cape near Ticonderoga, on the west side of Lake Champlain, and put them to flight. The honors gained in this victory with fire-arms over bows and arrows, was of little account; but in the progress of civilization it marked an important period, as the campaign discovered a new lake, to which Champlain attached his own name, and inaugurated a war that was only permanently terminated by the surrender of Canada to the English, one hundred and fifty-one years afterwards. The war which Champlain voluntarily assumed in 1609, became a necessity the following year, for a considerable war party of the Iroquois invaded Canada, seeking revenge for their misfortunes of the previous year.

Champlain, by presents, and the terror produced by his fire-arms, succeeded in winning over to the side of the Algonquins, the Hurons, who were kindred of the Iroquois, and engaged them to join him in the war against their brethren. Thus strengthened, he attacked the war party of the Iroquois, who had hastily fortified themselves on the St. Johns river, and totally defeated them, even before the arrival of his 200 Huron allies.

This defeat, together with the defection of the Hurons, seems to have struck the Iroquois with terror, and it was probably under these circumstances that the five Iroquois bands formed themselves into a confederacy, offensive and defensive, which made them so powerful in subsequent years. They were also greatly exasperated at the Hurons, who had thus voluntarily abandoned them, and had gone over to their enemies, and ever afterwards held against them the spirit of revenge. Profiting by their experience, the Iroquois fortified their villages against fire-arms, and prepared for the war with the judgment of more civilized nations. The northern allies, impatient for new victories, and having been attacked by war parties north of Lake Ontario, induced Champlain to head another war party in 1615. This party was organized at the east end of the

Georgian bay, which point Champlain reached by way of the Ottawa river and Lake Nipissing, on the first day of August. On the first day of September the allied forces started on their expedition. They passed through Lake Simcoe, made a portage to the head waters of the Trent river, which stream they passed down, and discovered Lake Ontario. This country was found destitute of inhabitants, they having lately been driven back by war parties of the Iroquois. Crossing at the foot of Lake Ontario, Champlain hid his canoes, and journeyed by land five days in a southerly direction, and on the 10th of October reached the Iroquois fort, near a considerable lake, supposed to be Cayuga. This fort the allied forces besieged until the 16th of the same month, when Champlain, having been twice wounded, and many of his allies killed and wounded, the Indians refused to continue the siege, and the allies retreated. Champlain returned to the Georgian bay, where he was forced to remain until spring, on account of the ice, and only reached Quebec the following year, apparently disgusted with his Indian war.

In 1629 the English took possession of Quebec, and carried Champlain to England; and for three years the Indians were left free from French intrigue to settle their own difficulties. The Iroquois, taking advantage of the absence of their new French enemies, mustered their warriors, and marched into the Huron country. The Hurons gathered together their allies, and fought a great battle, some where between Lakes Ontario and Huron, and were defeated. They then sued for peace, which was granted, and the Hurons and Iroquois were again united and the tomahawk buried; and when the French returned to Canada in 1632, the Hurons and Algonquins positively refused to renew the war, or permit the Jesuit priests to establish a mission on Lake Huron. The French brought to bear upon the untutored savages all their arts in diplomacy, and in 1634 finally obtained leave for their priests to renew the mission to Lake Huron.

The Iroquois continued to regard the French as their enemies, and a kind of semi-war existed for some years, until finally, in 1648, the pent-up volcano broke forth, and the powerful war parties of the Iroquois, fully armed with fire-arms obtained from the Dutch, swept the whole Huron country, and both shores of Lake Huron. The allied tribes, in great numbers, rallied and fortified the Island of Mackinaw, where, in about 1652, they were again attacked by about 3,000 Iroquois warriors, and totally defeated. A remnant of the Ottawas and Chippeways took shelter in the dark pine forests of Lake Superior, while the Sacs and Foxes, and the Mascotens and Miamies, and their kindred the Kickapoos, planted themselves on the territory of the Winnebagoes, along the Fox and Wisconsin rivers, and a fragment of the Hurons passed across the State of Wisconsin, and obtained a resting place on the Iowa river, on the borders of the territory of the Dakotas. A small number of the Christian Hurons, with their surviving priests, escaped their enemies, and formed a village below Quebec. The larger portion of the Huron nation were either killed or taken prisoners and adopted into the families of the Iroquois, where they were afterwards recognized by their Catholic priests.

The Erie, or Cat bands of the Huron-Iroquois nation, living along both shores of the Niagara river, and the southeastern shore of Lake Erie, called by the Iroquois the *Kah-Kwah*, positively refused to join their brethren in that fratricidal war, and continued neutral; but when the Hurons had finally been expelled the country, the neutrals were charged by the Iroquois with giving protection to their enemies, and failing to render satisfaction, they too were attacked, and after a severe struggle of three years, were, in the fall of 1655, finally defeated, and shared the same fate as their brothers the Hurons, except no remnants of the

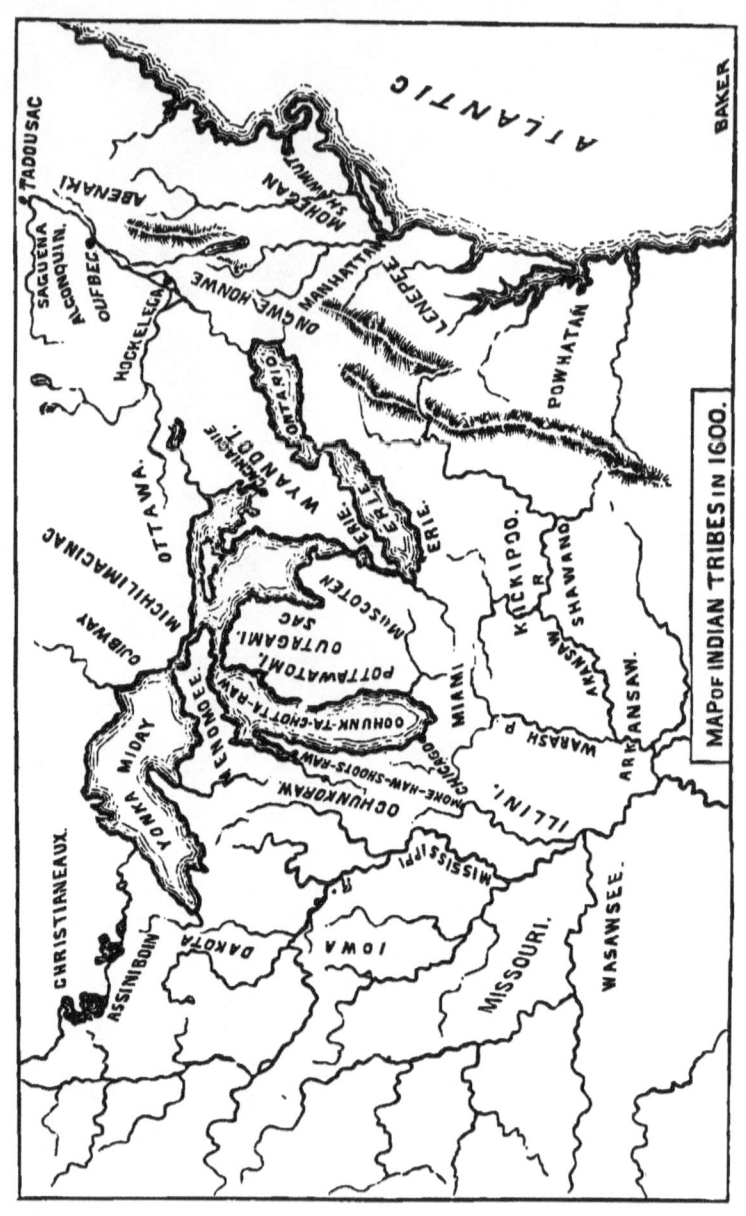

tribe have ever since been heard of, that were not prisoners in the hands of their captors. The French are supposed to have originated this war, as their priests urged its vigorous prosecution early in 1655.

Suggestions have been made by some authors that the Shawnees, who were afterwards driven from the Ohio to Tennessee, might have been a remnant of the Eries; but that hypothesis is destroyed by the fact that the Shawnees spoke a dialect of the Miami-Algonquin, while the Eries spoke the dialect of the Huron-Iroquois.

It is not, however, probable that a nation numbering in 1625 nearly 15,000, were so nearly annihilated; and we may reasonably suppose that hundreds of them fled to friendly tribes in the west, where they became merged and lost sight of in a single generation. The same suggestion might be made with force with reference to the Hurons, who were also very numerous before the war.

After the defeat of the Eries, war parties of the Iroquois sought their old enemies in their hiding places in Wisconsin, and in 1660, one of these parties became involved in difficulties with the Indians of Illinois, and a furious war followed; and in the short period of two or three years, by the potency of fire-arms obtained from the Dutch, the fierce Iroquois drove a bleeding remnant of the Shawnees of Northern Kentucky and Southern Ohio back upon the Tennessee river; the tall Arkansea, of the lower Ohio valley, down the Mississippi to Arkansas river; the powerful Illinois, west of the Mississippi; and the Mascotens, Kickapoo and Miamies, to the Wisconsin river. This fierce war was short, as the Iroquois in the mean time became involved, probably by French intrigue, in a war with their powerful neighbors, the Mohegans and Delawares. This latter war commenced probably about 1664, and the French claimed in 1680 that the Iroquois had nearly annihilated the Andastognés and Mohegans. We know that the Delawares, in 1675, were driven by the Iroquois south upon the lower

Potomac, where they committed some depredations upon the white settlers in Maryland and Virginia, and that six of their chiefs visited Captain Washington, the great-grandfather of General Washington, who was captain in the Militia of Virginia, to settle the difficulties, and Captain Washington murdered the whole of them; whereupon the Governor of Virginia reprimanded him, by saying that he would not have murdered them, under the circumstances, if "they had killed his own father and mother." This act of barbarity of Captain Washington was revenged by the Indians, when the Militia of Maryland and Virginia attacked the Delawares, and drove them back upon the Iroquois. The Delawares then sued for and negotiated a peace with their northern conquerors. By the traditions of both tribes, it is said that, at the conclusion of a peace between them, after a long war, which was probably the aforesaid treaty, the Iroquois prescribed as the terms of the peace, that the Delawares should take the condition of squaws, and not go to war without the consent of their conquerors, which the latter tribe agreed to, and were only restored to the condition of warriors by Colonel Johnson, the Indian agent in New York, in 1756.

The bold and warlike Iroquois, however, did not neglect their old enemies the French in the midst of their complicated warfare, but repeatedly sent their war parties to harrass them, and compelled them to keep constantly fortified. A record of about 1651 said: "Hardly do those savages let us pass a day without alarms. They are ever at our skirts; no month passes that our bills of mortality do not show, in lines of blood, indications of the deadly nature of their inroads." The *Jesuit Relations* of 1653, speaking on this subject, said: "The war with the Iroquois has dried up all sources of prosperity. . . . Crowds of Hurons no longer descend from their country with furs for trade. The Algonquin country is dispeopled; and the nations beyond it are retiring further away still, fearing the musketry of the Iroquois."

In these exigencies, the Canadians asked France for help, and in 1653 received a considerable reinforcement of picked colonists, under the prestige of which they made a treaty of peace with the four western bands of the Iroquois the following year, but the Mohawks refused to join. Under this treaty, in 1656, the French sent Captain Dupuis with fifty men, and established a fort among the Onondagas, but this excited the alarm of this band. Forewarned of their danger by a dying Indian, the French fled from the country. The Mohawks followed with four hundred warriors, but failed to overtake the fugitives. They, however, passed beyond Quebec, and captured ninety of the Hurons on the Island of Orleans. Wars and alarms followed, and in the fall of 1658 the Governor of Canada represented to France that if "succor were not accorded, Canada would be irretrievably lost to France," and demanded 3,000 regular troops or six hundred colonists.

During this period the French repeatedly attempted to break up the Iroquois Confederacy, by negotiating a peace with the separate bands, and involve them in a new civil war, but all these efforts were defeated by the confederacy. In 1662 the Governor again applied to France for help, and obtained 400 soldiers. The following year 165 colonists were received. The whole subject finally came under discussion by the French ministry, and in May, 1664, the government of Canada was turned over to the "West India Company" by a royal edict, and Marquis de Tracy appointed viceroy over all New France. He landed at Quebec in June of the following year, with four companies of troops; and twenty companies more, with many colonists, followed by December. He immediately set himself to fortifying the country, and during the following winter sent an army into the Mohawk country, which found the Indian country nearly deserted, but succeeded in burning the Indian cabins and corn. With this display of force, and by negotiations, a peace was concluded in the summer of 1666 with the whole Iroquois Confederacy, which lasted nearly eighteen years, and was hailed with great joy by the whole of New France.

We have thus seen that the inauguration of the plan to disregard the rights of the Indians, and make them subservient to the interests of the whites, by the French of Canada, nearly ruined their early attempts to establish an empire in the new world, and added new proof that the great law of justice could not be trifled with, even against the American "savages;" but it took more than a century for our ancestors to become convinced of its truth. Massachusetts, however, learned it in King Phillip's war; and the Dutch of New Amsterdam learned it after the massacres of the Indians by the orders of Director Keift; while the pious Quakers of Pennsylvania proved the truth of the proposition, by practicing "good faith and good will" to the warlike Delawares, for not a drop of Quaker blood was ever shed by that nation.

Soon after the close of the Iroquois war in the north-west, the Knisteneux, or Christenaux, a powerful Algonquin nation to the south of Hudson's bay, having obtained fire-arms from the English traders at that bay, and being probably joined by many of the fugitives from Canada who had escaped into that country, commenced a war on the Dakotas of the upper Mississippi. This war in 1671 became general all along the line of the Algonquin nations on the east, who had taken possession of Dakota territory, as far south as the Wisconsin river. In the spring of that year the chivalrous Dakotas returned to the Jesuit missionaries at the head of Lake Superior the presents they had received from them, and notified the eight fugitive nations at that point, whom the missionaries declared were the aggressors, to leave the country, and soon followed up the notice with fierce war parties, who speedily swept the whole Lake Superior region of their new enemies. These bands of warriors, however, still respected the territory of the Ha-ha-ton-wa, or dwellers at the Falls of St. Mary, and stopped their advance a few leagues short of that point. This war continued until 1679, when the French interceded, and Captain Du Lut visited the head of Lake Superior and negotiated a peace between the Knisteneux and Chippeways, and the Assiniboins, the northern band of the Dakotas, which inhabited the country from the head of Lake Superior west, leaving the southern bands of the Dakotas to continue their war with the several Algonquin tribes on the Wisconsin river, and the Illinois, who had become allies of the latter tribes. This peace was another intrigue of the French, like that with the Hurons, and produced another civil war.

While the war was progressing with the Delawares, an Illinois chief, in open council, at the French post at Mackinaw, unprovoked, stabbed and killed a chief of the Iroquois. This outrage never having been settled, the Iroquois, in 1680, sent a war party of about 600 to take the usual revenge on the Illinois. This war party was joined by the Miamies, and in September attacked the Illinois, then on the river of that name, and killed and took prisoners over 1,200, and drove the balance of the tribe, as fugitives, west of the Mississippi. This attack was while the party of La Salle was on the Illinois river, some of whom were wounded in attempting to negotiate for the Illinois. About three years subsequent to this, another war party of the Iroquois of about 1,000 attempted to surprise the Foxes of Wisconsin in their winter's hunt. They passed along the north shore of Lake Huron late in the fall, and sought the Foxes near the head-waters of the Wisconsin river, as it was supposed; or, as some have it, near the Kewenaw bay of Lake Superior. The Foxes, fortunately warned by two Chippeways who had seen the party, fortified themselves on a narrow neck of land between two small lakes, and after a desperate struggle for several days, repulsed the Iroquois with heavy loss. Indeed, the Foxes claimed that they nearly destroyed the whole party. The story of this battle was related to La Hontan, while he was on the upper Mississippi in 1688, by three Fox chiefs, with great pomp and flourish; and Captain Carver, who visited that region in 1766 and 1767, had repeatedly related to him by the Chippeways the tradition of the battle. This defeat seems to have mainly closed the war of the Iroquois in the northwest, inaugurated by Champlain by his alliance with the Hurons seventy-three years previous.

But if the Iroquois sent no more powerful war parties to the north-west, it was not on account of a lack of ability to do so, but because the French took up the cause of the Illinois, and threatened to renew the war against the Iroquois unless the latter tribes desisted in their attacks on the French allies of the north-west. This demand of the French the Iroquois flatly denied, and to show their contempt for the French, sent a war party against Fort St. Louis. The French sent their popular traders to the north-west, who brought down to Niagara large bands of the Hurons, Ottawas, Foxes and other tribes; but the Governor of Canada, wasting his time in corresponding with Governor Dongan, of New York, failed to meet them at Niagara as agreed, to the great disgust of his allies. The Governor of Canada finally reached the south shore of Lake Ontario, at a point above Oswego, ever since called "Anse de la Famine," where many of his troops died with famine and local diseases. Here he met a delegation of Iroquois, and concluded a treaty with them, leaving out the chief point of their dispute, to the disgust of all Canada. Indeed, " the arrogant chief of the Mohawks" told the governor in council, that " so far from leaving the Illinois in peace, war against them is meant, till one of our tribes is exterminated." As soon as the report of this treaty reached France, it was rejected by the French ministry, the governor was removed (1685), and M. Denonville, with 600 troops, was sent to Canada to supersede him and conquer their Indian enemies. The summer of 1686 was spent by the French in preparing for war, and in hypocritical negotiations for peace. In the spring of 1687 eight hundred more troops arrived to reinforce the Canadian army. With all this force Governor Denonville opened the campaign with an act of treachery that shocked the moral sensibilities of his most savage allies. He sent a Jesuit priest to the Iroquois, to summon a large delegation of their chiefs to hold a council and settle all difficulties. When these chiefs arrived and took their place in council, a position sacred in the eyes of even the King of Dahomey, the governor meanly arrested and sent them in chains to France, leaving the poor priest as a kind of hostage in the Indian country, to the mercy of the Iroquois. To the credit, however, of the Indians, they scorned to revenge themselves on the poor priest, but sent him under a safe escort to his friends in Canada. The governor then led his troops into the Indian country, had a skirmish with 300 Mohawks, who burned their own town and fled. The French obtained a quantity of the Indians' corn, and then retired from the country, making no attempt to invade the balance of the confederacy.

The retreat of Governor Denonville from the country was the signal for the rallying of the fierce old warriors to revenge and punish an accumulation of grievances; and during the balance of the summer and fall they ravaged all western Canada with fire and tomahawk, and even assaulted the block-houses about Montreal.

During the following winter the French made a truce with the Iroquois, which their allies were suffered to continually break; but finally, in the spring, the Governor of Canada was notified by the Governor of New York, that as the Iroquois occupied a part of the British territory, the king had taken those Indians under his protection. Thus the Indian affairs were suffered to rest during the year 1688, as both English and French turned their attention to the revolutions in Europe. The right of succession to the British crown having been contested by the King of France, he declared war against the English in June, 1689, and the most distant colonies prepared for their defense against invasion, and their respective Indian allies were armed anew, and urged on by the exciting influence of spirituous liquors to deeds of blood and carnage.

The Iroquois, still smarting from an accumulation of injuries, opened the campaign; and on the 5th of August, 1689, with 1,400 warriors, disembarked on the Island of Montreal in the dark hours of the night, and for several leagues devastated the garden of Canada with fire and tomahawk, and Lachine was laid in ashes by daylight. They then passed to other parishes, and for ten weeks, almost unresisted, held high carnival in the richest portion of that country.

The following winter, the French made a descent on New York, burned Schenectady, massacred sixty of its inhabitants, and carried off twenty-seven prisoners. Another party burned Dover, in New Hampshire, killed twenty-three of its inhabitants, and carried off twenty-nine captives. The Abenakis, with a party of French, were sent against the settlements of Maine, where they massacred two hundred whites, and burned Casco and the houses for some distance around. The beautiful settlement of Salmon Falls was also burned. In this conflict, nearly all the north-western tribes were hired by the French and sent against the English and Dutch colonists.

During this severe contest, and until the peace of 1700, the Foxes and their allies kept up their war parties against the Sioux, which very much offended the French, as the latter nation desired all the strength of the north-west against the English. It had the effect, also, to nearly destroy the French trade with the Sioux, as the Foxes insisted during the time, that the French traders should not sell guns and ammunition, " articles contraband of war," to the former tribe. The French, acting on the principle that the Indians had no rights which white men were bound to respect, persisted in their contraband trade, and consequently their traders were repeatedly plundered by the Foxes and their allies. The French vowed vengeance against those Indians, but admitted that they were in no condition to punish the Indians at that time, but treasured their wrath until it was well satiated by the massacre at Detroit, in 1712.

The great power of the Iroquois, backed and armed as they were by the Dutch and English, finally induced the French to try diplomacy instead of war with the confederates, and in 1700 they effected a treaty, which the following year was ratified with great pomp and flourish by more than twenty of the north-western tribes, in which the French "buried the hatchet" in untold depths of earth, and declared that they would exterminate the tribe that first renewed the war. The French evidently designed at first to split the confederacy and get up another civil war, and made their first treaty with the Senecas, but the whole confederacy ratified it, under their plea to the English, that it was necessary to get back their prisoners. This treaty the English opposed, but failed to defeat; and in 1700 the Earl of Bellomont made a treaty with the Iroquois, nearly the same month as that in which the treaty was made by the French, by which the English and Indians renewed their covenant chain. The following language of the Earl to the Indian chiefs, expresses the feelings of the parties: " I have been told that the Jesuits have warned you not to come hither and enter into a conference with me, assuring you that I should meet you with a great armed force here, to surprise and cut you off, and that when that failed, I should give you poison to drink in rum; but you shall find a treatment so contrary to what the Jesuits have insinuated to you, that if you do not give up your reason to those ill men, they will forever hereafter pass with you for the

4*

greatest liars and impostors in the world, and men that are a reproach to Christianity."

Frequent attempts were made by the English and Dutch of New York to establish posts and open trade with the north-western Indians, but these parties were generally plundered and taken prisoners by the French. For the purpose of opening such a trade, in 1686 seven Englishmen and five Indians visited Detroit, and the following year Major McGregor organized a party of sixty young men of Albany and several Mohegan Indians, and with thirty-two canoes, and merchandise for the Indian trade, started for Detroit; but they were met by the French on Lake Erie, their goods plundered, and the party sent prisoners to Canada, and not released until in the fall of that year, after considerable negotiation by the English authorities. Soon after this, the French established a military post above Detroit, and the English, for the time, abandoned the trade. After the general peace with the Indian tribes in 1700, the English made another attempt to extend their trade to the northwest, but with not much better success; and the French made the most strenuous efforts to keep the north-western Indians from even visiting Albany to trade.

To this end M. de Pontchartrain wrote from Versailles, June 6th, 1708, that "It is no way advisable that the Indians visit Orange (Albany) and other English settlements, and an effort should be made to excite a vigorous and general war between these Indians and the English." Again, in a letter of the same date, to the Governor of Canada, he says: "I request you to endeavor to so manage and engage them (Indians) to make war against the English, as to put a stop to all such commercial intercourse." Accordingly, M. de Tonty, the Commandant of Fort Frontenac, endeavored to stop all trading parties of the north-western Indians from having intercourse with the English, which produced much dissatisfaction among those tribes, but did not entirely stop that trade. The Indians had found that the English goods were nearly half cheaper than those of the French, and the open forests enabled them to escape their vigilance. From this time the English influence began to gain in the north-west.

The peace that had for a time existed between the Sioux and the Indians of the region of Hudson's Bay, was finally broken, as the French believed, by the influence of the English traders at that place; and in the fall of 1700 the great war broke out between the Sioux and the Christineaux, in which the "Assenipoils" (Assiniboins) and the Chippeways joined the latter tribe. This formidable array from the north created no little alarm among the warlike Dakotas; particularly as among their enemies were now arrayed the Assiniboins, a part of their own confederacy, and hence "Greek must meet Greek." The Dakotas, as skillful in diplomacy as in war, in 1702 made peace with the Foxes and their allies along the Fox and Wisconsin rivers, and, to the chagrin of the French, engaged the latter tribes against their fierce enemies of the north. The Iowas, and several other southern tribes, also joined the Dakotas. Thus was organized the second great Indian war of modern times, which was continued at intervals and with modifications for nearly one hundred and fifty years. In later years it has been called "the hereditary war between the Sioux and Chippeways," and baffled the diplomacy at times of both the English and French nations. The Sacs and Foxes, however, had had some difficulties with the Chippeways, and they took this occasion to redress them. This is confirmed by the Governor of Canada, in his dispatch of November 4th, 1702, wherein he writes that "the differences that have arisen between the Sauteurs (Chippeways) and Sacs and Foxes, had terminated in mutual acts of hostilities."

The treaty of 1700, formed with the different tribes under the solemn pledges of the Governor of Canada that the French would take up arms against any tribe of Indians who should make war on another tribe, was evidently designed by the French as a treaty to quiet the Iroquois, while the Governor used the other tribes to make war on the English. It had but just been ratified, when the Governor of Canada wrote to the French Government, that it "acquired for the king a certain and incontestable superiority in Canada over all New England," and that the New England people were "cowardly to an astonishing degree." In November, 1702, the Governor of Canada wrote M. de Pontchartrain that "I will not omit any thing to get the English and Iroquois at loggerheads and to attach the latter to us, in order then to make use of the power you sent me in your letter of the 17th of May, to undertake something with more certainty against the English."

So inconsistent did the French soon appear to even the untutored savage, that the Iroquois chief told the Governor of Canada that "you tell us that we remain quiet on our mats. Nevertheless, we see our brothers of the *Sault* and the *Mountain*, who ought to be neutral like us, strike the English. You have given them the hatchet, and they go to war against the English."

From the treaty of 1700, the French used their whole diplomatic art to engage the north-western Indians in a war against the English, but with little success, owing to the great war then progressing on the upper Mississippi among those nations. They soon found that scolding and threatening would not avail them, and therefore they appointed a special agent to visit the north-west, to stop the war, and make combinations for that purpose. On this subject, the Governor of Canada, in his dispatch of the 31st of October, 1710, remarked that, "As it is our interest to prevent these Indians waging war against each other, so as to have it in our power to make use of them in case of need, should the Iroquois happen to declare against us, M. Raudot and I have concluded to send an officer thither to arrest their hatchet, and have selected, at the request of M. de Ramezay, Sieur d'Argenteuil, his brother-in-law," etc.

In 1711 the eventful time arrived for renewing the war against the English, and Governor Vaudreuil dispatched De Tonty to Detroit and De St. Pierre, by way of Grand river, to bring down the upper Indians to Montreal, for the purpose of engaging them in a war against the English. He returned with 400 or 500, who were afterwards joined by others, and who, in the language of the Governor, after showing a great reluctance to "closing the path to the English; for, after all, my lord, all the upper nations, even to the Indians of Lake Superior, resort thither," consented to take up the tomahawk against the English.

But this force was far inferior to that desired by the French, and this was charged on the Foxes and their allies along the Wisconsin and Fox rivers, who positively refused to stop their war against the Chippeways, and engage against the English.

However, the sequel is briefly told in the dispatch to M. de Pontchartrain, dated November 6, 1712, wherein it is stated: "This is what occurred this year, for the man named Saguina, having discovered during the winter the secret to unite with the Pautawatimis in order to wage war together against the Maskoutens and the Outagamies (Foxes), not only destroyed a considerable number of them in the place where they were wintering, but having further found means to win over almost all the other tribes to his interest, pursued these unfortunate people as far as Detroit, where they have killed or taken prisoners nearly a thousand of both sexes."

The Governor of Canada, it will be observed, is extremely careful not to intimate that the French had any hand in the massacre at Detroit; and still he must have had the dispatch of the commandant at Detroit, which claimed it as a great French victory. The facts were evidently these: During the winter of 1711 and 1712, the French, by their agent, had gained over to their interest the Potawatomies and some other tribes, which were then in alliance with the Foxes and

Mascotens, and while a large band of the latter tribes were engaged in their winter's hunt in the present State of Michigan. Early in the spring, the Ottawas and their new allies, the Potowatomies, suddenly attacked and massacred 150 Mascotens at St. Joseph's, where they had wintered, and the Chippeways attacked and defeated a band of Foxes sixteen miles above Detroit; whereupon the bands of *Pemoussa* and *Lamina*, of Mascotens and Foxes, including women and children, numbering nearly 1,000, retreated to Detroit, and pitched their camp within fifty paces of Fort Pontchartrain.

This so alarmed the commandant, M. Dubuisson, that, to use his own language, he " did not know on what saint to call;" but he immediately dispatched messages to the hostile nations, and in a few weeks there came together large bands of the Chippeways, Ottawas, Hurons, Potowatomies, and lastly, a large force of Illinois, Missouris, Osages, Sacs, Menominies, and other remote nations. A short council was held by the French and war chiefs, powder and ball distributed to the allies, when a great war-whoop was given, "the earth trembled," and the battle commenced.

It progressed with great violence for nineteen days, all being fortified, when on a dark, rainy night, the Mascotens and Foxes fled four leagues to Presque Isle, near Lake St. Clair, where they again fortified, and were again besieged, and after four days surrendered at discretion. All but the women and children, and 100 men, were immediately killed. The 100 men were bound, but made their escape. What became of the women and children, the French commandant does not inform us, but from the number given as killed, we naturally infer that they belonged to that list. Indeed, he admits that the Hurons killed all their prisoners. During this terrible battle, the Foxes and Mascotens twice asked for peace, but the French commandant refused it, because, in his own language, he " understood they were paid by the English for our destruction."

The French commandant, in his boasting dispatch, assumed that these Indians came to attack him, but from the fact that they were there with their women and children, at the close of their winter's hunt, made no attack on a weak wood fort with only about a score of soldiers, for weeks, while the French Indian allies were still absent on their winter's hunt, openly protested their peaceable intentions, and had never broken the peace of 1700, the writer is perfectly satisfied that this was a wanton massacre on the part of the French, to punish them for not going to Montreal the previous year, and taking up the tomahawk against the English.

Nothing appears in the English documents that the Foxes or Mascotens were in alliance with the English; but in 1710 the Governor of New York told the Iroquois, "the only way to strengthen you and us, and to weaken ye enemy, is to have as many (of the "Far nations") brought into the covenant chain as possible."

The treaty of peace concluded at Utrecht, April 11, 1713, may have closed the series of universal wars for the balance of power in Europe, but it did not equalize the wrongs of their allies in America. The Foxes and Mascotens soon reëstablished their alliance with all the tribes along the Fox and Wisconsin rivers, closed the French path to the Sioux by the Wisconsin river, and in 1719 the war raged fearfully against both the Illinois Indians on the south, and the Chippeways on the north.

In 1714 the French fitted out an expedition of eight hundred French and Indians, all pledged to exterminate every Fox Indian in Canada, according to Charlevoix, (tom. iv., p. 155,) which attacked the Fox fort on the Fox river; but after carrying on the siege for several days, evidently with considerable loss, the French abated the extermination, made a peace with the Foxes, and returned home.

But the French again resorted to diplomacy, and June 7th, 1726, M. de Lignery, the commandant at Mackinaw, concluded a treaty of peace at Green Bay, with the Sacs,

Foxes, and Winnebagoes, while some of the war parties of those tribes were still on the war path against the Illinois and Chippeways. That fact may have made the treaty irregular; but the following year the French secretly resolved to exterminate the Foxes at all hazards. They made peace with the Sioux, and in the fall of 1727 established a fort on Lake Pepin, under the command of Sieur de Lapperriere, with the Rev. Father Guignas as Jesuit missionary. The Foxes so far gave effect to the treaty of peace, that they did not disturb the small force when on their way to establish that fort. The Governor of Canada also sent a circular in 1727 to the commandants of all the French forts in the western country, "to make all necessary preparations for the expedition;" and said, "it is of the highest consequence that the Foxes should not be informed of this design."

The expedition left Canada early in the spring of 1728, nearly 1,000 strong, and were joined by the western forces and Indian allies at Green Bay; but they signally failed, either in surprising or exterminating the Foxes or their allies. The good Father Guignas abandoned his Sioux mission, and fled towards the Illinois, but was captured by the Mascotens and Kickapoos, in October of the same year, remained a prisoner five months, and was condemned to be burned at the stake, but was saved by an old Indian's adopting him into his family. The French say but little of the misfortune of this expedition, got up in secret, in violation of their treaty of 1726, but it was evidently a disastrous affair.

The French then changed their tactics, and thought to cut them off by parties of the Iroquois; and we find, in 1732, the Governor of Canada asking his king for medals to bestow upon Indian chiefs, to redeem his promise. Said the governor: "The adventure of our Iroquois and Hurons against the Foxes, places me under the obligation of giving a few to the principal chiefs of the expedition."

This process proved too slow, and a new military expedition was gotten up, and a battle fought, in 1734, when the King of France writes to the governor, in 1735, that he had "learned with pleasure that Captain *Desnoyelle's* expedition against the Foxes and Sacs has not been attended by any bad consequences." The Foxes were, however, not yet subdued, and in 1741 the Governor of Canada again writes, "that he learns that some under-ground belts were sent by the English to diverse Indian nations, inviting them to rid themselves of the French;" that "the Foxes had sent out some war parties against the Illinois, whereby several Frenchmen have been killed;" "that some brilliant action would be necessary, in order to keep the nations in check;" and that "this project" must be "kept a secret;" that he had "nothing so much at heart as the destruction of that Indian nation, (Foxes,) and that they had "a secret understanding with the Iroquois to secure a retreat among the latter, in case they were obliged to abandon their villages," and a similar one with "the Sioux of the Prairies, with whom they are allied." Still further to circumvent the Foxes, Sieur de Lusignan, Commandant of the French, spent the winter of 1745-6 with the Sioux, to effect a peace between them and the Winnebagoes, Menomonies, and Chippeways, with whom they had been at war for a long time.

But the misfortunes of the French with their Indian allies in 1747, culminated in a general conspiracy, as the governor wrote in November, "fomented by the English, who, by force of presents and lies, excite the Indians against us," and among other overt acts, he says: "The Sauteurs (Chippeways) have defeated one French canoe and plundered the goods," and that "the Foxes at the Bay, the Sioux and the Sacs — in a word, all the nations, so to speak — have struck whenever an opportunity presented."

These difficulties had occurred after Captain de la Corne St. Luc, the commandant at Mackinaw, had mustered all the north-western Indians possible, and taken them to Canada to fight against the English. His first attack with these allies was on Fort Clinton, where he took some English scalps. This general conspiracy was soon arranged, but it still had the effect to bring back the most of these allies who had gone east.

Captain de Vercheres, the commandant at Green Bay, did not leave Mackinaw for the Bay, for fear of the Bay Indians, until the first of October, 1747, and about the middle of the same month wrote to Mackinaw that "he had not been able to speak to the Indians, who were, when he arrived, all gone to their winter quarters without having given any token of repentance for the outrages they had perpetrated. It is hence to be presumed," he said, "that they persist in their evil dispositions."

The spring and summer of 1748 was mainly devoted to various "talks" and negotiations with the different tribes in the north-west, with no definite results, until the 3rd of August, when the news of the treaty of peace between England and France having reached Canada, the governor, by his proclamation, "orders all the nations to be notified not to go to New England on any more war parties; that they will not be paid in future for prisoners or scalps." The Indians naturally resolved themselves into quietness when the whites no longer needed their services, and consequently lopped off their usual bribes and excitements to war.

Hon. Morgan L. Martin, in his address before the State Historical Society of Wisconsin, in 1851, speaking from the traditions extant at Green Bay among the half-breed population, said that in 1746 the Sacs and Foxes were defeated by Captain Morand, "and finally driven beyond the Mississippi." Mr. Grignon, in his "Recollections," published by the State Historical Society, speaks of the tradition, and thought that the occurrence was in 1745, and that his grandfather probably was in the expedition.

Captain John Carver, in 1766 spoke of the tradition, and fixed the time at sixty years previous, which would have made it in 1706.

From the narrative which is here given, and which has mainly been compiled from official French documents, it will be observed that each of the traditions are equally improbable, as the Sacs and Foxes were still powerful, and inhabiting the Wisconsin valley in 1712, 1728, 1748, and 1754.

The exploits of Captain Morand are believed to be no where alluded to in any of the public documents, and he was probably the mythical hero, or *Robin Hood*, over which the French fathers beguiled their dusky half-breed children at the old trading-posts of *La Bay de Puans*.

The important wars between the colonies and their allies so absorbed the attention of the Indians of the Upper Mississippi, that they do not appear to have done much damage for several years, and in 1754 the French commandant at Green Bay, Sieur Marin, succeeded in effecting a treaty of peace between the Sacs, Foxes, Winnebagoes, and other tribes of the Bay Indians, and their enemies, the Chippeways, Christinaux, and French.

This peace was of great advantage to the French, as it enabled them, the following years, on the breaking out of the French and Indian war, to muster over six hundred of the north-western Indians, and march them to *Fort Duquesne*, where they assisted the French in the defeat of the army under General Braddock.

CHAPTER III.

THE INDIAN TRIBES, FROM 1755 TO THE CLOSE OF THE PONTIAC WAR, IN 1763.

THE impending struggle between the French and British nations, which was to settle the question of the extent of their colonial possessions in America, induced the former to change their system of keeping the various Indian tribes embroiled in wars among themselves, to the great scandal of civilized humanity. Hence, the French Government instructed M. Duquesne, the Governor of Canada, as early as April, 1752, that "'Tis considered proper to direct M. Duquesne to lay down henceforward in Canada, a different system from that always followed hitherto, in regard to wars among the Indians. With a view to occupy and weaken them, the principle has been to *excite and foment these sorts of wars.* That was of advantage in the infancy of the settlement of Canada. But in the condition to which these nations are now reduced, and in their present dispositions generally, it is in every respect more useful that the French perform between them the part of protectors and pacificators. They will, thereby, entertain more consideration and attachment for us; the colony will be more tranquil in consequence, and we shall save considerable expense. Cases, however, may occur in which it will be proper to excite war against certain nations attached to the English; but even such cases call for two observations: one, to endeavor first to gain over these same nations, by reconciling them with ours; and the other, to be as sure as possible that our Indians will not suffer too much from these wars."

This new system, however, was evidently to be pursued as intimated, only when the French could not avail themselves of the Indians' services; hence, M. Duquesne reported to his Government, in October, 1754, that " the Poutwatomies, Kickapoux, Maskoutins, and Sioux of the Prairies, have assembled together, to go and destroy the Peorias, who, for a long time have regarded with insolence the other Indians; they are, moreover, people of no faith, who steal with impunity, even in their neighbors' cabins. This war, in which I am not at all interested, can be productive only of a good effect in putting down such banditti. I have, nevertheless, ordered the commandant to adjust all matters after these rascals will have received a sharp lesson."

The impending crisis seems to have been well understood by both governments, and as early as the summer of 1753, the French opened the campaign, by sending *Sieur Marin*, with about two hundred and fifty soldiers and some Indians, to take formal possession of the Ohio valley, who erected a fort at " *River au Bœuf*," at the present site of Waterford, Erie county, Pennsylvania.

In October following, Major George Washington was dispatched by Governor Dinwiddie, of Virginia, to the commandant at the French fort, remonstrating against the French occupying the Ohio valley. The English, about the same time, commenced the erection of a fort at the present site of Pittsburgh, Pennsylvania, but were soon dispossessed by the French, who proceeded with the work, and erected Fort Duquesne.

In April, 1754, Lieutenant-Colonel Washington was dispatched by the Governor of Virginia, with a force of about 400 troops, to drive out the French from the valley; but in the mean time, the French, having been reinforced, attacked

Colonel Washington at Fort Necessity, July 3, 1754, and forced him to surrender his troops.

Thus we find that the question of the right to the possession of the great valley of the Mississippi, at this early day, involved two continents in a murderous, destructive war, which continued over eight years, bringing untold sufferings upon both the white and the red men of the new world. The British government dispatched two regiments to Virginia from some Irish port, as early as January 13, 1755, under the command of General Braddock; and in April following, the French sent a fleet of six battalions of regulars, of about 3,000 men, under the command of Baron de Dieskaw, as major-general.

In February, the Shawnees, of Ohio valley, were excited to commence war against the English settlements, and took seventeen scalps and ten prisoners, and M. Duquesne sent a detachment of troops on the ice from Montreal to support the Indians. With no declaration of war between the home governments, but under the strongest protestations of peace, both nations hastened to send large armies across the Atlantic, while the recruiting drums rattled in every colonial village, and the war-whoop was heard in every savage tribe from the Atlantic to the Rocky mountains, and from the Gulf of Mexico to the frozen regions of the north.

The popular Sieur Marin, who commanded the French expedition to the Ohio in 1753, returned to Canada late in the fall of the same year, and in the following spring was assigned to the command of the post at Green Bay, where he effected a peace between the Sacs, Foxes and other Bay Indians, and the Christinaux of Lake Superior, thus reconciling the troublesome Foxes, with whom the French had been at war for nearly forty years, and brought the united Indian force of the north-west into the league against the English.

As the campaign of 1755 opened on the Ohio, all the popular Indian leaders of the north-west called Indian councils, distributed war belts, ammunition, arms, blankets and other presents, with a good supply of brandy, and rallied the dusky warriors for the murderous conflicts which ensued. The prominent Indian traders, believing that the exclusive possession of the Mississippi valley by the French was absolutely necessary to preserve to them their monopoly of Indian trade, seconded the efforts of the French officers, and in a few days long files of warriors, under their bravest chiefs, were on their way for the defense of Fort Duquesne, at Pittsburgh. Charles Langlade, a half-breed trader of Green Bay, De Carry, a French trader among the Winnebagoes, and father of a line of Winnebago chiefs, of whom one-eyed De Carry was grandson, and others too numerous to mention, trading among other tribes, joined the winding files as leaders and interpreters, and were often the most savage of their savage companions in arms. These bands were joined on the route by small parties of warriors from most of the tribes of the Ohio valley, and a considerable force soon congregated at Fort Duquesne for the defense of that post.

General Braddock, with nearly 1,200 regular veteran soldiers from Great Britain, and some provincials from Virginia, under Colonel Washington, who had cut his way, at great labor, over the mountains of Virginia and Pennsylvania, was met within four leagues of Fort Duquesne, on the 9th day of July, 1755, by an advance party of skirmishers, consisting of 72 French regulars, 146 Canadians, and 637 north-western Indians, all under the command of Captain de Beaujou; and after a severe battle of nearly four hours, General Braddock's army was routed with great slaughter, and put to flight. This action cost the English nearly 600 men dead on the field, according to the French account, besides wounded; fifteen brass field-pieces and mortars, and their entire ammunition and camp equipage. General Braddock was mortally wounded, and a large proportion of his officers killed. Captain de Beaujou, the French commandant, was killed at the first fire, but the losses of the French and Indians were claimed to be less than 100.

This decisive action for a time left the Ohio valley in the peaceable possession of the French, and their allies of the north-west. Baron de Dieskaw was quite as unfortunate in his campaign against Fort Lake George as his English cotemporary had been in Pennsylvania. The Baron left Montreal with 720 French regulars, 1,500 Canadians, and 760 Indians of the Huron, Iroquois, Abenakis, and Nepissing tribes. He passed along Lake Champlain, and with a large part of his regulars and Canadians, and all his Indian allies, on the 8th of September, 1755, attacked the advance of about 1,000 provincials and Indians, under Colonel Williams and the Mohawk Chief Hendricks, which he drove in with the loss of those two leaders and many of the men, and then assaulted the camp at Fort Lake George, commanded by General William Johnson. In this assault he was himself mortally wounded and taken prisoner, Captain St. Peter, who commanded the Indians, killed, his forces utterly defeated and routed, and pursued for some distance with great slaughter. General Johnson had about 250 Indians of the six nations in his command, but the most of those tribes either remained neutral or had joined the French. Baron de Dieskaw charged the loss of the battle "to the treachery of the Iroquois," and that "as the Iroquois perceived some Mohawks, they came to a dead halt;" but this statement was not corroborated in Governor Vaudreuil's dispatch, who, on the contrary, stated that the Indians charged up to the English barricades, led on by the Rev. Father Andran, the Jesuit missionary of the Abenakis.

After the defeat of General Braddock, the north-western Indians returned home, and the Governor of Canada ordered the commandants at Detroit and Mackinaw to send down a body to assist in the defence of Niagara as early as September of the same year; but those commandants reported that the Indians " were so fatigued after their campaign at Fort Duquesne, that they were unable to go."

The fierce battles which ended by the total defeat of the armies of Generals Braddock and Dieskaw, had so far brought to light the intrigues and hypocrisy of the courts of the two nations, that further secrecy was of no importance; and, December 21st, 1755, the French foreign minister publicly demanded " reparation for insults to the French flag," to which the British minister replied, January 13, 1756, that it could not be accorded while the " French armed posts to the north-west of the Alleghanies existed."

After the war had been carried on nearly two years, it was formally proclaimed by England, May 17th, 1756, and by France, June 16th following; but little had been accomplished, however, between the contending armies. During this year, crimination between the English and colonial officers run high. General Shirley was made commander-in-chief by the crown, but the colonists early refused to volunteer under him, and demanded General Winslow.

Colonel Washington, as early as February, visited General Shirley at Boston, to settle the rank between himself and Captain Dagworthy, holding a king's commission. In the mean time, the Indian forces were called in from the north-west by the French officials, and overran all the western parts of Pennsylvania, Maryland, Virginia, Carolina, and Georgia; and the French claimed that over 3,000 prisoners, men, women, and children, were captured and carried into the Ohio valley. Colonel Washington, with a regiment of Rangers, whom the French claimed were dressed and painted like Indians, acted on the defensive, but could not defend so extensive a frontier. The French had in their service this season, seven hundred Delawares and Shawnees, two hundred and fifty Miamies, and three hundred Indians from Detroit; also, seven hundred from Mackinaw, under the command of De Repentigny, Langlade, and Herbert, junior. They also had many from

Illinois and from Canada; — in all amounting to 3,250, as appeared by a French dispatch.

M. Marin, the commandant at Green Bay, with sixty Indians from his post, with De Villiers, the commandant from New Orleans, with four hundred French and Indians, on the 2nd July, 1756, attacked a large convoy of supplies for Oswego; and he claimed to have destroyed five hundred bateaux, and killed four hundred and fifty English. Lieutenant De Villiers, the 2nd of August following, with a detachment of fifty-five French and Illinois Indians, captured and burnt Fort Granville, within sixty miles of Philadelphia. Lieutenant Marin, with his Wisconsin Indians, went to Lake George, and with a party of one hundred, captured fifty-two English near that lake, some time in September. During the following winter, several scalping expeditions were sent against the English, but there were probably no north-western Indians among them, as they returned home in the fall.

The winter of 1756–7, in the north-west, was spent in recruiting Indians for the French army; and in June, 1757, 1,000 reached Montreal, ready for new scenes of fight and plunder. General Montcalm planned the attack on Fort William Henry, at Lake George, and moved in that direction. Lieutenant Marin, in charge of about two hundred Wisconsin Indians and Canadians, while on a scout in July, boldly attacked Fort Edward, and then retreated with one prisoner and thirty-two scalps.

General Montcalm, in his dispatch, complimented these Indians, by saying, "they generally have all behaved well." The general labored hard to gain the confidence of his Indian allies, having, as he said, "chanted the war songs" with them, given "feasts," and held "councils;" and was "obliged to pass" his "time with them in ceremonies as tiresome as they were necessary." He dare not mention to them the attempt to assassinate the king, for fear that "these barbarians, so ferocious in war, so humane in their lodges, might waver in their esteem for us, seeing us capable of producing such monsters."

He was obliged to submit all his plans of the campaign to the general councils, " for," said he, " these independent people, whose assistance is purely voluntary, require to be consulted; every thing must be communicated to them, and their opinions and caprices are oftentimes a law for us." But the greatest difficulty with all the white commandants was to keep the Indians from returning home after one battle, or even a skirmish in which a few scalps had been taken, for the reason, as wrote the general, that " these people scruple to incur again the risk of war after one success, pretending that such would be tempting the Master of Life, and bring down on them bad luck." After speaking of the praying Indians before the battle, he remarked: " But this pious exercise was not for the upper country nations, whose superstitions and excessively restless minds were juggling, dreaming, and fancying that every delay portended misfortune. On marching, these nations left suspended a complete equipment, as a sacrifice to the *Manitou*, to render him propitious."

Attached to the French army at the capture of Fort William Henry were 1,806 Indians, of which 820 were the " domiciliated" or Christian Indians of Canada, and the following from the north-west:

Ottawas,	340	Commanded by De Langlade, Florement, and Herbin, with Abbe Mealavet, missionary.
Chippeways,	157	La Plant and De Lorimer; Chesne, interpreter.
Potowatomies,	78	
Menomonies,	129	
Miamies,	15	
Winnebagoes,	48	De Tailly, interpreter.
Iowas,	10	
Foxes,	20	Marin and Langus.
Onillas,	10	Reaume, interpreter.
Sacs,	33	
Loups,	5	
Total,	986	

All of the Indian allies were placed under the command of *M. de St. Luc*, an old commandant at Mackinaw and in the north-west previous to 1748, who had often led the Indians against the English.

Thus it is apparent that these Indians required all the tricks and appliances of civilization to induce them to engage in war against the English; and while they have done no worse than they were hired to do, they have a counterpart in the Hessians of Germany, who fought as hirelings for the English in our American revolution.

Fort William Henry was attacked by General Montcalm, and surrendered August 9th, 1757, and the English soldiers paroled and sent to Fort Edward, under an escort, but were attacked on the way and plundered by the Indians, to the eternal disgrace of the French and their Indian allies; although many of the French officers, including General Montcalm, to their credit, risked their own lives in defence of the English soldiers.

While this affair has been termed by the English a massacre, but few of the English were killed. Nearly four hundred were taken as prisoners; but the most of them were immediately released by General Montcalm, and the balance, after their return to Montreal. This unfortunate affair, however, was not charged against the north-western Indians; but General Montcalm expressly says, in his dispatch, that it was commenced by the *Abenakis*, a "domiciliated" tribe of Canada, "who pretended to have experienced some ill treatment at the hands of the English." They were probably retaliating for the New England massacre of their own tribe at Norridgewock, in 1724, when the Rev. Father Rale, the aged Jesuit missionary, was mercilessly shot down while clinging to his mission cross, his church burned, and his Dictionary of the Abenakis language carried off and deposited in the Harvard college, where it still remains. Even as late as 1754, it appears by a letter of that date, from M. Duquesne, that the Abenakis were desiring to revenge the death of two of their chiefs, killed two years previous, near Boston.

The Iowas, a kindred tribe to the Winnebagoes, appear to have sent ten warriors this year to assist the French; but the Sioux, probably on account of their wars with the Chippeways, never joined the French during the war.

During the winter of 1757-8, several expeditions were made against the English by small parties of French and Indians; one of which burnt a village on the German Flats, and took one hundred and fifty prisoners; another defeated Major Rogers, and carried off one hundred and forty-six scalps and a few prisoners; but the Indians which accompanied these marauding parties were the Iroquois, and other domiciliated Indians of Canada, the north-western Indians having returned home in the fall; and, unfortunately, many of them on their way thither died with the small-pox, which generally proves fatal to them under their system of medicine. Many also died during the winter of the same disease, at Mackinaw and some other places. A difficulty also occurred at Green Bay, and a party of Menomonies killed eleven Canadians, burned the store-house, but missed the commandant, who was probably M. Marin.

But few of the north-western Indians went to Canada in 1758, and none of them were with General Montcalm when he defeated General Howe before Ticondaroga, July 8th; but soon after that, the Indians were sent to General Montcalm, under M. De St. Luc and M. Marin, who did some service in capturing an English convoy near Fort Edward, containing fifty-four wagons, on the 30th of the same month. M. Marin, "a colonial officer of great reputation," commanded another expedition, which was met by the "partisan Robert Rogers," and defeated with some loss; or, to use the more classic French, "he extricated himself very handsomely" from the English.

The probability that the English would attack Niagara in the spring of 1759, induced the military authorities of

Canada to make early preparations for the defense of that post. They dispatched orders early in the fall of 1758, to the north-west, to bring down in the spring all the available force of the upper country, including the Illinois region and the Ohio valley, with a rendezvous at Presque Isle, near the present site of Erie, Pennsylvania. *M. Pouchot*, "an experienced and intelligent" officer, was ordered to repair to the outlet of Lake Ontario, on the ice, in March, and with cannon; from thence to embark, at the opening of navigation, for Fort Niagara, in two corvettes, with two pickets of regulars.

M. De Montigny, with 300 Canadians, and provisions in thirty bateaux, was to go by the north shore of Lake Ontario to Niagara, at the opening of navigation, while M. De St. Luc, with some Canadians and Indians, was to reconnoiter about Oswego. He made an attack on that place, but was driven off, and M. De St. Luc wounded. M. de Ligneris, in command at Fort Machault, at the junction of the Alleghany and French creek, Pennsylvania, was ordered to repair to Niagara, if necessary for its defense.

Agreeable to the anticipations of the authorities of Canada, the Americans and English, with 2,200 troops and 600 Indians, mostly Iroquois, left Oswego July 1, 1759, for Niagara, under General Prideaux, with Colonel William Johnson, Indian agent, second in command, and were soon after joined by 300 additional Iroquois Indians, and on the 7th of the same month laid siege to Fort Niagara. Notice of this anticipated attack was early sent to M. de Ligneris, the commandant at Presque Isle, to come with his whole force to the assistance of the besieged.

On the 24th of July, M. de Ligneris, with his force from Ohio river, M. Aubry from Illinois, M. Marin from Green Bay, in charge of the Indians, and M. De Montigny, M. Repentigny, commandant at Mackinaw, and others, with a combined force estimated by the English at 850 Canadians, and 350 Indians, but by the French at 400 Canadians, and 30 Indians, attacked an English detachment, partly fortified, on the bank of the Niagara river, above the fort, under Lieutenant-Colonel Massey, and were totally defeated, with 200 killed, and 100 taken prisoners. The balance escaped back to the 150 Canadians left to guard the canoes and batcaux above the Falls, and under M. Belestre returned to Detroit with their Indian allies. Five captains and twelve subaltern officers, mostly wounded, were taken prisoners, among whom were Messrs. De Ligneris, De Aubry, De Marin, De Montigny, and De Repentigny. On the following day, M. Pouchot, having learned of the loss of this reinforcement, surrendered the fort to the English.

This misfortune to the French was attributed by them to the fact that the 900 Iroquois Indians on the side of the English, induced the western Indians, nearly 1,000 strong, not to fight, but with them to remain neutral, and when M. Marin rallied his warriors for the fight, but thirty of the most determined of them followed him to the attack, while only about 100 Iroquois assisted the English. This defeat, with the loss of Fort Niagara, cut off from the French of Canada nearly all their western resources and western allies, and enabled the English to concentrate their entire force on Quebec and Montreal. This obliged the French to evacuate Crown Point and fall back on *L'Isle au Noix*, near the outlet of Lake Champlain, on the 4th of August following.

The fall of Quebec, September 18th, and the surrender of all Canada to the English the following September, 1760, closed the French power in Canada, which had continued for one hundred and fifty years.

The English exercised no less zeal than the French to secure the Indians as their allies during the whole war. Early in the spring of 1755, General Braddock appointed Colonel William Johnson as Indian agent for the Six Nations in New York, and gave him £2,000, to be expended mainly in Indian presents.

In June of the same year, Colonel Johnson called an

Indian council, at which he called the Great Spirit to witness that the English had no evil designs against them, threw them the war belt in General Braddock's name, began the war-dance, and "ordered a large tub of punch out to drink the king's health." He armed, clothed and fitted out every Indian who would go to war against the French. The Indians complained of many frauds practiced on them in getting their lands, to which Colonel Johnson replied, with the present of a belt of wampum, that "I am convinced that many frauds have been made use of in the purchasing of your lands, for which I am very sorry," and pledged them redress. The Indians went to war, but the redress came not. The Indians of course became cold and neutral, and some joined the enemy, and the western nations laid waste the whole western frontier.

Again, in September, 1757, Colonel Johnson remonstrated to the lords of trade, "that the Indians are disgusted and dissatisfied with the extensive purchases of land, and do think themselves injured thereby. This is one main cause of their defection from the British interest." In 1758 the British government awoke to the importance of the question, and at the treaty at Easton, Pennsylvania, held by the Governors of that State and New Jersey, they agreed to surrender to the Indians certain lands, the purchase of which had caused so much complaint; and the deeds of surrender were delivered to an assembly of ten nations of Indians, being the Iroquois and some of their allies, April 17, 1759. At this time, Colonel Johnson remarked to them: "You see, while the French keep their forts in the midst of your country, and fight with us in order to secure the possession of them, we give up those lands which you had sold us." This was all very satisfactory to the Indians, and they delivered up their prisoners, and heartily engaged in the war against the French.

This amicable adjustment of their difficulties gave Colonel Johnson 900 warriors in July at Fort Niagara, who won over the western Indians, and thereby hastened the downfall of the French power in America. So important did these measures appear to the lords of trade, that they reported, and the king in council confirmed, November 23, 1761, the following language: "It was happy for us that we were early awakened to a proper sense of the injustice and bad policy of such conduct towards the Indians; and no sooner were these measures pursued which indicated a disposition to do them possible justice upon this head of complaint, than those hostilities which had produced such horrid scenes of devastation ceased, and the Six Nations and their dependants became at once, from the most inveterate enemies, our fast and faithful friends."

This war was sustained with great zeal by the French traders, and *courrier de bois* of the north-west, and probably two-thirds of them perished in the fearful conflicts which took place during its existence; but, being on the unfortunate side, no historian of that day has preserved their memory, and they are only known, at this day, from the obscure traditions of their half-breed descendants. Some were the husbands of the daughters of Indian chiefs, and were fathers of illustrious lines of chiefs, who are yet in the possession of power in their respective tribes. As an instance, might be named *De Carry*, the grandfather of the old Winnebago chief, "One-eyed De Carry." He married *Ho-po-ko-e-kaw*, or "the Glory of the Morning," the daughter of the principal chief of the Winnebagoes, and had two sons; the oldest, *Choo-ke-kaw*, or "the Ladle," was head chief at the Portage, in Wisconsin, 1801, and signed the treaty of peace with the United States in 1816: the younger son was *Chah-post-kaw-kaw*, or "the Buzzard," who came with a band to La Crosse, where he was killed, previous to 1800. The latter was father to *Wadge-hutta-kaw*, or "the Big Canoe, commonly called "One-eyed De Carry" by the English. He died at the Tunnel, in Wisconsin, August, 1864, very aged.

Wa-kon-ha-kaw, or "Snake Skin," another chief, brother to "Big Canoe," was alive in 1867. He was orator of the tribe, and known to the English as Washington De Carry. Old De Carry fought through the war, and was wounded April 28th, 1760, before Quebec, and soon after died at Montreal. The widow was chief of the tribe in 1766, and was visited by Captain Carver in that year, her father having probably died in the war.

Equally unfortunate were the popular French colonial officers, who had explored and developed so much of the north-west, and had wielded a controlling influence among the red men for many years. We mark their fall in the thickest of the fight, from year to year, and when the war closed by the surrender of Canada, Lieutenant *Charles De Langlade*, the half-breed Ottawa, almost alone survived, and was, by the Governor of Canada, September 3rd, 1760, ordered to take charge of and conduct the Canadians under his command to Mackinaw, and the Indians to their villages, and forward two companies of English deserters to Louisiana. Lieutenant De Langlade was the grandfather of the Grignons who, in the present century, have occupied prominent positions at Green Bay.

The rule of the French in the north-west was mainly like that of the libertine over his mistress, — full of coquetry and smiles, and they were generally called by the endearing name of "good spirits." The advent of the French trader to an Indian village was a day of rejoicing. He smoked their pipe of peace, chanted their songs, joined in the festive dance, gave feasts to the chiefs, and took to wife their daughters. The Indian maidens emulated each other to become the trader's mistress, and be decorated with the gaudy trappings of civilization. The French Jesuit missionaries, with breviary and cross, who had then threaded every forest and navigated every river in the Mississippi valley, and had had thousands of converts among the different

WA-KON-HA-KAW.
(WINNEBAGO CHIEF.)

tribes, generally left the country and returned to Europe on the fall of the Canadian government.

The change of government could not restore the dead fathers to their thousands of weeping children, and their sorrowing mothers could only tell them that their fathers had been scalped by the merciless "Long-knives." The small-pox, a fatal disease to the Indians, had raged fearfully among many of the tribes. Trade for a time was nearly suspended for want of goods, and the Indian missed his powder and ball, to kill the game to feed his family.

During the war, the English had been profuse in their promises to the Indians, as an inducement to take up the tomahawk against the French; that their lands should be returned, and supplies furnished at a far less rate than was done by the French; but, on the contrary, wrote Colonel Johnson, Indian agent, in June, 1761: "Instead of restoring their lands, we are erecting more forts in many parts of the country, and goods are still so dear that their warriors and women are very uneasy, and apt to believe very bad reports concerning the intentions of the English."

The French of Louisiana, who were very anxious to turn the channel of the Indian trade in that direction, and had continued to hold possession of the Illinois, industriously circulated among the Indians every damaging report possible against the English; and to give point to the charge of sinister motives of the English in erecting forts in the Ohio valley, alleged that it was the intention of the English to take the Ohio valley from the Delawares, Senecas, Shawnees, Miamies, and other tribes that then inhabited it, and give it to the Cherokees, who were friendly to the English, but with whom the Ohio Indians were at war.

To encourage the Indians to take up the war hatchet against the English, war belts were freely circulated by the French among the Indians during the winter of 1762–3, with a statement that early in the spring the King of France was coming with a great army to recover possession of

Canada, and inviting the Indians to anticipate their father by capturing all the English forts in the country. There is reason to believe that these were not idle, gossiping stories of the French, but that there was a serious disposition among many of the Canadians to revolt, and, with the assistance of France, to gain their former position. In 1762 England had refused to ratify a treaty of peace with France, and the latter nation had formed an alliance with Spain, and many in the colonies thought that France might, with the help of Spain, regain her Canadian possessions. Several memorials were addressed to the King of France to that effect, by prominent Canadian officers in the late war, but fortunately, perhaps, for them, the belligerent nations finally ratified a treaty of peace, February 10th, 1763, by which the French ceded Canada to England, and Louisiana to Spain, thereby terminating their possessions in North America.

But the poor Indians, buried in the depths of the primeval forests of the great west, knew nothing of the intrigues of the vacillating courts of Europe. Intent on the point of serving the French, ridding themselves of their hateful enemies, and revenging the murders still often perpetrated on them by the licentious soldiers, traders, and pioneers on the frontier settlements, unwittingly went on perfecting their leagues, and finally commenced an attack on all the English forts in the north-west.

Pontiac, a chief of a roving band of the Ottawas, then near Detroit, who had distinguished himself at the defeat of General Braddock in 1755, and at several other battles during the French wars in America from 1746, became the leading chief, and, assisted by the French, planned a simultaneous surprise of the English posts. Mackinaw, Miami, Presque Isle, Ouiatenon, St. Josephs, Sandusky, La Bœuf and Venango, were taken, and the most of the garrisons tomahawked. Detroit, the most important post in command of the English, was reserved by the cunning chief, on which to exercise his own prowess and stratagem; but failing to keep to himself his plan of surprise, it was disclosed to Major Gladwin, the commandant of the post, by a friendly squaw, and by that means saved from surprise and capture. Pontiac laid siege to the fort, but failed to reduce it. The Indians also laid siege to Fort Ligonier, Bedford and Loudon, of Pennsylvania, and Cumberland, of Maryland, and devastated the country about Fort Pitt. Nearly all the English traders among the Indians were plundered and massacred, and raiding parties sent against the frontier settlements of Pennsylvania and Virginia, with murderous effect.

The usual errors in dates have occurred among historians relating to this war, but Bancroft has collected them with considerable accuracy, and dates the commencement of the siege of Detroit, May 9; the capture of Sandusky, May 6; of St. Josephs, by a party of Potowatomies from Detroit, May 25; Miami, May 27; Fort Ouiatanon, near Lafayette, Indiana, June 1; Mackinaw, June 2; Presque Isle, June 22; and Le Bœuf, June 18.

Authors have generally enumerated Green Bay among the list, but Lieutenant Gorell, who commanded there when notified of the capture of Mackinaw, voluntarily abandoned that fort, and was guarded by the tribes about the Bay, who were friendly to the English, far on his way towards Montreal, to a place of safety.

It has also been customary to include the Sacs and Foxes, and other Indians of the Bay, as hostile to the English, and as having joined Pontiac's confederacy, but facts do not well sustain the allegation; on the contrary, they received presents from Sir William Johnson for their fidelity to the English. The Sioux, instead of joining Pontiac, offered Sir William Johnson 5,000 warriors to assist him in destroying the confederates. Neither did the Illinois Indians, nor the Chippeways of Lake Superior, become members of the Pontiac confederacy. The confederacy might be said to include a few Ottawas and Chippeways about Mackinaw, and to have extended to Lake Ontario and the Ohio river, including the Ottawas, lower Chippeways, Hurons, Miamies, Kickapoos, Potowatomies, Shawnees, Delawares, and the Geneseo band of the Senecas.

Soon after the war commenced, the Indians of Canada sent a message to their hostile brethren, notifying them that peace had been established between France and England; that the King of England had now become their father, and advising peace. Sir William Johnson held a treaty with the Six Nations, reconciled the Senecas, and sent parties of the Six Nations against the Delawares, which made some captures, and broke up the confederacy, the Delawares suing for peace.

In the mean time, Le Neyon de Villiere, the French commandant at Fort Chartres, in Illinois, sent belts and a proclamation, addressed to twenty-five nations, notifying them that the French had surrendered Canada; that peace was established; that the French were retiring west of the Mississippi, and advising peace. This message reached Pontiac at Detroit, the last day of October, 1763, and the next morning he sent overtures of peace to Major Gladwin, who notified the chief that he had no power to conclude a peace, but would refer it to General Gage. This was satisfactory to the chief, and the savages dispersed to their hunting-grounds, and the fort was relieved of its long and painful siege.

General Gage, early in 1764, dispatched an order to Major Gladwin, at Detroit, that if the western Indians were desirous of peace, to send them to Niagara, where they would be met by Sir William Johnson, the Indian agent, and a peace concluded. Consequently, over 2,000 Indians assembled at Niagara by the 25th of August, 1764, containing delegations from the Hurons, Senecas, Ottawas, Chippeways, Menominies, Foxes, Sacs, Winnebagoes, and some tribes from the north of Lake Superior. They were met by

Sir William Johnson, with about 600 friendly Indians, and Colonel Bradstreet, with an army designed for the west.

Treaties were formed with the Hurons and Senecas, but the balance of the tribes brought certificates from Major Gladwin and others, that they had not joined in the war against the English, except some individuals who had left the tribes for that purpose, but had continued friendly to the English. Colonel Johnson reported that he " admitted them into the covenant chain of friendship, on their agreeing to the reëstablishment of Mackinaw, and promising to get all prisoners out of the enemy's hands, as also to procure some restitution for the traders' losses; all which they engaged to perform."

Colonel Johnson also reported that " the Indians who did not attend at Niagara, were, I believe, doubtful of our sincerity, but they now seem desirous to make terms of concession," etc.; and that " Pontiac is, with some of the most obstinate, as yet in the Miami's country, near the west end of Lake Erie, but has sent to desire peace, and I believe is only apprehensive for his security and that of those with him, otherwise he would have attended the congress."

Colonel Bradstreet left for Detroit with his army, took the responsibility to treat with some of the Indians, to the great disgust of Colonel Johnson; and finally returned a part of his army in the fall in bad condition. Colonel Bouquet, in command of a small body of forces, left Fort Pitt, and penetrated the heart of the Delaware and Shawnee country; obtained over two hundred prisoners, and brought back hostages that they would go to Colonel Johnson and conclude a treaty. In May, 1765, the Delawares visited Colonel Johnson, and settled their difficulties by treaty; and the Shawnees followed their example, July 9th ensuing.

May 15, 1765, Colonel Croghan set out from Fort Pitt with a party to visit the Illinois and take the surrender of the posts in that region from the French, but they were taken prisoners on the way by the Kickapoos and Masco-

6*

tens, taken to Post Vincent, and from thence towards the Illinois, when Colonel Croghan met Pontiac, and returned with him to Detroit, where he arrived with that chief, August 17th. Here peace was concluded with the balance of the hostile Indians, to the general satisfaction of all parties; and Pontiac declared that he and the Indians had been imposed upon by the French for the purpose of obtaining the beaver, and called it the "beaver war," and sent his pipe to Colonel Johnson.

Captain Sterling, with a small detachment of troops, took possession of Fort Chartres in the Illinois, in October, 1765, without opposition; and finally, Pontiac, in July following, with several south-western chiefs, visited Colonel Johnson at Oswego, settled all differences, and in his closing speech, Pontiac eloquently remarked: "Father, it will take some time before I can make known to all the nations what has passed here, but I will do it even from the rising of the sun to the setting, and from north to south."

Pontiac was a chief of more than ordinary ability, as well as business capacity, and constantly kept two secretaries, one to read his letters, and the other to write. Colonel Croghan, who was with him for some weeks, said of him that he "is a shrewd, sensible Indian, of few words, and commands more respect among all those nations than any Indian I ever saw could do amongst his own tribe."

Some three years after the close of the war, and in 1767, this able chief was assassinated in Illinois by a Peoria Indian, for a reward of a barrel of rum from an English trader, to revenge which the Ottawas, Potowatomies, and some other tribes, are said to have nearly annihilated the whole band of Peorias.

CHAPTER IV.

THE INDIAN TRIBES, FROM 1764 TO THE CLOSE OF THE WAR WITH GREAT BRITAIN, IN 1815.

The desire of revenge, with the Indian, terminates when the belt of peace is presented by the adversary and accepted, and the pipe passed round and individually smoked by the dusky warriors; and one who has been the greatest enemy, may safely pass through two lines of wigwams, without danger of insult or injury; for their religion holds that an injury to an enemy of whom they have accepted the belt and the pipe, is an insult to the Great Spirit. But such is not the case with the white man of the frontier; and ever since the first settlement of this country, there have been large numbers who have believed that the Indians, as heathens, had no rights which the white men "were bound to respect."

After the conclusion of peace with the confederate tribes under Pontiac, the pioneers committed some of the most barbarous murders along the frontiers of Pennsylvania and Virginia, and it required many presents, and the greatest efforts of those in authority, to pacify the Indians, and save the country from a renewal of the war.

Upon this subject, Colonel Johnson, the British Indian agent, wrote to his government as early as June 28, 1766, that the war "was no sooner terminated at a considerable loss and expense, than the frontier inhabitants, from Virginia to this province (New York) (though they shewed but little alacrity at the time they ought), began, under the specious pretense of revenge, but in violation of the British faith, to murder, rob, and otherwise grossly misuse all Indians they could find in small parties, either on their way to or from the southward, or trading amongst them; whilst those who avoided imbruing their hands in blood added fuel to their jealousy by encroaching upon their rights, and treating the Indians with contempt, much greater than they had ever before experienced. This has at length thoroughly confirmed their opinion that we projected their ruin."

Colonel Johnson, who had become well acquainted with Indian character, writes further, in the same dispatch: "Our people in general are very ill calculated to maintain friendship with the Indians; they despise those in peace, whom they fear to meet in war. This, with the little artifices used in trade, and the total want of that address and seeming kindness practiced with such success by the French, must always hurt the colonists. On the contrary, could they but assume a friendship, and treat them with civility and candor, we should soon possess their hearts, and much more of their country than we shall do in a century by the conduct now practiced."

The encroachments upon the Indian rights increased from bad to worse, until 1774, when Captain Cresap, with a party near Wheeling, Virginia, murdered the whole family of Captain John Logan, a friendly chief of the Cayuga band of the Iroquois, who rallied his warriors and retaliated with fearful vengeance, until the fall of the year, when he was defeated in a battle at Point Pleasant, by 1,500 Virginians, and finally pacified by Lord Dunmore. It was at this treaty that Logan delivered the following speech, for which President Jefferson has immortalized him, by quoting it in his "Notes on Virginia:"

"I appeal to any white man to say, if ever he entered Logan's cabin hungry, and he gave him not meat; if ever he came cold and naked, and he clothed him not. During the course of the last long and bloody war, Logan remained idle in his cabin, an advocate of peace. Such was my love for the whites, that my countrymen pointed as they passed, and said, 'Logan is the friend of white men.' I had even thought to have lived with you, but for the injuries of one man, Colonel Cresap, the last spring, who in cold blood, and unprovoked, murdered all the relations of Logan, not even sparing my women and children. There runs not a drop of my blood in the veins of any living creature. This called on me for revenge. I have sought it; I have killed many; I have fully glutted my vengeance; for my country I rejoice at the beams of peace. But do not harbor a thought that mine is the joy of fear; Logan never felt fear. He will not turn on his heel to save his life. Who is there to mourn for Logan? Not one."

In this state of animosity were the western Indians at the commencement of our revolutionary war. Colonel William Johnson, the British agent, died July 11, 1774, and his son-in-law, Guy Johnson, was appointed by the king his successor. He had been in the Indian department for nearly twenty years, and was scarcely as humane as the Indians themselves, as subsequent events showed. The British government early determined to make allies of the Indians, to help suppress the rebellion in America, and, July 24, 1775, the Earl of Dartmouth instructed Colonel Guy Johnson that "the unnatural rebellion now raging there calls for every effort to suppress it; and the intelligence his majesty has received of the rebels having excited the Indians to take a part, and of their having actually engaged a body of them in arms to support their rebellion, justifies the resolution his majesty has taken, of requiring the assistance of his faithful adherents the Six Nations. It is therefore his majesty's pleasure, that you do lose no time in taking such steps as may induce them to take up the hatchet against his majesty's rebellious subjects in America, and to engage them in his majesty's service, upon such plan as shall be suggested to you by General Gage, to whom this letter is sent, accompanied with a large assortment of goods for presents to them upon this important occasion."

The colonial congress at Philadelphia, July 12th, 1775, determined to establish three departments of Indian affairs, the northern, middle, and southern; the northern to include the Six Nations and all other tribes to the northward of them; and that commissioners should be appointed, "with powers to treat with the Indians in their respective departments, to preserve peace and friendship, and to prevent their taking any part in the present commotion."

In the northern department the following commissioners were appointed: Major General Philip Schuyler, Major Joseph Hawley, Mr. Turbot Francis, Mr. Oliver Wolcott, and Mr. Volkert P. Douw.

Messrs. Douw and Francis met the Six Nations at German Flats, August 15th, 1775, acquainted them that twelve colonies had united, and invited the Indians to Albany, to hold a council, August 25th, of the same year. A general council was accordingly held at Albany, at which the Indians were told that "this is a family quarrel between us and old England. You Indians are not concerned in it. We don't wish you to take up the hatchet against the king's troops. We desire you to remain at home, and not join either side, but keep the hatchet buried deep." To which the Indians replied that Colonel Johnson, at Oswego, had also requested them to remain neutral, and they promised to follow the wishes of both parties in respect to neutrality.

Colonel Johnson, however, stated in his dispatch to the British government, that he was "threatened with an attack from the colonists, and left for Ontario the last of May, at which place he held a council with the Indians soon after, "who agreed to defend the communication, and assist his majesty's troops in their operations."

In the beginning of July, Colonel Johnson left for Montreal with two hundred and twenty Indians and tories; and at the latter place, the last of that month, assembled 1,700 Indians of the northern confederacy, who promised also to assist his majesty's troops. The Indians did some skirmishing that summer and fall, near St. Johns, and thirty-two officers and men of Colonel Johnson's department, and some of his Indians, assisted in the capture of Colonel Ethan Allen, three miles from Montreal, September 25th; but General Carlton, in command of Canada, refused to allow Colonel Johnson to send Indians south of Canada line, to the great disgust of Colonel Johnson and his Indian allies; whereupon Colonel Johnson, to settle the limits of his command, visited England with an Indian delegation the following winter, and returned to Staten Island, New York, July 29th, 1776. During this year the Indians assembled in considerable numbers at Niagara and in Canada, but were little employed.

The Indian campaign for 1777 was organized in Canada by Daniel Claus, the newly-appointed Indian agent for the northern department, by assigning the domiciliated Indians of Canada to the expedition of General Burgoyne, to advance up Lake Champlain, while the Six Nations and western Indians joined the expedition of General St. Ledger, which advanced into western New York, and laid siege to Fort Stanwix.

Soon after the commencement of the siege, General Ledger, hearing of the advance of General Herkimer for the relief of the fort, sent forward a large force of soldiers and all the Indians, and waylaid General Herkimer on the 6th of August, entirely defeating his force, with the loss of General Herkimer and over 400 of his troops. In the mean time a sortie was made from the fort, which captured the entire Indian baggage and most of their clothes, as the Indians had gone to attack General Herkimer nearly naked. This so discouraged the Indians that they fell off by degrees, and General St. Ledger hearing of General Arnold's force, which was coming to the relief of the fort, retreated to

Oswego, from which point General St. Ledger, on the 26th of August, was ordered to join General Burgoyne, which closed the western campaign. General Burgoyne, still more unfortunate, was forced to surrender his entire army, October 17th, at Saratoga.

At the close of the campaign of 1777, a special effort was made by the Indian agents to rally the north-western Indians for the following year, for the British service. Captain De Peyster, the commandant at Mackinaw, secured the services of Charles De Langlade, of Green Bay, and many other popular Indian traders; and a considerable force of all the Wisconsin and other north-western Indians was sent to Oswego, and the sequel may be found in the dispatch of Colonel Guy Johnson, the Indian agent, of September 6th, 1778, where he says: "Your lordships will have heard before this can reach you, of the successful incursions of the Indians and loyalists from the northward. In conformity to the instructions I conveyed to my officers, they assembled their force early in May, and one division, under one of my deputies (Mr. Butler) proceeded with great success down the Susquehanna, destroying the posts and settlements at Wyoming, augmenting their number with many loyalists, and alarming all the country; whilst another division, under Mr. Brandt, the Indian chief, cut off two hundred and ninety-four men near Schoharie, and destroyed the adjacent settlements, with several magazines from whence the rebels had derived great resources."

This victory is known over the civilized world as the "Wyoming Massacre," and being specially directed and controlled by the British officers and British troops, who were known to have been more savage than the Indians themselves, the English people should never thereafter complain of Indian cruelty.

It was after the close of this barbarous campaign, that Governor Haldimand, of Canada, presented Cha-kaw-cha-ka-ma, or *the Old King* of the Menominie Indians, a medal, with the date of August 17, 1778, which has been deposited in the cabinet of the Historical Society of Wisconsin.

During this year, Colonel G. R. Clarke, with a force from Virginia, captured the Illinois country; and during the following winter, Lieutenant-Governor Hamilton, of Detroit, planned an expedition for its recovery. For that purpose, their Indian allies were again summoned with the "war belt" to meet in council at L'Arbre Croche, to go again on the war-path. Again, Captain De Peyster, the commandant at Mackinaw, rallied his Indian traders, and De Langlade and others sang the war-song, danced the war-dance, and distributed the fire-water, and in due time the bold warriors of Wisconsin and Michigan were on their way to attack the "*Long-knives;*" but when they reached St. Josephs, at the head of Lake Michigan, they learned with sorrow that Colonel Clarke had turned upon his pursuers, and Governor Hamilton and his soldiers were prisoners of war, in the hands of the "Long-knives." Upon this the war party returned home.

Early in 1779 large bodies of Indians assembled in the heart of New York, under the deputy agent, Mr. Butler, for the purpose of reënacting the "Wyoming Massacre" on the western frontier, but were attacked by General Sullivan with nearly 5,000 American troops, driven to Canada, and forty Indian villages burned, and the Indian country laid waste. The exasperated Americans took no prisoners, but warriors, squaws, papooses and loyalists were alike fortunate in finding a common grave. Late in the fall, Colonel Guy Johnson attempted to make another Indian campaign, but was delayed by a storm on the Lake, and finally stopped by orders to go into winter quarters. This order found on the hands of Mr. Johnson, as he wrote, November 11, 1779, 2,628 Indians, whose country was devastated, and who must be supported at the public expense.

In the spring of 1780 Colonel Johnson colonized many of his Indian allies on the "route to Ohio," where they could "plant," and thereby greatly lessen the government expenses. During this year and the following, he carried on the "Petite Guerre" warfare against the western frontier, "which," he wrote, "has compelled the latter (rebels) to contract their frontier, and confine themselves within little forts." During these two years, Colonel Johnson appears to have had of the New York and Canada Indians all that he could feed and employ, and we find no evidence that he called down the north-western tribes.

The campaign of 1781, and the surrender of Cornwallis October 19, of that year, virtually closed the war, and quieted the fears of the mothers and children along our extensive frontier of nearly 3,000 miles, which for seven years had echoed with the merciless war-whoop of the Indian, and the more savage counterfeit of the tories.

The treaty of peace between Great Britain and the United States, signed September 3, 1783, did not adjust the differences between the United States and the various Indian tribes, which had grown out of the revolution; and the British, more bold than the French after the surrender of Canada, refused to yield up to the United States the western military posts, and reënacted the Pontiac conspiracy. The new chief around which the Indians rallied was Michikinigua, or the "Little Turtle," the head chief of the Miamies. Colonel John Johnson, one of the leaders of the Iroquois of New York, during the revolution, was made Indian agent, and Major Matthews commandant at Detroit; and that post became the central rendezvous for Brant and other leaders of the Iroquois, who had displayed such fearful barbarity during the late war, and who had been colonized in Ohio and Canada. Here was organized, by British advice, the new Indian confederacy, composed of the Hurons, Delawares, Shawnees, Miamies, Kickapoos, Ottawas, Chippeways, Potowatomies, and Iroquois, under the nominal leadership of "Little Turtle," although, in fact, the British not only directed the movements of the confederacy, but furnished the Indians an abundance of arms and ammunition.

A grand council of this confederacy was held at the mouth of Huron river, a little below Detroit, in December, 1786, and another soon after, in which the Indians, under British advice, insisted on the Ohio river as the old boundary line, notwithstanding they had allied themselves against the United States, and been defeated in the revolutionary war.

The north-western territory had been organized by Congress, July 13, 1787, and Major-General Arthur St. Clair was appointed Governor of the territory in October following. He made great exertions to pacify the Indians, and drew part of the Indian confederacy to make a treaty January 9, 1789, at Fort Harmer, but it was repudiated by the confederacy, and consequently no further attention was paid to its provisions. Governor St. Clair finally, believing that no peace could be established until the Indians were defeated, and the British forced to show their hands in their Indian intrigues, July 15, 1790, in pursuance of an order of the President, of the previous 6th of October, called on Virginia for 1,000, and Pennsylvania for 500 militia, to coöperate with the few regular troops on the Ohio, in suppressing the Indian hostilities.

These forces advanced upon and burnt several Indian villages, and a large amount of corn in October of the same year, but two of its detachments were defeated by the Indians, and the army returned to Fort Washington at Cincinnati. This expedition only exasperated the Indians, and they renewed their murders with greater violence.

The following year Governor St. Clair, having been appointed commander-in-chief of all the forces sent against the Indians, detached General Charles Scott, of Kentucky, to advance on the Indians upon Wabash river, where in June he took several prisoners, and burned a large quantity of corn and the village of "Ouiatanon," in which were several well-built French residences. Colonel Wilkinson was then sent with another expedition higher up the Wabash, and reached the mouth of Eel river on the 7th of August, where he burned a village, cut up a large quantity of corn, and took a few prisoners.

Governor St. Clair, having collected together his main army, numbering over 2,300, advanced from Fort Washington September 17, 1791, and reached a branch of the Wabash with only about 1,400 men. Here, on the 4th of November, he was boldly attacked by the confederate forces, and completely defeated with great loss. The fugitives retreated to Fort Jefferson, twenty-nine miles distant, which they reached before dark of the same day, the Indians having pursued them only four miles.

Nearly two years, following this defeat, were spent in fruitless negotiations with the Indians, and at last, August 13, 1793, at a general council held at Maumee, they decided that their ultimatum boundary line was the Ohio river.

Some years after this council, the notorious Brandt, who had advised that council to conclude a peace with the United States, said that such a treaty "was opposed by those acting under the British government, and hopes of further assistance were given to our western brethren, to encourage them to insist on the Ohio as a boundary between them and the United States." The Governor of Canada was evidently laboring under the impression that by holding on to Detroit, and fomenting the Indian war, the United States would, in the end, vary the treaty of 1783, and extend the British possessions to the Ohio river; and he carried that impression in his address to the Indian delegates in February, 1794; but in this he was bound to be disappointed.

In the spring of 1794 a new enemy of the United States appeared, from the Spanish settlements of the Mississippi, offering the aid of Spain to the Indians, if they would continue their war against the United States. Thus advised and led on by the crafty, civilized nations of Europe, the poor, ignorant red man renewed the war-whoop, and rushed forward to inevitable destruction. General Anthony Wayne, the hero of Stony Point, was appointed to succeed General St. Clair over the western troops, and spent the winter of 1792-3 in drilling his troops at Legionville, and moved down to Fort Washington, in May, 1793, where he spent the summer of that year. Having received news of the failure of the commissioners to negotiate a peace, he left Fort Washington, October 7th, and on the 13th of the same month encamped six miles in front of Fort Jefferson, and named his camp Fort Greenville, where he spent the winter. During the winter and spring of 1794, General Wayne erected Fort Recovery on St. Clair's battle-ground, buried six hundred skulls found on the ground, and made every proper arrangement for the summer campaign.

"Little Turtle" opened the campaign by attacking Fort Recovery, June 30th, with some 1,500 warriors and some British volunteers, but was finally driven off. July 26th, General Scott arrived from Kentucky with a reinforcement of 1,600 mounted militia, and in two days thereafter, General Wayne commenced his advance, and, on the 20th of August, met the Indians in force on the north bank of the Maumee river. The Indians were formed in three lines, with their left resting on the river, and right extending two miles, at right angles with the river, to a very thick brushwood.

General Scott was ordered to charge the Indians' right flank, and Captain Campbell the left, while the infantry, with trailed arms, were ordered to rouse the Indians from their coverts with the bayonet, and then deliver their fire as the Indians retreated. Such was the impetuosity of the charge of the infantry, that but part of General Scott's mounted force could get in position so as to take part in the battle. In one hour, the entire Indian force was driven two miles, and their defeat was complete, leaving the ground strewed with dead bodies, among which were found many Canadians, armed with British muskets and bayonets. About seventy of the Canadian militia were in the battle with the Indians. This battle was fought in sight of the new British fort, and the American troops burned the houses and stores belonging to the Indians and Canadians, as well as the house and store of McKee, the British agent, under the guns of the fort. This was the severest defeat ever received by the western Indians. After this battle, General Wayne laid waste the Indian country, and retired to Fort Greenville, to winter quarters.

Governor Simcoe, of Canada, knowing that the Indians would probably sue for peace after so severe a defeat, sought to forestall peace negotiations, by calling a council on the 10th of October of the same year, at which he urged the Indians to still insist on the Ohio river as the boundary line, and advised them to convey their lands to the king, so as to give the British a pretext for assisting them. and accompanied his advice with promises of large presents; but the Indians were divided in council as to the proper course for the future, and finally, on the 24th of January, 1795, the preliminary terms were agreed upon by a large delegation, who met General Wayne at Fort Greenville.

The new treaty between the United States and Great Britain was signed by Mr. Jay and others, November 19th, 1794, and finally ratified by the president, August 14th of the following year, by which the British agreed to surrender the north-western posts to the United States.

The British agents had continued to tamper with the Indians to induce them to renew the war, but the news of the treaty between Great Britain and the United States much abated their zeal, and the Indians finally assembled in great numbers, and concluded a treaty with General Wayne, August 3rd, 1795, by which they agreed to surrender all prisoners, and consented to the following boundary line: " Beginning at the mouth of Cuyahoga river, and run thence up the same to the portage between that and the Tuscarawas branch of the Muskingum; thence down that branch to the crossing place above Fort Lawrence; thence westerly to a fork of that branch of the great Miami river, running into the Ohio, at or near which fork stood Loromie's store, and where commences the portage between the Miami of the Ohio and St. Mary's river, which is a branch of the Miami which runs into Lake Erie; thence a westerly course to Fort Recovery, which stands on a branch of the Wabash; then south-westerly in a direct line to the Ohio, so as to intersect that river opposite the mouth of Kentucke or Cuttawa river."

The Indians also ceded to the United States the following tracts, viz.: "(1.) One piece of land, six miles square, at or near Loromie's store before mentioned. (2.) One piece, two miles square, at the head of the navigable water or landing on the St. Mary's river, near Girty's town. (3.) One piece, six miles square, at the head of the navigable water of the Au-Glaize river. (4.) One piece, six miles square, at the confluence of the Au-Glaize and Miami rivers, where Fort Defiance now stands. (5.) One piece, six miles square, at or near the confluence of the rivers St. Mary's and St. Joseph's, where Fort Wayne now stands, or near it. (6.) One piece, two miles square, on the Wabash river, at the end of the portage from the Miami of the lake, and about eight miles westward from Fort Wayne. (7.) One piece, six miles square, at Outanon or old Wcea towns, on the Wabash river. (8.) One piece, twelve miles square, at the British fort on the Miami of the lake, at the foot of the rapids. (9.) One piece, six miles square, at the mouth of the said river, where it empties into the lake. (10.) One piece, six miles square, upon Sandusky lake, where a fort formerly stood. (11.) One piece, two miles square, at the lower rapids of Sandusky river. (12.) The post of Detroit, and all the land to the north, the west, and the south of it, of which the Indians' title has been extinguished by gifts or grants to the French or English governments; and so much more land to be annexed to the district of Detroit as shall be comprehended between the River Rosine on the south, Lake St. Clair on the north, and a line, the general course whereof shall be six miles distant from the west end of Lake Erie and Detroit river. (13.) The post of Michillimackinack, and all the land on the island on which that post stands, and the mainland adjacent, of which the Indian title has been extinguished by gifts or grants to the French or English governments; and a piece of land on the main, to the north of the island, to measure six miles on Lake Huron, or the strait between Lakes Huron and Michigan, and to extend three miles back from the water of the lake or strait; and also the Island De Bois Blanc, being an extra and voluntary gift of the Chipewa nation. (14.) One piece of land, six miles square, at the mouth of Chikago river emptying into the south-west end of Lake Michigan, where a fort formerly stood. (15.) One piece, twelve miles square, at or near the mouth of Illinois river emptying into the Mississippi. (16.) One piece, six miles square, at the old Peorias fort and village, near the south end of the Illinois lake, on said Illinois river."

The United States, by article fourth of the treaty, relinquish to the Indians all their claim to lands from said boundary line to the Mississippi, except the following:

"1st. The tract of one hundred and fifty thousand acres near the rapids of the Ohio, which has been assigned to General Clark, for the use of himself and his warriors.

"2nd. The post of St. Vincennes on the river Wabash, and the lands adjacent, of which the Indian title has been extinguished.

"3rd. The lands at all other places in possession of the French people and other white settlers among them, of which the Indian title has been extinguished as mentioned in the 3rd article; and

"4th. The post of Fort Massac, towards the mouth of the Ohio. To which several parcels of land so excepted, the said tribes relinquish all the title and claim which they or any of them may have."

This treaty, so important to the north-west, was signed by the number of chiefs and warriors of the different tribes as follows: Wyandots or Hurons, 10; Delawares, 14; Shawnees, 9; Ottawas, 7; Chippeways, 11; Potowatomies, of St. Josephs, 22, and of Huron 7; Miamies, 5; Eel river band, 1; Weeas, for themselves and Piankaskias, 3; Kickapoos and Kaskaskias, 3; Delawares, of Sandusky, 3. In the treaty at Fort Harmar in 1789, by a part of these tribes, the Sacs were named, but none were named in the treaty of General Wayne.

It has been customary for authors to name all the Wisconsin Indians as belonging to this confederacy, but I find no evidence that the Winnebagoes, Menominies, Foxes, Sioux or Chippeways, of Lake Superior, took any definite part, although a few individuals of each tribe might have done so; but as the war between the Chippeways of the north, and the Sioux and their allies, the Sacs, Foxes, Winnebagoes, and Menominies of the south, was then raging, it is quite probable that the Wisconsin Indians, strictly speaking, should not be regarded as belonging to "Little Turtle's" confederacy. Even the two Sacs who signed the treaty at Fort Harmar, were probably insignificant warriors, as their names do not appear in any subsequent treaties with that tribe.

The difficulties which were fomenting between England, France, and the United States, during the wars of Napoleon, threatening every year to culminate in an open and bloody war between the United States on one side, and alternately with France or England on the other, tended to keep the partisans of the two latter nations, in the west, in constant communication with the various Indian tribes; and in that intercourse, being further moved upon by the rivalry of trade, they neglected nothing which would prejudice the

Indians against the Americans, and prepossess them in favor of the English and French.

Tecumseh and his twin brother, Elskwatawa, of the Shawnee tribe, were the two who constituted themselves as the leaders, to regenerate their race;—the former as war chief, and the latter as prophet. The plan of Tecumseh and his brother was certainly a good one to prejudice the Indians against the Americans, and in favor of both English and French, and was evidently generated in more civilized heads.

The prophet preached that while the Great Spirit made the English, French, and Indians, that he did not make the Americans, but that the latter grew from the scum of the great salt water, when it was troubled by the evil spirit, and the froth was driven into the woods by a strong east wind; and that the Great Spirit hates the Americans, as the children of the evil spirit. Among other things, the prophet taught the Indians that they must not give the Americans meat, nor sell them their land, and that each tribe must send two delegates to be instructed in the faith by the prophet, or else the tribe would be cut off from the face of the earth. All were positively prohibited from divulging the faith to the Americans, under the penalty of death.

Thus, armed with the new religion and the tomahawk, no uncommon weapons in the civilized world, they commenced proselyting among all the tribes west to the Rocky mountains, and two old chiefs of the Delawares, and one of the Wyandots, were known to have been tomahawked by order of the prophet, for refusing to be converted. The new faith found converts among all the western tribes from about 1805 to 1811.

The conduct of the Shawnees, and that of the prophet and Tecumseh, at their village at Tippecanoe, having alarmed the Americans, General Harrison, in the fall of 1811, was ordered with 1,200 men to advance on the Shawnee town, to ascertain the purposes of the savages. On the

6th of November he encamped within one mile of the town, where he met a delegation of Indians, who promised to meet the General in council the next morning. An hour before daylight on the morning of the 7th of November, it being dark and rainy, the Indians suddenly attacked General Harrison's army on all sides, and a fierce and bloody battle ensued; but the Americans, having the advantage of position, steadily held their ground until after daylight, when the Indians were fiercely charged with the bayonet and the sword, and routed at every point. Unfortunately for the Shawnees, Tecumseh was absent at the time, not expecting so sudden an attack by General Harrison, and his shrill voice was not there to direct the movements of the over-ardent warriors.

Thus prepared in advance for the war which was declared the following June against Great Britain, it required only the war-whoop to rally the thousands of fierce warriors to the deadly strife. Although war was declared the 18th of June, news of the declaration did not reach Governor Hull, at Detroit, until July 2nd, and not until some days after the news was possessed by the British at Malden, in Canada, opposite Detroit; which enabled the British to capture General Hull's baggage on its way to Detroit.

Colonel Robert Dickson, an old English trader at Prairie du Chien, and British Indian agent, had so well anticipated the progress of events, that with a large Indian force of Sioux, Winnebagoes, Menominies and others, he reached Mackinaw, and with some forces from the east, captured that post on the 17th of July, and communicated to Lieutenant Hanks, its commandant, the first news he had of the declaration of war.

Governor Hull, fearing a similar fate to the fort at Chicago, ordered Captain Heald to evacuate that post, and take his command to Detroit. Accordingly, that fort was evacuated on the morning of the 15th of August, but Captain Heald and his party were attacked by the Potowatomies soon after they left the fort; fifty men, women and children were killed, and the balance taken prisoners.

After the capture of Mackinaw, Colonel Dickson returned to Green Bay, when he sent messages to other tribes, and among the rest, to the Sacs and Foxes at Rock Island, and to the Potowatomies, to collect parties and meet him at the Bay, and receive presents, guns and ammunition.

The Sac chief, with two hundred warriors, reached the bay, was feasted and armed by Colonel Dickson, and appointed brigadier-general of the Indian forces. The following day, Colonel Dickson, Black Hawk, and about five hundred warriors, started for Detroit by way of Chicago, and passed the latter place soon after the massacre of Captain Heald's party. Tecumseh commanded the Indian forces near Detroit, at the surrender of General Hull, August 16th, which numbered about seven hundred warriors.

The north-western Indians continued in the British service, under General Proctor, in the region of Detroit and north-western Ohio, until the defeat of that general before Fort Stevenson, on the Sandusky river, August 1st, 1813, when that general retired to Malden, and the most of the north-western Indians, including Black Hawk, and about twenty of his Sac warriors, returned home disgusted with the service. The balance of the Indians, however, returned to Malden under Tecumseh, and were finally defeated by General Harrison, October 5th of that year, at the battle of the Thames, where the brave Tecumseh and one hundred and thirty Indian warriors were left dead on the field.

This serious defeat broke the Tecumseh confederacy, and, the following year, the most of the hostile bands of the Miamies, Delawares, Shawnees, Potowatomies, Ottawas, and Kickapoos, formed a treaty with the United States, in which they, among other things, "engaged to give their aid to the United States in prosecuting the war against

MACKINAW

Great Britain, and such of the Indian tribes as still continue hostile." It should be borne in mind, however, that many of the bands of the Senecas, Wyandots, Delawares, and Shawnees, never joined the Tecumseh confederacy, but fought throughout the war on the American side.

In the summer of 1814, Major Holmes, with a small force of Americans, attempted to recapture Mackinaw; but news of the expedition reaching Colonel Dickson, who rallied a large force of Indians from Wisconsin, with some two hundred Sioux, and most of the Indian traders of Green Bay, whom he conducted to Mackinaw, and, with the British troops and traders at that place, successfully resisted the attack of the Americans; and Major Holmes, and eleven others, were killed in the battle which ensued, on the 4th of August.

Immediately after this affair, the Americans having taken possession of Prairie Du Chien, Lieutenant-Colonel William McKay, of the British forces, was dispatched with a few regulars, two companies of Mackinaw militia under Captains Rolette and Anderson, and one brass six-pounder, to recover that post. Colonel Dickson remained at Mackinaw to defend the place, but detached two hundred Sioux, one hundred Winnebagoes, and some Foxes, to accompany the expedition to Prairie Du Chien. This force recruited at Green Bay one company of militia, seventy-five Menominies, and twenty-five Chippeways. The expedition passed the portage and down the Wisconsin in canoes and bateaux, and laid siege to the Fort at Prairie Du Chien, which contained about sixty American soldiers, July 17th, 1814. After four days' siege, Lieutenant Perkins surrendered the fort; but, in the mean time, the small gun-boat which contained the ammunition and most of the supplies, had escaped down the Mississippi.

About the same time, Major Campbell left St. Louis with a force of United States troops, to reinforce Prairie Du Chien, but was attacked above Rock Island by Black Hawk with an Indian force; one boat was captured, several soldiers killed, Major Campbell and others wounded, when the expedition returned to St. Louis. Soon after this affair, some troops and cannon were sent from Prairie Du Chien by the British to Rock Island, with a considerable Indian force, to defend Black Hawk and his band from the attacks of the Americans.

Major Zachary Taylor, with three hundred troops in boats, attacked Black Hawk, August 3rd, but were repulsed with some loss, and Major Taylor and his troops returned to St. Louis.

The total defeat of the British at New Orleans, January 8th, 1815, by General Jackson, and the ratification of a treaty of peace in February following, with Great Britain, again silenced the war-whoop in the Mississippi valley, and the great tide of immigration that rolled into it the few following years, removed all serious fears of its repetition for some time to come.

In the history of the Indian tribes in the north-west, set forth in the last three chapters, the reader will at once perceive that there was a constant rivalry between the governments of Great Britain, France, and the United States, as to which of them should secure the services of the barbarians, to scalp their white enemies; while each in turn were the loudest to denounce the shocking barbarities of such tribes as they failed to secure in their own service; and the civilized world, aghast at these horrid recitals, ignore the facts that nearly every important massacre in the history of North America, was organized and directed by agents of some one of these governments.

The system of warfare in vogue among the Indian nations of North America at the discovery of the continent, was of the *guerrilla* kind, in which the friends of the deceased organized a raid against their enemies, to revenge their friends' death, and a few scalps were quite sufficient to satiate their anger. Hence we learn from Champlain, Montcalm, and Sir William Johnson, that it required all their arts of persuasion to keep their Indian allies in the field after their first skirmish; and to the civilization of European warfare are we indebted for the most of our serious massacres.

The fact that Indians often killed women and children in war, and murdered some of their prisoners afterwards, has been taken as evidence that the Indian nature was innately brutal, and they have ignored the facts that it is not a century since the British burnt New London, in Connecticut, and put the garrison of Fort Griswold to the sword; that Napoleon massacred 3,000 Turkish prisoners, and turned over the city of Joppa to be sacked by his soldiers, after he had promised the city protection if they would surrender; while, still later, an organized confederacy of whites in the United States never repudiated the massacre at Fort Pillow, nor the starving of prisoners at Andersonville. We also ignore the massacre of nearly 2,000 Indians by Governor Kieft, of New Amsterdam, as early as 1645, in which not a woman or child was spared.

With this chapter we pass the period in which the northwestern Indians were used as " cats' paws" by rival governments, and made subservient only to foreign interest; and shall hereafter attempt to trace that under-current of Christian love, which often struggled for the mastery, but almost uniformly failed, from the effect of governmental power and interest. We here, also, take the opportunity to congratulate our readers that, after the close of the war of 1812, we find a change in government policy; and, thereafter, the government acting in harmony with the Christian interests, to improve the condition of the Indian race.

CHAPTER V.

THE CATHOLIC MISSIONS.

The nominal Christianity of the sixteenth and seventeenth centuries was so interwoven with bigotry, politics, superstition, and legerdemain, that the conscientious Christian of the present day at times doubts if Christianity then existed at all among the nations of Europe. To say the least, the stench of the blood then shed in the name of Jesus, is still offensive in the nostrils of all civilized society.

Unfortunately for the new world, this Christianity crossed the ocean, associated with avarice of the nominal pilgrims; and the untutored red man received his first lessons of Christianity from the same men that robbed his wigwam, and pillaged his corn and the graves of his ancestors. Even the pilgrims crossed the ocean to murder heretics; and, consequently, we find Melendez, of Spain, in 1564, the commandant of an expedition that murdered nearly eight hundred Huguenots in Florida; and De Gourges, of France, in 1568 the commandant of an expedition that retaliated, by exterminating the Spaniards, and hanging two hundred of them on the trees. With little less of cruelty, Catholics, Episcopalians, Baptists, and Quakers could not be tolerated in Massachusetts, nor Protestants in Canada; and a man's life often poised on the thread whether he believed in transubstantiation, predestination, immersion, or preaching for hire. But with all the faults attributable to nominal Christianity, Jesus still reigned over his kingdom, which was "not of this world;" and the seeds of true Christianity often germinated with vigor in the wilds of America.

Long before the gentle and pious Elliot had won over the bold Mohegans to Christianity within ten miles of Boston, the adventurous Catholic missionaries had converted villages of Hurons, on the north-eastern shore of Lake Huron, and had even planted the cross at the Falls of St. Mary, at the outlet of the great Lake Superior.

The English colonies in America were not planted for missionary purposes, but were designed more as a refuge for the persecuted non-conformists of England; and the main point for the consideration of the emigrant, was to make himself a home and a plantation, and secure the political power of the colony for his own protection against the mother country. But it was far different with the colonists of Quebec. Their religion was supreme in France, and they came to America to establish trade with the Indian tribes. Agriculture, on the frosty banks of the St. Lawrence, was but a secondary consideration; hence, few became farmers, and the great majority plunged into the forests and became the adventurous *courrier de bois*.

Sieur Champlain had only made a few treaties, and fought a few battles with the Indian tribes, before he sent to France for missionaries, and early in 1615 he procured three priests of the order of the Recollects, and commenced the missionary work at once. Although the primary object of the French colony was trade, yet Champlain soon found that it was no easy matter to successfully carry on trade with superstitious barbarians, and we may well believe that it was a happy idea when he conceived the project of Christianizing the Indians, to protect his trade with them. Rev. Father Dennis Jamay took post at Quebec, John D'Olbeau hastened to Tadoussac to learn the language of the Algonquins, and Father Joseph Le Caron was attached to Sieur Champlain's war party, then about to set out to explore Lake Huron. The party reached the lake by the Ottawa river of Canada, and while the priest was engaged in collecting a vocabulary of the Huron language, Sieur Champlain led an unsuccessful war party of the Hurons and Algonquins against the Iroquois of New York. The party returned to Quebec the following summer. In 1622, Rev. Father Poulain visited the Hurons, and some others from time to time thereafter, including the Rev. Father Brebeuf, until July, 1629, when the English took possession of Canada, and transported to England Sieur Champlain, the priests, and the principal men of the colony.

Three years after, Canada was restored to France, and the task of converting the savages assigned to the "Society of Jesus," and the Recollects refused admission to Canada. This so grieved the zealous Le Caron that he died of disappointment early in the spring of the same year. 1633 found the Rev. Father Brebeuf, with several of his Jesuit associates, returned to Canada, but unfortunately for them, the allied Hurons and Algonquins, during the absence of the French, had fought a great battle with the Iroquois of New York, and been badly defeated; and becoming alarmed at their misfortunes, caused by their alliance with the French, the Hurons were unwilling that the Jesuits should go to the old missions on Lake Huron, and the Algonquins of Ottawa river positively refused the missionaries a passage through their country. Thus matters stood through the following winter; but French diplomacy and presents again won over their old allies, and in 1634 the Rev. Fathers Brebeuf, Daniel, and Davost, planted themselves in the old mission on Lake Huron. They commenced their work with great zeal, but their former power was broken, and they met with great opposition from the medicine-men of the tribe. To add to their misfortunes, in the fall of 1636 the Rev. Fathers Garnier, Chatelain, and Jogues arrived as their assistants, but accompanying them came that terrible plague to the Indians, the small-pox. This disease raged with virulence for some years, and in 1637 the missionaries were

FATHER ISAAC JOGUES, S. J.

openly charged with producing this disease by witchcraft, for the destruction of the Indians; and their cabins were burned by the infuriated savages, and the missionaries daily expected to be tomahawked. But Brebeuf having eloquently defended himself and his brethren, before an Indian council in 1638, their principal accuser was tomahawked by his side, and the priests escaped. In the spring of 1639 the small-pox was brought in again, and the old charges revived against the priests, who suffered every thing but death from the savages.

The missionary force having increased to thirteen priests, the following year they began to extend their field of labor to other tribes, and in the fall of 1641 the Rev. Fathers Isaac Jogues, and Charles Raymbaut, planted the cross at the falls of St. Mary, at the outlet of Lake Superior, in an assembled multitude of 2,000 Chippeways and other nations.

From this time the misfortunes of the missionaries began to accumulate. Fathers Raymbaut and Jogues returned to Quebec in the summer of 1642, where the former died with the consumption, October 22nd; and the latter, in attempting to return to Lake Huron, was captured by the Iroquois. He repeatedly ran the gauntlet, had his finger-nails torn out, and his hands and body otherwise mutilated by the Mohawks. The Dutch of Albany, hearing of his captivity, raised a volunteer fund, and sent an agent to redeem him, but the Indians would not let him go. Having visited Albany with his captors, he escaped to a vessel in the river, and the Dutch pacified the infuriated Indians for their loss, with presents, and the good Father was sent to France. Here he was received at Court, and the Pope, by a special dispensation, authorized him to say mass, notwithstanding his hands were mutilated. While at Albany, he wrote in elegant Latin a history of his captivity, and of New Netherlands, and sent to France, which was afterwards published. Having returned to Canada, and a temporary peace having been made with the Mohawks, Father Jogues, in 1646, returned to the Mohawks, was captured on the way thither by a war party, was defended by the Wolf band, decreed his liberty by the general council, but privately assassinated by some of the Bear band the same night, October 18, 1646.

The Iroquois having obtained fire-arms of the Dutch, the war between them and the allied Hurons and Algonquins, inaugurated by Sieur Champlain as early as 1610, now burst upon the Huron country in all its power, and the Hurons and missionaries alike fell before grim-visaged war. From 1648 to about 1652, the allied Hurons and Algonquins were driven out of all the coasts of Lake Huron, and a part of the remnant took shelter in the dense and tangled forests of northern Wisconsin; while the heroic and devoted Fathers Brebeuf, Lalamant, Daniel, and Garnier, with many of their neophytes, were massacred by the warlike Iroquois. A few only followed the surviving priests to Quebec; but the greater part of those populous villages, estimated in 1640 as containing 16,000 inhabitants, were either killed or taken prisoners. The most of the prisoners were adopted into the families of the Iroquois as slaves, many of whom were recognized and instructed by Catholic priests in subsequent years.

Thus nearly perished the great Huron nation, by smallpox and war, which calamities were directly attributable to their contact and alliance with the French. For a time the north-west was closed against both Christianity and trade, but as events progressed, and Iroquois war parties diminished, flotillas of Indian canoes began to reach the trading-posts near Quebec by the north shore of Lake Huron, and the Ottawa river from the distant shores of Lakes Michigan and Superior. The missionaries sought the first opportunity to return with the Indians to their distant homes, and that opportunity offered in 1656. The Rev. Fathers Garreau and Druilletes, with a party of traders, left with the Indians for the north-west. The brutality of the Indians induced the traders to leave the expedition at the Three Rivers; but the bold missionaries having gone on, the expedition was soon after attacked by a war party of the Iroquois, and the good Father Garreau mortally wounded and taken prisoner; and Father Druilletes, having been abandoned by the Ottawas, returned to Quebec.

Time chafed the pious hearts of the missionaries until 1660, when sixty canoes arrived from the far-off Superior, and volunteers hastened to return with the Indians to their homes. Two good Fathers left with the returning expedition, but one abandoned it at Montreal, having been turned out of the canoe by the "fantastic humor of one of the savages," but the other, Rev. Father René Ménard, one of the survivors of the old Huron mission, was suffered to proceed. Writing to his superior under date of August 27, 1660, Father Ménard said: "In three or four months you may place me to the memory of the dead, as a consequence of the manner of life of these people, my age, and feeble constitution; notwithstanding which, I have felt such powerful instincts, and I have seen in this business so little of nature, that I can not doubt that having failed to take advantage of this occasion, I should feel therefor an eternal remorse."

The expedition took the usual route up the Ottawa river, thence to the Georgian bay, and along the north shore of Lake Huron to St. Mary, and thence along the south shore of Lake Superior to the Kewenaw bay, called by him St. Theresea Bay, where he arrived, October 15, 1660, after a long and fatiguing voyage of nearly seven weeks, in a bark canoe. Here for a time he was permitted to lodge with Pike, the chief of the band, but having offended the proud chief, he was turned out, and forced to construct a cabin of pine boughs, in which he spent the winter, and nearly perished with cold and hunger; and sustained life with pounded fish-bones and boiled moss.

Learning that a remnant of the Hurons, his old acquaintances and friends, were located on the Black river in Wisconsin, he resolved to visit them at all hazards; and June 13, 1661, he set out with one Frenchman and some Huron guides to visit them. They passed the iron and copper mountains of the northern peninsula of Michigan, the barren regions of the head waters of the Wisconsin river, and reached a small lake at the head of Black river. Here the Huron guides left the Father and went forward, promising to send back assistance. He remained fifteen days, and as provisions failed and no help came, they found a canoe hid in the brushwood, and started down the river. The low stage of water, and the interminable rapids between Rock creek and Black river falls, made the navigation very tedious. At the last important rapid, which was probably the latter falls, the Father passed round on the bank through thick pines, while the assistant Frenchman took the canoe over the falls; after which, looking round for the Father, he was not in sight. Guns were fired, but he responded not, and was never afterwards heard from. Thus ended the life of the good Ménard, about the 10th of August, after twenty-one years of missionary life among the Indians of North America. The following year some savages found his sack, and some of the furniture used in his chapel was seen in an Indian wigwam; but none of them would ever acknowledge that they had seen his body, and it is very probable that he became bewildered in the thick pines, and wandering off, was devoured by the wolves or other wild beasts.

For four years subsequent to the loss of Ménard, the north-west echoed to no Christian song; but Christianity lives although its disciples perish, and 1665 found the Rev. Father Claude Allouez impatiently waiting at the "Three Rivers," for an opportunity to follow the example of his predecessor, and plant again the standard of the cross on the inhospitable shores of the far-off Lake Superior. July 20th, after the pious father had "said a mass devoted to this project, in honor of Saint Ignatius and Saint Xavier," he was greatly delighted at the arrival of a trading expedition of savages from Lake Superior; and on the 8th of the following month, he embarked with six French traders and four hundred savages for the west end of the lake, where they arrived at the great village of the Hurons and Algonquins, at the head of Chagouamigong bay, October 1st, 1665. Here he opened his mission and erected his chapel. Subsequently, he established other missions along the lake, and spent a month with the Chippeways at St. Mary, at the outlet of Lake Superior.

In 1667 Father Allouez visited Quebec, tarried two days only, and returned to Lake Superior with Rev. Father Louis Nicholas, an assistant. The latter soon returned to Canada, and was succeeded by Rev. Father James Marquette and Le Bœsine, who came out in April, 1668, and were followed in the summer of 1669 by Rev. Claudius Dablon, as superior of the missions, who united his labors with Marquette in the work at Sault St. Mary. In September, Marquette relieved Allouez at Chagouamigong, at. the mission of the Holy Ghost, and the latter returned to St. Mary.

At the urgent request of some Potowatomies, who had got into difficulty with some French traders at Green Bay, the Rev. Father Allouez, left Sault St. Mary for the Bay, to establish a new mission. With two French companions and two canoes of Potowatomies, he set out on the 3rd of November, 1669, and after a perilous voyage, by reason of the lateness of the season, reached the traders, at the mouth of Fox river, December 2nd, on the eve of St. Francis Xavier. The next day he celebrated mass, at which six Frenchmen at the Bay joined in the devotions with the father and his two companions.

During the winter and the following spring, he established the mission of St. Francis Xavier, near the mouth of Fox river, and visited and instructed the Winnebagoes, Menominies, Potowatomies, Sacs, Foxes, Miamis, Mascotens, Kitchigamicks, and Kickapoos, who then inhabited the region around Green Bay, and the Fox and Wisconsin rivers. Indeed, the father went down the Wisconsin to within a few miles of the Mississippi. On the 20th of May, 1670, the father left the Bay, with one Frenchman, and returned to St. Mary. This summer the Rev. Fathers Gabriel, Druilletes, and Louis André, were added to the mission of the north-west.

In the spring of 1671 the Hurons and Algonquins, at the mission of the Holy Ghost, having provoked a war with the Sioux, the latter nation sent back to Marquette the presents they had received from him, and declared war against the allied tribes. The consequence was, those tribes all left the country with Marquette, and the Hurons pitched their wigwams on the Island of Mackinaw, and Marquette established the mission of St. Ignatius opposite the island, to the west on the mainland. The Algonquin nations generally stopped on the Manitoulin island of Lake Huron, where they came under the care of Father André.

September, 1670, found Allouez and his superior, Dablon, on their way to visit the nations along Green Bay and the Fox and Wisconsin rivers. After this task was performed, Father Dablon, the same fall, returned to Quebec, where he had been appointed superior of all the Canada missions, and was succeeded, as superior of the north-western missions, by Rev. Father Henri Nouvel. André was dispatched to Green Bay, to the assistance of Allouez.

In June, 1673, Jolliet, with Father James Marquette, were dispatched by the authorities of Canada to discover and explore the upper Mississippi, which they reached by the Wisconsin river, June 17th, 1673. They then proceeded down the river as far as Arkansas, after which they returned by the Illinois river and Lake Michigan to Green Bay, where they arrived the last of September of the same year. During the absence of Marquette, he had visited the Indians at Kaskaskia, and promised to return and establish a mission among them; but, unfortunately, during his journey he had contracted chronic diarrhœa, a disease which proved fatal to so many of our soldiers in the late rebellion, and was confined at Green Bay with this disease all the summer of 1674.

Late in the fall, his disease abating, he attempted to return to Kaskaskia, but was compelled, by the revival of his illness, to spend the winter near Chicago, and only reached the tribe the following spring, the 8th of April. Although very weak, he set vigorously at work in instructing the Indians, and named the mission the "Immaculate Conception of the Blessed Virgin." On Easter Sunday he celebrated the mass in presence of the whole tribe, and soon after left to return to Mackinaw. He soon became so weak that he could not help himself, and finally died, and was buried by his kind companions on the eastern shore of Lake Michigan. His bones were subsequently removed to Mackinaw. Father Marquette was evidently one of the best of men, and his memory will be ever fresh as long as civilization exists in the Mississippi valley.

The Illinois mission having become vacant by the death of Marquette, the Rev. Father Allouez was assigned to that post. He left Green Bay the last of October, 1676, to go by way of Lake Michigan, but winter having set in immediately, they tarried by the way until February, when the ice became strong. They then put their canoe on the ice, and, raising sails, made progress down the bay and into a small bay that led to a portage to Lake Michigan. On the 23rd of March, 1677, they embarked on the latter lake, and reached the Kaskaskia village, near Peoria, April 27th. Here he found a large village of three hundred and fifty cabins, and eight different tribes of the Illinois; the Kaskaskias having called in the dispersed tribes which had been scattered by the Iroquois war.

The good father baptized thirty-five children and one adult, and on the 3rd of May, "in the name of Jesus Christ," took possession of all the tribes, and, a few days after, returned north. He visited them again in 1678, and remained two years, but abandoned the mission on the arrival of La Salle, a personal enemy of the Jesuits.

Sieur La Salle reached the Indian village on the Illinois river in January, 1680, with three Recollect priests, and built a fort. In the spring he returned to Canada for supplies; and in September of the same year the Illinois Indians were attacked by the Iroquois, and the little French colony fled for Mackinaw.

One of the priests, Father Gabriel, was killed by a straggling war party of Kickapoos; one, Membré, reached the north safe, and one, Hennepin, having been dispatched to explore the upper Mississippi, also returned in safety to Green Bay, after a short captivity among the Sioux. La Salle and Father Membré returned to the Illinois in January, 1682, and from thence proceeded on their way for the exploration of the lower Mississippi.

Hitherto, the missions in the north-west had been comparatively successful, but they at last began to feel the effects of the sale of brandy to the Indians, which was destroying them with great rapidity in the region of Montreal and Quebec. Previous to 1662, the Jesuit priests had proscribed the sale of intoxicating liquors to the Indians, on pain of excommunication, and had thereby nearly destroyed its sale; but about this time the Governor of Canada interfered, and granted licenses. The Jesuits complained to the king, and the governor was removed in 1663. His successor, Sieur De Mezy, being distasteful to all parties, was continued in office but a few months, and was succeeded by Marquis De Talon, as viceroy, who took possession of the government of Canada in 1665.

The minister in France, in his instructions to De Talon, dated November 15th, 1664, speaking of the prohibition of the sale of brandy by the Jesuits, remarked: " This is doubtless a good principle, but one which is very ruinous to trade, because the Indians being passionately fond of these liquors, instead of coming to trade their peltries with us, go trade them among the Dutch, who supply them with brandy. This also is disadvantageous to religion. Having wherewith to gratify their appetites, they allow themselves to be catechised by the Dutch ministers, who instruct them in heresy. The said Bishop of Petrie and the Jesuit Fathers persist in their first opinions, without reflecting that prudence, and even Christian charity, inculcate closing the eyes to one evil to avoid a greater, or to reap a good more important than the evil." According to these views, M. Talon, the minister of justice in Canada, wrote M. Colbert, the king's secretary, November, 1666, that he had ordered to the Indians, "among the rest, the use of liquor, which has been prohibited them up to this time."

In 1668, the Rev. Father Pierron, a Jesuit missionary among the Mohawks, backed by the chiefs of the tribe, petitioned the Governor of New York for the suppression of the sale of intoxicating liquors to the Indians. The Governor, by letter of November 18th, 1668, acknowledged "the vast amount of liquors that some of Albany take the liberty to sell to the Indians, causing them thereby to commit excessive disorders," and declared that he had "adopted every possible precaution, and shall continue, by very certain fines, to restrain and prevent the supplying the Indians with any excess." These efforts to prevent "excess" in the sale of liquor to Indians, amounted to nothing definite.

The Jesuits of Canada still used all the means in their power to suppress the traffic, and prevented all the intercourse possible with the Christian tribes near Quebec and Montreal, and finally, in 1679, they procured an edict from the king, which afforded them some temporary assistance; but the governor and officials, more or less connected with the trade, neglected to enforce the edict, and brandy still composed a large item in every trader's outfit.

In 1716, Rev. Father Lafitan presented a petition to the

Canadian council, for the abolition of the brandy trade, in which, among other things, he stated that, "When the people (Indians), are intoxicated, they become so furious that they break and destroy every thing belonging to their household; cry and howl terribly, and go in quest, like mad men, of their enemies, to poignard them; their relatives and friends are not at these times safe from their rage, and they gnaw even their own noses and ears.

"Disunion and the dissolution of their marriages are always the result of their debaucheries, in consequence of the sorrow and despair experienced by their wives on beholding themselves robbed by their drunken husbands, who strip them of every thing in order to obtain drink, and the products of the chase, even, which belong to *them*, are taken away from their husbands by their creditors before arriving at their village.

"These Indians, loaded with debt and despoiled by their creditors, who do not leave them even their guns, are often obliged to abandon the country and go over to the English, despairing of being able to pay their debts.

"Several of their tribes have been almost wholly destroyed by brandy, particularly the Algonquin nation."

In answer to this petition, the Canadian council "All agree as to the inconvenience of the trade in brandy, but at the same time it is necessary." So they refused to prohibit it.

In October, 1729, the Governor of Canada writes the king that "The toleration his Majesty is pleased to entertain in favor of the distribution of brandy to the Indians, is so much the more necessary, as that liquor is the sole allurement that could attract and preserve them to us, and deprive them of all inducements to go to the English." Finally, in a dispatch from the King of France, of May 8, 1731, to the Governor of Canada, the king says that he has "Been pleased to see that Sieur Hocquart does not perceive any impropriety in his Majesty tolerating the distribution of brandy to the Indians."

The great success of the early Jesuit missions in the north-west, indicated an almost certainty of the conversion of the north-western tribes to Christianity; but this success raised a rivalry and hostility that ultimately proved their ruin. Count De Frontenac, the Governor of Canada, commenced hostilities on the Jesuits at an early date, and in his dispatch to the king, November 2nd, 1672, he remarked that, "To speak frankly to you, they think as much about the conversion of the beaver, as of souls; for the majority of their missions are pure mockeries, and I should not think they ought to be permitted to extend them further until we see some where a better formed church of those savages."

The enemies of the Jesuits had previously brought into Canada several of the Recollect priests, who had established a monastery. Sieur La Salle, a particular friend of the Governor, was also an enemy of the Jesuits, and took with him Recollect priests to the mission of Illinois.

The hostility to the Jesuits was severely felt by the society, and they appealed to the king for leave to continue their north-western mission. The king, by M. Colbert, wrote to Governor De Frontenac as follows, May 17th, 1674: "As to the request of the Jesuits, made to continue their missions in the far countries, his majesty thinks 'twould be more advantageous, both for the religion, and his service, if they attended to those more near, and whilst converting the Indians, led them to civilized society, and to abandon their manner of living, in which they can never become good Christians. His majesty, however, does not pretend that these good Fathers be in any wise circumscribed in their functions. He merely desires that you would communicate to them, and gently encourage them to second his majesty's views."

These views were communicated to the Jesuits by the Governor, and November 14th, of the same year, the Governor wrote M. Colbert that the former "Declared to me that they were here only to endeavor to instruct the Indians, or rather, *to get beaver*, and not to be parish priests to the French." The Governor then urges the sending of more Recollects. But the opposition to the Jesuits thus early manifested, although it must have embarrassed them, yet did not stop their efforts to convert the northwest. When La Salle went down the Mississippi in 1684, Rev. Father Allouez, with Father Durantaye as an assistant, again took possession of his Illinois mission, and when the survivors of La Salle's expedition returned in 1687, and reported La Salle also returning, Allouez retired to Green Bay. After that the good Father opened a mission at St. Josephs, where he died in August, 1690.

The success which at first had crowned the efforts of the missionaries under this opposition of the government, brandy, and the traders began to wane, and in a few years a few converts at each station was all there were left to encourage the despairing missionaries; and when the French surrendered Canada in 1760, there were probably but two missionaries west of Detroit; and the suppression of the Jesuits in 1763 by the king of France, it is said, left the north-west destitute of a resident Catholic priest for more than thirty years subsequent to that date. Indeed, as early as 1721, when the north-west was visited by Charlevoix, the missions had so far waned that he wrote: "The fathers are not much employed, having never found any great docility among the Ottawas."

Mr. Shea, in his history of the Catholic missions in North America, has compiled the following tables of the names of the missionaries to the Hurons, Ottawas, and Illinois, which probably contain some errors, but are as near the truth as can be attained at the present day:

LIST OF MISSIONARIES.

HURON MISSIONARIES.

MISSIONARIES.	ARRIVED.	ON MISSION.	DIED.
1 Joseph Le Caron, Rec.	May 25, 1615.	1615–16, 1623–24	1682
2 William Poulain, Rec.	June, 1619	1622	
3 Nicholas Viel, Rec.	June 28, 1623	1623–25	k. July, 1625
4 Theodat Sagard, L. B.	June 28, 1623	1623–24	left in 1624
5 Jos. de la Roche Daillon, Rec.	1625	1626–28	left in 1629
6 John de Brebeuf, S. J.	June 19, 1625.	1626–9, 34–41, 44–9	k. Mar. 16, 1649
7 Anne de Noue	July 14, 1626	1626–27	frozen Feb. 1, 1646
8 Anthony Daniel	June 24, 1633.	1634–36, 1638–48	k. July 4, 1648
9 Ambrose Davost	June 24, 1633.	1634–36	d. at sea in 1643
10 Francis Lemercier.	July 20, 1635.	1635–50	left after 1670
11 Peter Pijart	July 10, 1635.	1635–44	left in 1650
12 Charles Garnier	June 11, 1636.	1636–49	k. Dec. 7, 1649
13 Peter Chastellain	June 11, 1636.	1636–50	d. Aug. 14, 1683
14 Isaac Jogues	July 2, 1636	1636–42	k. Oct. 18, 1646
15 Paul Ragueneau	June 28, 1636.	1637–40, 1641–50	left Sept., 1666
16 Jerome Lalemant, S. J	Aug. 26, 1638.	1638–45	d. Jan. 26, 1673
17 Simon le Moyne	1638	1638–50?	d. Nov. 24, 1665
18 Francis Duperon	1638	1638–41	d. Nov. 10, 1665
19 P. J. M. Chaumonot	Aug. 1, 1639.	1639–50	d. Feb. 21, 1693
20 Joseph A. Poncet	Aug. 1, 1639.	1639–40, 1645–50	
21 Charles Raymbaut	1637	1640–42	d. Oct. 22, 1642
22 Claude Pijart	July 14, 1637.	1640–50	d. after 1668
23 Rene Menard	July 8, 1640	1641–50	k. Aug. 1661
24 Leonard Garreau	Aug. 15, 1643.	1644–50	k. Sept. 1566
25 Natalis Chabanel	Aug. 15, 1643.	1644–49	k. Dec. 8, 1649
26 Franc. J. Bressani	1642	1645–49	left Nov. 2, 1650
27 Gabriel Lalemant	Sept. 20, 1646.	1648–49	k. Mar. 17, 1649
28 Adrian Daran	Aug. 6, 1646.	1648–50	left in 1650
29 James Bonin	Aug. 14, 1647.	1648–50	left in 1650
30 Adrian Grelon	Aug. 14, 1647.	1648–50	died in China

OTTAWA MISSIONARIES.

MISSIONARIES.	ARRIVED.	TIME ON MISSION.	DIED.
1 Isaac Jouges, S. J.	July 2, 1636	1642	k. Oct. 1646
2 Charles Raymbaut	1637	1642	Oct. 22, 1642
3 Rene Menard	July 8, 1640	1660–61	k. Aug. 1661
4 Claude Allouez	July 11, 1658	1665–89	about Aug. 1690
5 Louis Nicholas	May 25, 1663	1667–68	
6 James Marquette	Sept. 20, 1666.	1668–75	d. May 19, 1675
7 Claude Dablon	1655	1668–71	
8 Louis Andre		1669–79*	
9 Gabriel Druillettes	Aug. 15, 1643.	1669–80	d. April 8, 1681
10 Henry Nouvel	Aug. 4, 1662.	1671–1700*	
11 Charles Albanel	Aug. 23, 1649.	1673–88*	
12 Peter Bailloquet	June 25, 1647.	1675–88*	
13 Philip Pierson	Sept. 25, 1667.	1675–81*	
14 Anthony Silvy		1676–78*	

OTTAWA MISSIONARIES—(continued).

MISSIONARIES.	ARRIVED.	TIME ON MISSION.	DIED.
15 Peter Andrew Bonneault		1676–79*	
16 John Enjalran		1678–88*	
17 Nicholas Potier		16 –84	
18 James Gravier		1688†	1706
19 Claude Aveneau		1688†–1703*	
20 Stephen de Carheil	Aug. 6, 1666	1688†–1703*	July, 1726
21 James Joseph Marest		1700†–1712*	
22 J. B. Chardon			
23 J. C. Guymonneau		1721–22	
24 Peter M. Guignas		1728–30	
25 O. M. Messaiger		1724	
26 J. B. Lamorinie		1749–50	
27 Justinian la Richardie			
28 Marin Louis Lefranc		till 1764	
29 Pierre Dujaunay		1764	
30 Peter Potier		1751†–81	d. July 16, 1781

* And perhaps later.   † And perhaps earlier.

ILLINOIS MISSIONARIES.

MISSIONARIES.	ARRIVED.	WHEN IN ILLINOIS.	DIED.
1 James Marquette, S. J.	Sept. 20, 1666	1673–75	May 19, 1675
2 Claude Allouez	July 11, 1658	1677, 1679–87	about Aug. 1690
3 Gabriel de la Ribourde, Rec.	Aug. 1670	1680	k. Sept. 19, 1680
4 Zenobius Membre	June, 1675	1680	k. 1686–7
5 James Gravier, S. J.	June 16, 1672 ?	1687–1706	k. about 1706
6 Sebastian Rale	Oct. 13, 1689	1691–92	k. Aug. 23, 1724
7 Francis Pinet		1700, 1703	d. before 1712
8 Gabriel Marest		1700, 1703, 1712	
9 James Marmet		1700, 1703, 1712	
10 Julian Binneteau		1700	d. before 1711
11 —— de Lymoges		1700	
12 —— Bovie		1700	
13 John B. Chardon		1700, 1703, 1721	
14 John Bergier, Priest of F.M.		1700, 1707, 1710	
15 Louis Mary de Ville, S. J.		1712	
16 Dominic Mary Varlet, F.M.		1712–18 ?	d. 1742
17 Joseph Ign. le Boulanger, S. J.		1721	
18 —— de Kereben		1721	
19 —— de Beaubois		1721	
20 J. C. Guymonneau		1721	
21 G. Calvarin, F. M.		1719	
22 D. A. R. Taumur de la Source, F.M., ord. Feb. 1717		1721	d. April 4, 1731
23 John le Mercier, F. M.; ord. May, 1718		1721	d. April 17, 1752
24 —— Senat, S. J.		1730	k. 1780
25 Louis Vivier		1750	d. after Aug. 1750
26 A. F. X. de Guyenne		1750	
27 —— Doutreleau		1727	
28 —— Dumas	1727	1727	
29 —— Tartarin	1727	1727–46	
30 —— Vattrin		1750	
31 Sebast. L. Meurin		1750	d. after 1768
32 Claude F. Virot		on Ohio in 1757	
33 Julian Duvernay		1763	

The successful close of our American revolution, and the adoption of our constitution having established the freedom of conscience and emancipated the worship of God from the control of political power, a fruitful field was opened to the hundreds of Catholic priests, who had fled from France at the breaking out of the Jacobin revolution in that country. Arriving in this country, they naturally turned their attention to the villages of the old French and half-breeds of the Mississippi valley and Canada; and, at an early date, Rev. Father Gabriel Richard, a Sulpician, established himself at Detroit, who, in 1799, visited the Ottawas at Arbre Croche, where he found one Indian seventy-five years old, who had been baptized, probably by Du Jaunay, the last of the old Mackinaw missionaries. This Indian and a few traditions were all that was left, so far as could be ascertained, of the several flourishing missions that in the olden time had existed along the shores of Lake Huron.

Several years passed before the Ottawas of Arbre Croche received another visit from a Catholic priest; but the Episcopal see of Cincinnati having been erected, and Michigan attached to it, it was determined that the Ottawas of that locality should have a priest, and Father Richard was sent in 1821 to visit them again. Again the Indians asked for a priest, and in July, 1825, Rev. J. V. Badin visited Arbre Croche, Drummond island, Mackinaw, Sault St. Mary's, and Green Bay. In 1826, Father Richard induced the secretary of war to pay two-thirds the expense of buildings, and twenty dollars per scholar instructed, and by this pecuniary assistance, was enabled to establish a regular mission and school at Arbre Croche, which was opened the following year, under the charge of Rev. Father De Jean, and two Catholic ladies from Mackinaw. In the mean time, Assaguinac, an educated Indian from Canada, of some prominence, settled at Arbre Croche, who catechized the Indians, taught them hymns, and thus prepared twenty-one for baptism on the arrival of De Jean. The priest, however, did not remain there permanently until 1829. In 1830 he had received six hundred into the church, and his school for boys and girls contained sixty-four pupils. As a consequence, intoxication was banished from the village. They had also erected a house, forty-six feet long and twenty wide, for their school, and a church fifty-four by thirty feet. The complete success of this mission encouraged the Catholic church to make a systematic effort to restore the missions to the different Indian tribes, and the Chippeways, Menominies, Potowatomies, and Kickapoos, along the lakes, received missionaries, who often came in collision with Protestant missionaries, and government was often appealed to on both sides for protection and assistance. The further progress of the Indian missions will be noticed when speaking of individual tribes.

The most prominent of the present Jesuit missionaries, in the north-west, is Rev. Father De Smet, who became a missionary to the Flatheads, on the upper Missouri, in 1840. He has secured a commanding influence with the nations in that region, and in 1865 was employed by the government to assist in making a peace with the warlike Sioux. He makes his head-quarters at St. Louis, and is the author of several books on the Indian tribes.

CHAPTER VI.

THE PROTESTANT MISSIONS.

The true formula for the conversion of the Indians to Christianity, was successfully followed by the good and pious Elliot of Massachusetts. Having been settled as pastor of the church in Roxbury in 1632, and having witnessed the straggling natives, as they wandered about, trading some moccasins and furs for food and rum, his love for them was aroused to activity, and he determined in the true missionary spirit, to strive for their conversion to Christianity. Unlike the Catholic priests who accompanied the expeditions of Cortez to Mexico, and Pizarro to Peru, who only presented the alternative of the sword or the cross, the good Elliot commenced by learning the Indian language; then by instructing them in their own language in the requisites of both Christianity and civilization; and in 1654, after a labor of love for twenty-two years, gathered his first Indian church at Natick. The following year he had completed the translation of the New Testament into the Mohegan dialect of the Algonquin language, and in two years after, he completed the translation of the Old Testament; and the Indian Bible thus translated, was the first Bible printed in America. By his ardent labors, in 1674 he had fourteen praying Indian villages, in which six regular churches were formed.

In the mean time, constant aggressions had been carried on by the traders and settlers against the uncivilized Indians.

The great chief, Philip, had repeatedly been imprisoned and robbed of his territory; and at last, goaded to desperation, the bold chief summoned his warriors, raised his tomahawk, and in 1675 commenced the terrible war that resulted in the extermination of the most of the Indians, and in the death of over six hundred whites. After the war, when the sorrowing Elliot sought out the remnant of his Indian churches, which had cost him the labor of forty-three years, he found that they had been plundered and murdered in turn by both whites and Indians; and that four bleeding and decimated villages were all that were left of the fourteen before the war.

But the mantle of Elliot seemed to fall upon David Brainard. Expelled from Yale College for having said "that one of the tutors was as devoid of grace as a chair," he was immediately appointed a missionary to the Indians, by a Scotch missionary society, and entered upon the duties of his mission in the spring of 1742 among the Mohegans, at Kau-na-meek, between Stockbridge and Albany. After a year's labor of Brainard, those Indians removed to Stockbridge, and Brainard turned his attention to the Delawares of Pennsylvania and New Jersey. Here his labors were crowned with success; but unfortunately for the cause of missions, in the fall of 1746, from his arduous labors his health failed, and in the following spring he returned to Massachusetts, and in October, died in the family of Jonathan Edwards at Northampton. About this time several unsuccessful attempts were made to establish missions among the Indians. Even the zealous Charles and John Wesley, failed after three years' efforts, in Georgia. But the indomitable Moravians, having, like the Wesleys, failed in Georgia, removed to Pennsylvania, and in 1740 opened a mission among the Delawares on the Susquehanna. This mission for a time proved successful, but the Pontiac war aroused the anger of a portion of the whites, who determined to avenge themselves on the Christian Indians. To avoid this calamity, Zeisberger, the leader of the missionaries, took his Indians in a body to Philadelphia, and the governor attempted to protect them by placing them in the common prison. Even here some of them were murdered. In 1767 Zeisberger removed a band of Christian Indians to the Allegheny river, and three years after, again removed to Beaver creek on the Ohio, where he was the same season joined by another party of the Delawares from the Susquehanna, under the missionary Heckewelder. The following year, Zeisberger, under an invitation of the Delaware chiefs, opened another mission on the Muskingum river, where he was soon joined by a band from the Susquehanna of two hundred and forty-one persons. Here, in the depths of the forests of Ohio, the pious missionaries labored with great zeal in their Master's work, and successfully overcame the crisis of the hostility of the Pagan Indians, which in after years proved so disastrous to the Sioux. But successful as they were against the Pagans, many of them finally fell a sacrifice to the inhumanity of the whites.

The war of the revolution having arrayed the western Indians on the side of Great Britain, the fierce Iroquois demanded the alliance of the Delawares, but the Christian Indians, having imbibed the peculiarities of the Moravians, refused to fight. This greatly exasperated the English and their Indian allies, and in the summer of 1781 the Christian Indians were compelled to abandon their crops and their settlements on the Muskingum, and remove to Sandusky. In the fall of the same year, to protect themselves from starvation the coming winter, they sent back to the settlements on the Muskingum a party of ninety-eight men, women, and children, to gather their abandoned crops. This party, when nearly ready to return to Sandusky, were secretly surrounded by Colonel Williamson, with about ninety Americans from western Pennsylvania, who disarmed the Indians, and murdered ninety-six of them in cold blood. Two boys alone escaped to report the disastrous news at Sandusky. This success of Colonel Williamson and his party, so elated them and their friends at home, that early the following March they fitted out an expedition of nearly five hundred men, under Colonels Williamson and Crawford, who marched upon Sandusky with the view of surprising and exterminating the balance of the Christian Indians at that place. Learning of the near approach of that force, the hostile Indians about Sandusky, including the Wyandots, laid in ambush for the American party, and attacked and cut them to pieces. Colonel Crawford, his son, and son-in-law, were taken prisoners, and burned at the stake. After the close of the revolution, and in 1786, the Christian Indians returned to Pennsylvania and to the Muskingum, and Zeisberger died on the Muskingum in 1808, aged eighty-seven, having been a missionary among the Delawares for the long period of sixty-two years. From the commencement of the mission to 1782, the missionaries baptized seven hundred and twenty Indian converts. Heckewelder returned to Pennsylvania, where he wrote a history of the mission, and some other books relating to the Indians, and finally died at Bethlehem, Pennsylvania, in 1823. With those two distinguished missionaries, probably terminated the Moravian missions among the Delawares, as that tribe in subsequent years do not appear to have had any Moravian teachers.

From the commencement of the revolution to the close of the war of 1812, the north-west was in an unsettled condition, by reason of the refusal of the British to deliver up to the Americans their surrendered posts, and the constant intrigues of English traders among the Indians to keep the latter in the condition of war against the United States; but the triumphant close of the war with Great Britain by the great victory at New Orleans, January 8th, 1815, fully placed the Americans in the enjoyment of the rights won by the revolution, and left the north-west free to American enterprise; and we might with safety date the dawning of north-western civilization from that eventful victory.

In this condition of affairs, even religion seemed to have put on a new phase, and adapted itself to the advance of civilization in the great west. The then comparatively new sect called "Methodists," originated by the Wesleys, of England, and planted in New York in 1766, had now become the religion of great numbers of the pioneers of the west. It could be preached without parchment or pulpit, grammar or diploma; could be learned without creed, prayer-book or breviary, and heard, too, without chapel or cathedral. It marched without crosier or cross in the emigrant train, and slept with the pioneer the first night in his log cabin. It assembled the scattered pioneers in the shady grove for the camp meeting, where the happy shouts of the new converts often excelled in noise the most extravagant Indian war dance.

The Methodists early embarked in Indian missions. Their first noted missionary in that department was *John Steward*, a free colored man, born near Richmond, Virginia, who was converted and united with the Methodist church in that State. Unadvised, and acting on his own impressions of duty, he journeyed alone and on foot from Virginia to upper Sandusky, in Ohio, where, in November, 1816, he commenced a mission among the Wyandots or Hurons. He found an interpreter in a negro, who had, many years before, been taken prisoner by the Wyandots, and had learned their language. He met with a determined opposition from the Pagan and Catholic parties, and to obviate a difficulty raised by the latter to his not being a priest, in March, 1819, he visited Urbana Quarterly Conference, and obtained a local preacher's license, and was appointed missionary to upper Sandusky.

The Ohio Conference, August 7th, 1819, appointed Rev. James B. Finley to the Lebanon district, which included upper Sandusky mission, which appointment gave him the supervision of that mission. Up to this time, Mr. Steward had won over to the Methodist church four prominent Wyandot chiefs, and about sixty other Indians. Schools were established, and in 1826 the church members numbered 303, and the schools 77 scholars. An important revival occurred in 1837; and when they removed west of the Missouri they carried Methodism with them, and continue to sustain a flourishing church to the present day.

In 1820, the fame of the success of the mission work among the Wyandots crossed Lake Erie, and aroused the attention of another band of the same tribe living near Fort Malden, in Canada. Two native preachers, and John Sunday, a converted Chippeway, visited and preached to them in the Wyandot language. Several were converted, and a mission established.

In 1823, two half-breeds, John and Peter Jones, brothers, who were chiefs at Credit river, in Canada, were converted at a Methodist mission under the preaching of Revs. Torry and Crawford. The two young Indians returned to their tribe, and commenced teaching. In 1827 they were visited by Indian missionaries, and an important revival commenced. A camp meeting was held during the summer near Cobourg, where hundreds of Indians attended, and many were converted. The shouts of the happy Indian souls might have been heard for miles around. The great work spread from band to band, until barbarism almost ceased in southern Canada West.

John Sunday and some other native preachers went as missionaries to Lake Superior in 1830, and were followed in 1834 by four others, including George Copway, as a teacher. They established, in 1833, a successful mission at Anse, near Kewenaw bay; and, in October, 1835, they established another at Ottawa lake, on the upper Chippeway river, one hundred and seventy-five miles nearly south from La Point. These missions were under the care of Rev. John Clark, whose head-quarters were at Sault St. Mary.

REV. ALFRED BRUNSON, D.D.

At the session of Pittsburgh Conference, Pennsylvania, in July, 1835, Rev. Alfred Brunson, then presiding elder of Meadeville district, was appointed superintendent of missions on the upper Mississippi. In September of that year he started on his work, and attended the Illinois Conference, which appointed him presiding elder of Galena district, extending from Rock Island north to the British possessions. He finally reached Prairie Du Chien in November, where he found a fort, and quite a settlement of Canadian French and half-breeds, but only three American families outside of the fort. Arrived at the head of civilization, he found himself entirely unqualified for the work of missions, as he did not know a word of any of the Indian languages in this region. Casting about for an interpreter, he fortunately found a negro slave at Fort Snelling who understood the Sioux language, and who could be purchased of an officer at the fort for $1,200. Sending the facts to the Methodist paper at Cincinnati, he was soon put in possession of the money by private donations, and with it procured free papers for the negro.

Father Brunson consumed the summer of 1836 in visiting Pennsylvania, bringing on his family, and holding quarterly meetings in his Galena district, south of Prairie Du Chien; and, finally, about the 20th of May, 1837, he availed himself of the first steamboat up the river that spring to go with his small party to Little Crow's village, at Kaposia, three miles below the present St. Paul, where he built a house and established a mission. Returning after several weeks to Prairie Du Chien for additional supplies, he first met George Copway, John Johnson, his cousin, and Peter Marksman, three young Chippeways, who had spent the last three years in the missions of Lake Superior, and whose superintendent, Rev. John Clark, had sent south to be further educated at the Methodist school at Jacksonville, Illinois, called the "Ebenezer Seminary." These young men accompanied Superintendent Brunson on his return to Kaposia, and assisted in building the school-house and church, and soon after acted as interpreters at a treaty with the Chippeways, in which Governor Doty, as government agent, purchased a large tract of the Chippeways' country. In the fall they were sent to the seminary, where they remained two years, and then returned to the missionary work. During the summer of 1837, Revs. Thomas W. Pope, James Whitford, and Hiram Delap were added to the mission, the latter with his family. In May, 1838, Mr. Brunson, with two other missionaries, Whitford and Randolph, visited *Hole-in-the-Day*, the head Chippeway chief, near Crow Wing, above St. Anthony falls, and got leave to establish a mission in his band, but the fierce war that broke out immediately with the Sioux delayed it for some time.

Late in the fall, Mr. Brunson was prostrated with the fever, which so destroyed his health that he failed to visit the Kaposia mission the following year, and in the fall of 1839 he was placed upon the superannuated list, and was superseded by Rev. B. T. Kavenaugh as superintendent. Mr. Kavenaugh took with him to his missionary field, Brothers Spates, Huddleston, Johnson, and Marksman, and established a new mission among the Chippeways, on the east bank of the Mississippi, at Elk river, some three hundred miles above St. Paul. In the fall of 1840, when the missionaries returned from Rock River Conference, they found the Indians had all fled, on account of the expected attack of the Sioux, and the mission was removed to Rabbit river the following February. However, on the 30th of December, before the removal, Rev. Mr. Huddleston died of dysentery, and was buried on the top of a little hill on the bank of the Mississippi. *Hole-in-the-Day* threw a heap of stones on the grave, "so," as he said, "that all may see and know where the good man lies; he who came to bless us."

In the fall of 1840 a new mission was established at Sandy Lake, under the charge of Rev. Mr. Spates, and a school organized. The Sioux having sent hostile war parties far into the interior of the Chippeway country, Superintendent Kavenaugh again changed his base, and established a new mission at Whitefish lake, and another at Fond du Lac, of Lake Superior. In July, 1841, the missions were consolidated into that at Sandy lake, under the charge of Rev. H. J. Bruce, assisted by Rev. Samuel Spates, with a school of thirty scholars; that at Whitefish lake, under the charge of Rev. John Johnson, (Chippeway); and that at Fond du Lac, under the charge of Rev. George Copway, (Chippeway), assisted by his wife, her sister, and James Simpson, as teachers.

The mission at Kaposia was much embarrassed in the spring of 1841, by the war parties, and the school was closed for the reason that "Little Crow" visited it, and entered his protest against any boys attending the school, under the ill-conceived idea that if they were educated they would not make warriors. But to his credit it should be stated that at the alarm in 1838, the night after the battle with the Chippeways on the St. Croix, when the missionaries had all embarked to go down the river, he ordered them back to their mission house, placed his son with them, and left a strong guard to surround their house, who reported hourly, "all quiet without." This son was then a young man nearly twenty, who became notorious as the head chief in the Sioux rebellion of 1862. During this fearful night "Little Crow" and his warriors had their war-dance over the Chippeway scalps, but a few rods from the mission-house. Superintendent Brunson was present at the dance a short time, and witnessed the barbarians holding high carnival over their trophies of war.

But the Methodists did not confine their efforts to the tribes above named. In 1823, Rev. Jesse Walker opened a mission among the Potowatomies, in the vicinity of Fort Clark, on Fox river, Illinois, and about 1837 over one hundred were converted. About this time, a prophet rose up among the Kickapoos, preaching the essential doctrines of Methodism, but adding many of his own peculiarities. His name was Kee-an-ne-kuk, or the "Foremost man." He was a chief of great eloquence, and preached every Sabbath to his tribe, denouncing intemperance with no sparing hand. The traders in that tribe told Mr. Catlin, who painted his portrait in 1835, that the chief got his knowledge of Christianity from a Methodist preacher, whom he would not allow to preach, but detained him some time, until he learned the essential doctrines of his religion, and then dismissed him. It has often been stated that the chief subsequently conformed to the orthodox church, but this is a mistake, as he died west of the Missouri with the small-pox about 1856, in the belief that he should rise again from the dead in three days. He had studiously opposed any innovation upon his teachings. His teachings, however, did not deter the Methodists from opening a mission among the Kickapoos in 1830, which flourished finely, and in 1834 numbered 230 members, with a school of twenty-four native children.

In 1829, a mission was commenced at Green Bay, among the Oneidas, by a young Mohawk, who had been converted in Canada among the Wesleyans. In a short time 100 were converted, and its influence spread to the Onondagas, Menominies, and Kewawenons, and schools were established.

Without following out in detail the various new missions, and their varied successes, we may say that in 1854, the Methodists claimed in Missouri, Wisconsin, Michigan, and Black river, thirteen missions, seventeen missionaries, 1,051 members, 176 probationers, and five local preachers; and the Methodist Church South, thirty missions, twenty-eight missionaries, 4,232 members, thirty-five churches, thirty-four Sabbath-schools, 1,394 scholars, nine manual labor schools, and 490 pupils. It should be observed, however, that the church south took possession of all the missions among the northern Indians, who removed west of the Missouri river, as well as the very extensive missions among

KEE-AN-NE-KUK.
(KICKAPOO PROPHET.)

the Cherokees, Choctaws, Creeks, etc., in the south; and so sensitive were the southern Methodists on this point, that they compelled the Rev. James Gurley, who had been appointed by the Ohio Conference, in 1849, to continue the mission with the Wyandots, to leave the country at the peril of his life, after he had been with that tribe nearly six months, to their entire satisfaction.

The American Board of Commissioners for Foreign Missions have not been neglectful of the Indians. A mission was commenced with the Ottawas at Maumee, Ohio, by the Western Missionary Society, in 1822, but subsequently came under the American Board. It flourished for a few years, and in 1828 had seventy pupils in their school, but the tribe having sold their land to government, became scattered, and the mission was abandoned in 1833.

In 1830, a mission was opened among the Chippeways, at Lapoint, Lake Superior, by Mr. Frederic Ayer, a teacher and catechist, who was followed the next year by Revs. Hall and Boutwell. They opened missions at Lapoint, Yellow lake, Sandy lake, and Leech lake. In 1834, the Sandy lake station, occupied by Mr. Ely, was removed to Fond du Lac; and the Yellow lake mission, in 1836, was removed to Pokeguma lake, where they were joined by the missionary from Leech lake. Fond du Lac mission was deserted in 1840, and in May, 1841, Pokeguma was attacked by the Sioux, and the Indians scattered with some loss. They did not return until 1843, and the post was abandoned by the missionaries a year or two after. In 1854, and for three years previous, they only held stations at Bad river and Crow Wing. The American Board also established a mission among the Sioux or Dakotas, in 1835.

The first missionaries were Rev. Thomas S. Williamson, and Jedediah D. Stevens, with their wives; Alexander Huggins, farmer, and his wife, and Sarah Poage, teacher, and Lucy C. Stevens, assistant. They selected two points, Lake Harriet, six miles west of Fort Snelling, and Lacqui

Parle, near the head-waters of Minnesota river. Mr. Williamson, who was a physician, Mr. Huggins and Miss Poage, remained at Lake Harriet, and the rest of the company proceeded to the other post. In 1850, they had six missions, three organized churches, thirty-one native, and thirty-two white communicants, with an average attendance of twenty-seven pupils in school. The Rev. S. R. Riggs was early added to the mission, who has performed much of the labor of compiling the Dakota Dictionary, and the translation of the Bible into the Dakota language. The mission continued to progress finely, until their labors were cut short by the outbreak of 1862.

Before we pass from the Sioux missions, it is proper to remark that an effort was made by some missionary society in Switzerland, to establish a mission among the Sioux, and Mr. Denton, a Swiss Presbyterian, was sent from Europe in 1834, who opened a mission at Red Wing in the spring of the following year, and Mr. Gavan, another Swiss Presbyterian, came out in the fall of 1836, and opened a mission at Mont Trempealeau, in Wabashas' band. They continued their missions for a few years with some success, and then returned to Europe. Their missions do not appear to have been named in any accounts published of missions in the north-west.

The American Board became possessed of the mission among the Osages, which was established by the United Foreign Missionary Society, in 1820. This mission was conducted with zeal and considerable expense until 1837, when it was finally abandoned as a useless effort. The same Board made a similar unsuccessful effort among the Pawnees, a tribe on the Platte numbering nearly 7,000. The first missionary company consisted of Rev. John Dunbar, missionary, Benedict Satterlee, physician and catechist, and Samuel Allis, assistant, who made their head-quarters at Bellevue, the government agency. Dr. Satterlee died on one of his excursions with a band towards the Rocky mountains, and, no adequate success attending the mission, it was abandoned in 1847.

The missions among the Tuscaroras and Senecas in New York, were, in 1826, transferred to the American Board. The following year, John Elliot, of Maine, entered the work among the Tuscaroras, and was joined by Rev. William Hall in 1829. In 1843, there were reported at Tuscarora, forty-nine members; Seneca, twenty; Cattaraugus, fifty-one; and at Alleghany, 114. The aggregate number of pupils in school at all the stations were reported at 200. Previous to 1854, these missions were consolidated into two, the Seneca and Tuscarora, and that year reported in the aggregate, six stations, five missionaries, nineteen female assistant missionaries, two hundred and sixty-five members of the church, and three hundred and eighty scholars.

The Presbyterian Board of Missions have also had some missions among the north-western Indians. They first opened a mission among the Iowas and Sacs in 1835, which has been continued with some success, and in 1854 they had with those tribes, one missionary, four teachers, and forty scholars. They opened a mission among the Olloes and Omahaws at Bellevue, in 1846, and in 1854 had one missionary and six teachers among them, and forty-two scholars in their school. Another mission was opened among the Chippeways and Ottawas, at Grand Traverse bay, Michigan, by Rev. Peter Dougherty, in 1838, and in 1854 they had one missionary, three teachers, thirty-four scholars, and thirty-two communicants. In 1852 a school was opened at Little Traverse, with two teachers and forty scholars; and at Middle Village, in 1853, with two teachers and thirty scholars.

There was a mission in 1835, not mentioned in the church missionary records, at Yellow river, Iowa, nine miles above Prairie Du Chien, conducted by Rev. David Lowry, a Cumberland Presbyterian, and the government agent and school teacher, among the Winnebagoes. Mr. Lowry subsequently came in collision with a Catholic priest, who claimed spiritual jurisdiction over the Winnebagoes, and we are not prepared to say what became of Mr. Lowry's mission.

The American Baptist Missionary Union, in the fall of 1817, appointed Rev. Isaac McCoy a missionary among the Indians on the Wabash river, who immediately repaired to Fort Wayne, in Indiana, then on the frontier, in the midst of bands of the Miamies, Kickapoos, Potowatomies and Ottawas. In a year he had made friends with a few Indian families, and obtained a few children, whom he taught in his family. In 1820 he had increased his school to forty-eight pupils. Two years after, he removed his station two hundred miles further west, and called his new station Carey, where the Indians were mainly Potowatomies. Here he gathered a church of some thirty members, part Indians and part whites.

On the solicitation of "Noonday," a principal chief of a band of Ottawas, Mr. McCoy established another mission with that band on Grand river, Michigan, which he named Thomas, which in 1827 was put under the care of Rev. Leonard Slater. The Potowatomies, having sold their land to government, and disappointed the missionaries by their indifference to religion, Mr. McCoy, in 1829, with all his associates except Rev. Mr. Sumerville, removed to Thomas. In 1830, this mission at Grand river was composed of five missionaries, six female assistants, and one farmer. In 1832, a revival of religion took place, and several Indians were converted, among which was the chief "Noonday." He proved a very consistent, active Christian; was of great service to the missionary in his work, and died triumphantly. His grave, in the Indian burial-place at "Richland," is marked by a white marble slab, with the name of "Noonday" carved upon it. In 1836 the Indians sold their land to government, and most of the tribes removed west of the Missouri. A small band, however, removed to Richland, fifty miles south of "Thomas," who were followed by Mr.

Slater. In 1853, this band also followed their brethren west of the Missouri, and Mr. Slater was relieved of his mission. The most of the expense of these missions, after 1825, was borne by government, under the act of Congress of 1819, appropriating $10,000 annually, to be expended by the President for the education of the Indians.

In 1828 the Baptist Board established a mission at Sault St. Mary, near the outlet of Lake Superior, and Rev. Abel Bingham was appointed missionary. The president made them an appropriation to assist in defraying the expenses of the mission. Suitable buildings were soon erected, and in 1832 forty persons were baptized and added to the church, of whom eleven were Indians, and the balance were generally connected with the American fort. Messrs. Meeker and Merrill, and their wives, were added to the mission in 1833. In 1854 the Chippeway Baptist mission numbered two stations, two out-stations, two missionaries, one female assistant, one native assistant, one church, twenty-one members, one boarding school, six pupils; two day schools and seventy-four pupils. The following year Mr. Bingham resigned his supervision of the mission. They also claimed the following at Shawanoe mission, west of the Missouri: three stations, three missionaries, five female assistants, two native assistants, three churches, one hundred members, two boarding schools, and forty-five pupils.

The Protestant Episcopal church established a mission at Green Bay in 1825, under the superintendence of Rev. Mr. Nash, but it was discontinued in 1827. It was revived in 1829, under the care of Rev. R. F. Codle, and again discontinued in 1837. December 2nd, 1838, Rev. Bishop Kemper consecrated a church at Duck Creek, erected by the Oneidas with funds received from government, and the following year Rev. Solomon Davis was placed in charge.

The American Missionary Association established a mission among the Chippeways at Red lake in 1843; Cass lake, 1846; St. Josephs and Belle Prairie in 1852. At these

10*

points, in 1854, they had two missionaries, seventeen assistant teachers, three churches, twelve native communicants, and thirty-nine scholars in boarding schools.

There were probably other missions of the foregoing churches and societies, as well as of other societies, but the writer has not the statistics from which to give their condition. Several of these missions were discontinued previous to 1867, and many new ones have been established, and the reader is referred to the sketches of the different tribes for the condition of the missions in 1867, together with their advancement in civilization.

The question has a thousand times been asked, " Why can't the Indian be civilized and Christianized?" The answer from the missionaries has been almost uniformly this, " that the Indian can be both civilized and Christianized;" but that the lack of success is mainly attributable to the hostility of the Indian traders, the lack of coöperation by government, and the sale of intoxicating liquors to the Indians.

We have previously given the testimony of the Jesuit Fathers on this subject, and now propose to submit some Protestant testimony of modern date to the same point, so that the reader can see that the evil is the same now that it was two hundred years ago. We will first introduce S. Cooper, Esq., the government sub Indian agent to the Sacs and Foxes at Council Bluffs, in October, 1841, by making an extract from his official report to his government:

" The principal reason of these people not progressing faster in civilization is *ardent spirits*, which are kept along the line of Missouri, and conveyed into the Indian country by half-breeds. The whisky trade has increased double this season, and can not be prevented by our Indian agents unless they can have *aid from government.* The Indian will sell any thing for liquor."

Our next witness is A. Hamilton, Esq., sub-agent to the Miamies, on their reservation in Indiana, who says, in his official report, September 10th, 1841, that "the tribe is diminishing yearly. More than half the adults who die, perish by the hands of their fellow-Indians. Frequently members of the same family destroy each other during their scenes of drunkenness and riot."

We next bring forward Rev. A. Bingham, the faithful Baptist missionary to the Ojibways, at Sault St. Mary. Here is his testimony to government on this subject, in August, 1841:

"And so long as our Indians are accustomed to frequent a place where twelve or fourteen houses are licensed to deal out intoxicating liquor to a population of two or three hundred souls, and while there are so many individuals who spend the most of their time in peddling the deadly stuff to Indians as well as others, and no check can be put to it; who, that knows the native fondness of an Indian for it, can calculate on any very extensive and beneficial results from the most faithful and self-denying labors of the missionary?"

It will be observed that the American Board had a missionary station among the Osage Indians from 1820 to 1837, which they abandoned the latter year. The following extract from the official report of the Indian agent for that tribe in 1841, will explain some of the difficulties:

"Hitherto, these people have lived in the world without law, or the fear of God before their eyes; and, in consequence, have repeatedly sinned against their neighbors, and for several years past have drank much more than formerly. The vendors of whisky are to be found at almost every other house, from the Cowskin to Missouri river, near the boundary line."

Further testimony from the same locality appears in the official report of J. B Luce, sub-agent to the Senecas, dated August 1st, 1841:

"There are two distilleries in Missouri, near the Seneca line, ready to absorb these toll grains, (of Seneca mill), and it is said one of them is supported and carried on entirely by grain bought *from* and whisky sold *to* the Indians. To such a pitch had this matter reached when I arrived, that every Monday, the day on which the tolls are distributed, three-fourths of these unfortunate people might be seen drunk about the mill."

By referring to the chapter on the history of the Chippeways of Lake Superior and the Mississippi, the reader will observe that all the efforts at Christianizing this tribe have been nearly fruitless; and the missionaries have from time to time abandoned them as past all hopes of recovery. Here are detailed some of the reasons of this failure in the official report of H. G. Gilbert, Esq., agent for the Chippeways, dated Detroit, Michigan, October 10th, 1855. Speaking of the bands at Lac Court, Oreille, and Lac de Flambeau, he says:

"They are seldom visited except by traders, who, from the very nature of their business, and the manner in which it has been conducted, have been directly interested in *preventing any advance in civilization* among them."
. . . "From their present appearance and condition, as well as from the most reliable information, I am led to believe that for many years they have been furnished with whisky in large quantities." . . . "The annuity payments are always attended by a set of miscreants, who rob and plunder the Indians of their goods and money, in exchange for intoxicating drinks. At the late payment at La Point, large quantities of whisky were brought to the place, and within a day or two after the distribution of goods had taken place, I learned that some of the interior Indians had been stripped in this way of all they had received. I had not yet made the money payments, but was ready to do so, and was well satisfied that if it was made under the then existing circumstances, a large proportion of the $20,000 to be paid in coin would find its way into the pockets of the whisky venders. There was but one course to take. With

the aid of my assistants and some other gentlemen present, every suspected place on the island was searched, and all the liquor found was destroyed. About 1,000 bottles, put up ready for sale, were broken, and twelve barrels emptied into the lake. Several hundred dollars worth of goods, that had been taken from the Indians in exchange for whisky, were reclaimed, and the traffic was effectually *broken up* for that time."

From the foregoing report, it appears that government has begun to wake up to the subject, and the following displays the shadows of coming events. Mr. Fitch, the Chippeway agent for 1859, sends the following advice to government: "This is a matter that admits of no compromise. The vender of intoxicating liquors among the Indians must be considered as their enemy, a disturber of the peace and good order of society, and should be treated as such at home and abroad, and as such dealt with according to law."

We next give agent Galbraith's report of the origin of the Sioux massacre, which report was dated January 27th, 1863: "On Sunday, the 17th day of August, A. D. 1862, at the village of Acton, in the county of Meeker, and State of Minnesota, four lower Sioux Indians, of the Sha-ka-pee's band, part of a hunting party composed of fourteen, obtained whisky, became intoxicated, and killed six persons, including a man by the name of Jones, from whom, it is alleged, they obtained the whisky. This was the immediate, exciting cause of the outbreak."

We close this testimony with an extract from the official report of the Governor of Dakota territory, dated September 20th, 1864. Speaking of the Sioux war, then pending, and its origin, he says: "It is in a great measure, if not wholly, attributable to the influence of disloyal persons, or rebels, who are so generously permitted by the government to have intercourse with them (Indians); and the practice which prevails to an alarming extent, doubtless much beyond the belief or even conception of the department, of allowing such persons to carry whisky into the Indian country, where it is sold to the Indians or exchanged for peltries, in such quantities as at times to make a whole camp drunk and unmanageable."

From these extracts, all of which are taken from the published documents of Congress, it appears that government is now fully advised that the whisky-trader with the Indians is a rebel, and should be treated as such by government; and that such rebels have constantly fought against all the efforts of government and of missionaries for over two centuries, and, unfortunately for civilization and Christianity, have, until lately, beat them both. But Congress has now passed strong penal laws against the whisky traffic with the Indians, and if the Commissioner of Indian Affairs shall hereafter select the proper Indian agents, who will sympathize with the missionaries, and, at all hazards, execute the laws, there is yet hope for the poor remnants of the once brave and powerful nations of the north-west.

In view of the premises, the zealous missionaries, remembering that even Jerusalem "killed the prophets and stoned them which were sent unto her," should take courage and renew the conflict, for the day of victory is evidently near at hand.

CHAPTER VII.

THE IROQUOIS, HURONS, DELAWARES, AND MOHEGANS.

ONGWE-HONWE, OR IROQUOIS.

THIS confederacy originally called themselves the *Ongwe-Honwe*, or real men; a name nearly synonymous in meaning with *Illini*, or the men of the Illinois confederacy. After the Iroquois had confederated, they called themselves *Konoshioni*, or people of the long house, meaning that their council-houses, from Albany to near Lake Erie, had become one. In the early times of Champlain, the French called them *Iroquois*, from their peculiar *eroh*, or grunt, which they gave at the close of a speech, with the affix of *ois*, probably thereby meaning the grunters, or eroh-ers.

They were originally six bands, known to the English as Mohawks, Oneidas, Onondagas, Cayugas, Senecas, and Tuscaroras. The latter band, according to their traditions, went down the Ohio to the Mississippi, and from thence to North Carolina. This probably occurred in about 1662, while they were in pursuit of the Shawnees. In North Carolina, while living near Newburn, they joined some local tribes, and made war on the whites in 1712, but were defeated, and the most of the band returned to New York in 1714. The Hurons and Eries were originally powerful bands of the same people, but having become alienated by the intrigues of Champlain, they were nearly exterminated by the Iroquois. A remnant, however, of the Hurons, called by the Iroquois *Quatoghies*, were readmitted, in

1723, as the seventh band or nation, under the English name of Necariages. This latter proceeding, however, does not appear to have been generally satisfactory with the Hurons, and they did not take up their residence with the confederacy. It was, nevertheless, a formal reunion of the whole great Ongwe-Honwe family, after the long, desolating civil war so unfortunately inaugurated by Champlain in 1610.

Like the Winnebagoes, Dakotas, and some other ancient tribes, they have no traditions of removals from other localities; but uniformly have declared that they were originally created or called forth from the bowels of a hill near the falls of the Oswego river. This miraculous birth, with their early history, are associated with spirits, beasts, reptiles, and war, in the best style of fabulous Greece and Rome; and even excelled the Puritans of Salem in the number and power of their witches.

Their traditions of wars, excepting those evidently fabulous, do not seem to extend beyond our history of the French settlement of Canada; but the Senecas always dwell with much emphasis on their war against the Kahkwas, or Eries, which we have given as having terminated in 1655. Beyond that, it is believed that there is no plausible tradition of a war extending to the Mississippi.

The wanderings of the Tuscaroras to the Mississippi, and thence to the rivers Roanoke and Neuse, in North Carolina, appear very reasonable, when we consider that the Shawnees were driven by the Iroquois up the Tennessee, until they were seen on the Santee in South Carolina. Had the Tuscaroras followed the Shawnees to the head-waters of the Tennessee, they would then have been in the western part of North Carolina, and near the head-waters of the Roanoke and other rivers running to the Atlantic. The custom of the Indians was to journey in canoes, and we must regard that custom in drawing inferences from their traditions.

In previous chapters we have traced this confederacy

through the heroic ages of their wars, and shall hereafter more particularly attempt to note their real progress in civilization. Long before the French and Indian war, the French missionaries were urging the Iroquois to settle within the bounds of Canada, for the double purpose of removing them from the Protestant Dutch influence, and that they might be available to the French in their wars against the English colonists. Hence the French finally planted a colony of these Christian Indians at St. Regis, on the south shore of the St. Lawrence river, on the north line of the present State of New York. This village often became the rallying-point for those raids into the English colonies, organized and directed by the French, which resulted in no good to, but eternally disgraced, the French name. Against this village the English directed their opposition, and the Iroquois refused them all political connection with their confederacy. In latter years, however, the St. Regis Indians have attained a respectable degree of civilization.

In a previous chapter we have detailed the circumstances of the breaking up of the confederacy by the American army in our revolution, on account of a large part of the tribe taking the part of Great Britain in that war. After that war, a considerable proportion of the hostile part of the confederacy settled on the Grand river in Canada, and founded Brantford, while others settled in Ohio, near the Hurons. At the present day, that branch in Canada have their schools and churches. After the close of the revolutionary war, and in October, 1784, the United States made a treaty with the Iroquois, who remained in New York, in which the Indians surrendered all their claim to the Ohio valley west of a line commencing on Lake Ontario, four miles east of Niagara; thence southerly four miles east of the falls carrying place to the mouth of Buffalo creek; thence south to the north line of Pennsylvania; thence following that State line to the Ohio river. This treaty cut off all rights of the hostile Senecas to territory in Ohio. Subsequent to this, treaties were made from time to time, until the territories of this once mighty nation were limited to small reservations in New York, where a remnant resided in 1867, apparently contented and happy.

The primary right to the soil of the territory held by these Indians, was purchased by a powerful land company in New York, which made a strong effort to induce the Indians to emigrate west, and Congress was induced to set aside nearly two millions of acres of land west of the Missouri river, for a reservation for the tribes, but only a few individuals ever emigrated to that region, who now live with the Shawnees. The Rev. Eleazer Williams, by his influence as a missionary with the Oneidas, finally succeeded in leading west, in 1823, a small company of that tribe to Fox river, near Green Bay. Difficulties, however, occurred with the Menominies, who gave the Oneidas their land, and nearly ten years were spent in negotiations, which were concluded in 1832; and soon after, the most of this band, and a part of the St. Regis band, removed and settled in Wisconsin. The Oneidas, in 1867, had a reservation near Green Bay of 61,000 acres, of which 3,307 acres were under cultivation, yielding the previous year 3,837 bushels of wheat, 18,875 of corn, 575 of rye, 830 of peas, 13,495 of potatoes, 11,156 of oats, and 584 tons of hay. They lived in forty-one frame, and one hundred and five log houses. In 1866 they had a mission school, conducted by the Methodists, with an average attendance of twenty-one scholars; and another by the Episcopalians, with an average attendance of twenty-six scholars. Agent Martin, in his annual report, September 23, 1866, said of the Oneidas: "There are upon the reservation many good farms and desirable houses, and a ride through their settlement exhibits evidence of thrift, industry, and good management, highly creditable to the resident population; their houses appear comfortable, their barns spacious and well filled," etc. Their lands had not been allotted to the individual members of the band, but are held in common. The band put 111 volunteers into the Union army.

The Iroquois in the State of New York, in 1865, had the following reservations: *Alleghany*, containing 30,469 acres, of which 2,436 were under cultivation, and having thereon 186 houses; *Cattaraugus*, containing 21,680 acres, of which 4,962 were under cultivation, having thereon 43 frame, 103 log, and 103 plank houses; *Tonawanda*, containing 7,000 acres, of which 2,006 were under cultivation, having thereon 18 frame, 38 log, and 63 plank houses; *Tuscarora*, containing 6,000 acres, of which 3,372 were under cultivation, having thereon 27 frame, and 44 log houses.

The Onondagas, residing at Onondaga castle, had 569 acres under cultivation, with 40 frame, 32 log, and 11 plank and block houses. The St. Regis band had 4,826 acres under cultivation, with 13 frame, 68 log, and 2 stone and brick houses. In 1845, that portion of the St. Regis band in the United States numbered 360 souls, but government have not taken them under their supervision, and they, consequently, do not receive any annuities.

The New York Indians are making progress in civilization, and have agricultural fairs annually at Cattaraugus and Tonawanda reservations. The Thomas Asylum for orphan and destitute Indian children, was entirely successful in 1866, and its embarrassment from lack of funds was relieved in 1865 and 1866 by annual grants of $1,000 from the United States national fund for education. The State of New York supports schools among the Indians, and had twenty-three in successful operation in 1866.

The Baptists, Methodists and Congregationalists have several churches, and a respectable number of church members among these Indians in western New York. The St. Regis band, however, are understood as being under the supervision of the Catholics. They were all loyal to the Union in the late rebellion, and furnished 195 soldiers to the army.

While two hundred years of our history of the Iroquois appear as worse than wasted in desolating wars, instigated and directed by the French and English influence, yet we have the pleasure of noting that a change of policy on the part of the white has in fifty years brought these "savages" up to a grade of civilization nearly equal to the whites of the States in which they live. This lesson, so dearly learned, ought to be remembered by both whites and red men, in the future of civilization in America.

WYANDOTS, OR HURONS.

This kindred band of the *Ongwe-Honwe*, called themselves the *Wyandots*. The French, however, called them *Hurons*, which name the historian Charlevoix (no very good authority) says was derived from *hure*, the French name of the head of a wild boar, on account of the fantastic manner in which the tribe dressed their hair. The Iroquois called them *Quatoghies*, and the English Necariages. A band of the Hurons, living to the south-west of the principal nation, were called by the French "Tobacco Indians" and "Tionontatics," and by the English in subsequent years, "Denondadies."

When Cartier visited the St. Lawrence in 1535, he found the sites of Montreal and Quebec in the possession of bands of Indians, of which he preserved some words of their language, which are found to be of the Huron or Iroquois dialect. When Champlain came in 1608, he found the Algonquins in possession of Quebec, and a war existing between them and the Iroquois. He heard of the Hurons at or above Montreal, and engaged them to join the Algonquins against the Iroquois in 1610.

We have traced them through that long and disastrous war, and find a remnant of them, about 1653, among the Sioux, on Iowa river; a few below Quebec, and the greater part either killed or prisoners among their enemies. The party among the Sioux soon quarreled with that tribe, and removed to the head waters of the Black river, Wisconsin, where they were visited by two Frenchmen in 1659. This point being ill adapted to agriculture, they returned down Black river, and fortified, probably, the site of the Winnebago village at Gale's Ferry, where they were visited by Jean Guerin, the associate of Father Ménard, in August, 1661; thence they were driven away by the Sioux, and in 1665 Father Allouez found them at the head of Lake Superior. Thence they were expelled with the Algonquin nations in 1671, and returned to the Island of Mackinaw. Here a portion of the band were stationed in 1723, when they were formally readmitted into the Iroquois confederacy. A party of the Hurons, however, had descended and settled near Detroit in 1700. The whole band finally settled at and near Sandusky, Ohio.

After the revolutionary war, they made several treaties with the United States, and finally, in 1842, engaged to remove west of the Missouri river. Here, the following year, December 14th, they purchased of the Delawares thirty-nine sections of land at the junction of the Kansas and Missouri rivers, where they settled. In 1850, by another treaty, their land was surveyed, allotted, and divided between them, and they were allowed to become citizens of the United States.

The Hurons numbered at Lake Superior, in 1668, about four hundred souls; at Detroit, in 1736, about two hundred men; in 1763, at Detroit about two hundred and fifty men, and at Sandusky about two hundred men; at Sandusky and in Michigan, in 1825, about five hundred and seventy-nine; and 1853, by a regular census, they numbered in Kansas five hundred and fifty-three.

By the treaty of 1855, it was provided that, upon the fulfillment of certain stipulations, the Wyandots should become citizens, and take patents of their lands, the existence of the tribe to cease; the greater part of them received their patents accordingly. Difficulties, however, accumulated from time to time. Certain of their lands set apart for orphans had been taxed by Kansas, and sold; whites had continued to trespass on their lands, and rob them of their property, and in 1866 nearly the whole band represented to government, " that, however much they may strive to live like whites, the people about them, in many cases, appear to think that Indians ' have no rights that white men are bound to respect,' and that they are constantly robbed of their stock and other property, and not able to obtain the same redress as white people;" and asked government to let them remove as a band and settle with the Senecas in the Indian country, south of Kansas, who, they said, had invited them to do so, in grateful remembrance for the home which the Wyandots had given the Senecas in Ohio, when the latter were fugitives from New York, at the time of the revolutionary war. The Wyandots have reached a grade of civilization nearly equal to the whites in their vicinity, and maintain schools and a Methodist society. Had they received fair and Christian treatment from the whites in Kansas, their posterity might, in a few years only, have been known as the " first families," like the " John Randolphs," of Virginia fame.

LENAPEE, OR DELAWARES.

This once powerful nation called themselves the *Lenapee*, but as bands of them lived along the Delaware river and bay when first settled by the whites, they became known to the English as the Delawares.

The French of Canada alluded to them in February, 1666, as the Wampum-makers, against whom the Mohawks and Oneidas had then sent a war party. They again speak of them in 1670, as " the Andastogues, a tribe bordering on New Sweden, well adapted for war." At a treaty between the Iroquois and French of Canada, in July, 1673, the former asked for the French assistance against " the Andastogues," who were then " strongly fortified with men and canoes," saying that they had not "the means of going to attack them in their fort, which was very strong," The French again speak of the Andastogues in February, 1684, as having previously "been conquered by the Iroquois and the English of 'Merilande,'" and that the English of Albany sent an Iroquois chief, who prevented William Penn from purchasing the Susquehanna valley of Andastogues. This long and destructive war was probably generated by the French of Canada about 1664, to engage the Iroquois, and prevent them from pursuing their successes against the Hurons and their Algonquin allies. As early as 1654, the French, for the same purpose, were urging the Iroquois to prosecute their war against the Eries; and the Mohegan band, at least, of the Delawares, were their allies against the Eries. On the defeat of the Eries, in 1655, the Iroquois soon renewed their old war against the French and their Indian allies, and about 1664 the Mohegans, by some influence, broke their allegiance with the Iroquois, which soon involved the whole Delaware nation, and led to their subjugation in 1675, and to their taking upon themselves the humiliating condition of squaws. In this condition William Penn found the Delawares in 1682, docile and very friendly; and in this condition he also found their great war chief, *Tamenend*, at his wigwam near Princeton, New Jersey, in 1683, who was afterwards canonized as "St. Tammany" by the Tammany Society in New York, soon after the close of the revolution, in derision of St. George, of the tories. Thus fell the acknowledged "grandfathers" of the Algonquin nations, victims to the intrigues of European civilization.

The original territory of the Delawares was situated on the south of the Iroquois nations, and north of the lower Potomac, extending from the Atlantic to the Alleghany mountains, while their powerful band with the totem of a wolf, or in their language, the *Mohegan*, extended to Massachusetts. Their leading tradition claims that they and their allies, the Iroquois, had a long war with the *Alleghans,* or *Allegewi,* which they finally conquered and drove down the Mississippi. From this tradition, some have imagined that the Alleghans might have been the Mound-Builders, but this hypothesis is not corroborated by the traditions of the Iroquois; but by applying this tradition to the defeat of the Eries, it becomes quite probable, as it is corroborated by the known fact that at least the Mohegans, the northern band of the Delawares, assisted the Iroquois in the defeat of the Eries; while the Delaware word "Alleghany" river, refers to a stream within the territory of the Eries, and the same tribe was beyond the "Alleghany" mountains.

The Delawares sold William Penn the site of Philadelphia in 1682, and some territory adjoining. The following year he attempted to purchase the Susquehanna valley, but the English of Albany dispatched the bold Cayuga chief *Orewakee,* who positively forbade the Delawares selling it, and the humiliated squaw nation dare not disobey their masters.

In 1694, a large band of the Shawnees were permitted to settle with the Delawares on the Susquehanna, by the Iroquois. Difficulties finally occurred between the whites and Delawares, and Shawnees, and in 1740 we find the Governor of Canada intriguing with the Delawares and Shawnees, and inviting them to settle in Ohio. In 1743 a large part of the war parties emigrated to Ohio, and the Christian bands were forced to follow in 1767. In a previous chapter we have traced their history in Ohio until after the war of 1812. A part of the Delawares and Shawnees of Ohio, being unwilling to continue the war with the whites, in 1793 emigrated west of the Missouri. The balance of the Delawares sold their lands in Ohio in 1818 and 1829, to the United States, and in 1832 joined their brethren in Kansas. The treaty of 1854 provided for a sale of part of their land in Kansas, and an allotment in severalty of the balance. In 1860 many of them had become good farmers, and maintained a mission school in charge of the Baptists, and their agents report them the richest nation *per capita* on the globe. They put 160 volunteers into the Union army during the rebellion.

In 1763 their various bands on the Susquehanna, Muskingum, and Lake Erie, were estimated at 600 men; in 1825, in Missouri, at 1,800 souls; and by the census of 1853, there were found 1,132 souls on their reservation in Kansas.

The Delawares have been much annoyed by their white neighbors, and many of them being desirous to move again to the Indian country, the United States made a treaty with them July 4, 1866, which was ratified, and published August 10, of the same year, by which their reservation of nearly 100,000 acres is to be sold to the Missouri River Railroad Company, "except such as is held by Indians who may elect to remain in Kansas and become citizens." Those wishing to remove are to be provided with a new home in the Indian country. A small band of the Munsee of the Delawares are associated with the Stockbridge Indians in Wisconsin.

MOHEGANS.

Mohegan, or in French orthography, *Mahingan*, according to the Algonquin language signified wolf; hence the French called them Loups. They belonged to the Delaware band, with the totem the wolf, which were located near Minisink, New York, at the first settlement of the country. They were often called the "River Indians," and "Canoe Indians," by the whites, as they were found along the Hudson and Connecticut rivers, and Long Island sound. They belonged to the great Delaware nation, and by them were called "Grandsons." Other bands of the Mohegans, called Pequods, Pokanoket, Narragansetts, and Massachusetts, occupied eastern Massachusetts and Rhode Island.

The first whites which landed in Massachusetts violated the hospitality of the Indians, by stealing a number of them and selling them into slavery in the West Indies; hence the

11*

whites became known only as enemies, and the first party of Pilgrims which landed in 1620 were boldly attacked by the Indians. In May, 1637, followed the Pequod war, and that band was annihilated or sold into slavery in the West Indies. The Dutch war followed in 1643, and, according to Dutch authority, the cruel Governor Kieft indiscriminately put to death 2,000 men, women, and children, in no instance sparing either age or sex.

The Mohegans became involved with their grandfathers the Delawares in the great war with the Iroquois in about 1664, and in 1675, with the Delawares, were content to assume the position of squaws.

King Phillip's war came on in 1675, and the Narragansetts, Pokanokets, and Massachusetts, ceased to exist as independent bands. The pious Elliot had spent forty years in learning the Massachusetts dialect of the Mohegan language, had translated the Bible into that dialect, and succeeded in establishing fourteen Christian villages, but when the war cloud cleared away, four decimated bleeding villages were all that were left of his forty years' labor, and his new Bible was found to be literally in a "dead language."

The surviving Mohegans of the Connecticut and Hudson rivers for many years continued a kind of wandering life, and were allies of the whites through the subsequent wars with the French and Canada Indians.

After the close of the French and Indian war, and in 1765, the census of Massachusetts showed 1,569 Indians and half-breeds, scattered through seven counties, as the relic of all the powerful tribes which once inhabited that region; and in 1860 that number was reduced to 317, nearly all of whom were in the Marshpee district.

Two small bands of Christian Indians, however, continued to exist, one the Brothertown, and the other the Stockbridge, or, as the latter called themselves, "Mohekunnucks." The latter band removed to New York previous to 1794, and the former followed soon after, and both were permitted to settle with the Oneidas, where they were joined by the small band of Delawares called the Munsees, from the Susquehanna. These three bands emigrated to Wisconsin with the Oneidas in 1821, and in 1831 were allowed to settle on three townships of territory purchased from the Menominies, on the east side of Lake Winnebago. The Brothertowns soon became citizens of the United States, but the Stockbridge and Munsees had divided councils, and part of them became citizens, and about one-fifth removed to Kansas soon after 1846.

The Stockbridges and Munsees, who remained in Wisconsin, sold their reservation, and in 1856 removed to two townships in the timbered country further north, being township twenty-eight, north of ranges thirteen and fourteen east. This new reservation proved to be too barren and frosty for agricultural productions, and in 1866 they were reported in a very destitute condition; but the commissioner of Indian affairs sent them $1,000 out of the fund to purchase "provisions for Indians," which, it was believed, would keep them from suffering. Their school averaged eighteen scholars in the summer of 1866, and was taught by Rev. J. Slingerland, a native teacher. They also organized a Methodist church the same year, with about twenty members of the class. In 1856 they numbered 409 souls, but the discontent on account of their poor reservation, had so scattered them in 1866, that there were but 152 left, only one of whom was a Munsee. These speak English, and are the "last of the Mohegans."

PUBLISHER'S NOTE. A small band of from three to five hundred of the Mohegans were settled in Connecticut on the Thames river, about five miles below Norwich, where a missionary, for several years, previous to 1845, Rev. Mr. Gleason, Congregationalist, a man of large heart and burning zeal, and a school-teacher, were for many years located, and labored with pretty good success. But their close proximity to whisky, and the indifferent quality of their soil, were constant drawbacks upon the progress in religion and civilization of these poor Indians. They have wasted away until only a mere remnant remains.

CHAPTER VIII.

THE ILLINOIS CONFEDERACY.

Under the name of this confederacy, we class:

1. The *Illini*, or "the men," who formerly occupied the country between the Illinois and Wabash rivers.
2. The Miami, who occupied the Wabash and Maumee rivers, and whom the early missionaries called an Illinois tribe.
3. The Mascotens, who occupied the eastern part of the State of Michigan.
4. The Kickapoo, a northern band, according to Shawnee tradition, of that tribe, who probably lived between the Miamies and Shawnees; and
5. The Shawano, or people of the south, who occupied the central valley of the Ohio river, and who in later years the English have called Shawnees.

We have classified these several tribes as a confederacy, not from any knowledge that they were the same people, or associated in government, but solely on account of their associations and similarity in customs and languages.

THE ILLINOIS.

This nation, consisting of the bands called Peorias, Kaskaskias, Kaokias, Tamarois, and Michigamias, occupied the country between the Illinois and Wabash rivers, and first became known to the French in the treaty with Nicolet, at Green Bay in 1639. The following year, they made a murderous assault on the Winnebagoes, but soon returned their prisoners and reinstated that tribe. In 1660 the Iroquois fell upon them, and drove the most of them beyond the Mississippi. Part of the Michigamias fled to the Wisconsin river, and the balance of that band to the Arkansas river. The most of the Illinois having returned to their country, they were again attacked by the Iroquois, September 10, 1680, and about 1,200 either killed or taken prisoners. This nation was constantly engaged in wars until modern times, when they became almost extinct. In 1736, they were estimated as follows: Michigamias, at Fort Chartres, 250 men; Kaskaskias, six leagues below, 100 men; Peorias at the Rock, 50 men; and Kaokias and Tamarois, 200 men.

The United States made a treaty with this tribe (except the Peorias), August 13, 1803, the first article of which is as follows:

"ARTICLE 1ST. Whereas, from a variety of unfortunate circumstances, the several tribes of Illinois Indians are reduced to a very small number, the remains of which have been long consolidated and known by the name of the Kaskaskia tribe, and finding themselves unable to occupy the extensive tract of country which of right belongs to them, and which was possessed by their ancestors for many generations, the chiefs and warriors of the said tribe, being also desirous of procuring the means of improvement in the arts of civilized life, and a more certain and effectual support for their women and children, have, for the considerations hereinafter mentioned, relinquished, and by these presents do relinquish and cede to the United States, all the lands in the Illinois country, which the said tribe has heretofore possessed, or which they may rightfully claim; reserving to themselves, however, the tract of about three hundred and fifty acres near the town of Kaskaskia, which they have always held, and which was secured to them by the act of Congress of the third day of March, 1791; and also the right of locating one other tract of twelve hundred and eighty acres within the bounds of that now ceded, which two tracts of land shall remain to them forever."

This treaty did not include the Peoria band of the Illinois, nor their territory; hence a new treaty was made, September 25th, 1818, with the Peoria, Kaskaskia, Michigamia, Cahoki, and Tamarois, specially describing the whole territory ceded by the united tribe as follows: "Beginning at the confluence of the Ohio and Mississippi rivers, thence up the Ohio to the mouth of Saline creek, about twelve miles below the mouth of the Wabash; thence along the dividing ridge between the waters of said creek and the Wabash to the general dividing ridge between the waters which fall into the Wabash and those which fall into the Kaskaskia river; thence along the said ridge until it reaches the waters which fall into the Illinois river; thence, in a direct line to the confluence of the Kankakee and Maple rivers; thence down the Illinois river to its confluence with the Mississippi river, and down the latter to the beginning."

For this cession the United States agreed to pay the Peoria band $2,000 in merchandise, an annuity of three hundred dollars for twelve years, and give them six hundred and forty acres of land, "including their village on Blackwater river, in the territory of Missouri."

By the treaty of October 27th, 1832, the Kaskaskias ceded to the United States their reservation in Illinois, except the three hundred and fifty acres near Kaskaskia, which they reserved "to Ellen De Coigne, the daughter of their late chief, who has married a white man;" also released to the United States their permanent annuity of $1,000, and salt annuity; and the Peorias ceded all their land in Missouri and Illinois, and all other claims. For which the United States ceded to the united bands of Illinois Indians one hundred and fifty sections of land, "as long as they live upon it," which was "to include the present Peoria village, west of the State of Missouri, on the waters of the Osage river, to be bounded as follows, to wit: North, by lands assigned to the Shawnees; west, by the western line of the reservation made for the Piankeshaws, Weas, and Peorias; and east, by lands assigned the Piankeshaws and Weas." Also, gave the united bands $3,000, as an annuity, for ten successive years; also, $1,600 to Kaskaskias for salt annuity; and horses lost, three hundred and fifty dollars; to Peorias for improvements on land left, two hundred and fifty dollars; to the united bands, four hundred dollars in stock, "three iron-bound carts, three yoke of oxen, and six ploughs;" also build for them "four log houses;" to pay for breaking and fencing, three hundred dollars; to buy iron and steel, fifty dollars annually for four years; to pay on ratification of treaty, eight hundred dollars in goods, and $1,000 for provisions and expenses of removal.

In 1858 these tribes, with the Piankeshaws and Weas, collectively, numbered only about two hundred souls, and had made some advance in civilization, and still occupied their reservation on the Osage. In 1865 the population of all these bands had increased to two hundred and thirty-six. Their individual personal property averaged one hundred and forty dollars each. By their treaty of 1854, the allotment system was adopted, and each Indian generally has his separate farm. They have no separate school, but several of their children attend St. Mary's school, among the Potowatomies. They often express a wish for a school and preaching. Several of them are members of churches. They have no annuities.

THE MIAMIES, MASCOTENS, AND KICKAPOOS.

The Mascotens, or "Fire nation," were known to the French in 1615, being then at war with the Eries. The three tribes were driven out of their country about 1660, and took shelter with the Sacs and Foxes on the Wisconsin river, on the borders of the Wisconsin forests, where they were found, April 30th, 1670, by the Jesuit missionary, Rev. Father Allouez, who said of the Miamies and Mascotens that they numbered " more than 3,000 souls, being able each one to furnish four hundred men to defend themselves against the Iroquois, who come even into these distant countries to seek them." Rev. Father Marquette, in 1673, found these three tribes on the Wisconsin river; but previous to 1680, according to Father Membre, the Miamies changed their residence to St. Joseph, Michigan, and had become allies of the Iroquois against the Illinois. La Hontan, who visited the upper Mississippi in 1680, and published his travels in France in 1705, locates the Miamies and a band of the Mascotens on the St. Joseph's river, and bands of the Miamies, called Aouiatinons, at Detroit, Maumee, and Wabash rivers. In 1751 the Miamies were on the Wabash. The Kickapoos, whom the Shawnees claim were a part of their tribe, with a band of the Mascotens, continued to occupy villages on the Wisconsin river, and were generally allies of the Sacs, Foxes, and Winnebagoes, up to 1754, when we find them associated with the Potowatomies and Sioux in a war against the Peorias of Illinois.

The Mascotens, who returned south-east with the Miamies, seem to have settled near the Sciota, for, according to the Governor of Canada, the Shawnees of Pennsylvania, in 1743, settled at the "Prairie of the Mascotens." In 1763, Colonel William Johnson locates near the Wabash a band of the Kickapoos, numbering one hundred and eighty, and one of the Mascotens, numbering ninety, and as belonging to the Miami confederacy. After our revolutionary war, the name of the Mascotens disappears from among the Indians of the north-west, and that tribe probably joined the band of Kickapoos, who many years ago emigrated south-west, and are now among the Creeks in the Indian country.

The balance of the Kickapoos sold their lands on the Wabash in 1832, removed south-west of the Missouri river, and in 1854 settled on their present reservation of 150,000 acres, located on the Grasshopper river, about thirty-three miles west of St. Joseph, Missouri. In 1859 they numbered on the reservation, 350, and were in about ninety families; some with farms which contained 100 acres. The wild bands return at the time of the government payments, and receive their proportion of the annuities. They had, in 1865, 800 acres under cultivation, with two frame, and forty log houses, and raised 600 bushels of wheat, 20,000 bushels of corn, 800 of oats, 1,500 of potatoes, and 200 of turnips.

The allotment of land was not generally adopted by the tribe, only thirty families having accepted farms; and the remainder occupy land in common. One hundred and twenty, who had been absent from the tribe since August 1, 1864, rumor says, had been cut off by the wild Indians in the south-west. At least, they had not returned in November, 1865. The unsettled condition of affairs during the rebellion had operated to create dissatisfaction, and many of their cattle and horses had passed into the hands of thieves. Many were anxious to sell out and remove to the south-west, but the chiefs refused to make a treaty to that effect in 1866. The mission-school, under the charge of the Methodists, which had been very successful, was finally discontinued in the latter part of 1864, but government reëstablished a school in June, 1866, from the educational fund. There is a great probability that part of the tribe have, or will, return to the wild state, and chase the buffalo in their annual circuits along the foot of the Rocky mountains. Their annuities are $5,000 interest, and an installment on principal of $5,000. They have been loyal to the government during the late rebellion.

There are small bands of Miamies still occupying the Eel river reservation in Indiana, but the most of them, including the Weeas and Piankashaws, sold their lands in Indiana in 1840, and removed to a reservation on the Osage river, the two latter bands associating with the Peorias of Illinois, with whom we shall further speak of them. By the treaty of 1854, the Miamies adopted the allotment in severalty of their lands, and each one has his separate farm. In 1865, they numbered one hundred and twenty-seven souls, had nine frame, and eleven log houses, cultivated 503 acres, and raised 200 bushels of wheat, 8,500 of corn, and 500 of potatoes. Their reservation contained 57,600 acres, and their personal property averaged $120 each. Their annuities were $1,540, for expense of smith-shop, mills, etc; $13,562.89 interest, and one annual installment of $7,500. They furnished three soldiers for the Union army.

The Eel river (Indiana) Miamies had an annuity of $1,100 of interest. A large proportion of these have become thoroughly civilized, and many of them devoted Christians, connected with the Baptist denomination. Two, brothers-in-law, were licensed to preach, and became very eloquent, effective preachers, among their tribe. Bruilette, the eldest of these, was an old warrior and a drunken fighter. But the grace of God subdued his wicked passions, and transformed the lion to the lamb. In that heart where sin abounded, grace did much more abound, and he lived several years exemplifying the spirit of Jesus, and in the summer of 1867 died the death of the righteous.

SHAWANO, OR SOUTHRONS.

The name of this tribe was Shawanons, according to the early French authors, which, in the Miami language, means Southrons, or the people of the south; evidently given them because they lived on the Ohio, to the south of the Miamies. The English contracted the word to Shawanees, and in later years, to Shawnees, by which they are known in modern times. According to Marquette, in 1673, they had thirty-eight villages on the Ohio river, near each other, and "are the people the Iroquois go far to seek, in order to wage an unprovoked war upon." According to the same authority in 1668, a party of the same tribe visited the Illinois Indians, after thirty days' journey from east south-east, with many glass beads, which showed that they had visited the whites, probably in Carolina. According to the Iroquois authority given the French in 1680, that nation attacked the Illinois Indians about 1660, and drove them out of the country. It is true the Iroquois do not mention the Shawnees as one of their bands, yet as the Illinois, Miamies, and Shawnees, spoke nearly the same dialect, it is reasonable to suppose, in connection with the statement of Marquette, that the Shawnees were driven out of the country at the same time with the Illinois, and retired to the south, where bands of them were seen on the head-waters of the Santee, according to Lawson, and on the head-waters of the Mobile, according to Adair; and a band of them might even have gone to Florida, according to General Harrison, where Black Hoof was said to have been born previous to 1750. Rev. Father Gravier, long a missionary among the Illinois previous to 1700, speaks of the Shawnees as living on the Tennessee river; and Charlevoix located a band of them, in 1721, between the Tennessee and Cumberland rivers. In 1693, the Shawnees made a treaty of peace with the Iroquois, with the help of the English of Pennsylvania, and a band of nearly 700 settled near the Delawares in Pennsylvania, the following year. They came to Pennsylvania by way of Pittsburgh. In about 1740, we find the Governor of Canada intriguing with the Shawnees, to induce them to return to the Ohio valley; and in 1743 the Pennsylvania Shawnees returned and settled on the Sciota, and a war with the Cherokees is understood as having driven the bands from the Tennessee to the same locality, about the same time. Mr. Schoolcraft puts this emigration to the Ohio from the south in 1640, which is evidently an error of 100 years, as we have no knowledge of the Shawnees previous to 1660. General Harrison, in his historical address in 1838, claimed that the Shawnees never occupied the Ohio valley until a short time previous to 1750, and based his statement on that of Black Hoof, who claimed to have been born in Florida. General Harrison does not even allude to the fact that a large band of the Shawnees lived in Pennsylvania, and was also evidently unacquainted with the French explorations in the north-west. Some authors have intimated that the Shawnees might have been the remnant of the Eries, but this hypothesis is destroyed by the fact that the Eries spoke a dialect of the Huron-Iroquois, while the Shawnees speak a dialect of the Miami-Algonquin. The name of the tribe is also fatal to this hypothesis.

A band of the Shawnees emigrated west of the Missouri river as early as 1793, but the balance remained in Ohio until 1832, when they sold out their lands to the United States, and, about four hundred strong, emigrated to and accepted a reservation of 200,000 acres of land west of the Missouri and south of the Kansas rivers.

In 1736 they were estimated to contain two hundred men; in 1763, three hundred men; in 1825, eight hundred souls; and in 1853, including the Delawares, 1,400. In 1865 the census numbered them at eight hundred and forty-five persons. Under their treaty of 1854, seven hundred of the Shawnees selected their farms in severalty, and the balance formed the Black Bob settlement, and continued to hold their lands in common. They have banished whisky, and many of them have fine farms under cultivation.

Their school is under charge of the Society of Friends, and in 1865 contained forty scholars, and was quite prosperous. Nearly twenty children attend the State schools. Both Methodists and Friends have religious services once each week among the Shawnees.

Their reservation contains 200,000 acres, on which there were forty-five frame houses, and one hundred and fifty log houses. They raised, in 1865, 3,000 bushels wheat, 20,000 bushels corn, 2,500 bushels oats, and a proportional of vegetables. They also had 300 horses, 600 cattle, 1,000 swine, and 580 sheep.

Being on the border of Missouri, they suffered from the

rebel raids, and particularly that of General Price in 1864. They furnished for the Union army one hundred and twenty-five enlisted men, and a company of home guards. They furnish an instance of the successful civilization of an Indian tribe. In the spring of 1866 a treaty was made with the tribe providing for the sale of lands, and authorizing such as desired it to remove to Indian territory, but it had not been ratified by the Senate in November of that year.

CHAPTER IX.

THE WINNEBAGO CONFEDERACY.

When Sieur Jean Nicolet visited the *O-chunk-o-raws*, or Winnebagoes, at Green Bay in 1639, he spoke of them as then "sedentary and very numerous;" but this fact has since been doubted, as the following year they were nearly exterminated by the Illinois, and if so easily exterminated, it was thought that they could not have been very numerous. Again, it was said by authors that the Winnebagoes were only an insignificant band of the Sioux, speaking a dialect of the Sioux language; but later investigations into the language of the *O-chunk-o-raws* and several other western tribes seem to establish the fact that they are the parent nation to a confederacy, of an independent language, reaching from Lake Superior south to the Red river, and composed of the Winnebagoes, Menominies, Iowas, Missouris, Osages, Kansas, Quapaws, Ottoes, Omahas, Ponkas, and Meandans, and perhaps some others.

On this subject the Rev. William Hamilton, who had previously for fifteen years been a missionary among the Iowas, and had published a grammar of their language, in answer to questions from H. R. Schoolcraft, wrote that gentleman in about 1853 as follows: "There is no more difference between the language of the Iowas, Otoes, and Menominies, than between the language of a New Englander and Southerner. A few words are common to one tribe, and not to the other. They say the Winnebago is the *first language.* This may be true; if so, the Iowa, Otoe, and Missouri language would be one dialect; the Omahas and Ponka another; the Konza, Osage, Quapaw, and Ahachae (a band of the Osages) another; or, perhaps, the Omahas, Pongkaws (Poncas,) Konzas, etc., might all be called one dialect." . . . "The Osage, Konza, Quapaw, etc., are the same language. The Omaha and Ponka are the same. Some say there is no difference between the language of the first and last named; others say there is some difference. I inquired of a Konza Indian, not long since, who said they were the same: he could understand all the Omaha. Many words of the Winnebagoes are the same in Iowa; so some of the old men who speak Winnebago tell me." (See *History of the Indian Tribes, by Schoolcraft. Part IV., pages* 405 *and* 406.)

In the same volume, at page 227, J. E. Fletcher, Esq., Indian agent to the Winnebagoes, writes: "The Winnebagoes claim that they are an original stock; and that the Missouris, Iowas, Otoes, and Omahas sprung from them. These Indians call the Winnebagoes their elder brothers; and the similarity of their language renders it probable that they belong to the same stock. Even in 1670 the Winnebagoes told Rev. Father Allouez that "there were only certain people of the south-west who spoke as they did."

To this testimony we may add that of Mr. Saterlee Clark, an old Winnebago trader, and one of the few who ever learned that language, that he could converse with and understand the Iowas, and that the Iowas called themselves O-chunk-o-raws; the late statement of the Winnebagoes to General Sully, that they spoke the same language as the Omahas; and the further statement of James Reed, Esq., of Trempealeau county, Wisconsin, to the writer, that he had not been able even to learn the Winnebago language, on account of its being so deeply guttural, notwithstanding he had many years spoken Sioux, been a farmer and trader amongst them, and had a cousin of the Chief

Wabasha as his wife. This, we imagine, makes a strong case against the assertion that the Winnebago is only a dialect of the Sioux.

When Sieur Nicolet assembled four or five thousand of Winnebagoes, Sioux, Illinois, and Potowatomies, at Green Bay, in 1639, for a general council, is it not probable that there came also the Menominies, Iowas, Osages, and other kindred bands of the Winnebagoes, and from their numbers he correctly came to the conclusion that the Winnebagoes were "sedentary and very numerous?" They then evidently occupied the territory from near Mackinaw south-west to the Red river, extending east as far as the Illinois river, the Mississippi, and the lower Ohio valley. For over thirty years later, and after the advent of the fugitive Algonquins, the eight Illinois bands were on Illinois river as their real homes, although Marquette, June 25th, 1673, found the Peorias on the Mississippi when descending the river; but they had returned to the Illinois when he came back, some two months after. Rev. Father Allouez also found the Illinois on the Illinois river in 1677. Thus was evidently situated the Winnebago confederacy in 1639, "sedentary and very numerous."

O-CHUNK-O-RAW.

The traditions of the *O-chunk-o-raw*, claim that that tribe was created at the *Moke-kaw-shoots-raw*, or red earth banks, on the south shore of Green Bay. They were known to the Algonquin tribe by the name of "Winnebagoee," or people of the salt water; and as the Algonquin word for salt water and stinking water was the same, the French gave them the name of *La Puants*, or stinkards. They, however, call themselves the *O-chunk-o-raw*.

This tribe was spoken of by Sieur Champlain, who visited Lake Huron in 1615, and the novelty of their name probably induced the French Governor of Canada to send Sieur Nicolet, his Indian interpreter, to visit them in 1639, in hopes of discovering the western ocean. They continued to occupy Green Bay, Fox river, and Lake Winnebago, until modern times, and were generally allies of the Sacs and Foxes in the old Indian wars. They were, after 1754, allies of the French while they held Canada; and afterwards of the British, until the close of the war of 1812.

In 1816 the United States concluded a treaty of peace with the Portage band, under the chief *Choo-ke-kaw*, or the Ladle; more commonly known by his French name, "De Carry." This band agreed to separate themselves from the balance of the tribe until they made a treaty of peace also, and delivered up their prisoners. The O-chunk-o-raws joined the tribes at the great council with the United States, held at Prairie Du Chien, August 19th, 1825. The treaty concluded at this council, defined the boundary of the Winnebago territory as follows: "It is agreed between the Winnebagoes and the Sioux, Sacs and Foxes, Chippeways and Ottawas, and Chippeways and Potowatomies of the Illinois, that the Winnebago country shall be bounded as follows: South-easterly by Rock river, from its source, near the Winnebago lake, to the Winnebago village, about forty miles above its mouth; westerly, by the east line of the tract lying upon the Mississippi, herein secured to the Ottawas, Chippeways and Potowatomies, of the Illinois; and also by the high bluff described in the Sioux boundary, and running north to Black river; from this point, the Winnebagoes claim up Black river to a point due west from the source of the left fork of the Ouisconsin; thence to the source of said fork, and down the same to the Ouisconsin; thence down the Ouisconsin to the Portage, and across the Portage to Fox river; thence down Fox river to the Winnebago lake, and to the grand *Kau-kaulin*, including in their claim the whole of Winnebago lake." The line mentioned as secured to the Ottawas, etc., extended from the Wisconsin river south, along "the sources of the small streams running into the Mississippi." The Sioux claimed to the bluffs east of the Mississippi from opposite the mouth of Iowa river, to the mouth of Black river. By the treaty of August 11, 1827, between the United States and the Chippeways, Menominies and Winnebagoes, our government stipulated that "the sum of $1,000 shall be annually appropriated for the term of three years; and the sum of $1,500 shall be annually thereafter appropriated as long as Congress think proper, for the education of the children of the tribes parties thereto, and of the New York Indians near Green Bay, to be expended under the direction of the President of the United States."

In 1827 a difficulty broke out between the Winnebagoes and Chippeways, which came near involving the whites in a war. It appears that some Winnebagoes attacked and killed eight Chippeways near Fort Snelling, whereupon the commandant of that fort took four of the offending Winnebagoes, and delivered them to the Chippeways, who immediately put them to death. Red Bird's band soon after attacked two keel boats at the mouth of Coon Slough, on the Mississippi, killing two, and wounding six whites; while Red Bird himself killed two whites at Prairie Du Chien. The alarm spread to the miners who were digging lead north of Galena, who fled to that town, and immediately organized for war, electing General Dodge for their commander. General Atkinson, with a small force of regular troops, marched up the Wisconsin river, and, being joined by the miners, under General Dodge, advanced to attack the Winnebagoes in force at the Portage; but on the arrival of the troops at that place, the Winnebagoes sent a flag and delivered up Red Bird, and six others, as the guilty parties, which ended the war.

The following year the United States made an attempt to purchase the Winnebago lands, including the lead mines, and failed; but by the treaty at Prairie Du Chien, concluded August 1, 1829, the tribe ceded their territory south of the Wisconsin river, and west of a line running south from

Lake Puckaway, by Duck creek, Fourth lake, near Madison, Sugar river, and *Pee-kee-tol-a-ka*, by which the Winnebago interest in the mines was secured to the United States. The consideration for the territory purchased was $8,000 paid annually for thirty years; $30,000 in goods paid down, and 3,000 pounds of tobacco, and fifty barrels of salt delivered annually for thirty years.

By the treaty of September 15, 1832, the Winnebagoes ceded to the United States all the balance of their lands south of the Wisconsin and Fox rivers, for which the government gave them an interest in the "neutral grounds" west of the Mississippi, an annual annuity for twenty-seven successive years, of $10,000, and further agreed to establish and maintain a school at Prairie Du Chien for twenty-seven years, at an annual expense not exceeding $3,000; support six agriculturalists for twenty-seven years; pay not exceeding $2,500 for twelve yoke of oxen and agricultural implements; pay the Rock river band 1,500 pounds of tobacco per annum; and pay $200 per annum each, for the services of two physicians, one stationed at Fort Winnebago, and the other at Prairie du Chien. The treaty contained some small grants of land to half-breeds, and required the tribe to surrender eight Indians, charged with the murder of some whites in the Black Hawk war.

By another treaty, of the first of November, 1837, the Winnebagoes ceded to the United States all the balance of their territory on the east side of the Mississippi river, and certain interests on the west side, for which our government paid $1,500,000. Of this amount, $100,000 was to be expended in goods, horses, provisions, opening farms, and expenses of the removal of the Indians west of the Mississippi, where the tribe engaged to go in eight months after the ratification of the treaty. However, they did not perform that agreement until 1840.

The eighth treaty with the Winnebagoes, was made at Washington, D. C., October 13, 1846, by which the tribe surrendered all their interests in lands in the United States, for which the United States engaged to give the tribe 800,000 acres of land north of the St. Peters, or Minnesota river, for a residence, and pay in addition, $190,000. Under this treaty, the chiefs of the tribe selected a tract of country north of the Watab, but the tribe were generally dissatisfied with the location, and the most of them remained scattered about the country. In 1853 a new treaty was made, by which they were allowed to change their location to the Crow river; but the ratification of this treaty was refused on the remonstrance of the people of Minnesota. The matter was compromised by the United States, and in February, 1855, the chiefs were permitted to select their lands on the Blue Earth river, south of the Minnesota. Here the tribe settled the same spring, highly satisfied with their land, and immediately commenced building houses and improving land. So well had they succeeded, that the government agent at St. Paul, in 1860, reported of them as follows: "There have been raised by individual Indians as high as sixty acres of wheat alone on a single farm. The reservation presents the appearance of as much improvement as the surrounding country; and in fact, when viewing the comfortable log and frame houses that dot the reservation as far as the eye can reach, it presents a far different scene than is usual to be found upon Indian reservations, for wigwams are becoming as rare as houses were but two years since."

The same year the teacher of the school reported 118 pupils enrolled, of which sixty-two were males, and fifty-six females; that they were instructed in the ordinary English branches, and had "as much educational capacity as can be found in any school of an equal size."

But in the midst of their prosperity, when their civilization had become almost a certainty, the occurrence of the "Sioux massacre," in June, 1862, dashed their fond hopes to the ground. Notwithstanding the Winnebagoes took no part with the Sioux in that affair, but offered the services of their warriors to our government, to help punish that rebellious nation, yet the exasperated inhabitants of Minnesota demanded the removal of the Winnebagoes, and Congress, by a special act, directed the President to transport them to the Missouri river with the friendly Sioux. Accordingly, in May and June, 1863, without any treaty, they were loaded upon steamers and taken to the Missouri river, where, in the language of a missionary to the writer, " they were, like the Sioux, dumped in the desert one hundred miles above Fort Randall." When the purposes of government became known to the tribe, the old chiefs, De Carry, Winneshiek, Dandy and their families, and some others, fled to Wisconsin, where, near the tunnel, in the fall of 1864, the venerable old chief, De Carry, who captured Black Hawk in 1832, and sent him to the government agent at Prairie Du Chien, died in poverty. He was very old, but remarkably intelligent, and was grandson of *Ho-po-ko-e-kaw*, or Glory of the Morning, the chieftess of the tribe when visited by Captain Carver in 1766, and of her French husband De Carry, who was mortally wounded at Quebec near the close of the old French and Indian war. In 1862 the writer spent several days with him, taking notes of his family and tribe, while his family were gathering their summer harvest of berries near Mont Trempealeau.

Soon after the Winnebagoes were landed at Crow creek, Dakota territory, they pronounced the country not fit for cultivation, and were greatly dissatisfied. They soon commenced the manufacture of canoes, to return down the river. Brigadier-General Sully visited their reservation, and July 15, 1863, sent a dispatch to General Pope, in which he remarked: "I find both tribes (Sioux and Winnebagoes) very discontented, and if troops are not constantly kept here, I think there will be trouble.

" The Winnebagoes I find hard at work making canoes, with the intention of quitting the agency and going to join the Omahas, or some other tribes down the river. I had a council with them yesterday, in which they said they had been promised, when they left their last reservation, to be settled on the Big Sioux river. How true that is I can not say.

"They also stated that nothing would grow here. They dare not go out to hunt, for fear of the other tribes, and they would all starve to death. This I believe to be true, without the government intends to ration them all the time. The land is dry, sandy, and parched up."

In a letter to the Secretary of the Interior, dated the following day, General Sully remarked:

"I state this from my own knowledge of the country. The land is poor; a low, sandy soil. I don't think you can depend on a crop of corn even once in five years, as it seldom rains here in the summer. There is no hunting in their immediate vicinity, and the bands of Sioux near here are hostile to them.

"They (the Winnebagoes) tell me they are friends of the Omahas, and speak nearly the same language. It is their wish to be united with them on the Omaha reservation, and, as they say, the Omahas are in favor of this also.

"Their last removal from Minnesota was hard for them, for they were not implicated in the late massacre," etc.

The Indian agent for the Omahas, October 16th, 1863, reported the continued arrival of small parties of Winnebagoes at that reservation in a destitute condition, and he was soon after instructed from Washington to provide for all that arrived. In September, 1864, over 1,200 had arrived, and the agent, with the consent of the Omahas, had assigned them a tract of land for temporary cultivation, and they had harvested one hundred acres of corn.

Soon after this, the Winnebagoes contracted with the Omahas for nearly one-third of their reservation, at about thirty-nine cents an acre, of which the Indian agent said, September 15th, 1865: "If this agreement be ratified by the Senate, the coming winter they will become possessed of lands (two hundred and forty sections) ample in extent for all the purposes of the tribe, abounding in wood and water, and for agricultural purposes equal to the best farming lands in Nebraska." This contract was finally ratified by the United States government.

Speaking generally of the Winnebagoes, the Indian superintendent of the Northern department, in September, 1865, said: "I cannot too strongly recommend this unfortunate and much-abused tribe to the fostering care and protection of the department. Hurried from their comfortable homes in Minnesota, in 1863, and located at the Crow Creek agency, where it is impossible, one year in six, to raise a crop, either of corn, wheat or potatoes, they have suffered more than any other tribe in the country. They are now subsisted by government on the Omaha reservation, in Nebraska, whither they have all sought refuge to escape starvation; and, under the most favorable auspices, they must continue a charge upon the government to a greater or less extent, for nearly two years to come."

The superintendent, in his August, 1865, report, again speaking of the same tribe, remarked: "This tribe is characterized by frugality, thrift, and industry to an extent unequaled by any other tribe of Indians in the north-west. Loyal to the government and peaceful towards their neighbors, they are entitled to the fostering care of the general government."

The removal and unsettled condition of the Winnebagoes broke up their schools and religious instruction, and in December, 1864, thirty-eight chiefs and head men, at their Omaha residence, petitioned their "Father," the President, among other things, as follows: "It is our sincere desire to have again established among us such schools as we see in operation among your Omaha children. Father, as soon as you find a permanent home for us, will you not do this for us? And, Father, as we would like our children taught the Christian religion, as before, we would like our school placed under the care of the Presbyterian Board of Foreign Missions. And last, Father, to show you our sincerity, we desire to have set apart for its establishment, erection, and support, all of our school funds, and whatever more is necessary."

The population of this tribe has been variously estimated at different periods. Thus we find in a French document, that they had two hundred and thirty warriors in 1736; according to Sir William Johnson, in 1763 they had increased to 360; Captain Carver, in 1766, reduced the number to 200. By a census of the tribe in 1859, they were found to number 2,256 souls, of which 1,055 were males, and 1,201 females; but by the census of 1865, the whole number had diminished to 1,900. The latter census probably did not include the stragglers in Wisconsin, which were still there in 1866. They have been a vigorous, athletic race, and received from the Sioux a name, O-ton-kah, which is said to mean, when interpreted, "the large and strong people."

In the spring of 1866, the Winnebagoes finally settled on their Omaha reservation, and commenced building houses, of which they had been destitute three years; they also put on white men's clothing, and have cheerfully settled down, hoping to have a permanent home.

The agent, in his report of August 20, 1866, said: "There has returned to the tribe, within the past few weeks, about 100 soldiers, who have served with credit to themselves and to their tribe, in the defense of their country. I consider the Winnebagoes one of the best tribes of Indians in the country, and with proper treatment, they will soon become a self-sustaining, prosperous and happy people."

By the treaty with the United States, ratified and proclaimed March 28, 1866, the Winnebagoes released their Crow creek reservation, and accepted their Omaha reservation, paid for by the United States. They also were to receive 100 cows, 400 horses, 20 yoke of oxen, and wagons; have a steam saw and grist mill, and necessary buildings for a complete agency erected, and are to be paid the expenses of removal and subsistence for one year.

13

CHAPTER X.

THE WINNEBAGO CONFEDERACY — CONCLUDED.

MENOMINIES.

This tribe early occupied the country between Green Bay and Lake Superior, and, anterior to the advent of the whites, were quite powerful; but having become involved in a war with the Chippeways, the Rev. Father Allouez, who visited them May 6, 1670, said they were then "almost exterminated." The date of this war is not given, but it probably occurred after the Algonquin nations and Hurons had been driven west by the Iroquois; that is, after about 1652 or 1653. Nicolet spoke of the Noquet, who inhabited the south shore of Lake Superior in 1639, but were at the Great and Little Bay De Noquet in 1659. This tribe might have been only a band of the Menominies, and were probably involved in the same war with that tribe, against the Chippeways. What became of the Noquets is not known, but they disappeared from history early in the eighteenth century, and probably were merged in the Menominies, who subsequently occupied their territory at Bay De Noquet. Their name, Menominie, or "the Wild Rice People," was of the Algonquin language, but by the French they were called, *Folles Avoines*, or the Wild Oats People.

The first treaty between this tribe and the United States, effecting a cession of territory to the latter, was that of August 11, 1827, by which it was provided as follows:

"ARTICLE 3. It being important to the settlement of

Green Bay that definite boundaries should be established between the tract claimed by the former French and British governments, and the lands of the Indians, as well to avoid future disputes as to settle the question of jurisdiction, it is therefore agreed between the Menominie tribe and the United States, that the boundaries of the said tracts, the jurisdiction and title of which are hereby acknowledged to be in the United States, shall be as follows: namely, beginning on the shore of Green Bay, six miles due north from the parallel of the mouth of Fox river, and running thence in a straight line, but with the general course of the said river, and six miles therefrom to the intersection of the continuation of the westerly boundary of the tract of the Grand Kaukaulin, claimed by Augustin Grignon; thence on a line with the said boundary to the same; thence with the same to Fox river; thence on the same course, six miles; thence in a direct line to the south-west boundary of the tract, marked on the plan of the claims at Green Bay, as the settlement at the bottom of the Bay; thence with the southerly boundary of the said tract to the south-easterly corner thereof; and thence with the easterly boundary of the said tract to Green Bay."

"In consideration of the liberal establishment of the boundaries, as herein provided for," the United States shall pay in goods, $15,682; $1,000 annually for three years, and $500 annually, "as long as Congress shall think proper, for the education of the children of the tribes, parties hereto, and of the New York Indians." This latter appropriation included the Winnebagoes and Chippeways, and the New York Indians then settled near Green Bay.

By another treaty, February 8, 1831, the Menominies ceded to the United States their territory south-east of Fox river and Green Bay, and east of Lake Winnebago, extending south to the "Milwauky, or Manawauky river," and extending east to Lake Michigan, estimated at 2,500,000 acres, of which tract three townships of land on the east side of Lake Winnebago were assigned to the Stockbridge, Munsee, and Brothertown Indians.

The Menominies also, for the location of "the Six Nations of the New York Indians, and St. Regis tribe," gave 500,000 acres north of the Fox river, for which cessions of territory the United States paid a fair consideration in money, goods, annuities, farm stock, and erection of houses, mills, etc. The original treaty was subsequently, on the 27th of October, 1832, by a new treaty, somewhat modified in the boundary for the Six Nations. By the treaty of September 3, 1836, they also further ceded the southern portion of their territory, east from Wolf river to their eastern boundary line between the Little and Great Bay De Noquet, a strip of land three miles wide on each side of the Wisconsin river, from near the Portage north, forty-eight miles, containing eight townships, for which the tribe received a large increase of annuities, and the payment of goods and the Indians' debts to the traders.

By the treaty of October 18, 1848, the Menominies ceded to the United States all the balance of their lands in Wisconsin, for which the United States gave them a reservation above the Crow Wing river, on the upper Mississippi, of 600,000 acres, and $300,000, and the tribe engaged to remove accordingly.

On the examination of this tract, the Indians being opposed to removing to it, the United States, May 12, 1854, accepted a recession of it, and gave the tribe a reservation on their old lands, of townships twenty-eight, twenty-nine, and thirty, north of ranges thirteen, fourteen, fifteen, and sixteen east, containing 432 square miles. For the difference between the two reservations, the United States gave them $242,686, in fifteen annual installments, commencing in 1867.

They moved on to their reservation and commenced improvements, and the following year the Indian agent reported that a majority of the Indians had adopted the American dress, and wore the coat and pantaloons. Oshkosh, the head chief, who had resisted the civilization of the tribe, this year, seeing the advancement of the civilized over the uncivilized Indians, gave in his influence for civilization.

The industrial school in 1855, under the care of Jane Dousman, manufactured one hundred and twenty-eight coats, two hundred and eighteen pants, one hundred and sixty-five shirts, one hundred and thirty-seven gowns, and forty-one pairs of socks and stockings. The school-houses being temporary shanties, the progress was slow in that department; but seventy-five male and fifty-two female children attended during the year. During the year, "five of the girls," said the teacher, "have left school, and have married, and are doing very well. I am happy to state they are good housekeepers, having been taught the more substantial branches of domestic work."

In 1853 the whole tribe numbered 2,708, and had much diminished from 1825, when they were estimated by the Secretary of War at 4,170, of course an over-estimate. In 1865, the whole tribe numbered 886 males and 993 females — total, 1,879 souls. They continued to reside on their reservation of 230,400 acres, but suffered considerably by the small-pox, having lost seventy-nine by death. They raised 150 bushels of wheat, 1,600 of corn, 550 of rye, and 3,975 of potatoes, and some other articles, and manufactured 90,000 pounds of maple sugar.

The educational and religious interests of the tribe are under the direction of the Catholics, but, unfortunately, for the last two or three years, a collision has occurred between the teachers of the schools and their priests, which led to the dismissal of the old priest for licentiousness and drunkenness. His successor gave offense by advising the Indians not to send their children to school, and was ordered off the reservation. A third, in 1865, took the dead bodies of those who died with small-pox into the church, and was run out of the county by the sheriff. The teachers of the schools are Catholics, and have long been connected with the educational and religious interests of the tribe. To their untiring zeal is attributed the partial civilization of the tribe; nearly two-thirds being Catholics, and the balance pagans.

The two schools have had about one hundred scholars annually for several years, and the pupils are represented as having made good progress in their studies. The sewing school, in 1865, notwithstanding the delays on account of the small-pox, manufactured twenty-six coats, seventy pants, forty-two shirts, thirty dresses, thirty-nine skirts, thirty-nine gowns, and socks and stockings one pair each.

The tribe has put into the Union army during the war one hundred and twenty-five soldiers, one-third of whom were killed in battle or died in hospital.

Intemperance has not been as prevalent as formerly, but still leads to difficulty, and some guilty whites have been indicted by the United States court.

The principal drawback on the civilization of the tribe is the poor quality of the soil of the reservation; much of it being sandy, black oak, barren; but there are some rich timber lands, which the agent has urged the Indians to occupy for farms, and which will probably soon be occupied instead of the barrens.

The United States owe the Menominies two annual appropriations of $916.66, for smith's shop, etc.; $3,000 balance to pay millers; and $242,686, divided into fifteen equal installments, to commence in 1867.

The report of agent Martin, in September, 1866, represents the Menominies as "very kind and tractable in their dispositions, easily controlled, and many of their chiefs manifesting a strong desire to have their children instructed;" that their "schools could not, in my judgment, be improved;" that their reservation was "perhaps the worst for farming purposes in this State;" and that "it is but an act of justice to Father Cajetan, the Catholic missionary resident at Kenosha, to mention his constant efforts, during the time he has been in charge, to promote the temporal and spiritual interests of the Indians, and the success which has thus far attended them."

IOWAS.

Of the O-chunk-o-raw confederacy, the Iowas evidently occupied northern Iowa, from the upper Iowa to the lower Iowa river, along the Mississippi; but, on the advent of the fugitive Algonquins, were crowded further back, and Le Sueur found them, in 1700, occupying the territory from the south bend of the St. Peter's river, extending south towards the Missouri; probably along the Cedar, lower Iowa and Des Moines rivers.

When the warlike Sacs and Foxes had conquered and driven south the northern bands of the Illinois, they extended their conquests into the present State of Iowa, and drove back the Iowas and other tribes of the Winnebago confederacy, and took possession of all the eastern part of the beautiful State. In this war, which was after 1760, they were assisted by the Ottawas of Mackinaw, and many of the confederates were captured and became slaves. Mr. Grignon, in his "Recollections," says he knew personally fourteen of these slaves, and that three of them were Osages, two Missouris, and one Mandan, but that they were commonly denominated Pawnees.

The first treaty with the Iowas was simply a treaty of peace and for the delivery of prisoners, made September 16th, 1815. By the treaty of August 19th, 1825, at Prairie Du Chien, the territory of the Iowas was not defined, but they were left jointly with the Sacs and Foxes, and some other tribes, in the possession of western Iowa. By the treaty of July 15th, 1830, the Iowas and other tribes cede to the United States, as a general reservation, for the location of Indian tribes, the country from the Big Sioux to the Missouri State line, and extending east from the Missouri and Big Sioux to the dividing waters between the Missouri and Des Moines, for which the United States paid the Iowas $2,500 annually for ten years, and gave them an assistant blacksmith, and six hundred dollars in agricultural implements.

In this treaty, the Iowas, Omahas, Ottoes, and Yankton and Santee bands of Sioux, set apart a tract for their half-breeds, "Beginning at the mouth of the Little Nemaha river, and running up the main channel of said river to a point which will be ten miles from its mouth, in a direct line; from thence, in a direct line, to strike the Grand Nemaha ten miles from above its mouth in a direct line (the distance between the two Nemahas being about twenty miles;) thence down said river to its mouth; thence up, and with the meanders of the Missouri river to the point of beginning."

By the treaty of September 17th, 1836, the Iowas released their claim to the south part of said reservation, now incorporated into the State of Missouri, and accepted a reservation on the west side of the Missouri river, of two hundred sections on the "Grand Nemaha river;" and by another treaty of the 23rd November, 1837, the Iowas relinquished all the balance of their claim to land on the east side of the Missouri, on said reservation, for the consideration of $2,500.

The last treaty would seem to cover all their claims on the United States; but by their own ingenuity, or more probably by that of their traders, diverse claims were made by the Iowas, under the treaty of 1824, 1825, 1830, and 1836, and to satisfy them, and assist in their civilization, the United States, by another treaty of the 19th of October, 1838, gave the Iowas $157,500, to be invested in stocks paying at least five per cent., the interest of which should annually be paid to the tribe as long as it exists; and also erect for them ten houses. These payments, however, included the annuities to be paid to the Indians by the treaties before mentioned.

The Iowas, in 1865, had limited their reservation, by a late treaty, to twenty-five sections, which are well watered, have rich soil, and plenty of timber, and are situated along the south side of the Great Nemaha, extending west from the Missouri river.

They had 289 acres under cultivation, and have 91 horses, 71 head of cattle, 210 hogs, besides agricultural implements valued at $7,250. Total value, $16,750, besides crops raised. They had a good school, averaging about thirty-eight scholars; but it does not receive its proper consideration from the Iowas.

The tribe sent forty-three soldiers to the war, who performed faithful services in several battles and severe campaigns, principally in the thirteenth and fourteenth Kansas regiments.

Their agent, September 1, 1865, remarked, in his report: "They may be seen daily, hauling their corn, vegetables, wood, etc., to market, and returning with flour, meat, coffee, sugar, etc., which they have received in exchange, or purchased with the proceeds of their loads." In 1866 they had a temperance organization, which made it a crime to get drunk or bring spirits on the reservation.

In 1825 the Iowas were estimated by the Secretary of War at 1,100. In 1853 there were 437, and in 1865, 294 souls.

They receive from the United States an annuity of $2,850 per year.

AKANSEA, OR QUAPAWS.

This powerful tribe, according to Rev. Father Gravier, an old missionary to the Illinois previous to 1700, formerly inhabited the country bordering Ohio river, and the Illinois and Miamies called that river the "river of the Akansea." Previous to Marquette's visit to the Mississippi in 1673, the Arkansas Indians had been driven from the Ohio by the Iroquois, and had settled on the Arkansas river, where he found them. He says that "their language is extremely difficult, and with all my efforts, I could not succeed in pronouncing some words." This shows that their language, like the Winnebagoes, was deeply guttural. Marquette, however, found among them one that could speak Illinois, who interpreted for him. The name Akansea was an Illinois word, for they called themselves O-qua-pas, or Qua-paw. La Salle found three villages of them along the Mississippi, near the Arkansas river, in 1681. De Tonty soon after names the "Kappas" on the Mississippi, and, inland, the Toyengan, or Tongenga, the Toriman, and the Osotonoy, or Assotoné. He commenced a settlement among them. Charlevoix, in 1721, makes four villages; and their missionary, Father Poisson, in 1727, places them all on the Arkansas river: "The Tourimans and Tongingas, nine leagues from the mouth by the lower branch; the Sauthouis, three leagues farther; and the Kappas still higher up." The Rev. Father Douay, however, returning from La Salle's expedition in 1687, said that the "Arkansas were formerly stationed on the upper part of one" of the branches of the Missouri, "but the Iroquois drove them out by cruel wars some years ago," and they settled "on the river which now bears their name." He was evidently ignorant of the fact that they were driven from the Ohio.

The Rev. Father St. Cosme, descending the Mississippi in 1699, to become their missionary, said: "We were much consoled to see ourselves in the places of our mission, but were sensibly afflicted to see this Acansea nation, once so numerous, almost entirely destroyed by war and sickness. It is not a month since they got over the small-pox, which carried off the greater part of them."

Father Gravier visited the Akansea in 1701, and found the Kappa and Tourima bands in a village of forty cabins, and the Sittëoüi five leagues up the river Arkansas "much more numerous than" the other two.

The Akansea became allies of the French, and in 1727 and 1728, assisted them in nearly exterminating the Natchez, for their massacre of a small French establishment amongst them, including Father Poisson, who was temporarily at Natchez.

The Arkansas bands continued to occupy their country until 1818, when the United States treated with them as the Quapaw nation, and purchased all their country between the Arkansas and Red rivers, and north of the Arkansas and east of the Mississippi, and allowed them a reservation. In 1824, the United States bought their reservation, and the tribe engaged to be "confined to the district of country inhabited by the Caddo Indians, and form a part of that tribe." The Caddos were probably a kindred tribe, and if so, the O-chunk-o-raw confederacy must have extended far into Texas. The Quapaws, agreeable to their treaty, settled on the south side of Red river, at Bayou Treache, on a tract given them by the Caddoes; but the latter tribe refused to incorporate them, and as the Raft on Red river so often flooded their land, they were finally obliged to abandon it, and in 1833 they made another treaty with the United States, by which they received one hundred and fifty sections of land west of the State line of Missouri, near the Osages, where they soon after settled on the Neosho river. They enjoyed the benefits of the Catholic manual labor and girls' schools with the Osages, and had become considerably advanced in civilization; but the war of the rebellion desolated their country with fire, and the Quapaws were driven from their country to the interior of Kansas, and their houses were plundered. They furnished in 1862, eighty Union soldiers. The Quapaws were estimated, in 1825, at 700; and in 1853 they numbered 314 on their reservation.

They receive from government $1,000 per year for educational purposes, and $1,660 for smiths, farmers, etc.

OSAGES, OR WA-SAW-SEE.

This band was first mentioned by Marquette, in 1673, as occupying the lower Missouri river, from which that river was generally called by the Recollect missionaries "the great river of the Osages." St. Cosme, in his voyage down the Mississippi in 1699, called the river "the great river of the Missourias," from which it obtained the name of Missouri river. They call themselves the Wa-saw-see. In 1687, Rev. Father Douay, who was with La Salle when he was killed, remarking of the Indians on the "famous river of the Missourias or Osages," locates the Osages with "seventeen villages" on a "river of their name, which empties into that of the Missourites." The Illinois were their common enemies previous as well as subsequent to the voyage of Marquette; but when the Illinois were driven west of the Mississippi in 1680, by the Iroquois, they fled to the Osages for protection, and were followed to Osage territory. The Osages were not well known until modern times, although they are mentioned from time to time by the French, and particularly in 1712, as assisting the French at Detroit to massacre the Foxes. They were a brave people, and never failed to hold their territory against all enemies, even to the present day. Mr. Catlin, who visited them in about 1835, pronounced them the tallest race of men in North America, either red or white. He found very few less than six feet high, and many six and a half and seven feet. They evidently have not degenerated from their Winnebago progenitors; and it goes to substantiate the probability that this was the confederacy referred to as the "Allegewi," in the traditions of the Delawares; and that the Delawares were allies of the Iroquois in the war against this people in 1660.

The first treaty made by the United States with the Osages was "concluded at Fort Clark, on the right bank of the Missouri, about five miles above the Fire Prairie, in the territory of Louisiana, the 10th day of November, 1808." By this treaty the Osages ceded to the United States all their territory east of a line running due south from Fort Clark to the Arkansas river, and down the Arkansas to the Mississippi, and all their territory north of the Missouri river; for which the United States furnished them a blacksmith, a store of goods "to barter with them on moderate terms for their peltries and furs," a sum not exceeding $5,000, to citizens, for the "lawless depredations" of the Osages, $1,500 in merchandise, and $1,200 in money. They also concluded the usual treaty, September 12th, 1815, of "peace and friendship," and that all previous hostile acts should "be mutually forgiven and forgot."

The next treaty, September 25th, 1818, ceded to the United States the following: "Beginning at the Arkansaw river, at where the present Osage boundary line strikes the river at Frog Bayou; then up the Arkansaw and Verdigris to the falls of Verdigris river; thence, easterly, to the Osage boundary line, at a point twenty leagues north of the Arkansaw river, and with that line to the place of beginning." In consideration, the United States pay not exceeding $4,000, for Indian depredations since 1814.

By a treaty of the 31st August, 1822, the United States paid the Osages $2,329.40, to be absolved from their contract to furnish a factory or store of goods, under the treaty of 1808.

By the treaty of June 2nd, 1825, the Osages ceded to the United States their "lands lying in the State of Missouri and territory of Arkansas, and all lands lying west of the State of Missouri and territory of Arkansas, north and west of the Red river, south of the Kansas river, and east of a line to be drawn from the head sources of the Kansas, southwardly through the Rock Saline," with the reservations as follows: "Beginning at a point due east of White Hairs village, and twenty-five miles west of the western boundary line of the State of Missouri, fronting on a north and south line, so as to leave ten miles north and forty miles south of the point of said beginning, and extending west, with the width of fifty miles, to the western boundary of the lands hereby ceded and relinquished by said tribes or nations;" also, some forty-five sections, for a long list of half-breeds;

also, fifty-four sections, to be laid off by the President and sold to raise funds for the support of Indian schools. The United States, in said treaty, release $4,105.80, due them from the Osages for goods furnished; and the Indians, in consideration thereof, "release their claim on the United States for regular troops to be stationed at Fort Clark, and also the furnishing of a blacksmith at that place, and the delivery of merchandise at Fire Prairie," under the treaty of 1808.

The United States agree to pay the Delawares $1,000; their own citizens not exceeding $5,000, for Osage "lawless depredations;" $6,000 in merchandise; $2,600 in "horses and equipage;" $100 to Paul Lois, and the same to Baptiste Mongrain, and $1,500 to three Indian traders, for debts.

By the treaty of January 11th, 1839, the Osages release all claim to any of their reservations "within the limits of any other tribe," and also "all claims or interests under the treaties of November 10th, 1808, and June 2nd, 1825, except so much of the latter as is contained in the 6th article thereof; and the said Indians bind themselves to remove from the lands of other tribes, and to remain within their own boundaries."

For the consideration of the above, the United States agreed:

1st. To pay to the Osages $20,000 annually for twenty years.

2nd. To furnish the Osages, for twenty years, two blacksmiths and two assistants, each to receive two hundred and twenty-five dollars per year; also, "each smith to be furnished a dwelling-house, shop and tools, and five hundred pounds of iron, and sixty pounds of steel, annually."

3rd. To furnish the Osage nation with a grist and saw mill, a miller to each for fifteen years, and an assistant to each for eleven years," etc.

4th. To supply them 1,000 cows and calves, 2,000 breeding hogs, 1,000 plows, 1,000 sets of horse gear, 1,000 axes, and 1,000 hoes; to be distributed to those which shall form an agricultural settlement.

5th. To furnish ten chiefs with a house worth two hundred dollars each, and eleven with a house worth one hundred dollars each; and also to furnish the chiefs six wagons, sixteen carts, and twenty-eight yoke of oxen, and yoke and log chains to each yoke.

6th. To pay all claims for Osage depredations not exceeding $30,000.

7th. To purchase the reservations to individuals at not exceeding two dollars per acre, made in the treaty of June 2nd, 1825, to be paid to the reservees.

8th. To reimburse $3,000 deducted from their annuity in 1825 to pay for property which has since been returned.

9th. To pay to Clermont's band their proportion of the annuity of 1829, which was wrongfully withheld from them, amounting to $3,000.

In 1862 the United States made a treaty purchasing the Osage reservation, but it had not in 1865 been ratified by the Senate. The Indians, however, had left their reservation, and retired some eighty miles to the south-west, under a state of dissatisfaction, complaining of the non-ratification of the treaty, and that the United States had not performed all their agreements in the treaty of 1839.

In September, 1865, a new treaty was made, which was ratified by the United States, September 21st, 1866. By this treaty the Osages ceded a large portion of their entire reservation, which is to be sold, and the funds invested for the benefit of the tribe; $80,000 of which are set apart as a school fund, and a provision was made for their mission school.

According to Charlevoix, the Catholics early sent missionaries to the Osages and Missourias; but one of them lost his life, and another was long held as prisoner.

In 1820 an effort was made by the Presbyterians to establish a mission among them, but was subsequently abandoned. The Catholics again renewed their efforts in 1846 for their conversion, under Fathers John Shoenmaker and John Bax, and the Sisters of Loretto opened a school for girls. Father S., in 1855, reports to the Indian agent that the "Osages advance but very little towards civilization," but he is willing "to bear them testimony that they are a nation of superior natural talents." He further said: "At our arrival in this nation we counted five farms; there are now twenty-five."

In 1860, Father Shoenmaker's manual labor school employed four male teachers, and had 125 pupils, and the Sisters of Loretto had fourteen engaged in teaching the girls' department, which numbered nearly as many as the boys; some of these pupils in both departments were Quapaws. The Indian agent of that year said the school was "prosperous beyond the most sanguine expectations of its founders."

The breaking out of the rebellion was disastrous to this tribe, as they were on the border. About 1,000 of them went south in 1861, but probably did not take up arms against the United States, and most of them had returned in 1865. The balance, about 2,500, remained loyal to the United States; and as early as 1862 two hundred and forty warriors enlisted in the Union army. The whole tribe were faithful guards to the frontier against guerrillas, and in June, 1863, captured and killed at one time twenty rebel officers and soldiers, who had come into their country for plunder. In 1864, the rebels burned all their houses and plundered their country.

The schools continued to diminish from year to year, and in 1865, the agency buildings were burned about the 10th of May, probably by guerrillas, and Father Shoenmaker's report is missing from the report of the Commissioner of Indian Affairs. They receive an annuity of $3,456 per year for educational purposes.

MISSOURIAS AND OTTOES.

The first knowledge we have of the Missourias is derived from Marquette, who marked them on his map as *Ouemessourit*, and located them on the Missouri river, next above the Osages. The word is evidently Algonquin, of the Illinois dialect, but the writer has never found it translated into English or French. Father Douay is believed by the writer to have been the first one to give their name to the great western branch of the Mississippi, in 1687, as the "river of the Massourites." During the next century we occasionally find their names mentioned, but nothing definite in regard to them.

The United States found them on the north side of the Missouri river, with the Ottoes, and made the usual treaty of peace with the two tribes, June 24th, 1817.

In the treaty of July 15th, 1830, the Missourias and Ottoes joined the Iowas, Sacs, and Foxes, and several other tribes, in ceding to the United States their territory on the east side of the Missouri river, from the Missouri State line extending up the river to the Big Sioux river, which territory so ceded was to be " assigned and allotted, under the direction of the President of the United States, to the tribes now living thereon, or to such other tribes as the President may locate thereon, for hunting and other purposes." For this cession the Missourias and Ottoes received $2,500, and one blacksmith, at the expense of the United States, and the necessary tools; also, instruments for agricultural purposes to the amount of five hundred dollars. In the same treaty, part of the territory of the Ottoes, on the west side of the Missouri, was set off for a half-breed tract, and it was stipulated that the Omahas, Iowas, and Yanckton and Santee bands of Sioux, should pay the Ottoes therefor $3,000.

By the treaty of the 21st of September, 1833, the Ottoes and Missourias ceded the following territory to the United

14

States: "Beginning on the Little Nemaha, at the northwest corner of the land reserved by treaty at Prairie Du Chien, on the 15th of July, 1830 (see Iowas, page 199), in favor of certain half-breeds, of the Omahas, Iowas, Ottoes, and Yanckton and Santee's band of Sioux, and running westerly with said Little Nemaha, to the head branches of the same; and thence running in a due west line as far west as said Ottoes and Missourias have, or pretend to have, any claim." By this treaty the two tribes agreed to locate themselves in such convenient agricultural districts as the President may think proper;" and also expressed "their entire willingness to abandon the chase for an agricultural life." The United States agreed, when they are settled by the President on their new reservation, to continue their annuity for ten years from 1840, for $500; also, $500 annually for five years for schools; also erect a horse-mill for grinding corn, and provide two farmers to reside in the nation to instruct and assist said tribe for the term of five years; also deliver them $1,000 value in stock, to be placed in care of their agent. In addition to this, the United States extended their annuity by treaty of 1830, $2,500, ten years from 1840; and also paid them, at the time of the treaty, $400 worth of goods.

By the treaty of October 15th, 1836, they relinquished their claim to the piece of land between the State of Missouri and the river, afterwards added to Missouri, for which the Ottoes received $1,250, and the Missourias $1,000. The Ottoes and Missourias also received 500 bushels of corn, having failed to raise a crop that season, on account of having removed that spring on to the tract which had been selected for them by the President.

By the treaty of 1854, amended and ratified April 10th, 1855, the Missourias and Ottoes ceded to the United States all their land west of the Missouri except their reservation on Big Blue river, defined as follows: Commencing five miles due east of a point in the middle of the main branch of the Big Blue river, at a place called by the Indians the Islands, south-west of Fort Kearney; "thence west twenty-five miles; thence north ten miles; thence east to a point due north of the starting-point, and ten miles therefrom; thence to the place of beginning." By this treaty they consented to a survey and allotment in severalty of their reservation. Upon this reservation these tribes removed in July, 1855, and the first of November of that year government had broke for them 100 acres of prairie, built one house and one smith-shop, and put up 100 tons of hay. In 1858 government put them up a steam saw and grist-mill. In 1860 their crops of 250 acres were an entire failure by drouth. In 1865 the farmer reported that the Indians had "manifested a much greater interest in agriculture than the year previous, and that their crops were good. The mills were doing well, and grinding for both whites and Indians.

In November, 1854, government arranged with the Presbyterian Board of Missions to open and conduct a mission school for five years, and paid them the $500 per year agreed to in the treaty of 1833, which expired in June, 1860, since which time no school has been open. This school was under the charge of the Rev. Mr. Guthrie, and proved a complete failure, he having failed to interest the Indians to send to the school. The agent, in 1858, said the Indians "never will, unless compelled to, send their children to this school," and the agent recommends that the school be discontinued.

In 1853, the two tribes were reported at 1,000 souls, but in 1855 the agent estimated them at only 600. By the census of 1865, they then numbered 508. They furnished only four soldiers for the Union army, but were involved in war with the south-western Indians, and were loyal to our government. They, however, enrolled fifty young men for General Lane's "Indian regiment," which, however, were not called for.

The total annuity now due the Indians, under the treaty of 1854, amounts to $221,000, which is divided into some thirty annual installments.

The report of 1866 urges the establishment of a school, which was earnestly requested by the tribes; alleges constant trespasses on their timber lands by the whites, and represents some progress in agriculture.

KANSAS, OR KAWS.

This tribe was located, by Marquette, west of the Osages, and next to the Pancassa or Pawnees, which seems to have continued as their locality to the present day. We know comparatively nothing of their wars, except that the whole O-chunk-o-raw confederacy were more or less at war with the Illinois in early times, the Sacs and Foxes at a later day, and almost continually with the Pawnees. Even the Winnebagoes, at Green Bay, have often sent war parties against the Pawnees within the memory of the old French.

The United States made their usual treaty of peace with the Kansas, October 28, 1815; and June 3, 1825, they made another treaty, the first article of which was as follows:

"The Kansas do hereby cede to the United States all the lands lying within the State of Missouri, to which the said nation have title or claim; and do further cede and relinquish to the said United States, all other lands which they now occupy, or to which they have title or claim, lying west of the said State of Missouri, and within the following boundaries: Beginning at the entrance of the Kansas river into the Missouri river; from thence north to the north-west corner of the State of Missouri; from thence westwardly to the Nodewa river, thirty miles from its entrance into the Missouri; from thence to the entrance of the Big Nemaha river into the Missouri, and with that river to its source; from thence to the sources of the Kansas river, leaving the old village of the Pania Republic to the west; from thence, on the ridge dividing the waters of the Kansas river from those of the Arkansas, to the western boundary of the State line of Missouri, and with that line, thirty miles, to the place of beginning."

The second article of said treaty provided for a reservation as follows:

"From the cession aforesaid, the following reservation for the use of the Kansas nation of Indians shall be made, of a tract of land, to begin twenty leagues up the Kansas river, and to include their village on that river, extending west thirty miles in width, through the lands ceded in the first article, to be surveyed and marked under the direction of the President," etc.

The consideration of this purchase was "$3,500 per annum for twenty successive years."

The United States also furnished the Kansas 300 head of cattle, 300 hogs, 500 domestic fowls, three yoke of oxen, and two carts, "with such implements of agriculture as the superintendent of Indian affairs may think necessary; and shall employ such persons to aid and instruct them in their agriculture, as the President of the United States may deem expedient; and shall provide and support a blacksmith for them."

Article fifth provides: "Out of the lands herein ceded by the Kansas nation to the United States, the commissioner aforesaid, in behalf of the said United States, doth further covenant and agree, that thirty-six sections of good lands on the Big Blue river, shall be laid out under the direction of the President of the United States, and sold for the purpose of raising a fund, to be applied under the direction of the President to the support of schools for the education of the Kansas children within their nation."

The United States also stipulated to give twenty-three half-breeds of the Kansas a section of land each of one mile square, commencing at the reservation on the north side of the Kansas river, and extending down the river. They also agree to pay, not exceeding $3,000, for Indian depredations since 1815; also pay François G. Choteau $500, towards the liquidation of Indian debts to him; also pay $4,000, "which, together with the amount agreed on in the third and fourth articles, and the provisions made in the other articles of this treaty, shall be considered as a full compensation for the cession herein made."

There were provisions for the delivery of stolen property and the punishment of offenders.

By another treaty of the 16th of August, 1825, the Kansas tribe cede the privilege of a highway through their land, for which they received eight hundred dollars.

Article I. of the treaty of 1859, proclaimed by the President November 17th, 1860, provides:

"The Kansas Indians having now more lands than are necessary for their use, and being desirous of promoting settled habits of industry amongst themselves, by abolishing the tenure in common by which they now hold their lands, and by assigning limited quantities thereof in severalty to the members of their tribe owning an interest in their present reservation, to be cultivated and improved for their individual use and benefit, it is agreed and stipulated that that portion of their reservation commencing at the southwest corner of said reservation, thence north with the west boundary nine miles; thence east fourteen miles; thence south nine miles; thence west with the south boundary fourteen miles, to the place of beginning, shall be set apart and retained by them for said purposes; and that out of the same there shall be assigned to each head of a family not exceeding forty acres, and to each member thereof not exceeding forty acres; and to each single male person of the age of twenty-one years and upwards not exceeding forty acres of land, to include in every case, as far as practicable, a reasonable proportion of timber. One hundred and sixty acres of said retained lands, in a suitable locality, shall also be set apart and appropriated to the occupancy and use of the agency of said Indians, and one hundred and sixty acres of said lands shall also be reserved for the establishment of a school for the education of the youth of the tribe." By article 4th of the same treaty, it is provided that the surplus, after locating all the said Indians as aforesaid, might be sold for the benefit of the said tribe, and for assisting in making agricultural improvements, and for the payment of Indian debts. The tribe also make further provisions for more half-breeds.

This tribe has not particularly attracted attention until lately; and in 1855, agent Montgomery wrote of them in his report, that their annuity " is mostly laid out for provisions and whisky;" that about the middle of June of that year " the small-pox broke out amongst them, and has continued to prove fatal with the greater number of them, it seems, to the great satisfaction and admiration of all those who have any acquaintance with the Kaws." . . . " They have no school, and it appears that what they have had has been only a dead expense to the government." . . . " The Kansas are a poor, degraded, superstitious, thievish, indigent tribe of Indians; their tendency is downward, and, in my opinion, they must soon become extinct; and the sooner they arrive at this period, the better it will be for the rest of mankind."

To this report Mr. Manypenny, the Commissioner of Indian Affairs, replied that the agent spoke " in very improper terms" of " those untutored wards of the government ;" and " that instead of designing their extermination, he should employ the best means within his reach calculated to promote their welfare and improvement," etc.

In March, 1862, their lands having been surveyed, were allotted to them in severalty, and that year they commenced civilization in earnest. The agent said of them that " they have been provided with comfortable and substantial stone houses, which they now occupy." . . . " They have cultivated, for the first time in many years, considerable fields of corn, potatoes and other vegetables. The new fields were broken too late for use." He also said that their new school buildings were ready for teachers; but they need a blacksmith, mill, etc.

In May, 1863, their mission school went into operation, under the charge of the Society of Friends, with thirty-five scholars, and was quite successful. Mr. Hauffaker their farmer, reported that they "were cultivating over three hundred acres, and are well pleased with their new mode of life;" but labored under the difficulty of having an "insufficient number of oxen, ploughs and other agricultural implements;" and that more than eighty of the Indians had "enlisted in the United States service during the past year."

In 1865 they cultivated four hundred acres, and raised 350 bushels of wheat, 9,000 bushels of corn, 500 bushels of oats, and 750 bushels of potatoes. Their annuities were $10,000 annually.

In 1853 the Kansas numbered 1,375; in 1860, 803; in 1862, 775; in 1864, 701; and in 1865, 631. This shows a large decrease annually, which is in part explained by the fact that they still continue their buffalo hunts in the summer to the west, and their probable losses in the late war of the rebellion. However, at that rate, the "wards of government" will soon disappear like the "children of the woods."

By the report of the agent in September, 1866, it appears that the most of this tribe spent the previous winter in the buffalo country, and killed 3,000 buffalo; that the Santa Fe traders constantly sold them whisky; that thirty of their children attended the mission school, and made some progress during the winter, twelve learning to read, but most of them returned home in the spring, when their parents returned from the hunt; that many of their horses had been stolen by white men; and that the children at school, "when treated kindly, seem to be of an affectionate disposition." The mission school is in charge of the "Friends," who are under contract to the government "to receive the

Indian children to the buildings and farm, and give them a good English education to the extent of their capacity; and, in addition, to teach the boys farming, and the use of tools and agricultural implements, and the girls the various branches of housewifery, including sewing and knitting, and dairy operations, and whatever may tend to their civilization.

The treaty of 1864, providing for the sale of their lands to the United States, and their removal to the Indian territory, had not been ratified by the Senate in November, 1866.

OMAHAS.

This tribe was also located by Marquette on the Missouri, north-west of the Missourias, under the name of *Mama*. They joined with the Missourias and several other tribes, in the treaty of July 15th, 1830, and in that of October 15th, 1836.

By the treaty of 1854 the Omahas ceded all their lands west of the Missouri, " and south of a line drawn due west from a point in the centre of the main channel of said Missouri river, due east of where the Ayoway river disembogues out of the bluffs, to the western boundary of the Omaha country, and forever relinquish all right and title to the country south of said line," reserving the country north of said line for their home.

The sixth article provided for a survey, and allotment in severalty of the reservation.

The United States also agree to protect them on their reservation from the Sioux and other hostile tribes; also " erect for the Omahas, at their new home, a grist and saw-mill, and keep the same in repair, and provide a miller for ten years; also to erect a good blacksmith shop, supply the same with tools, and keep it in repair for ten years, and provide a good blacksmith for a like period; and to employ an experienced farmer for the term of ten years, to instruct the Indians in agriculture." They gave the Presbyterian

14*

Board a section of land to include the then buildings, and gave a right of way for roads and railroads through their reservation.

The United States agreed to pay them $40,000 per annum for three years, $30,000 per annum for ten years, $20,000 per annum for fifteen years, and $10,000 per annum for twelve years; each annuity to commence when the other was paid in the aforesaid order; also the further sum of $41,000, to be expended by the President in establishing and maintaining them on the reservation.

The tribe went on their reservation and progressed finely, and in 1865 had 945 acres under a good state of cultivation. Their mission school was under the supervision of Rev. R. J. Burtt, with four assistant teachers, and had forty-five scholars. The school received $4,476.23 from the Presbyterian Mission Board, and $3,750 from the tribe, annually. The census of 1865 was 1,002, showing an increase of thirty-one over the previous year. Indeed, the tribe has increased a small per cent. for several years. They have banished whisky from the reservation. The tribe has been loyal, and have put 260 soldiers into the Union army. Of their annuities, $480,000 are yet to be paid.

This tribe invited the Winnebagoes, their "elder brothers," to settle with them, and sold them, through the United States, a part of their reservation.

The treaty, selling a part of their reservation to the United States for the benefit of the Winnebagoes, was ratified February 15, 1866, by the President, by which they get $50,000, besides the extension of the provisions of the eighth article of a former treaty for ten years, and $7,000 damages from the Winnebagoes.

By the agent's report of August 1, 1866, the tribe was in a prosperous condition, the most of the people had put on the white man's clothing, and lived in comfortable houses; and their mission school, then under the superintendence of Old School Presbyterians, had sixty-one scholars, of which nineteen were girls, and forty-two boys — all making good progress. They had been blessed with a revival of religion.

The tribe, during the summer of 1866, cultivated 1,830 acres — 485 more than the previous year — and raised 73,630 bushels of grain, besides potatoes, beets, carrots, and turnips. The chiefs and head men of the tribe have petitioned for a survey and allotment in severalty of their reservation.

PONCAS.

Marquette mentions a tribe near the Maha, by the name of Pana, which is probably the same as the Ponca of the present day. The United States made their usual treaty of peace with this tribe in 1817, and another for trade in 1825.

By that of May 12, 1858, they ceded to the United States all their lands, except the following reservation for their future homes: "Beginning at a point on the Neobrara river, and running due north so as to intersect the Ponca river twenty-five miles from its mouth; thence from said point of intersection, up and along the Ponca river twenty miles; thence due south to the Neobrara river; and thence down and along said river to the place of beginning."

For this cession the United States agreed to protect the Poncas on their reservation, pay them $12,000 per annum for five years, $10,000 per annum for ten years, $8,000 per annum for fifteen years; and expend $20,000 " in maintaining and subsisting the Poncas during the first year after their removal to their new homes, purchasing stock and agricultural implements, breaking up and fencing land, building houses, and in making such other improvements as may be necessary for their comfort and welfare."

" To establish, and to maintain for ten years, at an annual expense not to exceed $5,000, one or more manual labor schools, for the education and training of the Ponca youth in letters, agriculture, the mechanic arts, and housewifery; which school or schools shall be managed and conducted in such manner as the President of the United States shall direct; the Poncas hereby stipulating to constantly keep thereat, during at least nine months in every year, all their children between the ages of seven and eighteen years.

"The United States also pay not exceeding $10,500, to be expended in the erection of mills, dwelling-houses, shops, etc., for the benefit of the Poncas; and also to expend annually, for ten years, or during the pleasure of the President, an amount not exceeding $7,500, for the purpose of furnishing said Indians with such aid and assistance in agricultural and mechanical pursuits, including the working of said mill, as the Secretary of the Interior may consider advantageous and necessary for them; the Poncas hereby stipulating to furnish from their tribe the number of young men that may be required as apprentices and assistants in the mills and mechanics' shops, and at least three persons to work constantly with each laborer employed for them in agricultural pursuits."

The United States also set aside $20,000 for the payment of Ponca debts; also the United States gave scrip for 160 acres of land each, to eight half-breeds, and Francis Roy, their interpreter.

The Poncas agree that if any of them "shall drink, or procure for others intoxicating liquor, their proportion of the tribal annuities shall be withheld for at least one year."

The Poncas also reserve the right to allot in severalty, their reservation "among themselves, giving to each head of family or single person a farm, with such rights of possession or transfer to any other member of the tribe, or of descent to their heirs and representatives, as may be in accordance with the laws, customs, and regulations of the tribe."

The Ponca reservation proving a "barren waste, destitute of wood for lumber and for fuel, and of grass for hay," a new treaty was made with them in March, 1865, giving them a new reservation in the valley of the Missouri river, about twelve miles long, and from one to two miles wide, and containing an abundance of timber, grass, and water. That treaty had not been confirmed by the Senate in the fall of 1866.

The manual labor school provided for in the treaty of 1858, had not been opened as late as September 30, 1865, but the Poncas were still urging its establishment.

The population of the Poncas amounted, in 1865, to 1,100, according to government documents.

By the agent's report of September 10, 1866, it appears that this tribe were making some progress in farming, having five hundred acres under cultivation; but were in an unsettled condition on account of the non-ratification of the treaty of 1865. They have no school or mission.

MANDANS.

This tribe was not named in the list of Missouri river Indians by Marquette, but the Sacs and Foxes included them in their raids west of the Mississippi.

In 1825 they were at war with the United States, but July 30th, of that year, concluded a peace.

About 1833 Mr. Catlin visited this tribe, and painted many of the portraits of the principal men. At that time they inhabited two villages about two miles apart, on the west side of the Missouri river, two hundred miles below the mouth of the Yellow Stone, and numbered nearly 2,000 persons. Within the memory of many of those now living, their location was some eighty miles further down the river, and numbered ten villages.

Their traditions, related to Mr. Catlin, carry them back to the Ohio river, from whence they were driven to the Missouri. Mr. Catlin saw " many remains on the river below these places (and, in fact, to be seen nearly as low down as St. Louis), which show clearly the peculiar construction of Mandan lodges." These lodges were always surrounded with a ditch two feet deep, which long remains, and distinguishes unmistakably their locality. Mr. Catlin subsequently says that he noticed about twenty points down the river, where he found evidence of Mandan villages; and at one, five hundred miles below their then residence, he found two hundred skulls arranged in a circle in the peculiar Mandan order; but the skulls had so long been there that they would crumble to powder. This would indicate a residence there probably one hundred and fifty years previous. The name which the tribe call themselves, *See-pohs-kah-nu-mah-kah-kee*, or "people of the pheasants," may indicate an Ohio origin, as pheasants are a very scarce bird on the Missouri river. They claim to have been the original people created, to have once been very numerous, but had become much reduced by old wars.

In 1838 the traders carried the small-pox to the Mandan villages, and the greater part of them died. A few of them still maintain their tribal name in the Dakota territory, near the Gros-Ventres and Arickarees; and all three of those tribes in 1865 only contained 2,500 persons.

We have placed the Mandans in the O-chunk-o-raw confederacy, on account of their traditions, residences, and language; for by traditions they were from the Ohio, and the Rev. Father De Smet, the Oregon missionary, speaking of the Winnebagoes in 1865, said " they appear to be distinctly related to the Mandans, there being a similarity in their respective languages." They were probably a band of the " Akansea," driven from the Ohio by the Iroquois about 1660, and fled up the Missouri, instead of following their tribe to the Arkansas river.

Mr. Catlin, however, argues that they might have been the Mound-Builders of Ohio, and descendants of Modoc, the Welsh captain, who, it is said, left Europe for the west in the thirteenth century, with ten ships, and was never heard from afterwards. We answer that hypothesis by reference to the well-established fact, that a portion of the mounds of Ohio are more than 1,000 years old, and such is their extent that Modoc and his followers could not have built them in 2,000 years. Besides, the Welsh had no customs or superstitions at that day which would probably have led them to undertake such an amount of labor. Indeed, the writer believes that the Indians of America show no evidence of a European origin for the last thousand years.

At present, the Mandans are associated with the Arickarees and Gros-Ventres, who may be a kindred people. The government made a treaty with them collectively in 1866, by which they obtained a cession of a tract of land twenty-five by forty miles, together with the right of way across their territory. It also contained provisions in aid of the civilization of the bands.

CHAPTER XI.

DAKOTA, OR SIOUX CONFEDERACY.

This powerful confederacy was called by the Algonquin nations "Nadouessioux," or "Enemies," a word clothed in French orthography, which was abbreviated or contracted to "Sioux," (Soo,) the common name for the tribe among the English and French traders for the last two hundred years. They, however, called themselves Dakota, or Confederates.

They spoke the same language, and claimed in their traditions that they were originally created at Mille Lac, the seat of their empire, when first visited by Rev. Father Hennepin in 1680. Their territory extended from Lake Superior to the Rocky mountains. When the Algonquin nations were crowded back upon them, about the middle of the seventeenth century, they became involved with those nations in constant wars to defend their eastern frontier.

When the English settled Hudson's Bay, they furnished the Christinaux with fire-arms, and they thereby enabled that tribe to force a peace with the Assiniboins, or Rock Indians, the northern band of the Sioux, by which that band became alienated from the confederacy. This peace was the one probably negotiated by the French officer, De Lut, in 1679.

The aggressions of the fugitive Algonquins and Hurons upon the Sioux becoming unbearable, in the spring of 1671 they attacked those tribes at the head of Lake Superior, and cleared the lake of their enemies. The Chippeways returned to the falls of St. Mary, the Ottawas to the islands on the north side of Lake Huron, and the Hurons to Mackinaw island, while the Sacs, Foxes, Miamies, Mascotens and Kickapoos returned to the Fox and Wisconsin rivers, and the Illinois to their home on the river of that name. This war was settled by De Lut, in 1679, by peace between the Chippeways, Christinaux, and Assiniboins, but on the south it continued until 1702.

In 1700, the southern bands of the Sioux, who do not appear to have ever been reconciled to the Christinaux, killed some of the latter tribe which they found among the Assiniboins; upon which the war was renewed, the latter band taking the part of the Christinaux. The Chippeways joined the northern confederacy. The Sacs and Foxes, and their confederates, becoming dissatisfied with the Chippeways, in 1702 were induced by the Sioux to make peace and join the latter tribe. Here commenced the great war which, in later years, has been called the "hereditary war between the Sioux and Chippeways."

The Assiniboins, who lived on the west of Lake Superior, soon passed west of the Red river of the north, perhaps to avoid the war path, while many of the Ottawas and other northern Algonquin nations joined the Chippeways, and in process of time became known as the "Ojibwa confederacy." This powerful confederacy, constantly receiving reinforcements from the northern hordes, continued to press down upon the Sioux until the treaty of Prairie Du Chien, in 1825, when they made good their title to the territory extending south to St. Croix falls and Sauk rapids, and west to the Red river of the north. When Hole-in-the-Day, at that treaty, was asked by the commissioner why he claimed so far south and west, he arose and with great emphasis declared, "We conquered it." This left to the conquerors the ancient home of the Dakotas at Mille Lac,

15

where they claimed that they were created by Wakon, the Great Spirit.

When the Dakotas were visited by Le Sueur in 1700, they enumerated by name sixteen bands, without including the Assiniboins, which then constituted their confederacy.

It is not easy to name these bands at the present time, but the following are known to exist:

Wahpakoota, Medawakanton,	Resided in Minnesota, and originated the massacre in 1862.
Wahpaton, - Sisseton, -	Resided in Minnesota, and were called "upper bands." These four bands are often called Santees. Reservation at Fort Randall.
Yankton - Yanktonai, - Brule, - - Two Kettle, or Teton, - - Blackfeet, - Minnecongou, Oncpapas, - Sans Arcs, - Ogallallas, - Assiniboins, -	Reside in Dakota territory.

The language of the Dakota, or Confederates, is peculiar to that nation, and, although guttural, is readily learned by traders and missionaries. The latter have collected it into a dictionary with grammatical rules, and also translated the Bible into it.

After the war with Great Britain closed, the United States made treaties of peace with the most of the Dakotas. In 1825 the United States called together the several northwestern tribes at Prairie Du Chien, with a view of inducing the Indians to define and settle their territorial boundaries, and establish a general peace, but the scheme was only partially successful. They succeeded, however, in establishing a line between the Sioux and Chippeways, which, we believe, was acquiesced in by those two nations, and was as follows: Beginning "at the Chippewa river, half a day's march below the falls; and from thence it shall run to Red Cedar river, immediately below the falls; from thence to the St. Croix river, which it strikes at a place called the Standing Cedar, about a day's paddle in a canoe above the lake, at the mouth of that river; thence passing between two lakes, called by the Chippeways ' Green lakes,' and by the Sioux ' the lakes they bury the eagles in ;' from thence to the standing cedar that ' the Sioux split ;' thence to Rum river, crossing it at the mouth of a small creek called ' Choking creek," a long day's march from the Mississippi; thence to a point of woods that propels into the prairie, half a day's march from the Mississippi; thence in a straight line to the mouth of the first river which enters the Mississippi on its west side above the mouth of Sac river; thence ascending the said river (above the mouth of Sac river) to a small lake at its source; thence in a direct line to a lake at the head of Prairie river, which is supposed to enter the Crow Wing river on its south side; thence to Otter-tail lake portage; thence to said Otter-tail lake, and down through the middle thereof to its outlet; thence in a direct line so as to strike Buffalo river, half way from its source to its mouth, and down the said river to Red river; thence descending Red river to the mouth of Outard or Goose creek." . . . "The eastern boundary of the Sioux commences opposite the mouth of Iowa river (upper Iowa,) on the Mississippi, runs back two or three miles to the bluffs, follows the bluffs, crossing Bad Ax river to the mouth of Black river, and from Black river to half a day's march below the falls of the Chippewa river."

By the treaty of September 29, 1837, the Sioux " ceded to the United States all their lands east of the Mississippi river, and all their islands in the said river." A reference to the boundary aforesaid, described in the treaty of 1825, will show the extent of this purchase.

The following provisions of the treaty of 1837 will show the consideration paid the Sioux for said land, and for continuing the initiatory steps taken by the United States for civilizing those Indians in 1830:

"Article II. In consideration of the cession contained in the preceding article, the United States agree to the following stipulations on their part:

"1st. To invest the sum of $300,000 in such safe and profitable State stocks as the President may direct, and to pay to the chiefs and braves as aforesaid, annually, forever, an income of not less than five per cent. thereon; a portion of said interest, not exceeding one-third, to be applied in such manner as the President may direct, and the residue to be paid in specie, or such other manner, and for such objects, as the proper authorities of the tribe may designate.

"2nd. To pay to the relatives and friends of the chiefs and braves, as aforesaid, having not less than one quarter of Sioux blood, $110,000, to be distributed by the proper authorities of the tribe, upon principles to be determined by the chiefs and braves signing this treaty, and the war department.

"3rd. To apply the sum of $90,000 to the payment of just debts of the Sioux Indians, interested in the lands herewith ceded.

"4th. To pay to the chiefs and braves, as aforesaid, an annuity for twenty years of $10,000 in goods, to be purchased under the direction of the President, and delivered at the expense of the United States.

"5th. To expend annually, for twenty years, for the benefit of Sioux Indians, parties to this treaty, the sum of $8,250, in the purchase of medicines, agricultural implements, and stock, and for the support of a physician, farmers, and blacksmiths, and for other beneficial objects.

"6th. In order to enable the Indians aforesaid to break up and improve their lands, the United States will supply, as soon as practicable after the ratification of this treaty, agricultural implements, mechanics' tools, cattle, and such other articles as may be useful to them, to an amount not exceeding $10,000.

"7th. To expend annually, for twenty years, the sum of

$5,500, in the purchase of provisions, to be delivered at the expense of the United States.

"8th. To deliver to the chiefs and braves signing this treaty, upon their arrival at St. Louis, $6,000 in goods."

Under this treaty, the Sioux removed all their bands to the west bank of the Mississippi in 1838.

By the treaty of September 10, 1836, Wa-ba-shaw's band of the Sioux released to the United States their interest in the tract of country between the Missouri State line and Missouri river, which was afterwards attached to that State, and became slave territory. A similar release was obtained from the Yankton and Santee bands of Sioux, and from the Ottoes, Missourias, and Omahas, by the treaty of October 15th, 1836; and from the Wah-pa-kootah, Sissaton and upper Medawakanton bands of the Sioux, by treaty of November 30, 1836.

By the treaty of Prairie Du Chien, of August 19, 1825, the boundary line between the Sioux and Sacs and Foxes, was established as follows: "Commencing at the mouth of the upper Iowa river, on the west bank of the Mississippi, and ascending the said Iowa river to its left fork; thence up that fork to its source; thence crossing the fork of Red Cedar river in a direct line, to the second or upper fork of the Des Moines river; thence in a direct line to the lower fork of the Calumet river, and down that river to the Missouri river."

By article third of the treaty at Prairie Du Chien, July 15th, 1830, the Medawakantons, Wah-pa-koota, Wahpatons, and Sissatons bands of the Sioux, "cede and relinquish to the United States, forever, a tract of country twenty miles in width, from the Mississippi to the Des Moines river, situated north, and adjoining" the aforesaid line; and the same bands, with the Yankton and Santee bands of Sioux, and the Iowas, Ottoes, Omahas and Missourias, further cede to the United States the country from the following line to the State of Missouri, as Indian territory for colonization:

"Beginning at the upper fork of the Des Moines river, and passing the sources of the Little Sioux and Floyd's rivers, to the forks of the first creek which falls into the Big Sioux or Calumet on the east side; thence down said creek and Calumet river to the Missouri river."

This "Indian territory" was afterwards abandoned, and the Indians transferred to the west bank of the Missouri. It was in this treaty that the "half-breed reservation" was set off on the west side of the Mississippi and Lake Pepin, fifteen miles wide, and extending down the Mississippi from Red Wing thirty-two miles, to opposite the mouth of Buffalo river.

For these purchases, the United States agreed to pay annually for ten years, to the Yankton and Santee bands, $3,000, and to the other Sioux bands, $2,000; and also furnish the latter Sioux bands "one blacksmith and the necessary tools, at the expense of the United States; also instruments for agricultural purposes, and iron and steel to the amount of $700 annually, for ten years," and as much longer as the President may think proper; and also furnish for the same period to the former Sioux bands, a blacksmith and tools, and agricultural implements to the amount of $400. The United States also paid and distributed among the several tribes who signed the treaty, in goods, $5,132, and set apart for educational purposes $3,000, to be paid annually for ten years.

The great tide of emigration having in good earnest reached the upper Mississippi valley in 1850, the United States government were pressed for more Indian lands to accommodate the millions of all nations of the world, who were looking earnestly for homes in the finest agricultural region of the north-west; and the authorities at Washington consequently turned their attention to the rich territories of the chivalrous Sioux. The thousands of bold warriors from the mighty Mississippi to the snow-clad Rocky mountains, were summoned to meet the high officials at *Traverse Des*

Sioux, on the Minnesota river, in the summer of 1851, where they were feasted and petted at government expense for nearly a month, when the terms of the two following treaties were agreed upon, and signed by L. Lea, the commissioner of Indian affairs, and Governor Ramsey, of Minnesota territory.

The first was signed July 23rd, 1851, and the following is a copy of the several articles:

"ARTICLE I. It is stipulated and solemnly agreed, that the peace and friendship now so happily existing between the United States and the aforesaid bands of Indians shall be perpetual.

"ARTICLE II. The said See-see-toan and Wah-pay-toan bands of Dakota or Sioux Indians agree to cede, and do hereby cede, sell, and relinquish to the United States, all their lands in the State of Iowa; and, also, all their lands in the territory of Minnesota, lying east of the following line, to wit: Beginning at the junction of the Buffalo river with the Red river of the north; thence along the western bank of said Red river of the north to the mouth of the Sioux Wood river; thence along the western bank of said Sioux Wood river to Lake Traverse; thence along the western shore of said lake to the southern extremity thereof; thence in a direct line to the junction of Kampeska lake with the Tchan-kas-an-data or Sioux river; thence along the western bank of said river to its point of intersection with the northern line of the State of Iowa, including all the islands in said rivers and lake.

ARTICLE III. In part consideration of the foregoing cession, the United States do hereby set apart for the future occupancy and home of the Dakota Indians, parties to this treaty, to be held by them as Indian lands are held, all that tract of country on either side of the Minnesota river from the Western boundary of the lands herein ceded, east to the Tchay-tam Bay river on the north, and to the Yellow Medicine river on the south side, to extend, on each side, a distance of not less than ten miles from the general course of said river, the boundaries of said tract to be marked out by as straight lines as practicable, whenever deemed expedient by the President, and in such manner as he shall direct.

"ARTICLE IV. In further and full consideration of said cession, the United States agree to pay to said Indians the sum of $1,665,000 at the several times, in the manner and for the purposes following, to wit:

"1st. To the chiefs of the said bands, to enable them to settle their affairs and comply with their present just engagements; and in consideration of their removing themselves to the country set apart for them as above, which they agree to do within two years, or sooner, if required by the President, without further cost or expense to the United States, and in consideration of their subsisting themselves the first year after their removal, which they agree to do without further cost or expense on the part of the United States, the sum of $275,000. *Provided*, That said sum shall be paid to the chiefs in such manner as they hereafter, in open council, shall request, and as soon after the removal of said Indians to the home set apart for them as the necessary appropriation therefor shall be made by Congress.

"2nd. To be laid out, under the direction of the President, for the establishment of manual labor schools, the erection of mills and blacksmith shops, opening farms, fencing and breaking land, and for such other beneficial objects as may be deemed most conducive to the prosperity and happiness of said Indians, $30,000.

"The balance of said sum of $1,665,000, to wit, $1,360,000, to remain in trust with the United States, and five per cent. interest thereon to be paid annually to said Indians for the period of fifty years, commencing the first day of July, 1852, which shall be in full payment of said balance, principal and interest; the said payment to be applied, under the direction of the President, as follows, to wit:

"3rd. For a general agricultural improvement and civilization fund, the sum of $12,000.

"4th. For educational purposes, the sum of $6,000.

"5th. For the purchase of goods and provisions, the sum of $10,000,000.

"6th. For money annuity, the sum of $40,000.

"ARTICLE V. The laws of the United States prohibiting the introduction and sale of spirituous liquors in the Indian country, shall be in full force and effect throughout the territory hereby ceded, and lying in Minnesota, until otherwise directed by Congress or the President of the United States.

"ARTICLE VI. Rules and regulations to protect the rights of persons and property among the Indians, parties to this treaty, and adapted to their condition and wants, may be prescribed and enforced in such manner as the President or the Congress of the United States from time to time shall direct."

The Senate, June 23rd, 1852, amended the said treaty by striking out all of article third and adding the following, which was afterwards consented to by the Sioux:

"1st. The United States do hereby stipulate to pay the Sioux bands of Indians, parties to this treaty, at the rates of ten cents per acre for the lands included in the reservation provided for in the third article of the treaty as originally agreed upon.

"2nd. It is further stipulated, that the President be authorized, with the assent of the said bands of Indians, parties to this treaty, and as soon after they shall have given their assent to the foregoing *article* as may be convenient, to cause to be set apart, by appropriate landmarks and boundaries, such tracts of country, without the limits of the cession made by the first [2nd] article of the treaty, as may be satisfactory, for their future occupancy and home:

Provided, that the President may, by the consent of these Indians, vary the conditions aforesaid, if deemed expedient."

The second treaty purports to have been signed August 5th, 1851, at Mendota, at the mouth of Minnesota river, and was made between the United States and *Med-ay-wa-kan-toan* and *Wah-pay-koo-tay* bands of the Dakota, or Sioux, by which those bands ceded to the United States all their interest in the lands in Minnesota or Iowa, and in consideration of such cession those bands were made tenants in common of a reservation along the Minnesota river, ten miles wide on each side, and the United States agreed to pay them $1,410,000. The further provisions of the treaty were substantially the same as were contained in the treaty with *See-see-toan* and *Wah-pay-toan* bands, of the 23rd of July of the same year. The treaty was amended by the Senate substantially as the other, and the amendment ratified by the bands at St. Paul, September 4th, 1862. Both treaties were ratified by the President's proclamation, dated February 24th, 1853.

In 1858 the United States concluded a treaty with the Yankton band of Sioux, by which that band ceded all their lands, except a reservation of 400,000 acres, extending thirty miles along the east bank of the Missouri river, above the Chouteau river, for which the United States engaged to pay annuities amounting to $1,600,000. The treaty contained the usual provisions for schools and agricultural improvements. It was ratified by the Senate, and published by the President's proclamation, dated February 26th, 1859.

The Sioux bands being unwilling to leave their reservation under the treaty of August 5th, 1851, as required by the amendment of the Senate in striking out article third, a new treaty was made with them at Washington, June 19th, 1858, with the following provisions:

"ARTICLE I. It is hereby agreed and stipulated that, as soon as practicable after the ratification of this agreement, so much of that part of the reservation or tract of land now held and possessed by the Mendawakanton and Wahpakoota bands of the Dakota or Sioux Indians, and which is described in the third article of the treaty made with them on the 5th day of August, 1851, which lies south or southwestwardly of the Minnesota river, shall constitute a reservation for said bands, and shall be surveyed, and eighty acres thereof, as near as may be in conformity with the public surveys, be allotted in severalty to each head of a family, or single person over the age of twenty-one years, in said bands of Indians, said allotments to be so made as to include a proper proportion of timbered land, if the same be practicable, in each of said allotments. The residue of said part of said reservation not so allotted shall be held by said bands in common, and as other Indian lands are held: *Provided*, however, that eighty acres thereof, as near as may be, shall, in like manner as above provided for, be allotted to each of the minors of said bands on his or her attaining their majority, or on becoming heads of families by contracting marriage, if neither of the parties shall have previously received land.

"All the necessary expenses of the surveys and allotments thus provided for, shall be defrayed out of the funds of said bands of Indians in the hands of the government of the United States.

"As the members of said bands become capable of managing their business and affairs, the President of the United States may, at his discretion, cause patents to be issued to them, for the tracts of land allotted to them respectively, in conformity with this article; said tracts to be exempt from levy, taxation, sale or forfeiture, until otherwise provided for by the legislature of the State in which they are situated with the assent of Congress; nor shall they be sold or alienated in fee, or be in any other manner disposed of except to the United States, or to members of said bands.

"ARTICLE II. Whereas by the treaty with the Mendawakanton and Wahpakoota bands of Sioux Indians, concluded at Mendota on the 5th day of August, 1851, said bands retained for their 'future occupancy and home,' 'to be held by them as Indian lands are held, a tract of country of the average width of ten miles on either side of the Minnesota river,' extending from Little Rock river to the Tchatamba and Yellow Medicine rivers, which land was to 'be held by said bands in common.'

"And whereas the Senate of the United States so amended said treaty as to strike therefrom the provision setting apart said land as a home for said bands, and made provision for the payment to said bands 'at the rate of ten cents per acre for the lands included in the' said tract so reserved and set apart for the 'occupancy and home' of said bands, and also provided in addition thereto, that there should be 'set apart, by appropriate landmarks and boundaries, such tracts of country without the limits of the cession made by the first article of the' said treaty, as should 'be satisfactory for their future occupancy and home,' said Senate amendment providing also 'that the President may, with the consent of these Indians, vary the conditions aforesaid, if deemed expedient;' all of which provisions in said amendment were assented to by said Indians.

"And whereas the President so far varied the conditions of said Senate amendment as to permit said bands to locate for the time being upon the tract originally reserved by said bands for a home, and no 'tracts of country without the limits of the cession' made in the said treaty *has* [have] ever been provided for, or offered to, said bands:

"And whereas by the 'act making appropriations for the current and contingent expenses of the Indian department, and for fulfilling treaty stipulations with various Indian tribes,' approved July 31, 1854, the President was authorized to confirm to the Sioux of Minnesota forever, the reserve on the Minnesota river now occupied by them, upon such conditions as he may deem just:

"And whereas, although the President has not directly confirmed said reserve to said Indians, they claim that as they were entitled to receive 'such tracts of country' as should 'be satisfactory for their future occupancy and home,' and as no such country has been provided for, or offered to, said bands, it is agreed and stipulated that the question shall be submitted to the Senate for decision whether they have such title; and if they have, what compensation shall be made to them for that part of said reservation or tract of land lying on the north side of the Minnesota river — whether they shall be allowed a specific sum of money therefor, and if so, how much; or whether the same shall be sold for their benefit, they to receive the proceeds of such sale, deducting the necessary expenses incident thereto. Such sale, if decided in favor of by the Senate, shall be made under and according to regulations to be prescribed by the Secretary of the Interior, and in such manner as will secure to them the largest sum it may be practicable to obtain for said land.

"ARTICLE III. It is also agreed that if the Senate shall authorize the land designated in article two of this agreement to be sold for the benefit of the said Mendawakanton and Wahpakoota bands, or shall prescribe an amount to be paid said bands for their interest in said tract, provision shall be made by which the chiefs and head men of said bands may, in their discretion, in open council, authorize to be paid out of the proceeds of said tract, such sum or sums as may be found necessary and proper, not exceeding seventy thousand dollars, to satisfy their just debts and obligations, and to provide goods to be taken by said chiefs and head men to the said bands upon their return: *Provided, however*, That their said determinations shall be approved by the superintendent of Indian affairs for the northern superintendency for the time being, and the said payments be authorized by the Secretary of the Interior.

"ARTICLE IV. The lands retained and to be held by the

members of the Mendawakanton and Wahpakoota bands of the Dakota or Sioux Indians, under and by virtue of the first article of this agreement, shall, to all intents and purposes whatever, be deemed and held to be an Indian reservation; and the laws which have been, or may hereafter be enacted by Congress, to regulate trade and intercourse with the Indian tribes, shall have full force and effect over and within the limits of the same; and no person other than the members of the said bands, to be ascertained and defined under such regulations as the Secretary of the Interior shall prescribe, unless such as may be duly licensed to trade with said bands, or employed for their benefit, or members of the family of such persons, shall be permitted to reside or make any settlement upon any part of said reservation; and the timbered land allotted to individuals, and also that reserved for subsequent distribution as provided in the first article of this agreement, shall be free from all trespass, use, or occupation, except as hereinafter provided.

"ARTICLE V. The United States shall have the right to establish and maintain upon said reservation such military posts, agencies, schools, mills, shops, roads, and agricultural or mechanical improvements, as may be deemed necessary, but no greater quantity of land or timber shall be taken and used for said purposes than shall be actually requisite therefor. And if in the establishment or maintenance of such posts, agencies, roads or other improvements, the timber or other property of any individual Indian shall be taken, injured, or destroyed, just and adequate compensation shall be made therefor by the United States. Roads or highways authorized by competent authority other than the United States, the lines of which shall lie through said reservation, shall have the right of way through the same, upon the fair and just value of such right being paid to the said Mendawakanton and Wahpakoota bands by the party or parties authorizing or interested in the same, to be assessed and determined in such manner as the Secretary of the Interior shall direct.

"ARTICLE VI. The Mendawakanton and Wahpakoota bands of Dakota or Sioux Indians acknowledge their dependence on the government of the United States, and do hereby pledge and bind themselves to preserve friendly relations with the citizens thereof, and to commit no injuries or depredations on their persons or property, nor on those of the members of any other tribe; but in case of any such injury or depredation, full compensation shall, as far as practicable, be made therefor out of their moneys in the hands of the United States; the amount in all cases to be determined by the Secretary of the Interior. They further pledge themselves not to engage in hostilities with the Indians of any other tribe unless in self-defense, but to submit, through their agent, all matters of dispute and difficulty between themselves and other Indians, for the decision of the President of the United States, and to acquiesce in and abide thereby. They also agree to deliver to the proper officers all persons belonging to their said bands who may become offenders against the treaties, laws, or regulations of the United States, or the laws of the State of Minnesota, and to assist in discovering, pursuing, and capturing all such offenders whenever required so to do by such officers, through the agent or other proper officer of the Indian department.

"ARTICLE VII. To aid in preventing the evils of intemperance, it is hereby stipulated that if any of the members of the said Mendawakanton and Wahpakoota bands of Sioux Indians shall drink, or procure for others, intoxicating liquors, their proportion of the annuities of said bands shall, at the discretion of the Secretary of the Interior, be withheld from them for the period of at least one year; and for a violation of any of the stipulations of this agreement on the part of any members of said bands, the persons so offending shall be liable to have their annuities withheld, and to be subject to such other punishment as the Secretary of the Interior may prescribe.

"ARTICLE VIII. Such of the stipulations of former treaties as provided for the payment of particular sums of money to the said Mendawakanton and Wahpakoota bands, or for the application or expenditure of specific amounts for particular objects or purposes, shall be, and hereby are, so amended and changed as to invest the Secretary of the Interior with discretionary power in regard to the manner and objects of the annual expenditure of all such sums or amounts which have accrued and are now due to said bands, together with the amount the said bands shall become annually entitled to under and by virtue of the provisions of this agreement: *Provided*, The said sums or amounts shall be expended for the benefit of said bands at such time or times, and in such manner as the said Secretary shall deem best calculated to promote their interests, welfare, and advance in civilization. And it is further agreed, that such change may be made in the stipulations of former treaties which provide for the payment of particular sums for specified purposes, as to permit the chiefs and braves of said bands, or any of the subdivisions of said bands, with the sanction of the Secretary of the Interior, to authorize such payment or expenditures of their annuities, or any portion thereof, which are to become due hereafter, as may be deemed best for the general interests and welfare of the said bands or subdivisions thereof."

The same difficulty existing with the Sisseton and Wahpaton bands of the Sioux, under their treaty of July 23rd, 1851, a new treaty was also made with them, of the date of June 19th, 1858, containing nearly the same provisions as the treaty with the other bands.

Both of the foregoing treaties were ratified, without amendment, by the President, March 31st, 1859.

The treaty of 1858, providing for the survey and allotment of eighty acres in severalty to each head of a family, and to each person under twenty-one years of age, placed the Sioux bands in position for civilization, and the energies of government were pointed in that direction. An attempt had been made soon after the treaty of 1837 to induce the Sioux to learn agriculture, by appointing farmers amongst them; but it was thoroughly demonstrated that an Indian would not become a farmer until he could be protected in the enjoyment of the fruits of his labor.

In 1835 attempts were successfully made to introduce Christianity among the Sioux, and from that time civilization began to attract their attention. In 1856 the "Hazelwood Republic" was formed, by the association of a few of the Sissetons and Wah-pay-tons most advanced in civilization, who desired to throw off their tribal relations. They elected a president and council, and a part of them put on the white man's dress. In the fall of 1857 twelve families of the Menda-wah-kan-tons and Wah-pah-koo-tah bands formed a similar association, and bound themselves to wear the white man's dress, and refrain from the use of spirituous liquors. During the year ending September 30th, 1858, some forty-five houses were built for individuals of the two latter bands, and from two to five acres ploughed about each house. Among the Sisseton and Wah-pay-ton bands nine houses were put up, mainly by the Indians, and some fields cultivated. The machinery of three steam saw-mills was sent for, and special efforts made for future improvement. The Hon. Joseph R. Brown had been appointed Indian agent for the Sioux, and being a man of judgment and ability, and long connected with those Indians as a trader, he well understood their necessities, and set himself vigorously at work to improve their condition.

Previous to the treaty of 1858, nearly a million of money had been expended by the government for the civilization of these Indians; but in despair the Commissioner of Indian Affairs stated in his official report of November, 1857, that "they have been indolent, extravagant, and intemperate, and have wasted their means without improving, or seeming to desire to improve their condition."

The inducements held out to the Indians for going to farming, under the treaty of 1858, was to give each Indian eighty acres of land, a yoke of oxen, one wagon, farming utensils and seed, and help him build a good, comfortable house, and break and fence a portion of the land. The evidence required of the Indians as a pledge on their part that they would continue as farmers, was that they should submit to have their hair cut in American style, and thereby lose their " scalp lock," and that they should put on the American dress.

In 1859, the agent reported that over two hundred, principally heads of families, including some chiefs, who had been " shorn of the scalp lock," had presented themselves as candidates for farmers, and were contemptuously called by their brethren the " white Indians." Thus these favorable omens of civilization were accompanied by sneers and the contemptuous treatment of other portions of the tribe, which at times extended to open violence. Much of this opposition was generated by the " medicine men," or pagan priests, who correctly imagined that the complete success of this movement would destroy their occupation and influence; hence they were assiduous in stirring up opposition. To defend the farmer Indians, the agent was obliged to call for military assistance from the United States troops.

During 1859, government furnished seeds and agricultural implements to the value of $2,450, and oxen, wagons, and plows to the value of $17,000, and plowed 1,816 acres of land. The machinery for three saw-mills, two shingle and two lath mills, were put in operation, and a considerable amount of lumber manufactured.

The educational department was not neglected, and two buildings for superintendent of schools, and two for manual labor schools, and some other school-houses were erected, at the aggregate expense of $2,985, and several schools put in operation.

Captain Gibson, of the second artillery, who attended at the payments to the Sioux in June, 1860, in his official dispatch, speaking of the Indian improvements, said: "The agent began this movement in 1858 with sixteen Indians, who were persuaded by Superintendent Cullen to be shorn of their 'scalp locks,' and put on the white man's dress. . . . The next year, two of the most noted chiefs, Wabashaw and Wakute, with more than a hundred others, submitted to the same ordeal. . . . Without the aid and shield of government, the farming Indian could not continue his work one moment; without that assurance, not one would dare to throw off the blanket; protection is the salvation of this work. . . . For want of protection, the 'Hazelwood Republic,' that commenced auspiciously, has already been broken up by the hostilities, the unchecked and still unpunished depredations and murders committed by the neighboring bands."

But in the midst of their prosperity came also adversity, and the demon of 1861 hurled his arrows of sorrow at the poor Sioux. Consequent upon the change of President was the change of officers connected with the civilization of the tribe, and the poor Sioux, who had so patiently toiled under the direction of the genial face of Hon. J. R. Brown, were obliged to look upon the strange face of a new agent. The troops which had protected them were withdrawn, to go to the defence of Washington, and the vague rumors of the great rebellion crept slowly into the suspicious mind of the untutored savage.

The new agent of schools found " scarcely a building on the reservation adapted for any kind of school use," and that, " if schools are kept, additions must be made to the shells called school buildings;" and further, that " not one dollar has been received from any quarter applicable to school purposes since my appointment, the first of June last, consequently but little has been done upon which to report." He even "discontinued the manual labor school."

The general agent for the Sioux, October 1st, 1861, reported that a military force was necessary, and further remarked: "I will simply say that there is no available force now for this purpose, and that if such force is not provided, the work of civilization must be greatly retarded, if not abandoned." The $6,000 received by the agent to pay the employees, was partly applied to settle their claims from April 1st to June 30th, 1861, leaving a small balance to apply on the future quarter.

Finally, October 5th, of the same year, the acting Commissioner of Indian Affairs called on the government for "seven companies, of one hundred each, of troops, one of which should be cavalry, as a guard for the frontier." These difficulties, which alarmed the government, were said by agent Thompson to have been caused by:

"1st. The allowance, by the department at Washington, last year, of a claim of $5,500, which was deducted from their annuity.

"2nd. The renewal of old questions by the Yanktons, in which they claim that they were part owners of the lands sold to the government by the treaty of 1851, by which the Sissetons and Wahpaytons, bands of Sioux, should be allowed to share in the annuities."

The Indians were temporarily pacified, however, at the payment, September 16th, at "Yellow Medicine," by the "presence of two companies of troops from Fort Ridgley, and by liberal presents of beef cattle," and liberal promises. The troops demanded by the commissioner of Indian affairs were not furnished by government, the difficulties and robberies accumulated, and the following year culminated in the "Sioux massacre."

CHAPTER XII.

THE SIOUX MASSACRE.

The Sioux massacre, coming so unexpectedly, like the avalanche from the mountain, and having been so destructive in its brief course, shocked the whole Union with horror; and the professional letter-writers, really ignorant of its origin, divided their invectives between the depravity of the Indian and the depravity of Thomas J. Galbraith, Esq., the Indian agent. A few, however, opponents of civilization and Christianity, with supercilious smiles, asked you to look at "the effects of twenty-seven years of missionary labor," and then turned on their heels with the most profound contempt for all the missionary labors of the world.

Through the country the reports of the cause of the massacre might be divided about as follows: The whisky-sellers charged it directly on the missionaries, with whom they were in open hostility. The traders charged it upon the agent, for delaying the payments so that he could speculate by exchanging the gold, which bore a large premium, for greenbacks, the traders having expected to reap a great harvest in getting the gold on their Indian debts, and thereby securing the premium for themselves. The cunning republican, who wanted to make a little capital for his party, charged the massacre to the influence of "rebel sympathizers;" and those "sympathizers," in return, charged it on the imbecility of the administration. The land speculators, who imagined that they could see fortunes in the tidy Indian houses and farms, charged the troubles to the total depravity of the Indian character; but some of the good missionaries, more charitable to their immediate neighbors, charged the whole affair to his majesty the devil, who was then engaged in one of his raids on mankind.

The people of Minnesota at large, believing that the most of the charges were true, clamored for the unconditional removal or extermination of the whole nation of Sioux, and accompanied their clamor with such threats as satisfied the government that they were in earnest; hence the government kept such Indians as had surrendered themselves under a military guard until the spring of 1863, when the most of them were sent and located high up the Missouri river.

Agent Galbraith, to turn the attention of the public away from himself, declared, in his report on the causes of the massacre, that "ignorance, indolence, filth, lust, vice, bigotry, superstition and crime, make up the ancient customs of the Sioux Indians, and they adhere to the code with a tenacity and stoicism indefinable." In speaking of the "hereditary war" between the Sioux and Chippeways, the agent ignored the fact, and declared that, "There is no war or cause of war existing." "The *feather* is the cause of those malicious murders committed on the Chippeways, and to get 'the feather,' they would just as soon kill any body else as a Chippeway."

It is too late in the nineteenth century to ignore that "hereditary war," for it is a notorious fact in Indian history, that that war has continued, with slight intervals, from 1700 to the present time, and that during that one hundred and sixty-seven years, the Sioux have been driven from Lake Superior to west of the Mississippi, and that among the numerous villages vacated to the victorious Chippeways, was Mille Lac, where was the seat of the

Dakota Confederacy in 1680, and where, by the Sioux traditions, they were created.

It is equally in conflict with history that the Sioux are so degraded and vicious, or such "inveterate cowards." Three successive attacks on Fort Ridgley, under a shower of shells from the cannon in the fort, besides a heavy fire of musketry, the last attack lasting nearly five hours, ought of itself to clear the Indians of the charge of cowardice; and their delivering up several hundred captives without ransom, ought to be passed to the credit of their " total depravity."

The Sioux, like the other tribes of Indians, have their peculiar manners and customs, with which the whites have long since become familiar, among which are killing women and children in war. Such being the Indian custom, we have almost uniformly retaliated in kind, and it has long since been understood, that an Indian war is extermination on both sides. This system of extermination was practiced in the King Philip's war by the people of Massachusetts, by the Dutch of Manhattan, and the battle of Bad Ax showed no change. Even in this Sioux war we have taken comparatively no prisoners, except such as the civilized Indians voluntarily delivered up to General Sibley, thirty-three of whom were tried, convicted, and hung, for aiding in the war, and nearly two hundred and seventy more were lately under the sentence of death, which the President refused to carry into effect.

But agent Galbraith evidently comes nearer the merits of the cause of the war, when he states in his report that the Sioux " recited that, at the treaty, it was promised them that each one of them should have one blanket at least every year, and plenty of pork, flour and sugar to eat, and that every hunter should have his gun, and all the ammunition he wanted; that white men would be hired to do all their work, and that coffee, tea, tobacco, hatchets, and such like, in large quantities, would be furnished them, and they should have 'all they wanted;' in addition to all of which things, money to the amount of $40,000 to the upper, and $46,000 to the lower bands, would be paid to them every year, and that they should be taken care of and never suffer from want any more." . . . "With such statements every speech teemed, whether made to the agent, superintendent, or in their own councils."

The agent further remarked in his report: "In addition to the natural hostility of the wild Indians to the white men, I soon discovered that evil-disposed white men, and half-breeds in their interest, were engaged in keeping up this hostility, and in fomenting discontent." . . . "Although my partiality to the white party was looked upon with great jealousy, yet I kept on as best I could, from the commencement until the outbreak, in aiding the work of civilization. During my term, and up to the time of the outbreak, about one hundred and seventy-five Indian men had their hair cut, and had adopted the habits and customs of white men." These, with the one hundred and twenty-five which had been civilized under agent Brown, made three hundred men, mostly heads of families. To see these three hundred receive each a suit of clothes, oxen, wagon, grain, farming utensils, house, and eighty acres of land of the value of more than five hundred dollars, while the blanket Indians could not get even their necessary subsistence, tended to keep alive these jealousies, which were constantly fomented by the whisky-sellers, who had been banished from the tribe for the protection of this very civilization.

This experiment at civilization was a part of the system which government had extended to most of the tribes that had lived on the borders of civilization, and it was the duty of government to protect it at all hazard against its enemies, either white or copper-colored. It was based on philanthropy for the race, for it has become definitely settled that the only other alternative is extermination, to which the whisky-seller is most happily devoted.

Such being the condition of the tribe, and the almost positive certainty of an outbreak on the first exciting cause, the Commissioner of Indian Affairs at Washington, as early as October 5th, 1861, called for seven companies of troops, of one hundred to each company, for "a guard to the frontier;" but Secretary Stanton, of the war department, neglected to furnish the guard, and when the outbreak occurred, nearly a year after, even Fort Ridgley was guarded by only eighty soldiers, while the whole frontier beyond was destitute of a single soldier.

About the 25th of June, 1862, near the usual time of making the Indian payments, several chiefs and head men of the Sissetons and Wah-pay-tons visited the agency, and inquired about the payments, and whether they were going to get any money, alleging that they had been told that they were not to be paid. Again, on the 13th of July, some 4,000 of the upper bands of the annuity Indians, with nearly 1,000 of the Yanktons, assembled at the agency. The agent inquired what they came for, and they "answered that they were afraid something was wrong; they feared they would not get their money, because white men had been telling them so." As the money was due and daily expected, the Indians were unwilling to return home, and there was but a limited supply of provisions to feed them. As day after day passed away, the Indians began to complain of starvation; and, finally, on the 4th of August, to the number of nearly five hundred and fifty, they broke open the warehouse, and carried off one hundred sacks of flour.

This outbreak was compromised the next day, by giving the Indians, at their request, their annuity goods, and a supply of provisions, and on the 9th of August they left for home.

During this time the Indians became informed of the defeat of General McClellan on the peninsula, and the call for 600,000 more troops by the President.

As soon as the Indians left, the war fever broke out

16*

among the employees of government and half-breeds at the agency, and the Indian agent, Galbraith, left with a party of these volunteers on the 13th day of August, for Redwood, where he enlisted some twenty more on the 14th. On the 15th, he proceeded to Fort Ridgley, and from thence, on the 16th, he changed his base to New Ulm; and on the fatal 18th, in the morning, the "Renville Rangers," fifty-five strong, might have been seen, under Captain Galbraith, filing out of New Ulm, and winding their serpentine course towards St. Peter. War fevers are known to be contagious, but the captain does not charge that it extended to the "cowardly" Sioux, although he asserted that Little Crow had repeatedly said to him: "When I arose this morning and looked towards the south, it seemed to me that I could see the smoke of the big guns, and hear the war-whoop of the contending soldiers."

From all the investigations made, no evidence was found that this outbreak was stimulated by rebel agents or sympathizers, nor that it was a preconcerted conspiracy; but, on the contrary, Little Crow himself had promised to have his hair cut and civilize, and the government was engaged in building his house, whilst he was contributing his personal attention to its erection, and three days before he expressed himself to the agent satisfied with its progress.

The proximate cause of this outbreak may therefore be summed up as originating:

1st. From the general dissatisfaction of the Indians over the treaty and the efforts at civilization, in a great measure generated by the whisky-sellers and traders.

2nd. The neglect of the Treasurer to make the payment in the usual time.

3rd. The neglect of the Secretary of War to furnish the guard for the frontier, as demanded by the Commissioner of Indian Affairs.

4th. The war fever, and the belief of the Indians that the

most of the men had left the country to go to the war, and that they were abandoned by the agent without payment.

There were doubtless many other difficulties that affected the bands to some extent; but, with less than these, the Chippeways commenced an outbreak at nearly the same time, which was happily put down by a military force, and the presence of the Commissioner of Indian Affairs, then on their way to Red river.

There was, however, a more direct, exciting cause, which ignited the tinder of their discontent, which occurred as follows: On Sunday, August 17, 1862, at the village of Acton, Meeker county, Minnesota, four of the Lower Sioux, of *Sha-ka-pee's* band, part of a hunting party of fourteen, returning from an expedition against the Chippeways, obtained whisky, became intoxicated, and killed six persons, including a man named Jones, from whom it was alleged they obtained the whisky. This party returned to their village at Rice creek, called a council of their relatives, and, according to agent Galbraith's report, discussed the matter as follows: "We have killed white men, and if caught, must die. Let us unite *now* and kill the whites at the agency. It is a good time to carry out our original and long-cherished designs. The whites are all gone to the war except the old men and women and children. We can kill them all, take their property, and repossess ourselves of the land which we sold them, and occupy it." The agent further reports that "This harangue and others like it had the desired effect. About twenty warriors at once united into a war party, and started for Redwood creek, and towards the agency. As they proceeded they were joined by the warriors of the bands of Sha-ka-pee, Little Crow, Black Dog, or Big Eagle, Blue Earth, and Passing Hail, all ripe for the work proposed. These bands all had their villages and plantings from four to ten miles above the lower agency, and most of their young men and soldiers belonged to the soldiers' lodge.

"By daylight on Monday, the 18th of August, this war party, now increased to about two hundred soldiers, armed and fierce for the fray, proceeded to the lower agency, having sent messengers to the bands of Saopi, Wabasha, Wakuta, Late-Comedu, and Husha-sha, who resided above and below the agency, informing them of the purpose, and asking and ordering them to join the war party forthwith, on pain of being punished, even to death, in case of refusal. As soon as the news of the uprising spread, the young men of these bands rushed up to the agency, and excitedly joined the war party, now being momentarily augmented in numbers, and stimulated with courage and resolution." . . .
"Many of the chiefs, old men and farmer Indians (generally friendly to the whites), remonstrated and even protested, but all was in vain; 'the die was cast;' madness ruled the hour. About six o'clock on this sad and eventful Monday morning, the work of death and devastation began."

This was an attack at the lower agency, fifteen miles above Fort Ridgley, on the trading house of Stewart B. Garvie, known as "Myrick's." It spread to the other stores, and soon reached the government stables, warehouses, shops and dwellings, which were plundered and burned, the people fleeing in all directions, panic-stricken. Some were shot down, some captured, and the balance fled for their lives.

According to the report of the agent, Little Crow and his associate chiefs, in the beginning intended to make regular war, but they failed to control their young warriors, and it soon turned into a massacre after the style of the eighteenth century.

News of the outbreak reached the Sisseton and Wahpay-ton bands in the afternoon, and after a division in council, one hundred and fifty of those bands resolved to join the war party, and at two o'clock the next morning attacked another store of Mr. Garvie, mortally wounding him, and seriously Mr. Patwell. The balance of the traders of that locality fled and escaped.

LITTLE CROW. OTHER-DAY.

At Yellow Medicine and Hazelwood missions, the missionaries and government employees, numbering twenty-two men and forty women and children, left the agency at early dawn of Tuesday morning, under the advice and guidance of Ampe-tu-to-kecha, or Other Day, a full-blooded Christian Indian chief, struck out into the open prairie, and in four days reached Shakopee village, above St. Paul, on the Minnesota river.

Rev. S. R. Riggs and Dr. T. S. Williamson, with teachers, assistants, and others, numbering forty-five, of the old Dakota mission, left Monday night, struck out into the prairie, and reached the settlements on the 24th, guided by Chaska and some other Christian Indians.

On Monday, at nine o'clock in the forenoon, news reached Fort Ridgley of the outbreak at the agency at Redwood, and Captain Marsh, with about fifty of his soldiers, left for the agency, but were attacked at the ford near the agency, and badly cut to pieces, with the loss of the captain and twenty-three men killed; fifteen, however, succeeded in returning to the fort the same evening. At twelve o'clock, noon, of Monday, the gold for the Indian payment reached Fort Ridgley, having left New York by express August 11, only seven days previous.

On Tuesday morning Captain Galbraith returned to the fort with fifty of his "Renville Rangers," which had been armed at St. Peter, and about the same hour Lieutenant Sheehan, of company C, 5th regiment, reached the fort with a force of fifty men. On Monday, about eleven in the forenoon, Indian parties commenced pillaging and murdering about the country.

After sacking the lower agency, the Indians, on Tuesday, the 19th, moved their camp to Little Crow's village, some four miles above, as a base for further operations, while a considerable force was dispatched to attack New Ulm, and several foraging parties were sent out in other directions.

The attack on New Ulm commenced on Tuesday, at three o'clock in the afternoon, but was successfully resisted by the inhabitants, who were reinforced by Captain Flandreau's cavalry at six o'clock in the afternoon, when the Indians were charged and driven away with some loss. This Indian force was estimated at over two hundred, but from the small amount of damage done to the town, the estimate was probably too high.

Failing in their attack on New Ulm, this force, with probably some additions, left for Fort Ridgley, distant eighteen miles, where they arrived at three o'clock in the afternoon of Wednesday, and marching up to the gateways and windows, fired a murderous volley at the men and women in the fort. According to the report of Lieutenant-Governor Donnelly, of Minnesota, made at Fort Ridgley the 29th of the same month:

"It was a surprise. The first announcement was a volley fired through one of the openings or entrances into the parade ground of the fort, doing at once deadly execution. The men were rallied to their posts. Sergeant Jones, ordnance sergeant, attempted to use his guns, but, to his surprise, found they would not work. A howitzer was brought into play, and in the mean time the sergeant drew the charges from his pieces, and found that old rags had been stuffed into them. This was the critical moment. Had the courage of the Indians been equal to the opportunity, the fort would have fallen. The garrison was alarmed, the women and children screamed with uncontrollable panic, and the guns for a time disabled. But the moment passed, never to return."

In reading the foregoing extract, we must bear in mind that Fort Ridgley was a government fort, and contained the remnant of Captain Marsh's company, fifty men under Lieutenant Sheehan, Captain Galbraith and fifty "Renville Rangers," $71,000 in gold for the Indian payment, and a large number of women, children, and refugees from the devastated country; and in open daylight, with the heavens lurid with burning buildings, and while their "war dogs" were stuffed with old rags, those "cowardly, sneaking, vicious Indians," set on by the "devil," were allowed to sneak up to the fort and fire a murderous volley at the men, women and children in the inside! No wonder that the brave Captain Galbraith should hold such Indians in such contempt, for firing on the "Renville Rangers!"

The report of the Lieutenant-Governor further says, " that the Indians continued the fight for three and a quarter hours, from the high grass and behind out-houses, logs, and every other object that could afford them shelter." The uneducated in Indian warfare will hardly be able to comprehend why a fort in an Indian country should be surrounded with such conveniences for "cowardly" Indians; but it is possible that the brave Captain Galbraith might enlighten us on this subject. This battle, however, was not very fatal to life, as there were only three killed and eight wounded in the fort.

The following day, Thursday, the attack on the fort was renewed at 9 o'clock, A. M., for half an hour, and at ten minutes to 6 o'clock, P. M., it was again renewed for another half hour.

On Friday, at ten minutes before 2 o'clock, P. M., a third

attack was made on the fort. This continued for nearly five hours, and was "most determined, bitter, and persistent, the guns sounding in one continuous rattle;" and "at one time a charging party was placed close to the fort, and the half-breeds could hear the chiefs shouting to the warriors to charge into the fort and seize the cannon; but without avail; their courage was not equal to the task." In this attack one was killed, and a few slightly wounded in the fort.

Failing in this final attack on the fort, the Indians, on Saturday morning, moved again upon New Ulm, and again attacked that place at half-past 11 o'clock, A. M. In a few minutes the Indians had fifteen houses in flames, and carried on their work of destruction with bravery until 5 o'clock, P. M., when Captain Flandreau rallied his cavalry, and at their head charged the Indians in the brushwood at the lower end of the town, driving them out. This partially relieved the town for the night. During the night, while the Indians were having their war dances near by, the forces in town contracted their line of defence, and burnt the buildings outside of the line, so that they would not afford a shelter to the savages.

On Sunday morning the attack was renewed at long range for an hour, the Indians not daring to charge across the ground made vacant during the night, after which they withdrew. During the siege ten men were killed and about fifty wounded. The Indian loss was supposed to be nearly forty. About noon a reinforcement of one hundred and fifty, under Captain Cox, arrived from St. Peter, and the following day New Ulm was evacuated without molestation.

After the repulse at New Ulm, Little Crow broke camp, and changed his base to Yellow Medicine, distant twenty-five miles above Little Crow's village, which took two days, as the train of teams loaded with plunder, etc., was nearly five miles long. At the head of this procession was unfurled an old British flag, while several American flags gave a military aspect to this dusky line.

At Yellow Medicine some time was spent in councils, and dispatches were sent off to the western band of Sioux, and to the British at the Selkirk settlement, notifying them that the Sioux had declared war against the United States, and asking them for their assistance. In these councils, "Little Crow" urged that they should immediately remove to the Selkirk settlement, and put themselves under the protection of the British, but he was overruled by the other chiefs. While encamped here, "Standing Buffalo," with two hundred warriors of the upper Sissetons, came down, and in council demanded of "Little Crow" the plunder taken at Yellow Medicine agency, as belonging to his band; but "Little Crow" refused, as he had done the fighting and was entitled to the plunder. "Standing Buffalo" then refused coöperation with "Little Crow," and returned home with his warriors, with some threats against the belligerent parties; but it is claimed that some of his young warriors afterwards took part with "Little Crow."

On the 28th of August, in the morning, Colonel Sibley arrived at Fort Ridgley with a detachment of troops for the relief of the fort, and to carry on offensive operations against the Indians. Three days after, Colonel Sibley sent out a detachment under Major Brown, consisting of one company of infantry under Captain Grant, and a company of cavalry under Captain Anderson, to reconoiter the country above the fort, and bury the dead. On the second morning, at daybreak, at their camp in Birch Coolie, this detachment were wakened from their slumbers by a deadly volley from over three hundred Indians, distant only one hundred and twenty-five yards. The horses and cattle were soon all killed by the enemy, and became breast-works for our men; the men also dug holes in the ground for their protection. Here they were held in siege until 11 o'clock the next morning, when they were relieved by Colonel Sibley; the loss on our side was twenty-four killed and sixty-seven wounded. The same day these troops were relieved, "Little Crow" in person, with one hundred and fifty warriors, made an attack on the town of Henderson, but were repulsed. They succeeded, however, in carrying off some plunder. About the same time a considerable force attacked Fort Abercrombie, on Red river, but were repulsed.

Colonel Sibley, having succeeded in arming his new troops, and in obtaining for them ten days' provisions, on the 18th of September he ordered an advance, crossed the river and pushed on for the Yellow Medicine agency, and arrived at Wood Lake, near the agency, on the evening of the 22nd. On the morning of the 23rd, the Indians in force attacked Colonel Sibley in camp some time after sunrise.

The Indians occupied the high grass, and had disguised themselves by tying tufts of grass around their heads and waists. The battle thus progressed until nearly noon, when the Indians, congregating in a ravine on our right, Colonel Sibley ordered the 7th regiment Minnesota volunteers to charge them. This charge was led by Lieutenant-Colonel Marshall, and the Indians were routed and put to flight. Unfortunately, however, Colonel Sibley had no sufficient mounted force to pursue the fleeing savages. In this charge, no prisoners were taken, and the wounded Indians were bayoneted by the first soldier who reached them; and their repeated cry of "me good Indian," was only answered with the bayonet and a curse.

The advance of Colonel Sibley had induced the Indians to remove their camp twenty miles further up the Minnesota river, above Yellow Medicine, where they were at the time of this decisive battle.

The fugitive Indians made no further stand, but fled immediately to their camp, and hastened the departure of their families for the wilds of the upper Missouri river; while those opposed to the war, and some others, took the prisoners, established for themselves a new camp, which they entrenched the same night, and sent a flag of truce to Colonel Sibley, offering to surrender themselves and prisoners.

On the 26th, at noon, Colonel Sibley reached this friendly camp, and marching partly round them, camped near the river, taking possession of the Indian camp, and relieving one hundred and fifty helpless women and children who were held as prisoners.

Lieutenant-Colonel Marshall was dispatched with two hundred men in pursuit of "Little Crow," but only succeeded in capturing by surprise a small band at Wild-Goose-Nest lake. "Little Crow" and his followers had separated into small parties, in the region of the Coteau Des Prairies, and Lieutenant-Colonel Marshall abandoned the pursuit, returning about the 21st of October, to "Camp Release," which name Colonel Sibley had applied to the friendly Indian camp.

In the mean time, Colonel Sibley had caused a log house to be erected in camp for a court house, and had organized a military commission to try these Indians, who had surrendered themselves, for murder. This commission, composed of Colonel Crooks, Lieutenant-Colonel Marshall, Captains Grant and Bayley, and Lieutenant Olin, progressed with their work until they convicted and sentenced to be hung three hundred and three, and to imprisonment for life eighteen, which were the greater part of all the male prisoners then secured. The finding of the commission was sent to Washington for the approval of the President. The Commissioner of Indian Affairs remonstrated against the execution of the sentence, and the President ratified the finding on thirty-eight of the most guilty, who were accordingly hung at Camp Lincoln, near Mankato, on the 26th day of December, 1862. Subsequently two others were hung at Fort Snelling. The ill-fated Indians, with characteristic decorum, ascended the platform singing their death-song, and in one long line, holding each other by the hand, they were sent to their final hunting-grounds, the Indian's elysium. The balance of the prisoners were kept under a strong military guard, to protect them from the repeated attempts of the mob to murder them; and on the opening of navigation the following spring, they were sent to Davenport.

The balance of the Sioux, being mostly women and children, about fifteen hundred, were shipped by steamer in May, 1863, to Crow creek, about one hundred miles above Fort Randall, on the Missouri river, where they were deposited, surrounded by a stockade fort, protected by a military force, and fed and clothed by government. No annuities have been paid the Sioux since the outbreak. Our losses during the difficulties were estimated by the Indian agent at 644 of men, women and children in the several massacres, and ninety-three soldiers killed in the various battles. We have no estimates of the losses of the Indians.

On the 29th of May, 1863, "Little Crow," and a party of about eighty, visited the British at Fort Garry, on the Red River of the north, and asked for assistance. Governor Dallas only gave them some provisions, but positively refused them ammunition. "Little Crow" complained that they were badly treated in the war, for that, while he yielded up the white prisoners, the whites had hung the Indian prisoners; and that they then had no alternative but to either fight or be hung, unless they could make peace on fair terms, which they much desired; and asked the governor to intercede for them.

But little was accomplished by the military forces in 1865, towards subjugating the Sioux. General Sully made a campaign from Fort Rice to Devil's Lake and Mouse river, and returned to Fort Sully by way of Fort Berthol, without meeting any considerable number of Indians. At the latter fort he heard that the Indians, numbering about 10,000, were encamped about fifty miles south-west, but with his small force of about 900 he did not deem it prudent to attack them. General Sully, however, reported that bands, numbering nearly 3,000 warriors, had made peace with him in 1864 and 1865.

During the summer of 1865 there was a difference of opinion between the War and Indian departments, as to the question of peace with the Sioux; but late in August they agreed on a joint commission to visit the upper Missouri, and conclude a peace, composed of Governor Edmonds, of Dakota Territory, Major-General Curtis, Superintendent Taylor, General Sibley, Rev. H. W. Reed, and Hon. Orrin Guernsey.

This commission visited the Upper Missouri country, and made treaties of peace with the following bands of the Sioux; Two Kettles, or Teton, Lower Brulé, Oncpapas, Minneconjous, Yanktonais, Sans Arcs, Upper Yanktonais, Ogallallas, and Black Feet. These bands were estimated at 16,020 souls. These treaties were ratified and proclaimed at Washington, March 17, 1866, and provide for a right of way through their country, and allow any of their people to become agriculturalists. Treaties were also made with the Assiniboins and Crows, securing the right of transit and small cessions of land, including Fort Union.

The Peace Commissioners having recommended that the Sioux of Crow creek be removed to a new reservation, Superintendent Taylor selected six townships at the mouth of the Niobrara river, in Nebraska, for the new reservation, and in June, 1866, the Indians of Crow creek, and the Davenport prisoners, were settled upon the new reservation; those prisoners having been pardoned by the President on the recommendation of their missionary and the war authorities.

A portion of the Christian Indians, who had rendered special service to the whites at the massacre, and afterwards acted as scouts to the troops, still occupied the old reservation in Minnesota; "but," said the Commissioner of Indian Affairs, in April, 1866, "many of these men have, for the past three years, been homeless wanderers, and actually suffering from want; a very poor return for services rendered to the whites at the risk of their lives." . . . "Action was taken by the department about a year ago, to select for them eighty acres of land each, upon the old reservation, but the feeling among the whites is such as to make it impossible for them to live there in safety."

These Sioux numbered in 1866, according to their missionary, two hundred and fifty, and contained, among others of like merit: An-pe-tu-to-ke-cha, or "Other Day," who "guided sixty-two missionaries and employees of Yellow Medicine and Hazelwood to Shakopee village, near St. Paul;" Taopi, or "Wounded Man," a chief who was "the leader in the rescue of two hundred and fifty prisoners;" Paul-maza-ker-ta-mane, who "openly denounced in council the hostile Indians, and at all times, at the risk of his life, declared his fidelity to" the whites; To-wante-toma, called Lorenzo Lawrence, who "at the risk of his life rescued ten white captives, and brought them to Fort Ridgley;" Simon An-ang-mani, who rescued four captives and brought them to Fort Ridgley; Wah-kin-yan-wash-to, or "Good Thunder," who assisted "Taopi," and "was threatened with death by 'Little Crow;'" Zoe Ha-pa, a squaw, who "at great risk brought provisions to the island where Rev. Mr. Riggs and party were secreted."

There were other inconsistencies among some of the people in Minnesota. New Ulm, a village where the massacre fell heaviest, was settled by German infidels, who, by the papers of the day, were reported as having burnt Jesus Christ in effigy, only a few days before the massacre. When the 25th regiment Wisconsin volunteers were stationed in the village for their protection, the chaplain asked for the use of the town hall, in which to have Sabbath religious services, there being no church, and was denied; whereupon, Colonel Montgomery marched his regiment into the hall, and Rev. T. C. Golden, the Methodist chaplain, preached the first Christian sermon in the village. Some of the religious writers of the day placed New Ulm in that class of villages which was headed by Sodom, and raised the question whether New Ulm was not punished for her unrighteousness.

In the spring of 1866, the Minnesota Sioux petitioned the Commissioner of Indian Affairs for leave to settle on the new reservation at Niobrara, which was granted; but as government could not arrange for their removal in time to put in a crop, their removal had not taken place in October.

Another party of Minnesota Sioux, who fled with "Little Crow," consisting of about eight hundred and fifty, have surrendered to General Sibley, protesting that they took no part in the massacre; and the Commissioner of Indian Affairs has recommended that they be located on a reservation near Fort Wardsworth, on the Missouri river. The treaty commissioners, however, failed to make any satisfactory treaty with them up to September, 1866, and they still remained in the region of Fort Wardsworth.

During all the trials incident to this unfortunate Indian war, the powers of the missionaries were brought in requisition to ease the misfortunes of the prisoners and persecuted friendly Sioux; and during 1866, Rev. Mr. Hinman and Bishop Whipple attended to the interest of those in Minnesota, Rev. John P. Williamson, at Crow creek and Niobrara, while Rev. Mr. Riggs had attended on the prisoners at Davenport the most of the time during their confinement.

The Yankton band, during the war, gave no aid or comfort to their brothers in arms, and in 1866 cultivated over 1,000 acres of corn, on their reservation on the Missouri river. According to the agent's report, October 1st, 1866, they were "peaceable, contented, and to a limited degree industrious." There are neither schools or missionaries among the Yanktons, or any other of the ten bands of Sioux in Dakota territory.

Those of the Minnesota Sioux who continued hostile to government in 1866, are reported to be in the region of Fort Garry, in the British possessions.

In the spring of 1867, General Sherman organized a strong military force against the hostile Indians, and the war, it is hoped, will close with a satisfactory peace during the summer.

CHAPTER XIII.

THE OJIBWA CONFEDERACY.

This tribe call themselves *Ojibwa*, or Leapers, contracting the name from people at the leaping water, or falls; hence the French called them *Saulteurs*, and the Sioux, *Hah-hah-ton-wah*. The English traders corrupted the word to *Chippeways*, which is the modern pronunciation in the northwest. This was originally a small band of Algonquins, found at the falls at the outlet of Lake Superior in 1641, by the Jesuit missionaries.

When the brave Iroquois had swept the confederate nations from Lake Huron, and with 3,000 warriors had stormed the fortified heights of Mackinaw island, the fugitive nations divided, and part fled to Green Bay, while the balance took shelter in the thick pines of the south shore of Lake Superior. The latter were pursued, and, according to Chippeway tradition, another battle was fought at *Nadowegoning*, or place of Iroquois bones, now believed to be Whitefish Point, at which the Chippeways claimed a complete victory. This was probably about 1652, as the following year the Iroquois were known to be fully engaged in a new war with the Eries near Buffalo, New York.

But this victory is very doubtful, as the confederate nations continued their flight, and in 1660 a small part of them were found at Kewenaw bay; and the greater part at the west end of Lake Superior, in 1665, where they remained until they were driven out by the Sioux in the spring of

1671, and after the peace made by the French with the Iroquois in 1666.

About this time the Christinaux, or Kilistinons, an Algonquin nation inhabiting the country between Lake Superior and Hudson's bay, having obtained arms of the English traders at the latter bay, according to French authority, attacked the Sioux on the north, and thereby became allies with the Chippeways, in a war against the Sioux. This war continued until 1679, when Captain De Lut visited the head of Lake Superior, took possession of the country in the name of the King of France, and made peace between the northern nations and the Assiniboins, the great northern band of the Sioux, without consulting the other bands of the Sioux Confederacy.

This gave offence to the southern bands, but as they were engaged in the war with the Sacs and Foxes, and other tribes of fugitive Algonquin nations of southern Wisconsin and Illinois, they did not appear to have specially continued the war at the north at that time; but subsequently, some of the southern Sioux visiting the northern band of Assiniboins, found among them some of the Kilistinons, and killed them as enemies. This caused a renewal of the war in 1700, in which the Assiniboins joined the northern nations against their own confederacy, the Chippeways uniting with the Kilistinons.

The brave Dakotas of the south, as skillful in diplomacy as in war, negotiated a peace with the Sacs, Foxes, Winnebagoes, and other nations of the Wisconsin and Fox rivers, and in 1702 engaged them to take up arms against the northern alliance. This new combination greatly disgusted the French, as they were using every art in their power to array all the northern nations against the English colonies. They scolded and threatened the Foxes, as the principal offenders, and in 1712 entrapped and massacred a hunting party of nearly 1,000 men, women and children, of the Foxes and Mascotens at Detroit. This war continued for fifty-two years, the French giving their influence for the northern alliance, and twice sending armies from Canada against the Foxes and other nations in southern Wisconsin. Finally, the necessities of the French increasing by the portentous struggle of 1755, they succeeded the previous year in drawing off the Sacs, Foxes, Winnebagoes, and other southern Wisconsin Indians from their Sioux alliance, and engaged them in the great war against the English. The Sioux, however, could never be coaxed into this latter war.

After the fall of Canada, the Sacs and Foxes renewed their war against the Illinois, who had long been allies of the French against them, and extended their conquests into the present State of Iowa; while the Chippeways of the north renewed their war against the Dakotas, which has continued at intervals until the present time. Thus the insignificant band of Ojibwas, by the aid of the French and their continued alliances with the Algonquins, or as called by the Iroquois, the Adirondacks, or bark-eaters, have become the mighty confederacy of Chippeways, and have conquered from the Dakotas all northern Wisconsin and Minnesota.

Various treaties were made with the Chippeways and Ottawas of Michigan, ceding lands to the United States, in the States of Ohio, Indiana and Michigan; but the first treaty of any importance reaching to Lake Superior, was that of the 28th of March, 1836. By this treaty, those tribes ceded all the country from Grand river, Michigan, north to Lake Huron and Lake Superior, and west to the Chocolate river of Lake Superior, and Skonawba river of Green Bay, making, however, several large reservations.

The next important treaty with the Chippeways, was that of July 29, 1837, by which they ceded a large tract of land in the then territory of Wisconsin, described in the treaty as follows:

"Beginning at the junction of the Crow Wing and Mississippi rivers, between twenty and thirty miles above where the Mississippi is crossed by the forty-sixth parallel of north latitude, and running thence to the north point of Lake St. Croix, one of the sources of the St. Croix river; thence to and along the dividing ridge between the waters of Lake Superior and those of the Mississippi, to the sources of the Ocha-sau-sepe, a tributary of the Chippewa river; thence to a point on the Chippewa river, twenty miles below the outlet of Lake De Flambeau; thence to the junction of the Wisconsin and Pelican rivers; thence on an east course twenty-five miles; thence southerly, on a course parallel with that of the Wisconsin river, to the line dividing the territories of the Chippeways and Menominies; thence to the Plover portage; thence along the southern boundary of the Chippewa country, to the commencement of the boundary line dividing it from that of the Sioux, half a day's march below the falls on the Chippewa river; thence with said boundary line to the mouth of Wah-tap river, at its junction with the Mississippi; and thence up the Mississippi to the place of beginning."

In the second article of the treaty it was provided that, "In consideration of the cession aforesaid, the United States agree to make to the Chippeway nation, annually, for the term of twenty years, from the date of the ratification of this treaty, the following payments:

1. Nine thousand five hundred dollars, to be paid in money.

2. Nineteen thousand dollars, to be delivered in goods.

3. Three thousand dollars for establishing three blacksmiths' shops, supporting the blacksmiths, and furnishing them with iron and steel.

4. One thousand dollars for farmers, and for supplying them and the Indians with implements of labor, with grain or seed, and whatever else may be necessary to enable them to carry on their agricultural pursuits.

5. Two thousand dollars in provisions.

6. Five hundred dollars in tobacco.

The third article of the treaty provided that "The sum

of one hundred thousand dollars shall be paid to the half-breeds" by the United States; and the fourth article required the additional sum of $70,000, to "be applied to the payment by the United States, of certain claims against the Indians" by the traders.

By the treaty of October 4, 1842, all the northern portion of Wisconsin was ceded to the United States, by the following boundaries:

"Beginning at the mouth of Chocolate river of Lake Superior; thence north-westwardly across said lake to intersect the boundary line between the United States and the province of Canada; thence up said Lake Superior to the mouth of the St. Louis, or Fond Du Lac river (including all the islands in said lake); thence up said river to the American Fur Company's trading-post, at the southwardly bend thereof, about twenty-two miles from its mouth; thence south, to intersect the line of the treaty of 29th July, 1837, with the Chippeways of the Mississippi; thence along said lake to its south-eastwardly extremity, near the Plover portage on the Wisconsin river; thence north-eastwardly, along the boundary line between the Chippeways and Menominies, to its eastern termination, on the Skanawba river of Green Bay; thence northwardly to the source of Chocolate river; thence down said river to its mouth, the place of beginning."

By Article IV., of the same treaty, it was provided: "In consideration of the foregoing cession, the United States engage to pay to the Chippeway Indians of the Mississippi and Lake Superior, annually, for twenty-five years, $12,500 in specie, $10,500 in goods, $2,000 in provisions and tobacco, $2,000 for the support of two blacksmiths' shops (including pay of smiths, asssistants, and iron, steel, etc.), $1,000 for pay of two farmers, $1,200 for pay of two carpenters, and $2,000 for the support of schools for the Indians parties to this treaty; and further, the United States engage to pay the sum of $5,000 as an agricultural fund, to be expended under the direction of the Secretary of War. And also the sum of $75,000 shall be allowed for the full satisfaction of their debts within the ceded district." Also, the United States paid $15,000 for the half-breeds of the tribe.

The next treaty with the Chippeways was made at Fond Du Lac, of Lake Superior, August 2, 1847, by which they ceded the following tract:

"Beginning at the junction of the Crow Wing and Mississippi rivers; thence up the Crow Wing river to the junction of that river with the Long Prairie river; thence up the Long Prairie river to the boundary line between the Sioux and Chippeway Indians; thence southerly along said boundary line to a lake at the head of Long Prairie river; thence in a direct line to the sources of the Watab river; thence down the Watab to the Mississippi river; thence up the Mississippi to the place of beginning; and also all the interest and claim which the Indians, parties to this treaty, have in a tract of land lying upon and north of Long Prairie river, and called 'One-day's Hunt.'"

For this cession, the United States paid the chiefs of the Lake Superior bands $17,000, and the same to the Mississippi bands of Chippeways; and agreed to pay to the latter bands $1,000 annually for forty-six years.

The foregoing tract of country was purchased by the United States with the view of locating thereon the Winnebagoes and Menominies, but these tribes disliking the tract, subsequently exchanged for other lands.

The most of the Chippeways of Lake Superior being unwilling to remove from the lands which they had ceded by the treaty of 1842, a new treaty was made September 30, 1854, by which those bands ceded to the United States certain additional lands, and received back the reservations at the places of their residence, with other provisions as follows:

"ARTICLE I. The Chippeways of Lake Superior hereby cede to the United States all the lands heretofore owned by them in common with the Chippeways of the Mississippi, lying east of the following boundary line, to wit: Beginning at a point where the east branch of Snake river crosses the southern boundary line of the Chippewa country, running thence up the said branch to its source; thence nearly north, in a straight line, to the mouth of East Savannah river; thence up the St. Louis river to the mouth of East Swan river; thence up the East Swan river to its source; thence in a straight line to the most westerly bend of Vermillion river; and thence down the Vermillion river to its mouth.

"The Chippeways of the Mississippi hereby assent and agree to the foregoing cession, and consent that the whole amount of the consideration money for the country ceded above, shall be paid to the Chippeways of Lake Superior; and in consideration thereof, the Chippeways of Lake Superior hereby relinquish to the Chippeways of the Mississippi, all their interest in and claim to the lands heretofore owned by them in common, lying west of the above boundary line.

"ARTICLE II. The United States agree to set apart and withhold from sale, for the use of the Chippeways of Lake Superior, the following described tracts of land: namely,

"1st. For the L'Anse and Vieux De Sert bands, all the unsold lands in the following townships in the State of Michigan: Township fifty-one north, range thirty-three west; township fifty-one, north, range thirty-two west; the east half of township fifty, north, range thirty-three west; the west half of township fifty, north, range thirty-two west; and all of township fifty-one, north, range thirty-one west, lying west of Huron bay.

"2nd. For the La Point band, and such other Indians as may see fit to settle with them, a tract of land bounded as follows: Beginning on the south shore of Lake Superior, a few miles west of Montreal river, at the mouth of a creek called by the Indians Ke-che-se-be-we-she, running thence south to a line drawn east and west through the center of township forty-seven north; thence west to the west line of said township; thence south, to the south-east corner of township forty-six, north, range thirty-two, west; thence west the width of two townships; thence north the width of two townships; thence west one mile; thence north to the lake shore; thence along the lake shore, crossing Shagwaw-me-quon point, to the place of beginning. Also, two hundred acres on the northern extremity of Madeline island, for a fishing ground.

"3rd. For the other Wisconsin bands, a tract of land lying about Lac De Flambeau, and another tract on Lac Court Orielles, each equal in extent to three townships, the boundaries of which shall be hereafter agreed upon, or fixed, under the direction of the President.

"4th. For the Fond Du Lac bands, a tract of land bounded as follows: Beginning at an island in the St. Louis river, above Knife portage, called by the Indians Paw-paw-sco-me-me-tig; running thence west to the boundary line heretofore prescribed; thence north along said boundary line to the mouth of Savannah river; thence down the St. Louis river to the place of beginning. And if the said tract shall contain less than one hundred thousand acres, a strip of land shall be added on the south thereof, large enough to equal such deficiency.

"5th. For the Grand Portage band, a tract of land bounded as follows: Beginning at a rock a little east of the eastern extremity of Grand Portage bay; running thence along the lake shore to the mouth of a small stream called by the Indians Maw-ske-gwaw-caw-maw-se-be, or Cranberry Marsh river; thence up said stream, across the point to Pigeon river; thence down Pigeon river to a point opposite the starting-point; and thence across to the place of beginning.

"6th. The Ontonagon band, and that subdivision of the La Point band of which 'Buffalo' is chief, may each select on or near the lake shore, four sections of land, under the direction of the President, the boundaries of which shall be defined hereafter. And being desirous to provide for some of his connections who have rendered his people important services, it is agreed that the chief, 'Buffalo,' may select one section of land, at such place in the ceded territory as he may see fit, which shall be reserved for that purpose, and conveyed by the United States to such person or persons as he may direct.

"7th. Each head of a family, or single person over twenty-one years of age at the present time, of the mixed bloods, belonging to the Chippeways of Lake Superior, shall be entitled to eighty acres of land, to be selected by them, under the direction of the President, and which shall be secured to them by patent in the usual form."

This treaty having been made with a view to the civilization of the Indians on the foregoing reservations, the United States further provided for defining the boundaries of said reservations, and for surveying and distributing to each person over twenty-one years of age, eighty acres of the land in severalty; and that missionaries, teachers, and other persons residing with the Indians, might enter their lands to the extent of one hundred and sixty acres each.

The Bois Forte Indians were given the right to select their reservations in proportion to their numbers, to the same extent as other bands.

Spirituous liquors were prohibited from manufacture, sale, or use on the reservations.

The United States paid for said cession, in addition to said reservations, annually for twenty years, $5,000 in coin, $8,000 in goods, $3,000 in agricultural implements, cattle, and building materials, and $3,000 for moral and educational purposes. Also $90,000 to pay their debts, and $6,000 for agricultural implements, household furniture, and cooking utensils, to the half-breeds; and furnished the Indians 200 guns, 100 rifles, 500 beaver traps, $300 worth of ammunition, and $1,000 " worth of ready-made clothing, to be distributed among the young men of the nation, at the next annuity payment."

The United States also, in lieu of previous engagements of the kind, agreed to furnish a blacksmith and assistant, with the usual amount of stock, during the continuance of the annuities, for each of said reservations. In addition, the United States agreed to pay the Bois Forte Indians $10,000 to pay their debts, and $2,000 annually for five years, in goods.

The treaty made February 22nd, 1855, at Washington, between the United States and the Mississippi, Pillager, and Lake Winnibigoshish bands of Chippeways, was probably the most important of any, touching the civilization of these bands, and we therefore copy the first three articles in full, as follows:

"ARTICLE I. The Mississippi, Pillager, and Lake Winnibigoshish bands of Chippeway Indians hereby cede, sell, and convey to the United States all their right, title, and interest in, and to, the lands now owned and claimed by them, in the Territory of Minnesota, and included within the following boundaries, namely: beginning at a point where the east branch of Snake river crosses the southern boundary line of the Chippeway country, east of the Mississippi river, as established by the treaty of July 29th, 1837, running thence, up the said branch, to its source; thence, nearly north in a straight line, to the mouth of East Savannah river; thence, up the St. Louis river, to the mouth of East Swan river; thence, up said river, to its source; thence, in a straight line, to the most westwardly bend of Vermillion river; thence, north-westwardly, in a straight line, to the first and most considerable bend in the Big Fork river; thence, down said river, to its mouth; thence, down Rainy Lake river, to the mouth of Black river; thence, up that river, to its source; thence, in a straight line, to the northern extremity of Turtle lake; thence, in a straight line, to the mouth of Wild Rice river; thence, up Red river of the north, to the mouth of Buffalo river; thence, in a straight line, to the south-western extremity of Otter Tail lake; thence, through said lake, to the source of Leaf river; thence, down said river, to its junction with Crow Wing river; thence, down Crow Wing river, to its junction with the Mississippi river; thence, to the commencement on said river of the southern boundary line of the Chippeway country, as established by the treaty of July 29th, 1837; and thence, along said line, to the place of beginning. And the said Indians do further fully and entirely relinquish and convey to the United States, any and all right, title, and interest, of whatsoever nature the same may be, which they may now have in and to any other lands in the Territory of Minnesota or elsewhere.

"ARTICLE II. There shall be, and hereby is, reserved and set apart, a sufficient quantity of land for the permanent homes of the said Indians; the lands so reserved and set apart to be in separate tracts, as follows, namely:

"For the Mississippi bands of Chippeway Indians: The first to embrace the following fractional townships, namely: forty-two north of range twenty-five west; forty-two north of range twenty-six west; and forty-two and forty-three north of range twenty-seven west; and, also, the three islands in the southern part of Mille Lac. Second, beginning at a point half a mile east of Rabbit lake; thence, south three miles; thence, westwardly in a straight line, to a point three miles south of the mouth of Rabbit river; thence, north to the mouth of said river; thence, up the Mississippi river, to a point directly north of the place of beginning; thence, south to the place of beginning. Third, beginning at a point half a mile south-west from the most south-westwardly point of Gull lake; thence, due south to Crow Wing river; thence, down said river, to the Mississippi river; thence, up said river, to Long Lake portage; thence, in a straight line, to the head of Gull lake; thence, in a south-westwardly direction, as nearly in a direct line as practicable, but at no point thereof, at a less distance than half a mile from said lake, to the place of beginning. Fourth, the boundaries to be, as nearly as practicable, at right angles, and so as to embrace within them Pokagomon lake; but no where to approach nearer said lake than half a mile therefrom. Fifth, beginning at the mouth of Sandy Lake river; thence, south to a point on an east and west line, two miles south of the most southern point of Sandy lake; thence, east to a point due south from the mouth of West Savannah river; thence, north to the mouth of said river; thence, north to a point on an east and west line, one mile north of the most northern point of Sandy lake; thence, west to Little Rice river; thence, down said river to Sandy Lake river; and thence, down said river to the place of beginning. Sixth, to include all the islands in Rice lake, and also half a section of land on said lake, to include the present gardens of the Indians. Seventh, one section of land for Pug-o-na-ke-shick, or 'Hole in the Day,' to include his house and farm; and for which he shall receive a patent in fee simple.

"For the Pillager and Lake Winnibigoshish bands, to be in three tracts, to be located and bounded as follows, namely: first, beginning at the mouth of Little Boy river; thence, up said river to Lake Hassler; thence, through the center of said lake, to its western extremity; thence, in a direct line, to the most southern point of Leech lake; and thence, through said lake, so as to include all the islands therein, to the place of beginning. Second, beginning at the point where the Mississippi river leaves Lake Winnibigoshish; thence, north to the head of the first river; thence, west by the head of the next river, to the head of the third river, emptying into said lake; thence, down the latter to said lake; and thence, in a direct line to the place of beginning. Third, beginning at the mouth of Turtle river; thence, up said river to the first lake; thence, east four miles; thence, southwardly in a line parallel with Turtle river, to Cass lake; and thence, so as to include all the islands in said lake, to the place of beginning; all of which said tracts shall be distinctly designated on the plats of the public surveys. And at such time or times, as the President may deem it advisable for the interests and welfare of said Indians, or any of them, he shall cause the said reservations, or such portion or portions thereof, as may be necessary, to be surveyed; and assign to each head of a family, or single person over twenty-one years of age, a reasonable quantity of land, in one body, not to exceed eighty acres in any case, for his or their separate use; and he may, at his discretion, as the occupants thereof become capable of managing their business and affairs, issue patents to them for the tracts so assigned to them respectively; said tracts to be exempt from taxation, levy, sale, or forfeiture; and not to be aliened or leased for a longer period than two years, at one time, until otherwise provided by the legislature of the State in which they may be situate, with the assent of Congress. They shall not be sold, or alienated, in fee, for a period of five years after the date of the patents; and not then without the assent of the President of the United States being first obtained. Prior to the issue of the patents, the President shall make such rules and regulations as he may deem necessary and expedient, respecting the disposition of any of said tracts in case of the death of the person or persons to whom they may be assigned, so that the same shall be secured to the families of such deceased persons; and should any of the Indians to whom tracts may be assigned, thereafter abandon them, the President may make such rules and regulations, in relation to such abandoned tracts, as in his judgment may be necessary and proper.

"ARTICLE III. In consideration of, and in full compensation for, the cessions made by the said Mississippi, Pillager, and Lake Winnibigoshish bands of Chippeway Indians, in the first article of this agreement, the United States hereby agree and stipulate to pay, expend, and make provision for, the said bands of Indians, as follows: namely, for the Mississippi bands,

"Ten thousand dollars ($10,000) in goods, and other useful articles, as soon as practicable after the ratification of this instrument, and after an appropriation shall be made by Congress therefor, to be turned over to the delegates and chiefs for distribution among their people.

"Fifty thousand dollars ($50,000) to enable them to adjust and settle their present engagements, so far as the same, on an examination thereof, may be found and decided to be valid and just by the chiefs, subject to the approval of the Secretary of the Interior; and any balance remaining of said sum, not required for the above-mentioned purpose, shall be paid over to said Indians in the same manner as their annuity money, and in such installments as the said Secretary may determine; provided, that an amount not exceeding ten thousand dollars ($10,000) of the above sum shall be paid to such full and mixed bloods as the chiefs may direct, for services rendered heretofore to their bands.

"Twenty thousand dollars ($20,000) per annum, in money, for twenty years, provided, that two thousand dollars ($2,000) per annum of that sum, shall be paid or expended, as the chiefs may request, for purposes of utility connected with the improvement and welfare of said Indians, subject to the approval of the Secretary of the Interior.

"Five thousand dollars ($5,000) for the construction of a road from the mouth of Rum river to Mille Lac, to be expended under the direction of the Commissioner of Indian Affairs.

"A reasonable quantity of land, to be determined by the Commissioner of Indian Affairs, to be ploughed and prepared for cultivation in suitable fields, at each of the reservations of the said bands, not exceeding, in the aggregate, three hundred acres for all the reservations, the

Indians to make the rails and enclose the fields themselves.

"For the Pillager and Lake Winnibigoshish bands:

"Ten thousand dollars ($10,000) in goods, and other useful articles, as soon as practicable after the ratification of this agreement, and an appropriation shall be made by Congress therefor; to be turned over to the chiefs and delegates for distribution among their people.

"Forty thousand dollars ($40,000), to enable them to adjust and settle their present engagements, so far as the same, on an examination thereof, may be found and decided to be valid and just by the chiefs, subject to the approval of the Secretary of the Interior; and any balance remaining of said sum, not required for that purpose, shall be paid over to said Indians, in the same manner as their annuity money, and in such installments as the said Secretary may determine; provided that an amount, not exceeding ten thousand dollars ($10,000), of the above sum, shall be paid to such mixed bloods as the chiefs may direct, for services heretofore rendered to their bands.

"Ten thousand six hundred and sixty-six dollars and sixty-six cents ($10,666.66) per annum, in money, for thirty years.

"Eight thousand dollars ($8,000) per annum, for thirty years, in such goods as may be requested by the chiefs, and as may be suitable for the Indians, according to their condition and circumstances.

"Four thousand dollars ($4,000) per annum, for thirty years, to be paid or expended, as the chiefs may request, for purposes of utility connected with the improvement and welfare of said Indians; subject to the approval of the Secretary of the Interior. *Provided*, That an amount, not exceeding two thousand dollars thereof, shall, for a limited number of years, be expended under the direction of the Commissioner of Indian Affairs, for provisions, seeds and such other articles or things as may be useful in agricultural pursuits.

"Such sum as can be usefully and beneficially applied by the United States, annually, for twenty years, and not to exceed three thousand dollars in any one year, for purposes of education; to be expended under the direction of the Secretary of the Interior.

"Three hundred dollars' ($300) worth of powder, per annum, for five years.

"One hundred dollars' ($100) worth of shot and lead, per annum, for five years.

"One hundred dollars' ($100) worth of gilling twine, per annum, for five years.

"One hundred dollars' ($100) worth of tobacco, per annum, for five years.

"Hire of three laborers at Leech Lake, of two at Lake Winnibigoshish, and of one at Cass lake, for five years.

"Expense of two blacksmiths, with the necessary shop, iron, steel and tools, for fifteen years.

"Two hundred dollars ($200) in grubbing hoes and tools, the present year.

"Fifteen thousand dollars ($15,000) for opening a road from Crow Wing to Leech Lake; to be expended under the direction of the Commissioner of Indian Affairs.

"To have ploughed and prepared for cultivation, two hundred acres of land, in ten or more lots, within the reservation at Leech lake; fifty acres, in four or more lots, within the reservation at Lake Winnibigoshish; and twenty-five acres, in two or more lots, within the reservation at Cass lake: *Provided*, That the Indians shall make the rails and enclose the lots themselves.

"A saw-mill, with a portable grist-mill attached thereto, to be established whenever the same shall be deemed necessary and advisable by the Commissioner of Indian Affairs, at such point as he shall think best; and which, together with the expense of a proper person to take charge of and operate them, shall be continued during ten years: *Pro-*

vided, That the cost of all the requisite repairs of the said mills shall be paid by the Indians, out of their own funds."

The revolt of the Sioux, and the massacre of several hundred whites by those savages, spread through the country like an electric shock. "Hole-in-the-day," the head chief of the Mississippi Chippeways, with a few of his warriors, immediately commenced stealing and killing the cattle about the Indian agency and Fort Ripley. Agent Walker fled to the fort, and directed the arrest of "Hole-in-the-day," but that chief retreated across the river with his family, when pursued by troops, and then fired back upon his pursuers, and shots were exchanged. Agent Walker set out for St. Paul, but laboring under the excitement of the occasion, he committed suicide on the way.

Commissioner Dole, of Washington, then at St. Paul, on his way to Red river, obtained two companies of volunteers from Governor Ramsey, and immediately set out for Fort Ripley. He reached that point, and held several councils with "Hole-in-the-day" and other chiefs of the bands, but with no definite result. Mr. Dole, in the mean time, persuaded the Mille Lac and some other bands to abandon "Hole-in-the-day," and thereby diminished that chief's strength one half. He then left for St. Paul. The Indians held a council, and although many chiefs were for peace, they came to no decision. Those favorable to peace went to the fort, surrendered the stolen property, received rations, and left for home. "Hole-in-the-day," having thus lost more than half of his warriors, soon after followed their example, restored his plunder, and delivered his war-club as a token of peace.

In the mean time, the legislature of Minnesota appointed commissioners to visit "Hole-in-the-day" and make a treaty. Judge Cooper, the attorney of the chief, was placed at the head of the commission. They concluded a treaty, but government refused to ratify it, and the treaty of 1863 was the consequence. The depredations of this outbreak were not extensive, and were settled under the treaty last named.

"Hole-in-the-day," with some forty of his principal chiefs and warriors, visited St. Paul soon after, and offered the whole force of his tribe to General Pope, to go against the Sioux, but their services were refused. Had they been accepted, they would have made valuable scouts against their old enemy, and might have been the means of having given success to the first expedition of General Sibley. It was arming tribe against tribe that gave the first success to the English arms in the Pontiac conspiracy; and the animosity of two hundred years might well have spent itself against the merciless Sioux.

By the treaty of March 11th, 1863, with the Chippeways of the Mississippi and the Pillager and Lake Winnibigoshish bands of Chippeways, they relinquish their reservations at Gull lake, Mille Lac, Sandy lake, Rabbit lake, Pokagomin lake, and Rice lake, and agree to accept, "for the future homes of the Chippeways of the Mississippi, all the lands embraced within the following described boundaries, except the reservations made and described in the third clause of the second article of the said treaty of February 22nd, 1855, for the Pillager and Lake Winnibigoshish bands; that is to say, beginning at a point one mile south of the most southerly point of Leech lake, and running thence in an easterly course to a point one mile south of the most southerly point of Goose lake; thence due east to a point due south from the intersection of the Pokagomin reservation and the Mississippi river; thence on the dividing line between 'Deer River lakes' and Mashkorden's river and lakes until a point is reached north of the first named river and lakes; thence in a direct line north-westerly to the outlet of 'Two Routes lake;' thence in a south-westerly direction to the northwest corner of the Cass Lake reservation; thence in a south-westerly direction to Karbekaun river; thence down said river to the lake of the same name; thence due south to a point due west from the beginning; thence to the place of beginning."

By article third it is further provided: "In consideration of the foregoing cession to the United States, and the valuable improvements thereon, the United States further agree:

"1st. To extend the present annuities of the Indians, parties to this treaty, for ten years beyond the periods respectively named in existing treaties.

"2nd. And to pay towards the settlement of the claims for depredations committed by said Indians in 1862, the sum of $30,000.

"3rd. To enable said Indians to pay their present just engagements, the sum of $30,000, as the chiefs in council may direct.

"4th. To the chiefs of the Chippeways of the Mississippi, $16,000, (provided they shall pay to the chiefs of the Pillager and Lake Winnibigoshish bands, $1,000,) to be paid upon the signing of this treaty, out of the arrearages due under the ninth article of the treaty concluded at La Point, in the State of Wisconsin, on the 30th of September, 1854.

"5th. And to pay the expenses incurred by the legislature of the State of Minnesota, in the month of September, 1862, in sending commissioners to visit the Chippeway Indians, amounting to $1,338.75."

By the fourth article of the same treaty, " the United States further agree to clear, stump, grub, and break in the reservation hereby set apart for the Chippeways of the Mississippi, in lots of not less than ten acres each, at such point or points as the chiefs of each band may select, as follows, viz.: For the Gull Lake band, seventy acres; for the Mille Lac band, seventy acres; for the Sandy Lake band, fifty acres; for the Pokagomin band, fifty acres; for the Rabbit Lake band, forty acres; for the Rice Lake band, twenty acres; and to build for the chiefs of said bands one house each, of the following descriptions: to be constructed of hewn logs; to be sixteen by twenty feet each, and two stories high; to be roofed with good shaved pine shingles;

the floors to be of seasoned pine plank, jointed; stone or brick fire-places and chimneys; three windows in lower story, and two in the upper story, with good, substantial shutters to each, and suitable doors; said houses to be pointed with lime mortar."

By article fifth it is further provided, that "the United States agree to furnish to said Indians, parties to this treaty, ten yokes of good, steady, work oxen, and twenty log chains, annually, for ten years, provided the Indians shall take proper care of, and make proper use of the same; also, for the same period, annually, two hundred grubbing hoes, ten ploughs, ten grind stones, one hundred axes, handled, not to exceed in weight three and one half pounds each; twenty spades. Also, two carpenters, and two blacksmiths, and four farm laborers, and one physician."

In addition to the foregoing, there were several other provisions tending to promote agriculture and education, and otherwise to aid the Indians in the advancement of civilization.

The Red Lake and Pembina bands of Chippeways not having joined in the foregoing treaty, a treaty was made with them, October 2nd, 1863, by which those bands ceded to the United States all their rights to the territory within the following boundaries: "Beginning at the point where the international boundary between the United States and the British possessions intersects the shore of the Lake of the Woods; thence in a direct line south-westwardly to the head of Thief river; thence down the main channel of said Thief river to its mouth on the Red Lake river; thence in a south-easterly direction, in a direct line towards the head of Wild Rice river, to the point where such line would intersect the north-western boundary of a tract ceded to the United States by a treaty concluded at Washington on the 22nd day of February, in the year 1855, with the Mississippi, Pillager and Lake Winnibigoshish band of Chippeway Indians; thence along the said boundary line of said cession to the mouth of Wild Rice river; thence up the main channel of the Red river to the mouth of the Shayenne; thence up the main channel of the Shayenne river to Poplar Grove; thence in a direct line to the 'Place of Stumps,' otherwise called Lake Chicot; thence in a direct line to the head of the main branch of Salt river; thence in a direct line due north to the point where such line would intersect the international boundary aforesaid; thence eastwardly along said boundary to the place of beginning."

As the price of the said purchase, the United States agreed to pay $20,000 per annum for twenty years, and $100,000, out of which the Indians were to pay their debts, together for damages for depredations committed on the whites.

This treaty was amended by the Senate, by striking out the annuity, and providing that "the United States will pay annually, during the pleasure of the President of the United States, to the Red Lake band of Chippeways, the sum of $10,000, and to the Pembina band $5,000." Also, expend annually, for fifteen years, for the Red Lake band, in goods, $8,000, and same for the Pembina band, $4,000; and furnish said bands, for a like period, one blacksmith, one physician, one miller, one farmer, and pay them annually, for the like period, $1,500 worth of iron, steel, and other articles for blacksmithing purposes, and $1,000 for carpentering and other purposes; also, "one saw-mill, with a run of mill-stones attached."

A new treaty was made with the Chippeways of the Mississippi, May 7th, 1864, by which the President was to select locations for the different bands on their reservation, on the extreme upper Mississippi. With this point in view, agent Clark visited the upper country in the summer of 1865, and on his return recommended to the Indian department "to contract for the clearing, stumping, grubbing, breaking, and planting, except planting in lots of not less than ten acres, provided the cost shall not exceed twenty-five dollars per acre, as follows: For the Gull Lake band, twenty acres at Leech lake; for the Rice Lake band, twenty acres at Long lake; for the Pokegama band, fifty acres at Oak Point; for the Rabbit band, forty acres at Lake Winnipeg; for the Sandy band, twenty-five acres at Lake Winnipeg; for the Sandy band, twenty-five acres at Oak Point." The agent also recommended that the new agency buildings be located at Leech lake, to consist of "one dwelling for the agent, one for the physician, two for carpenters, two for the blacksmiths, two for the farmers, one for the interpreter, one for the engineer; one school-house, two warehouses, one blacksmith's shop, one carpenter's shop, and two stables; all of which buildings, except shops and stables, to be inclosed on three sides with good, substantial stockades: provided the entire cost of buildings and stockade shall not exceed $25,000, as per fourth article, treaty 7th May, 1864."

The discovery of gold in 1865, near the Indian reservation at Lake Vermillion, and the advent of the gold-seekers upon Indian territory, forced the United States and the Bois Forte band of the Chippeways to make another treaty, and the following were the first articles of the treaty concluded at Washington, D. C., in April, 1866, which was soon after ratified by the Senate, and published by the President:

"ARTICLE I. The peace and friendship now existing between the United States and said Bois Forte bands of Indians shall be perpetual.

"ARTICLE II. In consideration of the agreements, stipulations, and undertakings to be performed by the United States, and hereinafter expressed, the Bois Forte bands of Chippeways have agreed to, and do hereby, cede and for ever relinquish and surrender to the United States, all their right, title, claim and interest in and to all lands and territory heretofore claimed, held, or possessed by them, and lying east of the boundary line mentioned and established in and by the first article of the treaty made and concluded by and between the United States of the one part, and the

Chippeways of Lake Superior and the Mississippi of the other part, on the 30th day of September, A. D. 1854, and more especially in and to all that portion of said territory heretofore claimed and occupied by them at and near Lake Vermillion as a reservation. The Bois Forte band of Chippeways in like manner cede and relinquish for ever to the United States all their claim, right, title, and interest in and to all lands and territory lying westwardly of said boundary line, or elsewhere within the limits of the United States.

"ARTICLE III. In consideration of the foregoing cession and relinquishment, the United States agree to and will perform the stipulations, undertakings, and agreements following, that is to say:

"1st. There shall be set apart within one year after the date of the ratification of this treaty, under the direction of the President of the United States, within the Chippeway country, for the perpetual use and occupancy of said Bois Forte band of Chippeways, a tract of land of not less than 100,000 acres, the said location to include a lake known by the name of Netor As-sab-a-co-na, if, upon examination of the country by the agent sent by the President of the United States to select the said reservation, it is found practicable to include the said lake therein, and also one township of land on the Grand Fork river, at the mouth of Deer creek, if such location shall be found practicable.

"2nd. The United States will, as soon as practicable after the setting apart of the tract of country first above mentioned, erect thereon, without expense to said Indians, one blacksmith's shop, to cost not exceeding five hundred dollars; one school-house, to cost not exceeding five hundred dollars; and eight houses for their chiefs, to cost not exceeding four hundred dollars each; and a building for an agency-house, and store-house for the storage of goods and provisions, to cost not exceeding $2,000.

"3d. The United States will expend annually, for and in behalf of said Bois Forte band of Chippeways, for and during the term of twenty years from and after the ratification of this treaty, the several sums and for the purposes following, to wit: For the support of one blacksmith and assistant, and for tools, iron and steel, and other articles necessary for the blacksmith's shop, $1,500; for one school teacher, and the necessary books and stationery for the school, $800, the chiefs in council to have the privilege of selecting, with the approval of the Secretary of the Interior, the religious denomination to which the said teacher shall belong; for instructions of the said Indians in farming, and the purchase of seed, tools, etc., for that purpose, $800; and for annuity payments, the sum of $11,000, — $3,500 of which shall be paid to them in money *per capita*, $1,000 in provisions, ammunition, and tobacco, and $6,500 to be distributed to them in goods and other articles suited to their wants and conditions.

"Article IV. To enable the chiefs, head men, and warriors now present to establish their people upon the new reservation, and to purchase useful articles and presents for their people, the United States agree to pay to them, upon the ratification of this treaty, the sum of $50,000, to be expended under the direction of the Secretary of the Interior."

From the examination of the several treaties between the United States and the Chippeways, it will be observed that a special effort has been made by the government, for the civilization of this tribe or nation of Indians. Several different denominations of Christians, the principal of which are the Methodist, Congregationalist, Episcopalian, and Catholic, have from time to time seconded the efforts of government, and attempted the introduction of Christianity, but their united efforts have produced no adequate results. Indeed, Mr. Bonga, the Indian interpreter to the Mississippi bands, and a half-breed, declared, in his report in 1865, that "it is now full thirty years since the government and missionaries have been trying in every way to get these Indians to adopt in some way the habits of the white man, but all their efforts have been to no purpose." Agent Webb, of the Lake Superior bands, in his annual report dated November 8th, 1865, represented that those bands "seem to have been almost constantly engaged in grand medicine dances, jugglery, and conjuring. I am unable to report any progress or interest manifested in the schools. The Protestant mission, under the control of the American Board of Commissioners of Foreign Missions, has been sustained among these Indians for over twenty years. The Board have decided to abandon it, for want of sufficient encouragement to continue their labors."

The physician to the Mississippi bands has added much to these discouraging reports, by his statement that the venereal disease, contracted by the natives in their intercourse with the vicious whites, almost threatens the extermination of those bands.

The efforts of government, and of the missionaries, to exclude spirituous liquors from these Indians, have been constantly thwarted by the whisky-selling traders, who thread the native forests of these bands from every point of the compass; and the failure in their agricultural enterprises is answered quite as readily, by stating the fact that their frosty, timbered country, mainly situated between 47° and 49° north latitude, is almost totally unfit for agriculture. If it is true that these Indians are the "wards of government," will not posterity demand why they were taught agriculture in a non-agricultural region, and instructed in Christianity while they were surrounded by the most vicious of the white race, constantly tempting their savage appetites with liquid poison, which has proved quite as fatal to Indian chastity as to Indian industry?

By the report of the Indian agent of the Mississippi bands in September, 1866, it appears that the agency buildings were being constructed on the south side of Leech lake, but that the Indians had not then removed to their new reservations. The agent had also caused five whisky-traders to be arrested and sent to St. Paul, to be indicted by the United States District Court, which was accordingly done, adding thereto several of their runners about Crow Wing. The agent also complains that whisky is sold to some extent by travelers.

The agent's report from Lake Superior, shows that one hundred and fifty-eight Catholic Indians of Bad river reservation, had petitioned for leave to build a church at that point, and that he had granted the petition, notwithstanding the remonstrance of a Protestant missionary at the same place. He represents the Catholic Indians to be on the increase among the Chippeways of Lake Superior, and that Catholic missionaries were producing "very salutary results among these Indians in many different ways, especially in restraining the use of ardent spirits."

When government places the Chippeways on permanent reservations, and protects them from vicious whites, we may hope for their regeneration.

CHAPTER XIV.

THE SACS, FOXES, AND POTOWATOMIES, AND A TABLE OF ALL THE TRIBES, IN 1866.

The Sacs and Musquakies, or people of the "Red Land," first became known to the whites as inhabitants of northern Michigan, about the Saginaw bay. Black Hawk claimed that the Sacs anciently lived near Quebec, but in the early wars of the Iroquois had been driven west to Mackinaw, and from thence to Wisconsin, from which place they had emigrated to Rock Island, where he was born. The Musquakies were called Outagamies, or Foxes, by the Algonquin tribes, from their totem, "a fox." From the fact that the two tribes had the same customs, spoke the same Algonquin dialect, have always lived together since they have been known to the whites, and are now merged into one tribe, we readily come to the conclusion that they were originally two bands of the same tribe near Quebec, and in the early Iroquois war fled to Michigan; from there were swept off by the Iroquois raids against the Hurons in 1649, and with the Hurons took shelter at Mackinaw; and that about 1652 were again defeated, and fled to the Fox river in Wisconsin.

In previous chapters we have traced their wars with the Sioux to 1702, then with the Chippeways and French to 1754, when the French effected a peace between them, the Chippeways and Christinaux, and themselves, after which they were allies of the French until the fall of Canada in 1760. From 1702 to 1754, the French exhausted every art of both war and diplomacy, to break up their alliance with the Sioux, and make them take up the tomahawk against the English, but without effect. Hence the French called them all kinds of hard names, and repeatedly had them all exterminated and driven out of Wisconsin. After the fall of Canada, these tribes united again with the Sioux, Kickapoos, and Winnebagoes, and soon nearly exterminated the Illinois. They were also joined by the Ottawas after the assassination of Pontiac, who revenged the assassination on the Peorias. After this war, they joined the British against the colonies in our revolution, and after the close of that war, they crossed the Mississippi, and drove the Iowas, Missourias, and Mandans, out of the greater part of the present State of Iowa.

About in this position Governor Harrison found them when he took possession of the west side of the upper Mississippi, after its purchase from France. At this time our government adopted the policy of extinguishing the Indian title to all lands east of the Mississippi, and locating the Indians on the west side. This policy soon alarmed the Shawnees and Miamies, as well as the Sacs and Foxes, and led to the Tecumseh Confederacy, which was only broken up by the battle of Tippecanoe, in November, 1811.

Among the first treaties negotiated by Governor Harrison, to carry into effect the removal of the Indians west of the Mississippi, was that of November 3, 1804, at St. Louis, with the Sacs and Foxes.

This treaty ceded to the United States the following territory: "Beginning at a point on the Missouri river opposite to the mouth of the Gasconade river; thence, in a direct course, so as to strike the river Jefferson at the distance of thirty miles from its mouth, and down the said Jefferson to the Mississippi; thence, up the Mississippi to the mouth of the Ouisconsing river, and up the same to a point which shall be thirty-six miles in a direct line from the mouth of said river; thence, by a direct line, to the point where the Fox river (a branch of the Illinois) leaves the small lake called Sakuegan; thence, down the Fox river to the Illinois river, and down the same to the Mississippi."

For this large tract of land, covering large parts of Wisconsin, Illinois and Missouri, the government engaged to give $2,234.50 in goods, and an annuity of $1,000 per year forever in goods, at costs at the place where purchased.

This was a small price in proportion to what was afterwards paid for Indian lands, but as the title to a portion of the territory was subsequently disputed, it may not have been a very unreasonable price at the time.

But, however, it gave great dissatisfaction to the tribes, and Black Hawk charged, in subsequent years, that the chiefs were not authorized to sell the land; besides that, they were made drunk, and did not know that they had made any such treaty. During the war of 1812, Black Hawk, with his belligerent warriors, went to Detroit, and the balance of the tribe of Sacs put themselves under the protection of the United States, and settled on the Missouri river, and at the close of the war signed a treaty of peace, as did the Foxes also, both confirming the treaty of 1804. Black Hawk, being threatened with an armed force, finally concluded to go down to St. Louis, and the 13th of May, 1816, signed a treaty of peace, ratifying the treaty of 1804; and further engaged to "deliver up all the property they had stolen or plundered from the United States since they were notified of the treaty of peace with Great Britain." To this treaty Black Hawk acknowledged that he "touched the quill," but denied that he understood that by it he surrendered his village on Rock river.

By another treaty of the 3rd September, 1822, the Sacs and Foxes relinquished their right to have the United States establish a "trading house, or factory," at a convenient point at which the Indians could trade, and save themselves from the imposition of traders, for which the United States paid $1,000 in merchandise.

By another treaty of the 4th August, 1824, the Sacs and Foxes sold the United States all their lands in the State of Missouri, north of the Missouri river, for which they received $1,000 the same year, and an annuity of $1,000 per year for ten years; to a half-breed, $500, for his losses during the late war; and the United States agreed to furnish a blacksmith during the pleasure of the President of the United States, and some other gratuities, as the President ":may deem expedient."

By a treaty held with the various Indian tribes of the upper Mississippi, by the United States, August 19th, 1825, at Prairie Du Chien, to settle the old Sioux and Chippeway war, and a war lately commenced between the Sacs, Foxes, and Iowas, against the Sioux, and establish peace, by agreeing on the boundary lines between the different tribes, our government found that the various tribes had many conflicting claims; but between the Sioux, and Sacs, and Foxes, they agreed to a line " commencing at the mouth of the Upper Iowa river, and ascending said river to its left fork; thence up that fork to its source; thence crossing the fork of Red Cedar river, in a direct line to the second or upper fork of the Des Moines; and thence in a direct line to the lower fork of the Calumet river, and down that river to its junction with the Missouri;" but from the Des Moines to the Missouri the line was held subject to the claims of the Yankton band of Sioux, and the Iowas and Ottoes.

By another treaty with the Sacs, Foxes, and Indians west, made July 15th, 1830, a large tract of country in the south-western part of the State of Iowa, extending west from the Des Moines river to the Missouri, was set apart, and the President was authorized to locate thereon the tribes which then inhabited it, as well as other tribes. The Sacs and Foxes in this treaty ceded to the United States a strip of land twenty miles wide, from the Mississippi to the

Des Moines, on the north side of their territory, and on the south side of the line agreed upon between them and the Sioux in the treaty of 1825, and the Medawah-kanton, Wah-pay-koota, Wahpeton and Sisseton bands of the Sioux; also cede to the United States a similar tract of twenty miles wide, on the north side of the tract above ceded by the Sacs and Foxes.

The time having arrived for the Sacs and Foxes to leave the east bank of the Mississippi, under the treaty of 1804, Ke-o-kuck, or "Watchful Fox," the leader of the friendly Sacs and Foxes, erected his wigwam on the west side of the river, and was followed by perhaps two-thirds of the two tribes; but Ma-ka-tai-me-she-kia-kiah, or the "Black Sparrow-Hawk," commonly called "Black Hawk," with his band, refused to leave their village near Rock Island. They contended that they had not sold their village, evidently believing that the Americans would not drive them off by force.

"Black Hawk" and his surviving warriors of the war of 1812, were evidently no friends of the Americans, and associated with his brother, Wau-ba-kee-shik, the "Prophet," sent his war belts to neighboring tribes, and sought to establish another confederacy, after the manner of Pontiac and Tecumseh, claiming to have had promises of assistance from the English at Malden, and the Potowatomies, Winnebagoes and other tribes; but as the sequel proved, he evidently imposed on his too credulous warriors.

In the spring of 1832, Governor Reynolds, of Illinois, ordered out 1,800 militia, and notified General Atkinson, then in command of the regular troops, of the movements of Black Hawk. The General moved up the Mississippi early in April, and ordered "Black Hawk" to leave the country. The 27th of April, the Illinois militia, under Brigadier-General Samuel Whitesides, of the State militia, commenced their march up the Mississippi to Rock river.

"Black Hawk," hearing of the advance of forces, retreated up Rock river, and sent word to General Atkinson that he was going to raise corn at the prophet's town above.

General Whiteside was ordered to follow "Black Hawk" fifty miles, to the prophet's town, and await the arrival of the regular troops under General Atkinson, with provisions.

Pursuant to the order, General Whiteside advanced to the prophet's town, which he burnt, and forty miles further, to Dixon's ferry, where he met Majors Stillman and Baily, with 275 additional militia from the region of Peoria, and halted for the regular troops.

Majors Stillman and Baily asked leave to follow after "Black Hawk," to watch his motions, and were allowed to do so. They advanced with their forces the 12th of May, to a place now called Stillman's Run, and encamped for the night. Soon after the camp was pitched, they discovered three Indians a mile distant, approaching with a white flag, when a few of Stillman's men, without orders, mounted their horses, advanced upon and took the Indians prisoners. "Black Hawk" dispatched five more Indians to look after the first three who were attacked; two of these were killed by Stillman's men, and the balance escaped. "Black Hawk," being near at hand, raised the war-whoop and attacked the advance party, who, retreating back to their camp, spread the alarm, when the whole of Stillman's force broke and fled to Dixon, and were pursued by some forty Indians several miles. Eleven whites were killed. The Indians lost three, and received the plunder of the camp.

"Black Hawk" then advanced up the river, and pitched his camp near the four lakes, in Wisconsin. General Atkinson soon joined General Whiteside at Dixon, when the militia insisted on going home, and were discharged from further service.

When the news of the advance of "Black Hawk" up Rock river reached the mining region in Wisconsin, General Dodge, of Dodgeville, raised a party of twenty-seven volunteers, and started for Rock river, to confer with General

Atkinson, but met an express from Governor Reynolds, advising him of the fight at Stillman's Run, when he turned home, and rallied the miners to defend the country. They in a few days erected thirteen forts or block-houses, for the security of their families, and General Dodge occupied Fort Union at Dodgeville.

Black Hawk dispatched numerous parties to the settlements, to kill and plunder. One of these parties came to the mines and commenced depredations.

General Dodge immediately rallied twenty-eight men, followed the trail of the Indians to the Pickatonica river, when, leaving their horses with seven men, General Dodge and the balance waded the river, and as they raised the opposite bank, received the fire of the Indians then in ambush. Nothing daunted, the General and his party charged the Indians before they could load, killing every one in less than five minutes — *seventeen* in number — while the loss of the miners was only three killed and one wounded.

This affair showed to good advantage the character of General Dodge, who had been raised in the Indian country. Several other skirmishes were had before the advance of General Atkinson.

After the return of the militia, General Atkinson had too small a force to advance, and Governor Reynolds again called for volunteers, when 4,200 men hastened to the general's standard, and by the 22nd of June commenced ascending Rock river. They found that "Black Hawk" was at the mouth of White Water river, above Lake Koshkonong. General Atkinson sent a part of his forces by way of the mines, where they were joined by General Dodge and 250 miners, and formed a junction with General Atkinson at Koshkonong. The commander of the expedition being short of provisions, he sent Generals Henry, Alexander, Posey, and Dodge, with their commands, to Fort Winnebago for supplies. Generals Posey and Alexander returned with the provisions, and Generals Henry and Dodge struck across the country to Rock river, at the rapids, where they discovered the Indian trail and gave immediate pursuit. On the 21st of July they reached the south bank of the Wisconsin river, opposite Sac Prairie, where they found "Black Hawk" engaged in transporting his squaws and children across the river. "Black Hawk" led a part of his warriors against the whites to hold them in check, while the balance aided in crossing the river. The battle lasted until dark, and the Indians crossed the river with small loss.

"Black Hawk" bent his course through the heavy forests to the north-west, hoping to escape across the Mississippi; and as his poor fugitive band toiled over those high and interminable bluffs, they left the trail literally strewed with those who had died from wounds and starvation. At length they reached the Mississippi some two miles below the mouth of Bad Ax river, and commenced crossing in canoes, but were stopped by a steamboat sent up the river with some troops and a cannon. On the 2nd day of August, the American forces, the advance of which was led on by General Dodge, and supported by Colonel Zach. Taylor, with his regulars, came up on the trail, and commenced an immediate attack. The warriors attempted to check the troops, while the squaws, with their children on their backs, attempted to swim across a branch of the river to an island, but were mercilessly shot down by the exasperated soldiers. "Black Hawk," with the Prophet and their families, escaped to the Winnebago village at La Crosse, and delivered themselves up to De Carry, the chief of that band. About one hundred and fifty escaped across the river, but were pursued by the Sioux, then allies of the Americans, and nearly half of them massacred by those savages.

Prisoners were not reckoned among the trophies of the victory. Mr. James Reed, who visited the battle-ground the same day, declared to the writer that it was literally a slaughter of squaws and children; and that, drifted against some flood-wood, he counted a dozen Indian girls from fourteen to sixteen years of age, who had been shot in attempting to swim the river. He rescued a little girl who was clinging to her dead mother, and took her to the prairie.

The Winnebago chief, Winnoshiek, whose wife was sister to the "Prophet," remained neutral; but his son, about eighteen years old, acted as guide to "Black Hawk," and, together with a son of the "Prophet," about the same age, were wounded and taken prisoners early the next morning after the battle, while engaged in helping some squaws to cross the river from the island.

De Carry, another Winnebago chief, assisted the Americans with a company of warriors, and aided a party of whites in capturing a few Indians and squaws who went down the Wisconsin; but he had returned to La Crosse, at the time of the battle at Bad Ax.

"Black Hawk" and his party, in all twenty-one, delivered themselves to De Carry at La Crosse, who sent "Black Hawk" and the "Prophet" to the government agent at Prairie Du Chien, by *Khay-rah-tshoan-saip-kaw*, or "Black Hawk," an under chief of the Winnebagoes, and a canoeman, who was half-breed Sioux and Winnebago. Mr. James Reed saw the party land at Prairie Du Chien.

The newspaper speeches put into the mouths of De Carry and Charter, if made by any Indians, were made by the Winnebago "Black Hawk" and his boatman, as De Carry informed the writer that he did not go to Prairie Du Chien at the time. Through the influence of Mr. Saterlee Clark, then an Indian trader at the Prairie, and perhaps some others, the government paid $1,000 for the capture of "Black Hawk" and the "Prophet," which was distributed between Mr. Clark, De Carry, one of the "Thunders," and probably some others.

This war having closed by the killing or capture of the greater part of "Black Hawk's" and the "Prophet's" band, the government convened at Rock Island the balance of the Sacs and Foxes, and on the 21st day of September, 1832, concluded a treaty with them, of which the following is the preamble:

"Whereas, under certain lawless and desperate leaders, a formidable band, constituting a large portion of the Sac and Fox nation, left their country in April last, and, in violation of treaties, commenced an unprovoked war upon unsuspecting and defenceless citizens of the United States, sparing neither age nor sex; and whereas the United States, at a great expense of treasure, have subdued the said hostile bands, killing and capturing all its principal chiefs and warriors, the said States, partly as indemnity for the expense incurred, and partly to secure the future safety and tranquility of the invaded frontier, demand of the said tribes, to the use of the United States, a cession of a tract of the Sac and Fox country bordering on said frontier, more than proportional to the number of the hostile band who have been so conquered and subdued.

"ARTICLE I. Accordingly, the confederated tribes of Sacs and Foxes hereby cede to the United States for ever, all the lands to which the said tribes have title or claim (with the exception of the reservation hereinafter made,) included within the following bounds, to wit: Beginning on the Mississippi river, at a point where the Sac and Fox northern boundary line, as established by the second article of the treaty of Prairie Du Chien, of the 15th of July, 1825, strikes said river; thence up said boundary line to a point fifty miles from the Mississippi, measured on said line; thence in a right line to the nearest point on the Red Cedar of the Iowa, forty miles from the Mississippi river; thence in a right line to a point in the northern boundary line of the State of Missouri, fifty miles, measured on said boundary, from the Mississippi river; thence by the last men-

KEOKUK.

BLACK HAWK.
(SAC CHIEF.)

tioned boundary to the Mississippi river, and by the western shore of said river to the place of beginning."

The Sacs and Foxes further agreed to remove from said land by the 1st of June, 1832, and not hunt or fish thereon after that date.

The reservation above named was of four hundred square miles, on both sides of the Iowa river, which was to include Ke-o-kuk's village, located twelve miles from the Mississippi.

In addition to our losses in the war, the United States agreed to pay the Sacs and Foxes an annual annuity of $20,000 for thirty years, and also pay "Farnham and Davenport, Indian traders at Rock Island, the sum of $40,000," for Indian debts, and grant to Le Claire, interpreter, two sections of land, and maintain among the Sacs and Foxes a gun and blacksmith, with steel, etc.

The United States restored all prisoners, but stipulated that the remnant of "Black Hawk's" band should be distributed equally among the two tribes; and "Black Hawk," the "Prophet," their sons, Napope, and two other warriors, should remain, during the pleasure of the President, as hostages for the good conduct of their band.

The United States, also, "to give a striking evidence of their mercy and liberality," gave the tribes "thirty-five beef cattle, twelve bushels of salt, thirty barrels of pork, and fifty barrels of flour, and cause to be delivered, for the same purpose, in the month of April next, at the mouth of the lower Iowa, 6,000 bushels of corn." The treaty was signed by Major-General Winfield Scott and Governor John Reynolds, on the part of the United States, and by Ke-o-kuk and thirty-two chiefs and warriors on the part of the United States.

This treaty opened the whole eastern part of the present State of Iowa for settlement, and in June and July of 1833 the great tide of emigrants poured into and founded that State. The reservation named in the foregoing treaty was finally ceded to the United States, September 28th, 1836, for which the government paid *seventy-five* cents per acre in coin.

By another treaty, made October 21st, 1837, the Sacs and Foxes ceded 1,250,000 acres lying along the west line of the cession of 1832, for which the United States gave $377,000.

The Sacs and Foxes of the Missouri river, by a separate treaty of the same date, ceded to the United States all the land belonging to that band east of the Missouri river, for which the government paid them $160,000.

And finally, on the 11th of October, 1842, the confederate tribes of Sacs and Foxes ceded all the balance of their lands west of the Mississippi, for $1,058,566, besides some items of provisions, etc.; and in addition, the United States engaged to procure them another tract of land, for their residence, on the Missouri river or its branches, and the Mississippi bands were accordingly located by the President on a reservation of 435,200 acres on the Osage river; while the Missouri band occupied a reservation on the south side of the Great Nemaha river, nearly in the south-eastern corner of the territory of Nebraska.

By a new treaty, the Sac and Fox band of the Missouri, in 1863, were located on twenty-five sections previously belonging to the Iowas, while their own lands were to be sold for the joint benefit of the Sacs and Foxes and Iowas.

The accounts which have been given by authors from time to time of the numbers of the Sacs and Foxes, have varied much more than the tribe would be likely to change, and the inaccuracies probably originated from the lack of proper information.

When the Rev. Father Allouez first met these tribes at

Cha-goua-mi-gong bay, Lake Superior, in 1665, he estimated the Foxes at 1,000 warriors and hunters; and while he did not pretend to estimate the Sacs, he remarked that he had seen two hundred of their warriors. When the Rev. Father visited the Foxes at their residence on Fox river, in 1670, he remarked, that "this nation is renowned for being numerous; they have more than four hundred men bearing arms; the number of women and children is greater, on account of polygamy, which exists among them, each man having commonly four wives, some of them six, and others as high as ten;" and that the previous March, "six great lodges," containing about one hundred, were cut off by the Iroquois. In 1718 the Foxes were estimated by the French to have five hundred men, and the Sacs one hundred and twenty; and in 1736 they were again set down at one hundred and fifty Sac and one hundred Fox warriors. In 1763 Sir William Johnson estimated them at three hundred Sac and three hundred and twenty Fox (men.) Lieutenant Gorrill, commandant at Green Bay, in 1761, estimated the Foxes on Fox river at three hundred and fifty warriors, and Sacs, near the Mississippi, at the same number.

Captain Carver, who visited these tribes in 1766, estimated the Sacs at 300 warriors, who spent their summers in wars against the Illinois and Pawnee Indians; and stated that the Sacs then lived on the Wisconsin river at a great village of ninety houses, one day's journey below the portage. Their houses were "built of hewn plank, neatly jointed, and covered with bark," each large enough to hold several families. About this time the band probably located at Rock Island. The Foxes he found at Prairie Du Chien, which then contained about three hundred houses, "well built after the Indian manner."

In 1841, it appears from a public document, that the Sacs and Foxes of the Mississippi, by estimation, numbered 6,400, and those of the Missouri river, 500 souls. In June, 1858, the former numbered 1,330, and the latter, 322; while in 1863, the former numbered in May only 975, and the latter, between the ages of eighteen and forty-five, sixty, of whom thirty-seven were, in October of that year, volunteers in the United States military service.

By the census of May 15, 1865, the Sacs and Foxes of the Mississippi in Kansas numbered 364 men, and 441 women, while those of the Missouri in the Great Nemaha agency, numbered only 44 men and 51 women, or a total of 900 souls.

It is believed, however, by the writer, that this diminution is not caused by the absolute decay of the tribes to the extent indicated, but mainly to the uncivilized portions emigrating to the regions of the buffalo and the Rocky mountains. In 1859 a chief, with six lodges, dissatisfied with the efforts of government to establish civilization, removed, and settled in Iowa, where they were in 1866. It is a fact well known, that many of the trappers and traders of Wisconsin and Minnesota, passed on before the tide of emigration, and their log huts for years after might have been seen among the beaver dams in the dark canons of the sources of the Columbia and Missouri rivers; and it is reasonable to infer that most of those took with them their Indian friends, with whom they had become connected in marriage or in trade. The Indian loves hunting, and when game became scarce in one locality, it was his custom to go where it was more plenty; and thus probably thousands have joined the tribes of the Rocky mountains, thereby decimating the eastern tribes, and leading us to believe that civilization is working their extermination.

The Sacs and Foxes of the Kansas agency, in 1865, raised 7,500 bushels of corn, and had 1,700 horses and ponies; and the total of all their personal property was estimated at $71,910. They are, however, what are called "Blanket Indians," having as yet not availed themselves, to much extent, of the allotment of the land, as provided by an act of Congress, although their land has lately been surveyed for that purpose.

In April, 1863, the Rev. R. P. Duval, and lady, of the Methodist Episcopal church, commenced a mission school in the tribe; also a Sabbath school, with preaching on the Sabbath. They received some help from some members of the tribe, and in 1866 the government rendered them some assistance from the educational fund; and the latter year were reported as well sustained by the Indians, and as accomplishing much good. Drunkenness in 1865 had nearly disappeared from the tribe, and Superintendent Murphy, the following year, said of them, that "They are, as a tribe, the most intelligent Indians I have yet met, and I believe as a general thing mean to do right." During 1866, traders sowed dissensions among them, and much embittered the uncivilized portions, headed by their chief, Mo-ko-ho-ko, and nearly produced a civil war; but these differences were harmonized by special agent W. R. Irwin, and peace was restored. The chiefs Keokuk, Che-ko-skuck, and Pah-teck-quaw, head the party for civilization, and themselves live in houses and cultivate land. The duty of government in this case to render prompt protection was made apparent by the Sioux massacre.

The Sacs and Foxes of the Missouri, in 1866, were reported by agent Norris as not as much advanced in civilization as the Iowas, but were "a remarkably civil, well-disposed tribe."

POTOWATOMIES.

This tribe, according to the Jesuit missionaries, originally occupied, with the Sacs and Foxes, that part of Michigan between Saginaw Bay and Lake Michigan. In 1639 a band of them occupied the northern islands in Green Bay, and were by the Sioux, the next year, driven off, and took refuge at the falls of St. Mary. The identity of their language and customs with the Sacs and Foxes, leaves no doubt that they were originally a kindred band to those tribes, and expelled with them from Canada previous to 1639, by the Iroquois. After that war subsided, and previous to 1700, the Potowatomies divided into two principal bands, and one located near Detroit, and the other at St. Joseph's, Michigan; while a few stragglers, with others of a like character from several other tribes, located at Milwaukee, which were afterwards known as "the united tribes of Ottawas, Chippeways and Pottawatamies, residing on the Illinois and Milwaukee rivers, and their waters, and on the south-western parts of Lake Michigan." Captain De Peyster, the British commandant at Mackinaw in 1779, called these bands "runegates of Milwaukee — a horrid set of refractory Indians." It was these bands that attacked and captured the retreating command of Captain Heald, at Chicago, August 15, 1812.

These lawless bands having no land of their own, naturally enough claimed all the land of their respective tribes, and the United States got into difficulty with them in their purchase of the Sacs and Foxes of the south-west part of Wisconsin, and north-west part of Illinois, by the treaty of 1804.

To settle all cause of complaint, the United States treated with them August 24, 1816, obtained a release of their claim of the land purchased of the Sacs and Foxes south of "a due west line from the southern extremity of Lake Michigan to the Mississippi," and the United States released to them the balance of their purchase north of said line, except five leagues square at the mouth of the Wisconsin river, including Prairie Du Chien. The United States also purchased of them the following tract: "Beginning on the left bank of the Fox river of Illinois, ten miles above the mouth of said Fox river; thence, running so as to cross Sandy creek ten miles above its mouth; thence, in a direct line, to a point ten miles north of the west end of the portage, between Chicago creek, which empties into Lake Michigan, and the river Desplaines, a fork of the Illinois;

thence, in a direct line, to a point on Lake Michigan ten miles northward of the mouth of Chicago creek; thence, along the lake, to a point ten miles southward of the mouth of said Chicago creek; thence, in a direct line, to a point on the Kankakee ten miles above its mouth; thence, with the said Kankakee and the Illinois river, to the mouth of Fox river; and thence, to the place of beginning." This tract included Chicago, which had previously been purchased by General Wayne in 1795.

As the consideration for the cession in the treaty, the United States delivered "a considerable quantity of merchandise," and agreed "to pay them, annually, for the term of twelve years, goods to the value of $1,000, at cost price."

By the treaty of 1825 with the various tribes, to settle their respective boundaries, and to establish peace between the Sioux on one part, and the Chippeways, Sacs, Foxes, Iowas, and probably other tribes on the other, it was found that nearly all the tribes had conflicting boundaries; but the United States recognized the rights of these bands of Ottawas, Chippeways, and Potowatomies to the mineral country about Galena, and in 1828 the United States made an unsuccessful attempt to purchase that country of these bands. They renewed the effort the following year, and, July 29th, obtained the following cession: "Beginning at the Winnebago village, on Rock river, forty miles from its mouth, and running thence down the Rock river to a line which runs due west from the most southern bend of Lake Michigan to the Mississippi river, and with that line to the Mississippi river opposite Rock Island; thence up that river to the United States reservation at the mouth of the Ouisconsin; thence with the south and east lines of said reservation to the Ouisconsin river; thence southerly, passing the heads of the small streams emptying into the Mississippi, to the Rock river aforesaid, at the Winnebago village, the place of beginning.

"Also, one other tract of land, described as follows, to

wit: Beginning on the western shore of Lake Michigan, at the north-east corner of the field of Antoine Ouitmette, who lives near Gross Pointe, about twelve miles north of Chicago; thence running due west to Rock river, aforesaid; thence down the said river to where a line drawn due west from the most southern bend of Lake Michigan crosses said river; thence east, along said line, to the Fox river of the Illinois; thence along the north-western boundary line of the cession of 1816 to Lake Michigan; thence northwardly, along the western shore of said lake to the place of beginning." From these tracts, the Indians reserved eleven sections for three Indians, and several more for certain half-breeds.

The consideration paid for this purchase was: $11,601, for Indian debts; $12,000 worth of goods the following October, and $16,000 " annually for ever in specie;" and " make permanent, for the use of the said Indians, the blacksmith's establishment at Chicago."

By a treaty with the Potowatomies, without naming any other bands, made October 20th, 1832, they ceded the following additional territory: "Beginning at a point on Lake Michigan ten miles southward of the mouth of Chicago river; thence, in a direct line, to a point on the Kankakee river, ten miles above its mouth; thence, with said river and the Illinois river to the mouth of Fox river, being the boundary of a cession made by them in 1816; thence, with the southern boundary of the Indian territory, to the State line between Illinois and Indiana; thence north with said line to Lake Michigan; thence, with the shore of Lake Michigan, to the place of beginning."

From this tract nearly forty sections were reserved to various chiefs and half-breeds. The government gave the Indians for this tract an annuity for twenty years of $15,000, and $600 annually to Billy Caldwell, $200 to Alexander Robinson, and $200 to Peter Le Clerc, during their natural lives; also, paid Indian debts to traders, $28,746; $75,000 in merchandise, and $1,400 for horses stolen during the "Black Hawk" war; and the Indians were allowed to hunt and fish on the land and vicinity as long as it remained the property of the United States, in consideration that said tribe had been "the faithful allies of the United States during the late conflict with the Sacs and Foxes."

The other bands of the Potowatomies that emigrated to Detroit and to St. Joseph's, above mentioned, by diverse treaties sold the most of their land in Indiana, Ohio, and Michigan, except some reservations, and emigrated west of the Mississippi, where a general treaty was formed in 1846, uniting the different bands, with the following preamble: "Whereas, the various bands of the Potowatomie Indians, known as the Chippeways, Ottawas, and Potowatomies, the Potowatomies of the Prairie, the Potowatomies of the Wabash, and the Potowatomies of Indiana, have, subsequent to the year 1828, entered into separate and distinct treaties with the United States, by which they have been separated and located in different countries, and difficulties have arisen as to the proper distribution of the stipulations under various treaties, and being the same people by kindred, by feeling, and by language, and having, in former periods, lived on and owned their lands in common; and being desirous to unite in one common country, and again become one people, and receive their annuities and other benefits in common, and to abolish all minor distinctions of bands by which they have heretofore been divided, and are anxious to be known only as the POTOWATOMIE NATION, thereby reinstating the national character; and whereas the United States are also anxious to restore and concentrate said tribes to a state so desirable and necessary for the happiness of their people, as well as to enable the government to arrange and manage its intercourse with them: now, therefore, the United States and said Indians do hereby agree that said people shall hereafter be known as a nation, to be called the POTOWATOMIE NATION."

By the second article of said treaty, "the said tribes of Indians hereby agree to sell and cede, and do hereby sell and cede to the United States, all the lands to which they have claim of any kind whatsoever, and especially the tracts or parcels of lands ceded to them by the treaty of Chicago, and subsequent thereto, and now in whole or in part possessed by their people, lying and being north of the river Missouri, and embraced in the limits of the territory of Iowa, and also all that tract of country lying and being on or near the Osage river, and west of the State of Missouri; it being understood that these cessions are not to affect the title of said Indians to any grants or reservations made to them by former treaties."

The consideration for this cession was $850,000; $87,000 of which were to be paid by the cession to the Indians of 576,000 acres of land on both sides of the Kansas river, west of the Missouri river, on to which land the consolidated tribe was to remove and permanently settle, within two years from the date of the ratification of the treaty.

They promptly removed to their reservation, with few exceptions, and numbered, on the "annuity roll of 1854," 3,444. Two hundred and fifty, who had intermarried with the Kickapoos, remained with that tribe, a few families with the Sacs and Foxes, and a few more remained back in the States of Illinois, Indiana, and Michigan, so that the whole tribe in 1854 was estimated to contain about 4,000 souls.

The political difficulties which originated in the organization of the Kansas territory in 1854, tended to demoralize the Indians of that territory, and the new emigrants trespassed upon their lands, and sold them whisky; and the anti-legislative party opened the ballot-box and attempted to make partisan speeches among them, notwithstanding the Indian reservations were expressly excluded from the operations of the law organizing the territory. The "Prairie" or "Blanket" Indians, who were adverse to the civilization of the tribe, committed depredations on the

"Farmer" Indians, by killing some of their stock and burning some of their cabins, but, fortunately for the Indians, they did not so far approximate to civilization as to imitate their white neighbors in their midnight assassinations.

The Indians complained that the government had not complied with their promises to induce the Indians to emigrate, and finally refused to accept their annuity.

The most of these troubles were only temporary, and in 1858 the Indian agent reported that a portion of the "Prairie band" had commenced improving farms and sending their children to the schools, which were very prosperous.

The desire of the farmers to have their farms set off to them in severalty, was carried into effect by a treaty, in 1861, and the government caused a survey of the reservation for that purpose, and in September, 1863, the agent reported that "allotments had been made to 1,375 persons, seven of whom were chiefs, drawing one section each; seven head men, each one-half section; and the balance, eighty acres each, making in the aggregate about 136,240 acres." Many of those farmers intended to become citizens of the United States under the act of Congress for that purpose. The uncivilized portions of the tribe continued to hold their lands in common.

The census of the tribe in June, 1863, then numbered 648 men, 593 women, and 1,033 children; total, 2,274. This was a large decrease since 1854, part of which was occasioned by deaths, but the greater part by stragglers to the hunting regions of the west, and to their old homes in the States. This year, they raised 3,720 bushels of wheat, 45,000 bushels of corn, 1,200 bushels of oats, 20 acres of potatoes, and had 1,200 horses, 1,000 cattle, 2,000 hogs, and 1,000 tons of hay.

The Catholic school averaged, during the year, ninety-five male pupils, under the care of four male teachers of the "Society of Jesus," and seventy-five girls under the care of "four ladies of the Society of the Sacred Heart," both under the general supervision of Rev. J. F. Diel. This school had then existed twenty years, and was conducted on the manual labor principle.

Independent of this, there was a select school of fifteen scholars under a female teacher. The Baptist manual labor school, being under the patronage of the church south, was discontinued early in 1861, on the breaking out of the rebellion, but was revived in 1866 by other persons.

The population of the Potowatomies June 1, 1865, was 1,874, being a decrease, since the previous year, of 404, which the agent accounted for by "forty going south," and "about 400 going north. Of those who went south, nothing certain is known. Of the other party, a few have returned, the main body having scattered through parts of Iowa and Wisconsin, some having gone as far as Michigan."

That part of the tribe which remained, cultivated 1,900 acres, of which 1,600 were put to corn, and 100 to wheat. Their total valuation of personal property in 1865, was estimated at $184,200. The agent further says that "a large proportion of that part of the tribe who have received lands in severalty, are industriously engaged in opening farms upon their allotments," and that many of those "are already sufficiently intelligent to be intrusted with the management of their own affairs." Seventy-one of the young Indians entered the Union army, being thereto advised by the chiefs.

The St. Mary's Catholic mission school had 240 scholars of both sexes, and was in a prosperous condition in 1865.

In 1866 this school was still in successful operation, and the superintendent, speaking of the pupils, said: "They not only spell, read, write, and cypher, but they study with success the various other branches of geography, history, and book-keeping, grammar, algebra, geometry, logic, philosophy, and astronomy. Besides, they are so docile, so willing to improve, that between their school hours they employ themselves, with pleasure, in learning whatever handiwork may be assigned to them," and particularly " to become good farmers." The girls, in addition to their studies, are "trained to acquire whatever may be deemed useful to good housekeepers and accomplished mothers of families."

The tribe, in 1866, were still troubled by white trespassers and whisky-sellers, although the agent had caused several of them to be indicted and punished every year. A limited number of farmers had become naturalized citizens, and others were about making application for citizenship.

We close our sketches of the Indian tribes with a table, compiled by the Commissioner of Indian Affairs in October, 1866, giving the superintendencies, agencies, names of tribes and their population, of all the Indians in the United States up to that date.

Table shewing the population of the various Indian tribes, by superintendencies, as corrected by the reports of 1866.

Superintendency and Agency.	Tribes.	Population.
WASHINGTON.		
Tulalip	Tulalips, Lummis, etc	1,900
Skokomish	Sklallams, etc	1,500
Makah	Makahs, etc	1,400
Puyallup	Puyallups, Nisquallies, etc	2,000
Quinaelt	Quinaelts, Quillehutes, etc	600
Yakama	Yakamas, etc	8,000
Fort Colville	Spokanes, Colvilles, Pend d'Oreilles, etc	3,400
		14,800
OREGON.		
Umatilla	Walla-Wallas, Cayuses, and Umatillas	759
Warm Spring	Wacoes, Deschutes, etc	1,070
Grande Ronde	Fifteen tribes and bands	1,144
Alsea	Cooses, Umpquas, etc	530
Siletz	Fourteen tribes and bands	2,068
Klamath	Klamaths, Modocs, and four bands of Snakes	4,000
	Other Indians	900
		10,471
CALIFORNIA.		
Round Valley	Pitt Rivers, Wylackies, Ukies, etc	1,889
Hoopa Valley	Various bands	623
Smith River	Humboldt and Wylackies	625
Tule River	Owens River and Tule River	725
Mission Indians	Various bands	8,800
	Coahuillas and other tribes	4,400
	King River and other bands	14,900
		25,062
ARIZONA.		
Papagos	Papagos 5,000, Pimas and Maricopas, 7,500	12,500
River Tribes	Yuhmas, Mohaves, etc	9,500
	Apaches	10,000
	Moquis	2,500
		34,500
NEVADA.		
Carson City	Pi-Utes	4,200
	Washoes	500
	Bannacks	1,500
	Shoshonees	2,000
		8,200
UTAH.		
Fort Bridger	Eastern Shoshones and Bannacks	4,500
	North-western Shoshones	1,800
	Western Shoshones	2,000
	Goships and Weber Utes	1,600
Uintah Valley	Utahs	7,100
	Piedes	600
	Pah-Utes	1,600
		19,800

TABLE.

Superintendency and Agency.	Tribes.	Population.
NEW MEXICO.		
Bosque Redondo	Navajoes at reservation	6,500
	Navajoes at large	1,200
Pueblos	Pueblos	7,010
Abiquiu	Capote Utes	350
	Webinoche Utes	700
Cimarron	Maquache Utes	600
	Jicarilla Apaches	800
Mescalero Apache	Mescalero Apaches	550
	Mimbres Apaches	200
	Captives held in peonage	2,000
COLORADO.		19,901
Denver	Grand River and Uintah Utes	2,500
Conejos	Tabequache Utes	2,500
DAKOTA.		5,000
Yankton	Yankton Sioux	2,530
Ponca	Poncas	980
Upper Missouri Sioux	Lower Brules	1,200
	Lower Yanctonais	2,100
	Two Kettles	1,200
	Blackfeet	1,820
	Minneconjoux	2,220
	Uncpapas	1,800
	Ogalallahs	2,100
	Upper Yanctonais	2,400
	Sans Arcs	1,680
Fort Berthold	Arickarees	1,500
	Gros Ventres	400
	Mandans	400
	Assiniboines	2,640
IDAHO.		24,470
Nez Perces	Nez Perces	2,830
	Cœur d'Alenes, Kootenays, etc.	2,000
	Boise and Bruneau Shoshones	500
	Kammas Prairie Shoshones	2,000
MONTANA.		7,330
Flathead	Flatheads	558
	Upper Pend d'Oreilles	918
	Kootenays	287
Blackfeet	Blackfeet	2,450
	Piegans	1,870
	Bloods	2,150
	Gros Ventres	1,500
	Crows	8,900
NORTHERN.		18,633
Winnebago	Winnebagoes	1,750
Omaha	Omahas	997
Ottoe	Ottoes and Missourias	511
Pawnee	Pawnees	2,750
Great Nehemaha	Sacs and Foxes of Missouri	102
	Iowas	303

Superintendency and Agency.	Tribes.	Population.
NORTHERN (continued).		
Upper Platte	Brule and Ogalallah Sioux	7,865
	Cheyennes	1,800
	Arapahoes	750
Santee Sioux (Niobrara)	Santee Sioux	1,850
CENTRAL.		18,178
Potowatomie	Potowatomies	1,992
Sac and Fox	Sacs and Foxes of Mississippi	766
	Chippeways and Munsees	80
Osage River	Miamies	127
	Peorias, Piankeshaws, Kaskaskias, and Weas	236
Shawnee	Shawnees	660
Delaware	Delawares	1,064
Kansas	Kansas or Kaws	670
Kickapoo	Kickapoos	242
Ottawa	Ottawas	200
Kiowa and Comanche	Kiowas and Comanches	2,800
Arapahoe, Cheyenne, and Apache	Arapahoes, Cheyennes, and Apaches	4,000
SOUTHERN.		12,837
Creek	Creeks	14,896
Cherokee	Cherokees	14,000
Choctaw and Chickasaw	Choctaws	12,500
	Chickasaws	4,500
Seminole	Seminoles	2,000
Neosho	Osages	8,000
	Quapaws	350
	Senecas and Shawnees	210
	Senecas	130
Wichitas	Wichitas	392
	Keechies	144
	Wacoes	135
	Tawacairoes	151
	Caddoes and Ionies	362
	Shawnees	520
	Delawares	114
	Other Indians	1,000
		58,904
INDEPENDENT AGENCIES.		
Green Bay	Stockbridges and Munsees	152
	Oneidas	1,104
	Menominies	1,376
		2,632
Chippeways of Mississippi	Mississippi bands	2,166
	Pillager and Winnebagoshish bands	1,809
	Red Lake bands	1,183
	Pembina bands	981
		6,179
Chippeways of L'ke Superior	Various bands	4,500

Superintendency and Agency.	Tribes.	Population.
INDEPENDENT AGENCIES (continued).		
Wandering bands in Wisconsin	Winnebagoes	700
	Potowatomies	650
		1,850
Mackinac	Chippeways of Lake Superior	1,058
	Ottawas and Chippeways	5,207
	Chippeways of Saginaw, etc	1,562
	Chippeways, Ottawas, and Potowatomies	232
	Potowatomies of Huron	46
		8,105
New York	Cattaraugus	1,886
	Cayugas with Senecas	150
	Onondagas with Senecas	188
	Allegany	845
	Tonawandas	529
	Tuscaroras	360
	Oneidas	184
	Oneidas with Onondagas	96
	Onondagas	825
		4,013
	Total	295,774

CHAPTER XV.

THE STATES OF OHIO, INDIANA, ILLINOIS, AND MICHIGAN.

OHIO.

This word, in French orthography, is the Iroquois name of the Alleghony and Ohio rivers, and the French used as an equivalent word, "la belle," or the beautiful." According to French and Iroquois pronounciation, the *i* has the sound of *e* long. The word does not include "river," and might have been Oheao, or duck, in the Cayuga dialect, and thus originally been called by that band, *Oheao kihade*, or Duck river.

The name of the first white man who discovered the State of Ohio is not known, but it was probably the Jesuit missionary who, it is said, visited the Eries, or neutral nation, from Lake Huron, in 1616. La Salle sailed along its shore in 1679; a party of English visited Detroit in 1686, and Captain De Vincennes, of Canada, was ordered to establish a military post among the Miamies in 1697, and passed up the Maumee river.

After the establishment of a military post at Detroit in 1701, trading posts are often mentioned by French documents at Maumee and Sandusky; and "Sandusky," and "Miamies on Maumee," are enumerated in an English pamphlet, printed in 1755, as old French military posts. They were surrendered to the English in the transfer of Canada. The fort at Sandusky was captured by Pontiac, May 16th, 1763; but was returned to the English after the

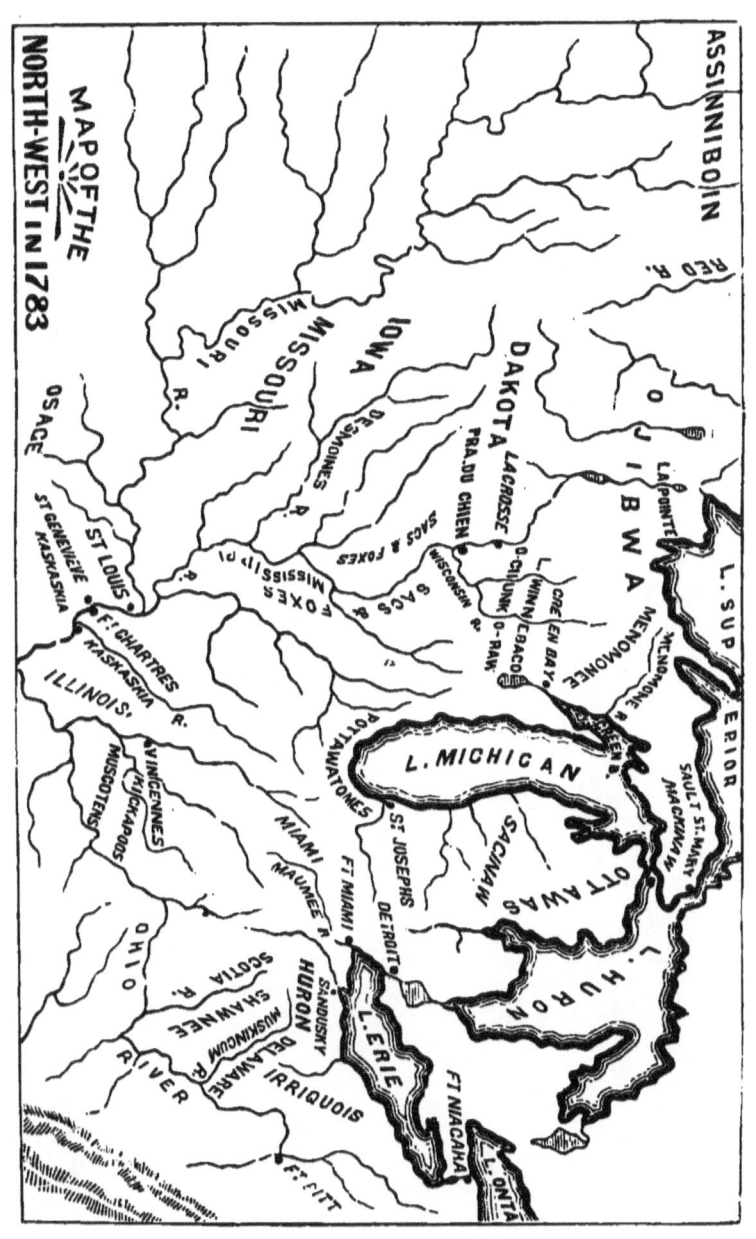

close of that war. The French also, in 1755, had a trading post at the mouth of the Sciota, according to the London pamphlet, which was spoken of also in Post's journal. In April, 1794, the British built a fort at Maumee rapids, and General Wayne, in August of the same year, built Fort Defiance at Grand Glaize.

After the close of the war of the revolution, the United States took military possession of the Ohio valley; and in 1785 Major Doughty built Fort Harmer, at Marietta, and Major Finny, the same year, built Fort Finny, at the mouth of the Miami river.

The primitive soil of Connecticut affording but poor encouragement to their agriculturalists, a plan was originated there in March, 1786, to plant a colony on the rich banks of the Ohio, and a subscription was begun to raise funds to purchase a large tract of land for a New England colony. The subscribers to this fund met March 8th, 1787, and elected General Parsons, General Rufus Putnam, and Rev. Manasseh Cutler, as directors of the colony, which they called the Ohio Company. On the 5th of July following, Dr. Cutler was sent to New York to negotiate with Congress, then in session, for the purchase of a tract of land on the Ohio, for the settlement. After a large number of "manœuvres," in the classic language of the Puritan divine, but in the more descriptive language of the west, "of log rolling and bribery," a favorable contract was made, July 27th, and a plan was arranged for the political organization of the north-west. This happy result was chronicled in the Rev. Doctor's journal as follows: "By this ordinance we obtained the grant of near 5,000,000 acres of land, amounting $3,500,000; 1,500,000 acres for the Ohio Company, and the remainder for a private speculation, in which many of the principal characters of America are concerned. Without connecting this speculation, similar terms and advantages could not have been obtained for the Ohio Company." With this ordinance, Dr. Cutler closed his contract with the Board of Treasury, October 27th, 1788. By referring to dates, it will be observed that, July 13th, 1787, the "Ordinance for the government of the Territory of the United States north-west of the River Ohio" was passed by Congress; and as Dr. Cutler had the names of all the officers of the new territory "in his hat," he, July 23rd, found himself in a tight place; and here again, in his journal, he tells how he escaped this crisis in his affairs: "Having found it impossible to support General Parsons as a candidate for governor, after the interest that General Arthur St. Clair had secured, I embraced this opportunity to declare, that if General Parsons could have the appointment of first judge, and Sargent secretary, we should be satisfied; and that I heartily wished his excellency General St. Clair might be the governor; and that I would solicit the eastern members in his favor. This I found rather pleasing to southern members." Among the arguments which he tells us in his journal he urged with effect, were the following: "The uneasiness of the Kentucky people with respect to the Mississippi was notorious. A revolt of that country from the Union, if a war with Spain took place, was universally acknowledged to be highly probable; and most certainly a systematic settlement in that country, conducted by men thoroughly attached to the federal government, and composed of young, robust, and hardy laborers, who had no idea of any other than the Federal government, I conceived to be an object worthy of some attention."

The tract of land which was thus secured was located on the north side of the Ohio, and extending from the Sciota river east, to the seventh range of townships; but as politicians did not meet their part of the engagement when money was required, and even the Ohio Company got short of funds, the tract was cut down in 1792 so as to only include the country between the seventh and tenth ranges of townships, and extending from the Ohio river north so as to include 750,000 acres, besides reservations. For this tract the Ohio Company was to pay one dollar per acre, deducting one-third of the whole tract for waste land.

Pursuant to this plan for a colony, General Rufus Putnam, as superintendent, set out with forty-seven emigrants, soon after the 1st of January, 1788, and reached the site of Marietta April 7th of that year, having traveled by way of Cumberland, Maryland.

Governor St. Clair received his appointment as governor October 5th, 1787, and reached Marietta July 9th of the following year; and on the 27th of July, by proclamation, organized the new county of Washington. The second county, Hamilton, including the new settlement at Cincinnati, was not organized until January 2nd, 1790. Cincinnati was made a town January 2nd, 1802, and a city by charter in 1819. Notwithstanding the Indian war, settlers continued to flock to the north side of the Ohio, of which many came from Kentucky; and in 1800, Congress set off the Indian territory.

By an Act of Congress, passed April 30th, 1802, Ohio was permitted to call a convention to form a State constitution. The constitution was adopted, in convention, November 29th, 1802, and Ohio became a member of the Union February 19th of the following year.

By the census of 1800, Ohio was found to contain 45,365 inhabitants. From this time the increase was rapid, and it contained, in 1810, 230,760; 1820, 581,295; 1830, 937,903; 1840, 1,519,467; 1850, 1,980,329; and in 1860, 2,339,502. From a comparison with the population of other States, it appears that Ohio became the third State in the Union in 1840, in population, which position it held in 1860, New York and Pennsylvania only exceeding it.

For educational purposes, Congress has donated to the State 675,094 acres for public schools, and 24,320 acres for colleges. In 1863, the permanent school fund amounted to $2,879,379, yielding an annual interest of $173,712. In addition to this, there was raised by State taxes for school purposes, $1,155,221; and by local taxes, $1,021,012.

In 1857, 838,037 children between the ages of five and twenty-one were enumerated, of which the average daily attendance at school was 350,867. In 1862, the enumeration was 920,820; and average daily attendance at school, 433,343.

In 1862 there were common schools, 14,728; high schools, 144; German and English schools, 108; and colored schools, 172; total, 15,152. The same year there were employed 10,459 male, and 10,931 female teachers; total, 21,390.

Ohio has also the following State institutions; four Insane Asylums, a Reform School, Institution for the Education of the Blind, Institution for Deaf and Dumb, Asylum for Idiotic and Imbecile Youth, and State Penitentiary.

In November, 1863, Ohio had twenty-four colleges and universities, which belonged as follows: three to the State, one to the Presbyterians, new school, one to the Presbyterians, old school, two to Presbyterians and Congregationalists, one to the Episcopalians, one to the Baptists, one to the Congregationalists, three to the Catholics, four to the Methodist Episcopal Church, two to Methodists, two to Evangelical Lutherans, one New Jerusalem church, one, Christian, and one United Brethren in Christ. The aggregate number of students in all the institutions, was about 3,300.

The newspaper, according to modern civilization, travels with the emigrant; hence we find, as early as July 29, 1786, the "Pittsburg Gazette," christened as the first child in that family in the upper Mississippi valley. With no violation of the course of nature, the second child in that family was christened the "Kentucky Gazette," at Lexington, in August, 1789; while "The Sentinel of the North-western Territory," at Cincinnati, November 9, 1793, which was changed to "Freeman's Journal" in 1796; and the "Western Spy and

Hamilton Gazette," also at Cincinnati, of May 28, 1799; all succeeding each other in the period of nearly three years; these certainly established their right to the name of "periodical literature."

This good name must not have been lost, for in Ohio alone, in 1810, we find there were fourteen weekly papers; while in 1828 the number had increased to sixty-six.

The census of 1840 gave them 9 daily, 107 weekly, 7 semi-weekly papers, and 20 periodicals; total, 143. In 1850, Ohio had 26 dailies, with the annual circulation of 14,285,633; 10 tri-weeklies, with a circulation of 1,047,930; 201 weeklies, with a circulation of 13,334,204. They had also 23 semi-monthly, with an annual circulation of 1,781,640; 1 monthly, with circulation of 24,000; total, 261. Total number of copies printed annually, 30,473,407.

In 1860 the census report shows: *Political*, 22 daily, 4 bi-weekly, 8 tri-weekly, 219 weekly, and 3 monthly; total, 256. *Religious*, 27 weekly, 8 monthly, 2 annually; total, 37; *Literary*, 1 daily, 6 weekly, 17 monthly; total, 24. *Miscellaneous*, 1 daily, 8 weekly, 13 monthly, 1 annual; total, 23.

The total number of copies circulated annually, was 71,767,742.

INDIANA.

The Rev. Father James Marquette, and his party, were probably the first white persons who visited any part of the territory of Indiana.

Returning from the newly-established mission of "the Immaculate Conception," among the Kaskaskias, Father Marquette passed up the Kankakee, across the portage, and down the St. Joseph's river to Lake Michigan, about the first of May, 1675; but died on the 17th day of the same month, before he reached Mackinaw, of chronic diarrhœa, a disease he contracted two years previous, while exploring the Mississippi.

The second party of white persons who visited Indiana,

was that of La Salle, which passed down the Kankakee river in December, 1679, on their way to explore the Mississippi.

In 1697, Captain De Vincennes was ordered by the Governor of Canada, with a small military force, to the Miamies on the Wabash, who established post Vincennes. He was popular among the Miamies, and remained the most of the time until his death there in 1719. His post was called Fort Vincennes after 1720, and was continued a trading-post as long as the Indians remained in the country.

By the act of Congress of July 13, 1787, Indiana was included in the territory north-west of the Ohio, but was made a separate territory May 7, 1800. In April, 1816, Congress passed an act authorizing Indiana to form a State government. On the 29th of June, of the same year, the people adopted a State constitution, and December 11, 1816, the State of Indiana was admitted into the Union of States.

While Indiana was an Indian territory, Congress, by an act approved March 26, 1804, established three land offices in the territory: one at Detroit, one at Vincennes, and one at Kaskaskia.

For the disposal of the lands along the Ohio river, between Vincennes and Cincinnati districts, a new land office was established at Jeffersonville by the act of the 3rd of March, 1807. By the act of the 3rd of March, 1819, additional land offices were established at Brookville and Terre Haute; and by the act of May 8, 1822, an additional office was established at Fort Wayne. By the act of March 2, 1833, another land office was established at La Porte, which in December, 1839, was removed to Winamac.

By the act of 1816, authorizing Indiana to form a constitution for a State government, Congress gave the new State the sixteenth section in each township for schools; all the salt springs, including the lands not exceeding thirty-six sections; five per cent. of the net proceeds of the sales of the public lands lying in said State; two townships of land for a seminary of learning; and four sections of land as a site for the seat of government.

By the census of 1840, Indiana was reported as then having 1,521 primary schools, with 48,189 scholars; 54 academies, with 2,946 scholars; and 4 colleges and universities, with 322 students. In 1850 the school fund was estimated at $3,628,215. There were, in 1851, 5,899 schools, and 225,318 scholars. In 1850, Indiana was reported by the census as having 4 colleges, with 295 students; 1 theological school, with 15 students; 2 medical schools, with 154 students; and 2 law schools, with 18 students.

In 1862, the common school fund was estimated at the value of $4,991,202. The whole number of children between five and twenty-one years, was 528,583; school districts, 7,921; number of schools taught, 5,995; number of high schools, 103; number of pupils attending primary schools, 273,450; number attending high schools, 7,318; number of private schools, 1,932; number of pupils attending private schools, 39,658.

The Hospital for the Blind, Institution for the Education of the Deaf and Dumb, and the Hospital for the Insane, all at Indianapolis, are flourishing institutions. In 1863, Indiana had thirteen colleges and universities, which belonged as follows: One to the State, two to the Presbyterians, four to the Methodists, two to the Baptists, one to the United Brethren in Christ, one to the Evangelical Lutherans, one to the Catholics, and one to the Christians, with an aggregate of 1,810 students. The Catholics and Lutherans had each a Theological School.

The population of 1800, which included Detroit, Kaskaskia, Prairie Du Chien, Green Bay and Mackinaw, and all the Indian territory, was enumerated in the census at 4,875. The census of 1810 gave a population of 24,520 for Indiana, without including Illinois or Michigan, as those regions had previously been set into new territories. In

1820 there were 147,178; 1830, 343,031; 1840, 685,866; 1850, 988,416; and 1860, 1,350,428.

In 1810, Indiana had one weekly newspaper, which circulated during the year 15,600 copies. In 1828, the number had increased to 17. By the census of 1840, there were 4 semi-weekly, 69 weekly, and 3 periodical papers.

The census of 1850 shows that the number had increased to 9 daily, 2 tri-weekly, 95 weekly, and 1 semi-monthly; total, 107, with a total annual circulation of 4,316,828 copies. These papers were classified as 21 literary, 84 political, and 2 religious.

In 1860, Indiana had the following papers: *Political*, 13 daily, 5 bi-weekly, 154 weekly; total, 172. *Religious*, 3 weekly, and 3 monthly; total, 6. *Literary*, 3 weekly, 2 monthly; total, 5. *Miscellaneous*, 3 monthly. The aggregate circulation of these papers, per annum, was 10,090,310.

ILLINOIS.

We have seen that Sieur Joliette, with Marquette, were the first to explore Illinois, by passing down the Mississippi in June, 1673, and returning north by the Illinois river and Lake Michigan.

Agreeably to a promise made to the Kaskaskia Indians, Marquette started from Green Bay, October 25, 1674, to return and establish a mission amongst them, but was detained by sickness during the winter at Chicago, and only succeeded in reaching the Kaskaskias, on the Illinois river, April 8, 1675. Here his stay was short, as he continued to grow weaker; and he died on his way to Mackinaw, May 17th, of the same year.

The Rev. Father Allouez, the honored founder of the Wisconsin missions, left Green Bay in October, 1676, to renew the mission at Illinois, but winter setting in earlier than expected, he only reached the Kaskaskias April 27, of the following year.

Here he found congregated eight tribes, of whom he

baptized thirty-five children and a sick adult. He continued in charge of this mission until near the time of the arrival of La Salle, when he retired to Green Bay, fearing the hostility of La Salle to the Jesuits. La Salle and his party descended the Kankakee river from St. Joseph's, and reached the site of the Indian village on the Illinois at the "Rock," near the close of December, 1679; but as the Indians were further down the river, he, January 1, pushed on, and on the 4th day of that month, found the tribe at the head of *Pimiteoui,* "or lake of plenty of fat beasts," since called Lake Peoria, where he built Fort *Crévecœur,* or "heart-breaking," so named on account of their many disappointments.

Rev. Father St. Cosme, who passed down the Illinois river in 1699, spoke of an "old fort," built by La Salle, at the upper village of the Indians, on a "rock which is on the bank of the river, about a hundred feet high," which La Salle "abandoned." If so, La Salle might have built a temporary fort during the few days that he remained at the deserted Indian village, but there is no mention of it by his historian.

Fort Crévecœur was made the head-quarters of the French missions for many years. About 1700 the Kaskaskias removed down, and settled at the mouth of Kaskaskia river, with their missionaries, leaving the Peorias at the lake. About 1722, the Peorias and other bands, at the Rock and Peoria lake, being pressed hard in their wars with the Foxes and their allies, also settled on the Mississippi near the Kaskaskias. The congregating of so many Indians near the mouth of the Kaskaskia river, induced the French to build a strong fort a few miles above the mouth of that river, in 1720, which they called *Fort Chartres.* This fort was strongly built of stone masonry. In the article for its surrender in 1765, it was described as eighteen feet high, and $334\frac{1}{2}$ toises in circumference. The south side, fronting the Mississippi, was $80\frac{1}{2}$ toises. The fort was pierced with

204 loop-holes. Besides the fort, there were the guard-house, government house, intendant's house, barracks, powder-house, bake-house, prison, and store, all built with stone, with "windows in cut stone, with shutters, iron-work," etc.

Fort Chartres was the center of French power and missionary labors on the upper Mississippi, until the surrender of Canada to the English in 1760. The fort was finally surrendered to the English, October 10, 1765, and it was held by them until it was partly undermined by the river about 1771, and abandoned by the English. The English had another fort above Kaskaskia, which Colonel Clark captured July 4, 1778; after which the French settlements at Kaskaskia and Cahokia, near the Mississippi, became a part of Virginia, and that State, in October of the same year, organized the country north-west of the Ohio into the county of Illinois. Thus continued the political affairs of the north-west, until the passage of "An ordinance for the government of the territory of the United States north-west of the river Ohio," July 13, 1787. May 7, 1800, Illinois was included with Indiana, and the territory north, in the "Indian Territory." In 1809, Illinois was made a separate territory, and August 26, 1818, formed a constitution, and December 3rd, of the same year, was admitted into the Union by a special act of Congress.

After the close of the revolutionary war, American emigrants occasionally passed the Ohio to the Indian territory, and in 1810 Illinois numbered 12,282, including the old French villages. In 1820 they had increased to 55,162, including 917 slaves. In 1830, 157,445; 1840, 476,183; 1850, 851,470; 1860, 1,711,951. The first American settlers were mainly from the slave-holding States, and many brought with them their negro slaves, notwithstanding the prohibition in the ordinance of 1787. These slaves numbered 331 in the census of 1840, but disappear before that of 1850. These settlers generally remained in the south

THE UNIVERSITY OF CHICAGO.

part of the State. After the Black Hawk war in 1832, emigration commenced entering the State by way of the lakes, and in 1837 the great tide was setting in heavily, and soon overspread the great prairies of the north.

By the act authorizing Illinois to form a State constitution, Congress donated to the State, for school purposes, the sixteenth section in each township, and three per cent. of the net proceeds of the sales of the public lands in the State after 1819; and for a seminary of learning, two entire townships, or seventy-two sections of land. In 1850, the permanent school fund amounted to $790,120; the Seminary fund, $58,788; and the State University fund, $90,889. Illinois has an excellent system for public education. In addition to her public State institutions, individual enterprise and benevolence have given her several excellent academies and colleges.

In 1862, there were in Illinois, 9,811 public schools, and 516,037 scholars attending those schools; 720 private schools, and 22,577 scholars. In 1864, Illinois had fifteen colleges and universities, three of which belonged to the State, four to the Methodists, two to the Baptists, one to the Presbyterians, new school, one to the Catholics, one to the United Presbyterians, one to the Presbyterians and Congregationalists, one to the Evangelical Lutherans, and one to the Universalists. These, in the aggregate, had 2,203 students. One of the most prosperous of these institutions is the University of Chicago, founded by the late Senator S. A. Douglas, in 1855, and now belonging to the Baptist denomination.

In 1862, the entire educational funds belonging to the State were $4,973,842, the interest of which, with the annual taxes levied, are expended for the different educational institutions belonging to the State.

Newspapers were not a very early institution in Illinois, as there were none in 1810, and but four weekly papers in 1828. In 1840, there were three dailies, two semi-weeklies, thirty-eight weeklies, and nine called "periodicals." In 1850, the number had increased to eight daily, four tri-weekly, eighty-four weekly, three semi-monthly, seven monthly, and one quarterly, with an aggregate circulation of 5,102,276 per annum. In 1860, the census showed, political papers: twenty-three daily, one bi-weekly, six tri-weekly, two hundred and twenty-eight weekly, and one monthly. Of religious papers, there were five weekly and six monthly. Literary, three weekly and five monthly; and miscellaneous, one bi-weekly, two weekly, and five monthly, with an aggregate circulation per annum of 27,464,764.

MICHIGAN.

The name of this State is abbreviated from two Chippeway words, *Michau,* or *Misho,* great, and *Sakiegan,* a lake, and literally means the great lake. The territory of this State was probably first visited by Sir Jean Nicolet, the Canadian interpreter, who appears to have visited the Winnebagoes at Green Bay in 1639. Rev. Fathers Joques and Raymbaut, Jesuit missionaries, next appear to have passed along the north shore of lake Huron, and visited the falls of St. Mary in 1641, where Rev. Fathers Dablon and Marquette established a missionary station in 1669, which must be regarded as the first permanent settlement of the State; leaving Wisconsin as the older State in point of settlement by four years. Mackinaw was made a missionary station by Marquette, in 1671, and the Canadian government raised it to a military post in 1688, and built a fort. In the mean time the Detroit, or straits between Lakes Huron and Erie, had been explored by Indian traders; and La Salle sailed from Niagara to Green Bay in the "Griffin," in 1679; and in 1687 the Canadian government built Fort St. Joseph, or De Lut, at the foot of Lake Huron, in Michigan; La Durantaye, in the name of the French king, having taken formal possession of all the east coast of the State June 7th of the same year.

La Salle, in November, 1679, built Fort La Salle, at the mouth of a river in the south-western part of the State, which was afterwards changed, probably by Allouez, the missionary at that point, to St. Joseph's.

Fort Pontchartrain was built by the Canadian government in 1701, at the present site of the city of Detroit, which laid the foundation of that enterprising city of the west. This point thus became the head quarters of the Indian trade in Michigan, Ohio, and Indiana, and for many years following. Its history has been given in the Indian wars in previous chapters.

By an Act of Congress, approved January 11th, 1805, all that part of the then Indian territory lying north of a line running east from the southern extremity of Lake Michigan, was organized with a territorial government under the name of "Michigan Territory." By an Act in 1818, the present territory of Wisconsin was attached to Michigan, and remained so attached until 1836, when it was also organized into a territorial government.

Without any enabling Act of Congress, the territory of Michigan held a convention and formed a State constitution, but its admission was long opposed in Congress; and they were finally compelled to surrender a part of their territory on the south, and in lieu thereof take the upper or Lake Superior peninsula; and after so amending their constitution, they were admitted as a State by an Act of Congress, approved January 26th, 1837.

The new State received from Congress the grant of seventy-two sections, or square miles of land, as an endowment of a university; the sixteenth section in each six miles square for the support of common schools.

In 1850 Michigan had 3,097 common schools, and 132,233 children between the ages of four and eighteen which attended school during the year. Besides these, there were 2,056 under four, and 8,346 over eighteen, which attended school. The public money, or interest of the school fund, that year distributed was $42,794.44; in addition to which, there were raised by tax to pay teachers, $81,392.44. To this, if we add funds raised to build school-houses, library funds, etc., we have a total paid out for schools during the year of $194,330.78.

In 1855 the number of scholars attending school were 142,307; and the number of teachers, 1,600 male, and 3,474 female. In 1860, the total number of scholars over four and under eighteen years of age were 240,684; number of scholars attending school, 192,937; number of teachers 2,599 male, and 5,344 female.

In 1862 the whole number of children over five and under twenty years of age were 261,323; number attending school, 207,332, with 2,380 male teachers and 5,958 female.

The State Normal School, at Ypsilanti, was opened for students in April, 1853, and in 1862 had 407 students in the normal department, and 86 in the model school. Students pledge themselves to teach in the State schools after they graduate.

The University of Michigan, at Ann Arbor, was opened in 1837, and their endowment funds from the seventy-two sections granted by Congress amounted in 1862 to $525,000, from the interest of which the University is mainly supported. A medical department was added in 1850, and a law department in 1859. It has also a fine astronomical department. In 1862 the University had, in the department of literature, 270 students; department of medicine, 216; and department of law, 129.

In 1857 Michigan founded a "State Agricultural College," at Lansing, and has now assigned to it the land granted by Congress to agricultural colleges. It has a farm of seven hundred acres, together with a fine laboratory, library, museum, etc. Students are required to labor on the farm three hours daily.

Besides these, there are the "State Reform School," at Lansing; the "Michigan Asylum for the Deaf and Dumb and Blind," at Flint; the "Asylum for the Insane," at Kalamazoo; and State Prison, at Jackson. All these institutions are doing a good work in their several departments of education and discipline. In addition to these State institutions, there are many private schools and academies, supported by private benevolence, and three colleges, viz.: Kalamazoo College, founded in 1833 by the Baptists; Hillsdale College, founded in 1853 by the Freewill Baptists; and the Albion College, founded in 1862 by the Methodist Episcopal church, having for several years previous been an academy. All these are owned by the denominations founding them.

The population of Michigan has been steadily progressive. There were, in 1810, 4,762; 1820, 8,765; 1830, 31,639; 1840, 212,267; 1850; 397,654; and 1860, 749,113.

Newspapers were a luxury in which Michigan did not early indulge. None had greeted them in 1810; and but two in 1828. The writer has not the date of the first paper, but the "Detroit Gazette" was being published as early at least as May, 1819. In 1840 they could boast of having 6 daily, 26 weekly, and 1 magazine. In 1850 the census gave the State 3 daily, 2 tri-weekly, 47 weekly, 3 semi-monthly, and 3 monthly publications; total 58, with an aggregate circulation for the year of 3,247,736.

In 1860, the papers had increased to: *Political*, 8 daily, 3 bi-weekly, 1 tri-weekly, 96 weekly, 1 monthly; total, 109. *Religious*, 3 weekly, 1 monthly; total, 4. *Literary*, 3 weekly. *Miscellaneous*, 1 weekly and 1 monthly. The aggregate circulation per annum was 11,606,596.

CHAPTER XVI.

WISCONSIN.

In writing of the introduction of civilization into the northwest, we have no fables to relate to prepossess the minds of a credulous generation, that our country has been specially favored by Deity; but, like the French commandant at Detroit, when attacked by the Indians, we don't "know on what Saint to call," and when driven to the necessity of making a selection, we are perfectly at liberty to take St. George of England, St. Andrew of Scotland, St. Patrick of Ireland, or St. Xavier of Japan, with full assurance that either of them will be equally serviceable to us in our necessities.

But if the day of Saints had passed away at the time of the advent of the whites to our shores, the day of imposition had not, and if the reader had been standing on the *Moke-kaw-shoots-raw*, or red earth banks of Green Bay, in the summer of 1639, there might probably have been seen advancing, in a pompous procession of Hurons and O-chunk-o-raws, a Frenchman, dressed in a long, full robe of china damask, covered over with flowers and birds of all colors, and carrying a pistol in each hand. To the reader, such a pompous display of brilliant colors would have excited only a smile of contempt; but not so with the untutored savage. The timid *Enog-ga-raw*, and her little flock of *Nink-sing-in-graws*, screamed, "*Wau-kon-ga-raw!*" or the "spirit man," and fled to the shelter of their wig-

wams, while the dusky warrior, whose courage of a hundred battles, welling up in his soul until it sparkled in his brilliant eyes, with his hands firmly grasping his bow and tomahawk, looked on with profound silence.

The message delivered was " Peace "— a fit message to be always borne by civilization. Peace between the great Huron, Iroquois and Algonquin nations. Perhaps the reader imagines this message was received by the old warriors with scorn and contempt, but they mistake even the Indian character. It was received with great joy. The news spread through the surrounding country, and soon after, an assembly of 4,000 or 5,000 of different nations came together, and great feasts were given by the chiefs, one of which served up six score beaver at a single banquet. Here were the *O-chunk-o-raws*, "sedentary and very numerous;" the proud *Illinois*, or "The Men;" the bold and warlike Dakotas, or the confederates; and the wandering Potowatomies, a stray band of Algonquins; all rejoicing with the Frenchman, at the temporary peace among a portion of the tribes that lived along the great lakes, foolishly thinking that a peace proclaimed by such a wonderful man would be permanent, and that thereafter their slumbers would not be broken by the murderous tomahawk. But this delusion was nearly fatal to the O-chunk-o-raws, who were nearly exterminated the following year by the Illinois, and but two years after, the Potowatomies fled to Lake Superior, from the victorious Dakotas.

War is generated among barbarous nations precisely as among civilized. Aggressions are committed by a few malicious and discontented persons; retaliation follows, when the war cry is raised, and but few have the moral power to resist its potent influence. Blood flows freely until the original instigators are destroyed, or the people become satiated with revenge. Christianity is the only power that can be brought to oppose war; but, alas! this has often proved too weak to calm the baser passions of our human natures.

The Frenchman whom I have introduced was *Sieur Jean Nicolet*, the Huron and Algonquin interpreter for the government of Canada. The governor of that colony, having heard of the "*Gens de Mer*," whom the Algonquins called *Winnebagoue*, or men of the Salt water, conceived the idea of exploring their country, and dispatched *Sieur Nicolet* for that purpose. He passed to the Hurons, took seven of that tribe as an escort, and coasted Lake Huron to the Winnebagoes, on the Green Bay. Here he concluded a treaty of peace with several tribes, and on his return, having reported "that had he sailed three days more on a great river which flows from that lake (Green Bay) he would have found the sea," it has been inferred that he reached the Wisconsin river, and was the first Frenchman that floated on the waters of the upper Mississippi.

The exact time of this exploration is not given in the Jesuit records; but, having been first spoken of in their Relations for 1639 and 1640, it is believed that it took place the former year.

Sieur Nicolet continued in the service of the Canadian government until October 31st, 1642, when he was capsized in a storm, near Quebec, and drowned. Thus perished the discoverer of Wisconsin, leaving but a paragraph of history.

Soon after Sieur Nicolet visited Green Bay, the Iroquois renewed their war against the western tribes, and the writer finds no record of any other white person having visited Wisconsin until the winter of 1659–60, when two Frenchmen, probably from Kewenaw bay, Lake Superior, visited the Tionontaties, on the head waters of Black river, "six days' journey towards the south-west;" and again, in the spring of 1661, Father René Menard, a Jesuit missionary, dispatched three Frenchmen from St. Theresa bay (probably

Kewenaw bay,) who found the "poor tribe of Hurons" far down the Black river, nearly in a state of starvation.

Finally, the good Father Menard, aged and infirm, with his lay assistant, Jean Guerin, left St. Theresa bay, June 13th, 1661, to visit the poor nation of Hurons far down the Black river,—lost his way in passing the portage, probably at Black River falls, August 10th, 1661, and perished in the woods.

After the death of Father Menard, his lay assistant, Jean Guerin, returned to St. Theresa bay, Lake Superior, and continued his missionary labors until October, 1662, when he was accidentally killed by the discharge of a gun.

But these misfortunes only quickened the missionary spirit of the zealous Jesuits, and, August 8th, 1665, found Father *Claude Allouez* embarking at "Three Rivers," Canada, with six Frenchmen and four hundred returning savages for Lake Superior.

The long, serpent-like flotilla of bark canoes slowly passed up the Ottawa river, in Canada, coursed the north shore of Lake Huron, passed the Falls of St. Mary, danced over the boisterous waves of the south shore of Lake Superior; and finally the tiny fleet was safely moored on the sandy beach of the main land, at the foot of what the Indians called "Chagouamigong" bay, in Wisconsin, October 1st, 1665. Here the pious Father established the mission of "The Holy Ghost," erected a chapel and cabins, and entered upon his great work; while his no less industrious French associates opened their little shops of Indian trinkets, and bartered for furs with the dusky natives.

But the good Father and his little party were unconsciously doing a still greater work. They were commencing the first settlement, and laying the foundations of the present flourishing, christian, and commercial State of Wisconsin. This proved a very important post to the French until the spring of 1671, when they and their Indian allies were driven out by the brave Dakotas, on whose territory they were trespassers.

For a few years the Dakotas held undisturbed possession of the shore of Lake Superior; but, in 1679, the adventurous *De Lut* visited the south-west coast of that lake, made peace with the Dakotas and Christinaux, and set up the arms of the king of France at three distant points; and in June of 1680, with two canoes, one Indian, and four Frenchmen, passed up the St. Louis river, and down the Rum river to the Mississippi, where he redeemed Father Hennepin from captivity, and conducted him to Mackinaw, by the way of the Wisconsin river.

A military post was established at Chegouamigong Point, under the charge of Lesueur, in 1692. From that time to the present, it is believed that that point, or "La Point," on Madeline island, has been occupied by the white traders, and most of the time as a military post.

At the close of the Iroquois war, in 1666, many of the savages having left Chegouamigong bay, at Lake Superior, and the Foxes, Sacs, Mascotens, Kickapoos and Pótowatomies, having returned to Green Bay and the Fox and Wisconsin rivers, Father Allouez resolved to follow them, and establish a church in that region. Consequently, on the 3rd of November, 1669, we find the good Father setting out from the Falls of St. Mary, Lake Superior, with two companions, for Green Bay. As the Father said: "Two canoes of Pouteouatamis wishing to take me to their country, not that I might instruct them, they having no disposition to receive the faith, but to mollify some young Frenchmen, who were among them for the purpose of trading, and who threatened and ill-treated them." On the second day, "the difficulties of the route, in consequence of the lateness of the season," induced them to "have recourse to Saint Francis Xavier, the patron of the mission," and on the fifth day they were involved in snow, delayed six days by bad weather; and finally he said: "The snow and frost menacing us with ice, my companions had recourse to Saint Anne, to whom we recommended our voyage, praying her, with Saint François Xavier, to take us under their protection." On the eleventh, near the Island of Mackinaw, they found two Frenchmen, with Indians, on the main land, and doubled in safety the cape south-west of that island. "Finally, after many difficulties," said the Father, " our navigation came to a close on the 2nd of December, the eve of the day of Saint François Xavier, by our arrival at the place where the Frenchmen were, who aided us to celebrate the festival with all the solemnity that was possible. The next day I celebrated the holy mass, at which the Frenchmen, to the number of eight, performed their devotions."

Here Father Allouez found one village of six hundred souls, composed of "Ousaki, Pouteouatamis, Outagami, and Ouenibigoutz," in which he soon commenced teaching, and named it the "Mission of Saint François Xavier." The location of this Indian village was on Fox river, near the bay.

For what length of time these six Frenchmen had occupied the point as a trading post previous to the arrival of the Jesuit Father, we have no intimation. They may have come in the summer of 1666, immediately after the conclusion of the peace with the Iroquois; but it is more probable that they commenced trade at the bay in the spring of 1669. But from the arrival of the Jesuit Fathers its importance as a trading post was established, and from that time may be dated its permanent settlement, thirty years after it was first visited by Sieur Nicolet, the Canadian interpreter.

From this date, the French appeared to make special efforts to press westward missionaries and the trade in furs, and finally, June 14th, 1671, at the Falls of St. Mary, in presence of large numbers of the Bay and Lake Superior savages, took solemn and formal " possession of the said place of St. Mary of the Falls, as well as of Lakes Huron and

Superior, the Island of Caientolon, and all other countries, rivers, lakes, and tributaries, contiguous and adjacent thereto, as well discovered as to be discovered, which are bounded on the one side by the northern and western seas, and on the other side by the south sea, including all its length or breadth; in the name of the most high, most mighty, and most redoubtable monarch Louis, the XIV. of the Christian name, king of France and Navarre."

These imposing ceremonies were had under the personal supervision of "Sieur De St. Lusson, commissioner sub-delegate of my lord the intendant of New France, to search for the copper mine . . . near Lake Superior;" and were witnessed by the Rev. Fathers Dablon, Drouillets, Allouez, and Andre, " all of the company of Jesus; Sieur Nicholas Perrot, his majesty's interpreter in these parts;" Sieur Jollyet, and fourteen other Frenchmen.

The desire so often expressed to explore the Mississippi, finally induced Comte De Frontenac, the Governor of Canada, to appoint for that service Sieur Jollyet, a young man born in Canada, and well acquainted with the Ottawa language, having resided with them several years; and assigned as his assistant Father James Marquette, of Mackinaw, who had fitted himself for the position by the study of the language of the Illinois while in charge of the mission of the Holy Ghost, at Lake Superior. The party, consisting of the two named, with five Frenchmen, embarked in two bark canoes from the mission of St. Ignatius, at Mackinaw, on the 17th of May, 1673. They passed by way of Green Bay and the Wisconsin portage, and reached the Mississippi the 17th of June, precisely one month after they left Mackinaw. They descended the river to the "Akansea" tribe, in about the 34° of latitude, and started on their return, July 17th, by way of the Illinois river and Chicago, and reached Green Bay the last of September.

The exact time at which a military post at Prairie Du Chien was established, has been the subject of much speculation, some putting it as late as 1775, while it is stated in a report of a committee in Congress to have occurred in 1755, which was the year following the reconciliation of the French and Sacs and Foxes. The latter date may be true, as the French surrendered Canada to the English in 1760, and the French made no pretensions to occupy the upper Mississippi after the abandonment of their fort at Lake Pepin, and the renewal of the Fox war in 1728; and in fact, the French trade to the Mississippi was nearly ruined from and after their barbarous massacre of the Foxes at Detroit in 1712.

But there must have been a French fort at or near Prairie Du Chien at a much earlier period. That it was *at* Prairie Du Chien is more than probable, as that has always been a point of general resort for the savages, and the "Mound-Builders" before them. The evidence of this early occupation is found in the document of the taking possession of the Mississippi valley in the name of the French king, by "Nicholas Perot, commanding for the king at the post of the Nadoue Sioux," "at the post of St. Anthony, May 8th, 1689," to which documents, among other names of witnesses, was "Monsr. De Borie-Guillot, commanding the French in the neighborhood of Ouiskonche, on the Mississippi."

Indeed, as early as 1686, the Governor of Canada, in his dispatch to the king, speaks of having received letters "from the upper Mississippi, where they propose wonders to me, were I to establish posts for the missions, and for the beavers which abound there." In reply, March 8, 1688, the king ordered the governor to send men to formally take possession of the country of the lakes and the Illinois, "in order to render incontestable his majesty's right." From these data, we may safely infer that the country about Prairie Du Chien was occupied as a French post, at least as early as the 20th of April, 1689, and possibly the previous fall.

But if the country was occupied as early as 1689, it does not follow that its occupation was continuous, for the Sacs, Foxes and kindred tribes were at war with the Sioux, from their first settlement on the Wisconsin river about 1655, to their peace with the Sioux about 1701; and as the French traders with the Sioux continued to sell powder, balls, guns, and other articles contraband of war, to that tribe, against the repeated remonstrance of the Foxes, their traders were often plundered by the latter tribe and their allies.

Neither did the condition of affairs improve on the alliance of the Sacs, Foxes, and Sioux, in 1701, as war was immediately commenced by the allies against the Chippeways and their allies of Lake Superior and the northern country, which continued with slight intermission until the reconciliation between the Foxes of the Wisconsin river, and the Christinaux of Lake Superior, in 1754. It is true that this war would at times subside, and traders would again reach the Mississippi. Thus in the fall of 1727, the French built Fort Beauharnois on the north side of Lake Pepin, but were driven out the following year; and Father Guignas, who had there established the "Mission of St. Michael, the archangel," was taken prisoner by the Mascotens, an allied tribe of the Foxes.

If the French ever had a permanent fort at Prairie Du Chien, in latter times, as tradition confirms, it was probably established in the fall of 1754, or the spring of the following year, when they rallied powerful bands of all the northwestern tribes against the English, with which they defeated General Braddock, near Pittsburgh, at the opening of the old French and Indian war, in 1755.

The Rev. A. Bronson, of Prairie Du Chien, in the Collections of the State Historical Society (Vol. 4, page 249), on the authority of B. W. Brisbois, Esq., a native of that place, states that the first settler of Prairie Du Chien was probably one Cardinell, who came with his wife to the Mississippi, from Canada, as a trader and trapper, between the years

1720 and 1730, and first fixed his residence on Cannon river, at the present site of Red Wing, Minnesota; but soon changed it to Prairie Du Chien, a more central point for trade, and opened the first farm at the latter place. Mr. Brisbois, who was personally acquainted with Cardinell's widow, who died very aged in 1827, had "heard her say that when she came to the place first, the waters were so high that they came up from the Wisconsin, next to the bluffs, where the ground is some feet lower than the rest of the plain, in their bark canoe." If this statement is true, Cardinell probably came to this prairie at the time of the great freshet on the Mississippi, in the spring of 1728, which flooded the fort on Lake Pepin, and was said by the Sioux to be the highest water they ever knew. The woman's statement has been quite generally doubted, because in modern times the river has not been high enough to flood the land next to the bluffs; but the great flood of 1728 having been established by official French documents, it goes strongly to corroborate her statement.

However, it does not follow, of course, that Cardinell was not driven out of the country with the other traders by the Foxes the same year, and even remained out until permitted to return after the general peace in 1754. The same authority makes the second settler one *Ganier*, whose descendants still live at the Prairie, but the date of his arrival is not given.

The Prairie derived its name from a Fox chief, by the name of *Alim*, or Dog, whose band occupied the bank of the Mississippi at that point as late as 1781, and the French name, "Prairie Du Chien," literally means, "Dog's Plains." By the French traditions, the "Dog's Plains" were purchased of the Fox Indians, probably at the time the French established the military post, about 1755, and evidence of the fact having been lost, the purchase was confirmed by *Nanpouis*, a Fox chief, about 1802, at Cahokia, near St. Louis.

Captain John Carver, of Boston, visited Prairie Du Chien in 1766, and wrote of it as then containing "about three hundred families," and that the houses were "well built, after the Indian manner," but does not say that it then contained any French inhabitants. He, however, said that it was a great mart for Indian trade, from which we can reasonably infer that it had a good supply of French traders; but as Canada had been surrendered to England, the French had of course evacuated their fort, which tradition said was burned the second year of the American revolution.

All Canada having been surrendered to England by the treaty of Paris, February 10, 1763, the most important posts were taken possession of by the British government, and in 1781, Lieutenant-Governor Patrick Sinclair, of Canada, negotiated with the Indians, and purchased Mackinaw, Green Bay, and Prairie Du Chien, and held possession of them until they were finally surrendered to the United States, July 1, 1796. Peter Lapoint was the interpreter at the treaty with the Indians, and was present at the Prairie when Bazil Guird, Pierre Antya, and Augustin Angé delivered the goods to the Indians, pursuant to the treaty, and with Michael Brisbois, became a permanent resident of that place in 1781 or 1782, from which time the post became one of importance, and its history easily traced. During the next ten years, nearly the whole prairie was claimed and reduced to cultivation by the adventurous *courriers de bois*, who had abandoned their wanderings, taken to their sweet embraces the daughters of the red men, and retired to the enjoyment of that connubial bliss which is often less appreciated by those much more advanced in the scale of civilization. Their numerous but dusky progeny, in which often flows the blood of mighty Indian warriors, now constitutes a portion of the aristocracy of the ancient villages of Prairie Du Chien and Green Bay.

Charlevoix, who visited Green Bay in 1721, dates the

first settlement of this place in the previous year, but strangely ignores authentic points in the early history of Wisconsin, and replaces them with vague traditions, which has tended so much to confuse the otherwise authentic histories of the early travelers. We have heretofore stated that we date the first settlement at the time that Father Allouez established the mission of St. François Xavier, in 1669. This mission had been so successful that, in 1673, Father Marquette stated that the "Fathers" had baptized over two thousand of the natives. In 1680, Father Hennepin found Frenchmen trading there without license, on his return from his exploration of the Mississippi. In the "Memoir of M. De Denonville," in 1688, he speaks of "some French established at the Bay Des Puans." In 1699, Father St. Cosme, in his journal across Green Bay and down the Mississippi, said that "the Jesuit Fathers have a mission at the head of the bay." In the "Memoir on the Indians of Canada," dated 1718, published in Vol. 9, of New York Colonial Documents, in speaking of Green Bay, says, "there are some Frenchmen there also."

Indeed, authorities can be multiplied to almost any extent, to show a continuous occupation by the French from 1669 to the surrender of Canada to the English.

At what time the first government fort was established at the Bay, there is considerable doubt, as the writer finds no mention of a commandant at that post until Captain De Vercheres was appointed, who reached that place about the first of October, 1747. Mackinaw had long been the headquarters of the fur traders, and a fort at that point was commenced as early as the fall of 1688, under the orders of the French king, dated March 8th of that year.

The renewal of the difficulties with the Foxes, by the murder of a Frenchman by that tribe, at the Bay, in the spring of 1747, may have led to the fortification of Green Bay by the French government for the safety of the traders, although in the return of a list of forts in Canada, in 1749, none are mentioned at the Bay; but Mackinaw was returned as then having four very small brass guns, and one four-inch mortar. Forts, however, were often mentioned at the Bay, by early travelers, particularly La Hontan, in 1689, and Charlevoix, in 1721; but such forts may have been stockades without cannon, constructed by the French traders for their own protection.

Captain De Vercheres evidently did not long remain at the Bay, as he was ordered to Lake St. Francis the following June. In 1754, Sieur Marin, who the previous year had commanded an important French expedition to take possession of the Ohio valley, was assigned to Green Bay, and fortunately succeeded in settling a peace between the Bay Indians and the Christinaux of Lake Superior.

The next year opened the old French and Indian war, which only terminated with the surrender of all Canada to the English. This war was the last great struggle on the American continent between the English and French for their territorial possessions, and for the supremacy of the Catholic or Protestant religion; and the French drew from the north-west every available Indian and white man to war against the English, and every battle-field of that war was strewn with the bodies of the natives of the western country.

The Governor of Canada having surrendered that province to the English, by articles dated September 8th, 1760, the following year forces were dispatched to take possession of the north-west; and, October 12th, Captain Balfour reached Green Bay with detachments from the 60th and and 80th regiments of Royal Americans, and "found the fort quite rotten, the stockade ready to fall, the houses without cover, our fire-wood far off, and none to be got when the river closed." The 14th of the same month, Captain Balfour departed for St. Joseph's, leaving Lieutenant James Gorrell, with "one sergeant, and corporal, and fifteen privates, a French interpreter, and two English traders, viz.:

Messrs. McKay from Albany, and Goddard from Montreal," to hold the post at the Bay, who erected Fort Edward Augustus.

The Fox Indians, so often exterminated by the boasting French, still occupied the Fox river, where they had been located for more than a hundred years, and numbered three hundred and fifty warriors, their usual strength.

Lieutenant Gorrell, in speaking of the Indians dependent on that post for supplies, includes the Sioux and Iowas, which precludes the probability of there being a military post at Prairie Du Chien at that time.

In 1763 occurred the Pontiac conspiracy, gotten up by the old French traders in the north-west, to drive the English out of the country; and, June 4th of that year, Mackinaw was treacherously captured by the united forces of the Chippeways and Ottawas, and Lieutenant Jamet and twenty privates were massacred.

News of the affair was sent by Captain Etherington, the commandant, a prisoner, to Lieutenant Gorrell, with orders to evacuate the post at the Bay and go to Mackinaw. A council of the Bay Indians, including the Foxes, was immediately called; speeches were made, presents delivered, and the Indians offered not only to protect the English, but to reinstate the garrison at Mackiñaw. Lieutenant Gorrell accepted one hundred warriors as an escort beyond Mackinaw, and on the 21st of June, 1763, proceeded with his small force and English traders to Montreal.

This war was of some importance; but peace was concluded with the western tribes on the 18th of July, 1767, at Niagara, and with Pontiac, July 18th, 1765, in the region of the Wabash river.

The post at Mackinaw was reëstablished in the fall of 1765, under the command of Captain William Howard, but I find no evidence that a military post was ever reëstablished at Green Bay while it remained under the government of Great Britain, nor until after the close of the war of 1812.

According to "Grignon's Recollections," in 1785 Green Bay contained only seven families, mostly half-breeds, and none above, on Fox river. This number increased slowly, and at the close of the war of 1812, there had been added about thirty Canadians and half-breeds from Canada, so that in his opinion the total number of men, women and children might have reached one hundred and fifty souls at the commencement of 1816.

About 1809 was erected the first saw-mill and grist-mill in the State, on Devil's river, near the Bay, by Mr. Franks. A second saw and grist-mill was erected in 1813, on Reaume's creek, about four miles from the Bay. In 1818 Colonel John Shaw erected a grist-mill at Fisher's Coulee, four miles above Prairie Du Chien, and the following year a saw-mill on Black river, at the first falls. In 1822, Mr. Perkins, of Kentucky, erected a saw-mill on the Menomonee branch of the Chippeway river, which was soon carried off by a flood; and in 1830 was successfully replaced by a new one, erected by Joseph Rolette and James H. Lockwood, of Prairie Du Chien.

The Indians along the Mississippi being restless and troublesome, early in the spring of 1814 Governor Clark, of St. Louis, visited Prairie Du Chien with a military force, held a council with the Indians, established a military post, and constructed a fort at that point. He left about sixty men, under the charge of Lieutenant Perkins, to hold the post. This force was captured, July 21st of the same year, by Colonel McKay, with a large force of British and Indians, after a four days' siege, and the men paroled and sent with their arms on a gunboat to St. Louis. Colonel McKay left at the fort the company of regulars and the two companies of militia from Mackinaw, under the command of Captain Pohlman, of the regulars, who probably held the post until the close of the war.

On the 21st day of June, 1816, a detachment of United States troops, under the command of Colonel Willowby Morgan, took possession of Prairie Du Chien, and immediately commenced the erection of a fort near the present site of the dwelling-house of Colonel H. L. Dousman, at the "upper town." This fort was flooded by the high water of 1828; a new site was selected, and the present Fort "Crawford" erected between the years 1829 and 1834, and was some time under the command of Colonel Taylor, afterwards President of the United States; and his son-in-law, Jefferson Davis, President of the Confederate States, was long a lieutenant at the same post, and conducted Black Hawk to St. Louis in 1832.

About the 16th of July, 1816, Colonel John Miller, afterwards Governor of Missouri, with a detachment of three companies of the 3rd regiment United States infantry, reached Green Bay in three sail vessels, the first to reach that point; and soon after Fort Howard was constructed, and the old trading posts of Prairie Du Chien and Green Bay began to emerge from half-breed jurisdiction to regular American civilization.

During this long night of advancing civilization, the traders and settlers were "a law unto themselves," and generally redressed their own grievances, and many a poor man perished by the deadly missile of his comparatively white neighbor, who charged the offence on some straggling Indian; but, to their credit, these offences were never approved, and the code of the *Courrier de bois* was generally like that of the Irishman, to give every one "fair play."

While justice to some may be intuitive, yet it is not safe always to leave its administration to either the guilty or injured party; and that being the opinion of General Harrison, then governor of the territory of Indiana, he occasionally appointed officers for Green Bay and Prairie Du Chien, but as these appointments were regarded as a slight interference with the established order of things, they were never very popular. This, however, may not be true in reference to Justice Reaume, who was said to have been commissioned about 1808 at Green Bay, and long balanced the scales, if reports be true, in the true style of the monkey in the fable. He, however, was brought to sorrow by the competition of Mr. Justice Porlier, who was commissioned by the Governor of Canada in 1812, claiming British jurisdiction of the Bay, and also recommissioned in January, 1815, by the same authority.

The advent of the troops and American population to Green Bay and Prairie Du Chien, the admission of Illinois as a State, and the annexation of Wisconsin to the territory of Michigan, attracted so much attention that it was deemed proper to give this new territory a civil government, and to that end the three judges in Michigan, then constituting the legislature, passed an Act organizing the present territory of Wisconsin into two counties, with the division line running north and south through the portage between the Fox and Wisconsin rivers, calling the eastern county Brown, and the western Crawford. This Act was approved by Governor Cass, October 16th, 1818, and Wisconsin became a civilized portion of the United States.

The mines of Wisconsin have figured largely in connection with its history, and have contributed much to attract the pioneer to its soil. Nicholas Perrot, the early French interpreter and commandant on the upper Mississippi, in 1689, has the credit of first discovering lead on the Des Moines, in Iowa, the mines of which long bore his name.

Le Sueur, in his voyage up the Mississippi, in 1700, speaks of a lead mine, seven leagues up the " River a la Mine," which, by his distances, was evidently Fever river, at Galena, Illinois; and the same authority further said: " From the 25th to the 27th of July, made ten leagues, passed two small rivers, made an examination of a lead mine, of which we took a supply. This mine was probably at Dubuque.

The exact date of the discovery of lead in Wisconsin does not appear; but Captain Carver visited the Blue Mounds in 1766, and speaks of lead as abounding there. He also visited the Sacs at Sauk Prairie, on the Wisconsin river, and remarked that "so plentiful is lead here, that I saw large quantities of it lying about the streets in the town belonging to the Saukies." It is quite probable that lead was known to exist in Wisconsin long anterior to its discovery by Captain Carver. The Indians owned the mines, and dug, smelted, and sold it to the French traders for goods, who shipped it to market when they went to St. Louis for their winter's supply.

In 1822 the lead trade began to attract some attention, and James Johnson, a government contractor for the United States army, made a kind of treaty with the Indians, and obtained leave to work the mines for a limited time, probably four years, as they left about 1826. Johnson made some arrangements by which he let in others also to dig, and Messrs. John and Joseph Ward, of Kentucky, brought in from fifty to four hundred negro slaves. Several others also worked slaves in the mines. Mr. John Armstrong came to Galena July 10th, 1822, about ten days after Johnson, and worked at different points in Illinois and Wisconsin. In 1826 there was a great rush of miners to Galena, somewhat like the California excitement, from which point they scattered through that country, and the following year found many of them still digging ore and opening farms. John S. Miller was at Gratiot's Grove; Ebenezer Brigham and John Ray were near Plattville; William Adney near Hazel Green; John Armstrong and Jesse W. Shulls at Shullsburg, and several others in south-western Wisconsin.

This advent of the miners upon the territory of the Winnebago Indians without any treaty, deprived them of their previous profit in the lead trade, and, with the difficulty at Fort Snelling, nearly produced an open war. Murders were committed on the whites by that tribe. The miners fled to

Galena, organized military companies, elected Henry Dodge as their general, and, with the government troops, made a campaign to the portage of the Wisconsin and Fox rivers, where the difficulties were compromised and peace restored without much bloodshed.

In this campaign to the site of Fort Winnebago (the fort having been erected the following year,) General Dodge discovered the Indian diggings at Dodgeville, and in the fall of 1827 he took possession of those diggings, and thereby founded the village of Dodgeville.

In the spring of 1828 lead was discovered at Mineral Point, and by fall Dodgeville had about five hundred inhabitants, Mineral Point about six hundred, and the whole mining district in south-western Wisconsin about 8,000 inhabitants. In the fall of 1829 a public meeting was held at Mineral Point, and John L. Chastine, Esq., a Kentucky lawyer, was appointed to attend the next session of the legislature of Michigan, and procure the organization of a new county south of the Wisconsin river. He performed the duty assigned him, and early in the winter Iowa became the third county in the new State.

The rapid ingress of population to the Mississippi valley at this period alarmed other Indian tribes; and in 1832 broke out the Sac war, and that tribe, under their leader, "Black Hawk," was driven through the eastern part of Wisconsin, by way of Rock river, the four lakes, and the Wisconsin Heights, and finally defeated at the battle of Bad Ax. This campaign brought the beautiful groves and prairies of that delightful region to the notice of thousands, and led to its prompt occupation by the adventurous emigrant within the next ten years.

The Rev. Father Zenobius Membré, speaking of the Indian tribes with whom he had become acquainted, and of their location, having incidentally remarked that "the Maskoutens and Outagamies, who dwell at about 43° north latitude, on the banks of the river called Melleoki, which empties into Lake Dauphin, very near their village," etc., we infer that he had learned those facts when he passed that point with the party of La Salle, in the month of October, 1679, on their way to the Illinois, to explore the Mississippi, and therefore that La Salle and his party, consisting of the Jesuit Fathers Hennepin, Gabriel, Membré, and Watteaux, and seventeen *voyageurs*, were the first white men who ever visited the location now known as Milwaukee.

It is true that Father Marquette, returning to Illinois, passed Milwaukee in November, 1674, and also that the Rev. Father Alloucz, on his way to Illinois, passed it again in the month of April, 1677 ; but as neither of them mention the name of Milwaukee, or the Indians on its bank, we are not allowed the inference that they landed and made themselves acquainted with its name and locality, although they probably saw the site of the city.

Again we find the name mentioned by the Rev. Father St. Cosme, on his way to the Illinois, in the following language: "We arrived on the 7th (October, 1699) at Melwarick. This is a river where there is a village which has been considerable, and inhabited by Motarctins and Foxes, and even some Poux. We remained there two days, partly on account of the wind, and partly to refresh our people a little, as duck and teal shooting was very plenty on the river. On the 10th of October, having left Meliwarick early in the morning, we arrived in good season at 'Kipikawi,' which is about eight leagues from it. Some Indians had led us to suppose that we might ascend by this river, and that after making a portage of about nine leagues, we could descend by another river called Pistrui, which empties into the Illinois." They remained five days at "Kipikuskwi," exploring, found no water, and went on the lake to "Chicago."

The writer was not well settled in the orthography of these names, as he changed each time he wrote the words.

The meaning of the word *Meliwarik*, or as now written,

Milwaukee, is not very clear, some traders rendering it "rich or beautiful land." Mr. Grignon, on the authority of an old Indian, renders it, Man-a-wau-kee, or place of an aromatic root called man-wau; but Governor Doty is quite positive that it means "the place of the hazel brush." The difference in the orthography of traders, probably results, in part, from the dialects of the Foxes, Mascotens, and Potowatomies, who have inhabited it at different times.

"Kipikawi" is also rendered "Root," for which the French give as an equivalent, "Racine," and therefrom we derive the name of another beautiful city on the western bank of Michigan, or Great Lake.

Milwaukee, like the most of the lake and river towns, has been occupied from time to time by Indian traders, from an early period of our State history; but the last one, more permanent than the rest, and whose stay reached down to civilization, was Solomon Juneau, Esq., a native of Canada, who erected his trading shop the 14th of September, 1818, the year that Brown county was organized. From this time to 1834, the region of country along the west shore of Lake Michigan seemed to afford little or no attraction to the white settlers; but in the latter year, Colonel George H. Walker, Hon. Byron Kilbourn, and some others, made claims at Milwaukee; Captain Gilbert Knapp and two associates, at Racine; Messrs. M. D. and A. R. Cutler, John Menderville, and Mr. Luther, at old Prairie Village, now Waukesha, and perhaps a few others, when application was made to the Michigan territorial legislature for another new county, and on the 6th of September, 1834, Milwaukee, or "the Land of the Hazel," was inaugurated as the fourth sister county of our growing family.

The two following years, the "Land of the Hazel" attracted comparatively a large emigration, which in 1836 and 1837, culminated in a wild town-lot speculation, and a general bankruptcy of speculators.

The territory of Michigan, east of the lake, including the

northern peninsula, having formed a State government, and been admitted into the Union of States, Congress passed an act, which was approved by the President April 20, 1836, " establishing the territorial government of Wisconsin."

The rapid settlement of the new territory soon made it necessary to adopt a constitution and become a State, and to that end delegates were elected, who met at Madison, the seat of government, October 5, 1846, and after a stormy session of seventy-three days, they adopted a constitution, which, on being submitted to a popular vote of the people of the territory, was rejected by a considerable majority. The difficulty in the convention arose mainly from the fact that, as the democratic party was largely in the majority in that body, the visionary theorists of the leaders succeeded in pressing into the constitution some of their wildest schemes, which proved more objectionable to the rank and file of the party than supposed; hence the "bolters," joining the whigs, who were all united in opposition, a large majority was secured against it.

A second convention was called, and new delegates elected, who met December 15, 1847, and on the 1st day of February, 1848, they signed the present constitution of the State, which, having been submitted to a vote of the people, was ratified and adopted without any serious opposition, whereupon Congress passed an act, which was approved by the President May 29, 1848, admitting Wisconsin as a State of the Union.

On the admission of the State into the Union, it became a district for a United States District Court, and Hon. A. G. Miller, a territorial judge, was appointed district judge by the President.

By an act of Congress, approved September 28, 1850, Wisconsin became a collection district, and Milwaukee the port of entry, and Kenosha, Racine, Sheboygan, Green Bay, and Depére, ports of delivery.

In 1834, Wisconsin territory, then belonging to Michigan,

was divided into two land districts, for the sale of government land, by a north and south line on the township line next west of Fort Winnebago; and the eastern district was called "Green Bay," and the western district the Wisconsin land district," registers and receivers being appointed in both districts. Other districts were afterwards established, as the Milwaukee in 1836, Western in 1849, Stevens' Point, July 30, 1852, La Crosse by the same act, Fond Du Lac, of Lake Superior, in 1855, and Chippeway district in 1857.

The population of a State, from period to period, is as good an index of the advance of civilization as can be obtained without the actual facts in the case. In Wisconsin, the population has been as follows: In 1840, 30,945; 1850, 305,391; 1860, 775,881; 1865, 863,326.

When this State was admitted into the Union, it became entitled to every sixteenth section in each township for the support of schools; also, to five hundred thousand acres as one of the new States, to balance the "surplus revenue" distributed to the older States in 1836. This amount was subsequently increased by one-fourth of the "swamp lands" donated to the State by the act of 1850.

Portions of these lands have been sold from time to time on contracts of ten years, for seven per cent. interest, some of which contracts have been forfeited to the State; and in 1865 the school lands held by the State, both unsold and forfeited, amounted to 515,081 acres. The amount of the funds yielding seven per cent. interest, since the organization of the State, has been as follows:

1849	$8,500.00
1850	538,094.41
1851	765,109.49
1852	819,200.50
1853	1,141,804.28
1854	1,670,258.77
1855	1,897,269.30
1856	1,859,242.82
1857	2,007,944.15

1858 - - - - - - - - - $2,845,846.34
1859 - - - - - - - - - 2,786,767.03
1860 - - - - - - - - - 2,339,694.49
1861 - - - - - - - - - 2,458,351.49
1862 - - - - - - - - - 2,219,905.59
1863 - - - - - - - - - 2,262,466.15
1864 - - - - - - - - - 2,118,423.56
1865 - - - - - - - - - 2,113,506.32

These funds for 1865 were invested as follows:

Amount due on land sold on certificates - - - $675,037.11
Amount due on mortgages - - - - - 289,123.75
Amount due on certificates of State indebtedness - - 897,000.00
Amount due on State bonds - - - - - 103,700.00
One quarter of the normal school fund - - - - 146,645.46

Total - - - - - - - - - $2,113,506.32

Statistical Table of Schools in Wisconsin.

YEAR.	Total number of children in the State over four and under twenty years of age.	Total number who attended school some portion of the year.	Average number in school a portion of the time, of each hundred of school age.	Average number of days schools were taught.	Apportionment in cents per scholar.
1849	70,457	82,147	45	71	
1850	92,947	61,507	66	74	8 8-10
1851	111,481	78,944	70	74	50
1852	124,783	88,042	71	75	48
1853	138,279	97,835	69	75	45
1854	155,125	108,938	65	77	72
1855	186,960	122,462	64	84	80 5-10
1856	213,686	134,358	64	99	70
1857	241,545	153,618	60		66
1858	264,077	171,795	63	122	75
1859	278,871	188,477	64	1 1	64
1860	288,984	194,357	67	136	64
1861	299,133	198,443	66	132	82
1862	308,056	191,866	62	109	50
1863	320,965	215,163	67	120	44
1864	329,906	211,119	64	120½	47
1865	335,582	228,067	66	134¼	46

In 1865 the whole number of school districts, and parts of school districts in the State, were 5,725, in which were employed 7,532 teachers. The total amount expended in the State for schools was $1,055,101.33, of which $151,816.34 were received from the State, and the balance raised by taxes. The number of public school-houses in the State was 4,338, which will accommodate 241,593 pupils. These houses and sites were valued at $1,669,770.06.

In addition to these public schools, there were, in 1865, 228 private schools, employing 242 teachers, and in which 7,986 scholars were registered who did not attend the public schools; 14 academies, employing 81 teachers, and having 1,950 students; and nine colleges and universities, employing 56 professors, and having 1,449 students. All of these institutions are supported by private means, except the State University, which had an endowment from the United States in public lands.

The "Normal fund," arising from the sale of "swamp lands," has been set apart to establish four Normal schools for the special training of teachers. The sites for the schools had not been selected in February, 1866. There has also been appropriated by Congress 240,000 acres of government land, for the special establishment of one or more agricultural colleges in the State, by the act approved July 2nd, 1862. These lands have been located in Wisconsin, and the whole fund has been set over to the State University, which has organized a department of agriculture.

To these educational institutions may be added, as institutions contributing greatly to the aid of civilization, the State Reform school at Waukesha, containing, September 30th, 1864, one hundred and seventeen males and twenty females; the State Prison at Waupun, containing at the same date one hundred and twenty inmates; the Institute for the Education of the Blind, at Janesville, which commenced with eight pupils in 1850, but had increased from year to year until October 1st, 1864, when the pupils numbered fifty-nine; the

Institute for the Education of the Deaf and Dumb, at Delavan, having, October 17th, 1864, forty-seven male and thirty-three female pupils; and the State Hospital for the Insane, at Fourth lake, near Madison, having in October, 1864, seventy-nine male, and ninety-one female inmates. These institutions are all in excellent condition, and are supported from funds derived from taxes on the whole property of the State.

The introduction of newspapers is also an important index of the progress of civilization in modern times; hence we find the first paper in Wisconsin started at Green Bay, December 11th, 1833, and called the "Green Bay Intelligencer," a four-column semi-monthly. The second paper was the "Wisconsin Free Press," started also at Green Bay in 1835. The third paper was the "Milwaukee Advertiser," commenced July 14th, 1836, at Milwaukee. The fourth was the "Belmont Gazette," commenced at Belmont in the fall of 1836. The fifth, the "Milwaukee Sentinel," a six-column weekly, commenced at Milwaukee in June, 1837. The sixth was the "Wisconsin Culturist," a large octavo, issued monthly, and commenced in 1837 at Milwaukee. The "Racine Argus" next came as the seventh, in 1839, and after six months was removed to Madison, and became the "Wisconsin Enquirer." In 1843 it removed to Milwaukee, and became the "Milwaukee Democrat" in August of that year. The next year it was changed to the "Freeman," and in subsequent years the "Free Democrat." In 1838 the "Miners' Free Press" was started at Mineral Point; in 1839, the "Northern Badger," at Plattville; 1840, the "Madison Express," at Madison; 1841, the "Southport American," at Southport; "Green Bay Republican" and "Green Bay Phœnix," both of Green Bay; and "Milwaukee Journal," at Milwaukee. In 1842 there were four more added: "Racine Advocate," "Wisconsin Democrat," at Madison; "Independent American," at Plattville; and "Mineral Point Free Press." In 1843 the "Grant

County Herald" was started at Lancaster. In 1844 five more were added: the "Wisconsin Argus," at Madison; the "Milwaukeean," a tri-weekly; the "Wisconsin Register," at Plattville; and the "Wisconsin Banner," a German paper at Milwaukee. Many of the papers enumerated were of short life, others changed their residences and names, and some became permanent.

The writer started the "Western Star," at Elk Horn, August 7th, 1845, the first paper in Walworth county, with which he was connected for nearly a year. At that time, the following were the newspapers of the territory, with their politics:

Whig.—Milwaukee Sentinel (daily and weekly); Southport American; Madison Express; Wisconsin Republican, Green Bay; Janesville Gazette; Western Star.

Democratic.—Milwaukee Courier; Southport Telegraph; Racine Advocate; Wisconsin Argus, Madison; Mineral Point Democrat; Wisconsin Banner, (German,) Milwaukee.

Abolition.—American Freeman, at Prairieville.

Neutral.—Wisconsin Herald, Lancaster; Independent American, Plattville.

The "Sentinel" then published the only daily paper in the territory, which was begun in October, 1844, and all the balance of the list were weekly.

The exact circulation of these papers at the time can not be given, but the daily did not exceed 300 per day, nor the weeklies 500 per week, on an average. This would give about 575,000 annually.

In 1850, Wisconsin had 6 daily, 4 tri-weekly, 35 weekly, and 1 monthly, with an aggregate circulation annually of 2,665,487.

In 1860, the papers had increased to 14 daily, 8 tri-weekly, 130 weekly, and 3 monthly, with an aggregate annual circulation of 10,798,670.

CHAPTER XVII.

THE STATES OF MISSOURI, IOWA, MINNESOTA, KANSAS, AND NEBRASKA; AND TERRITORIES OF COLORADO, DAKOTA, AND MONTANA.

MISSOURI.

WE have heretofore noticed that Missouri was first visited in 1673, by Jolyette and Marquette. From that time traders occasionally visited that region; and some time after the building of Fort Chartres, and said to be in 1751, a few houses were erected at St. Genevieve, nearly opposite the old town of Kaskaskia, which was the first settlement of Missouri.

In 1762, Mr. D'Abadie, the governor of Louisiana, granted to a company of merchants, of New Orleans, the exclusive privilege of the fur trade with the Indian nations of the Mississippi and Missouri rivers. This company bore the title of the firm of Pierre Liguest Laclede, Antoine Maxan and Co. In August, 1763, Mr. Laclede, the principal of the company, left New Orleans with his shipment of goods, and arrived at St. Genevieve, November 3rd of that year.

Failing to find at that place houses sufficiently large to hold his goods, he temporarily deposited them in Fort Chartres, and then passed up the Mississippi to find a suitable site for his trading establishment, finally selecting the ground on which St. Louis now stands. He cut down a few trees to mark the site, and returned to Fort Chartres, where he spent the winter. The 1st of February, 1764, he dispatched Auguste Chouteau, with thirty men and boats, who took possession, and commenced improvements at St. Louis, February 15th of that year. Log houses were erected, and in due time Laclede and Co., with their goods, were installed at the new city, which he named St. Louis.

At this period, the French commandant at Fort Chartres had received orders to surrender the east bank of the Mississippi to the English, and the French inhabitants and half-breeds were in great consternation about falling into the hands of the "heretics," as they called the English. Laclede took advantage of this alarm, and urged the inhabitants to pass over the river and settle at St. Louis. The French commandant, De Neyon, urged them to go down the river and colonize near New Orleans. The latter left with most of the troops and many of the inhabitants for New Orleans, July 10th, 1764. Many of these emigrants to the latter city not meeting with the success they expected, returned, and settled at St. Louis. The sequel showed that Laclede secured enough to constitute a small village at St. Louis. After De St. Ange De Bellerive had surrendered Fort Chartres to the English in 1765, he, too, passed over to St. Louis with his troops, and became a permanent settler. St. Louis thus became the capital of upper Louisiana, with Captain De St. Ange as commandant. Although Louisiana was transferred by the French to the Spanish in 1763, the latter nation never took possession of upper Louisiana until August 11th, 1768; and this possession only continued eleven months at first, as the difficulties at New Orleans called away the Spanish troops, who did not return until 1770.

The early pioneers have traditions of *l'anne de grand coup*, or the year of the great blow. It appears that about 1779, Jean Marie Ducharme, a Canadian fur trader of Mackinaw, had been on a trading expedition up the Missouri river, and returning to St. Louis with a valuable cargo of furs, was arrested by the Spanish commandant, thrown into prison, and his goods confiscated, because he had no Spanish license to trade. Proving that he had ransomed some Spanish, who were prisoners among the Indians, he was set at liberty, and returned to Mackinaw. Smarting under the loss of his property, he obtained the countenance and assistance of Governor Sinclair, the British commandant (England being at war with Spain), and mustered an expedition of Canadians and Indians, nearly nine hundred strong, which attacked St. Louis May 6, 1780, but were driven off by the French inhabitants. The Mackinaw expedition, however, succeeded in killing and scalping about sixty, principally women and children, who had not time to escape from the fields, where they were engaged in agricultural labors. The English also captured a few prisoners.

The emigration to Missouri was not confined to the Canadian French alone, for when the Americans had once passed the Alleghany mountains, their restless dispositions often led them to the very outskirts of civilization; hence we find that General Morgan, of American fame, procured a large grant of land of the Spanish government in 1788, and soon after planted an American colony at the present site of New Madrid; while General Dodge and his father, and others, settled at St. Genevieve in 1796. Even Daniel Boone, of Kentucky fame, spent the latter portion of his life in Missouri.

On "the 9th day of July, 1803, at seven o'clock P. M.," says the old record, St. Louis was thrown into a profound sensation on the receipt of the news that Spain had ceded Louisiana to France, and that Napoleon had sold it to the United States. This proved true, and on the 9th of March, the following year, Major Amos Stoddard appeared at that city with a company of the United States troops, and, as the agent of France, accepted the surrender from the Spanish to the French; and the following day, accepted the surrender from the French, and unfurled the stars and stripes over the territory of upper Louisiana. Major Stoddard became military governor, though soon after superseded by the arrival of General Wilkinson.

By an act of Congress passed March 6, 1804, Louisiana was divided on the parallel of the thirty-third degree of north latitude, and the southern portion was incorporated as the "Territory of Orleans;" while the northern portion was organized as the "District of Louisiana," and placed under the jurisdiction of the governor and judges of the Territory of Indiana.

By another act of Congress of the 4th of June, 1812, a portion of the "District of Louisiana" was organized under the territorial name of Missouri, with a civil government. By the act of Congress of March 6, 1820, the people of Missouri were authorized to hold a convention and frame a State constitution. The convention was accordingly held, a constitution adopted July 19th, 1820, and the State of Missouri admitted into the Union under the act of Congress of March 2nd, 1821, pursuant to the President's proclamation. A bitter opposition was made in Congress to the admission of Missouri as a State, for the reason that the inhabitants thereof had established slavery; but this opposition was finally compromised by a section in the act of March 6, 1820, prohibiting slavery in all the Louisiana purchase north of the parallel of 36° 30' north latitude; not, however, including any part of Missouri within the prohibition.

This was the postponement, only, of the great question of slavery, which the passions of men would only allow to be settled by the civil war of 1861.

The act authorizing the people to form a State government contained the usual grants for schools, a seminary, seat of government, salt springs, and five per cent. of the net proceeds of the sales of the public lands. The principal of the common school fund in 1850 was $575,667.96, which was loaned on bonds to the State bank. The seminary fund amounted to $100,000. In 1862 the school fund amounted to $687,968, and was invested in State bonds. The disorder in the State on account of the civil war suspended any distribution of the school fund to schools after 1860, until after the close of the war.

A State convention to amend the constitution of the State, assembled in February, 1861, and after refusing to vote the State out of the Union, adjourned until July. At the appointed day of adjournment, it met and deposed Governor Jackson, and the most of the State officers and members of the legislature, who had become rebels, and organized a provisional government — the convention assuming legislative functions for about two years. It finally adjourned July 1, 1863, after having, on that day, passed an ordinance abolishing slavery from and after July 4, 1870.

In 1769, upper Louisiana had a population of 891 souls. By the census of 1810, Missouri had a population of 20,845. In 1820 it had increased to 66,557, of which 10,222 were slaves. In 1830, 140,455; 1840, 383,702; 1850, 682,044; and 1860, 1,182,012, of which 3,572 were free colored, and 114,931 were slaves. The civil war which followed probably diminished the population of the State to some extent.

Of newspapers, Missouri had none in 1810, and but five in 1828. In 1840 there were 2 daily, 28 weekly, 1 tri-weekly; total, 31. In 1850 there were: Literary and miscellaneous, 17; political, 42; religious, 2; total, 61, with a circulation of 70,480, and an aggregate circulation for the year, of 6,195,560 copies. Five of them were daily papers.

In 1860, Missouri had : *Political*, 15 daily, 3 tri-weekly, 122 weekly, and 1 monthly, papers; *Religious*, 9 weekly and 2 monthly; *Literary* and *Miscellaneous*, 1 daily, 12 weekly, and 8 monthly papers; total of all, 173, with an aggregate annual circulation of 29,741,464 copies.

IOWA.

This State was visited by Marquette and Jolyette in 1673, and by Captain Perrot in 1689; and the latter has the credit of discovering the lead mine at Des Moines. Le Seuer saw lead at Dubuque in 1700. In 1780, the squaw of Peosta, a Fox warrior, discovered a vein of lead at Dubuque, and in 1788, Julien Dubuque, of Prairie Du Chien, obtained leave of the Indians to work the mine. He immediately settled at Dubuque, and became the pioneer of Iowa.

After the close of the Black Hawk war in 1832, the United States purchased the eastern part of Iowa of the Sac and Fox Indians, the Indians making a reservation of four hundred sections. In 1836, these sections were purchased, and the following year, 1,250,000 acres additional, along the west side of the purchase of 1832, which covered nearly all the balance of the present State of Iowa. The Indian title being extinguished to the eastern part in 1832, the following year, the settlements commenced, and were continued with rapidity.

In 1836 Iowa was included in the organization of Wisconsin territory, and July 4, 1838, was made a separate territory by the name of "Iowa." The 7th day of October, 1844, Iowa adopted a State constitution, and March 2, 1845, was admitted into the Union by act of Congress. The new State received the usual land grants of other new States.

The increase of population in the new territory was rapid, and in 1840 the census showed 43,112; 1850, 192,214; 1860, 674,948; and in 1863, 702,374.

The educational interests of Iowa are nearly the same as those of Wisconsin.

The newspaper press shows a fair advancement, the "Dubuque Visitor" having been the pioneer in 1836. In 1840, there were 4 weekly papers; 1850, 2 tri-weekly, 25 weekly, 2 monthly; total, 25, with an aggregate annual circulation of 1,512,800. In 186⁂ the number had advanced to: *Political*, 9 daily, 2 bi-weekly, 2 tri-weekly, 106 weekly; *Religious*, 1 monthly; *Literary*, 1 monthly; and *Miscellaneous*, 6 weekly, and 3 monthly; having an aggregate annual circulation of 6,589,360 copies.

MINNESOTA.

This name literally means, in the Sioux language, Smoky-water, and was applied by them to Minnesota river, which has a clay-colored appearance.

We have noticed that Father Hennepin and De Lut first visited this State in 1680, or at least the upper Mississippi part, but it is probable that Father Allouez first visited the territory west of Lake Superior as early as 1665.

Captain Nicholas Perrot, with a small military force, took formal possession, in the name of the King of France, of the whole upper Mississippi region, and made a record thereof May 8, 1689, at the post of St. Anthony.

Le Seuer visited the country again in 1700, and built a fort on the Blue Earth river, where he dug and shipped a quantity of the blue earth, supposing it to be copper ore.

From this time, the French had but little trade with the Sioux, as the French were the allies of the Chippeways, who were at war with the Sioux, and Sacs and Foxes. The massacre of the Foxes at Detroit, in 1712, cut off all communication with the Sioux by the Wisconsin, until after 1754, when peace was made with the Foxes.

After the revolution, England held possession of the north-west until 1796, when it was surrendered to the United States; but the upper Mississippi attracted little attention until after the peace of 1815. In 1816, the President sent a military force to take possession of Prairie Du Chien, and in 1819 Fort Snelling was commenced. In July, 1847, the writer visited St. Paul, Fort Snelling, Falls of St. Anthony, and Stillwater. At St. Paul he found two small log stores, with Indian goods, one of which was kept by Henry Jackson, a native of Virginia, who was the proprietor of the town site, and had resided there five years. A few half-breed log houses were on the prairie, towards St. Anthony's falls. Mendota was the only trading establishment of the fur company. Around Fort Snelling were three or four officers' houses. St. Anthony had a government mill and one log house on the west side, and one log house on the east side of the falls. Stillwater had a new water saw-mill, and about ten buildings. There were a few farms opened between Stillwater and St. Paul, and some trading-posts along the west bank of the river to Iowa. This was Minnesota in 1847.

On the 3rd of March, 1849, Minnesota, by act of Congress, received a territorial government. The settlement of the new territory was slow until after the treaty with the Sioux of 1851, which was amended and finally ratified by the President, February 24, 1853. This treaty opened for settlement nearly all Minnesota west of the Mississippi. In anticipation of the ratification of this treaty, settlers intrigued with officials, and occasionally got permits to trade with the Indians, thereby securing advantageous locations west of the river; but early in the spring of 1853, the great emigrant wave overspread all southern Minnesota, and extended high up the Mississippi. From this time the settlement continued rapid, and February 26, 1857, Congress passed a law allowing the formation of a State government. A convention was called, delegates elected, and a constitution adopted August 29, 1857. The constitution was ratified by the people, by a popular vote taken October 13th, of the same year. A peculiarity of this convention was, that in the early stages of its sitting, the delegates divided on party issues, which led to the division of the convention, and continued as two bodies, and each adopted a separate constitution. The compromising men of each division then put themselves to work to get up a compromise constitution,

and finally succeeded in agreeing on one, which was ratified by the people as above stated. The State was admitted into the Union by Congress, by act of May 11, 1858.

By the act of Congress of February 26, 1857, there were donated to Minnesota, every sixteenth and thirty-sixth section of land in each township for common schools, seventy-two sections for a State university, ten sections to complete the public buildings, seventy-two sections to include twelve salt springs, and five per cent. of the net proceeds of the sales of the public lands in the State, for internal improvements.

The following table, from the report of the superintendent of public instruction of Minnesota, dated December 31, 1865, will show the condition of the common schools of the State for the years 1864 and 1865:

	1864.	1865.	Increase.
Whole number of districts	1,738	1,824	86
Whole number of districts reported	1,402	1,495	93
Whole number partially reported	17	106	89
Whole number entirely unreported	119	223	104
Whole number of persons from 5 to 21 years.	74,965	87,244	12,279
Whole number in attendance, males	23,054	26,165	3,111
Whole number in attendance, females	21,733	24,399	2,666
Whole number in attendance, both sexes	44,787	50,564	5,777
Total average daily attendance	26,821	32,259	5,938
Total number of teachers	1,888	2,003	115
Total amount paid teachers	$110,024.97	$124,563.71	$14,538.74
Total number of school-houses	994	1,112	128
Total value of school-houses	$224,500.25	$280,329.51	$55,829.26

The population of Minnesota, which numbered only 6,077 in 1850, had increased, in 1860, to 173,855 souls.

The amount distributed in 1865, of the "current school fund," was $55,474.10.

A normal school was in successful operation at Winona, with fifty-eight students. A State University was located at St. Anthony, about 1859, and a building partly erected, but abandoned, probably for lack of funds. The writer is not advised that it has since been finished. The superintendent's report for 1865 makes no mention of it. There are, however, the Hamline University, at Red Wing, belonging to the Methodist Episcopal church; another at Hastings, in charge of the Baptists; and the North-western University at Wasioga, in charge of the Freewill Baptists; all of which are doing a good work for collegiate education. There are, also, several flourishing academies in different parts of the State.

The first newspaper of Minnesota was called the "St. Paul Pioneer," and was started by Mr. Goodhue, from Grant county, Wisconsin, April 28, 1849. The "Register" was started in July of the same year, the first number of which was printed in Cincinnati. About the same time, the "Chronicle" was issued at St. Paul. The two latter papers were soon after consolidated into the "Chronicle and Register." In 1860, there were: *Political*, 4 daily, and 43 weekly papers; *Religious*, 1 weekly; and *Miscellaneous*, 1 weekly, with an aggregate annual circulation of 2,344,000 copies.

KANSAS.

Long previous to the surrender of Canada, the French maintained a military post on the Kansas river, but the soldiers were withdrawn in 1764. After the region came into the possession of the United States, it was, by Act of Congress of June 30th, 1834, included in the "Indian country," and the most of the north-western tribes of Indians were subsequently located in Kansas. By the Act of Congress of May 30th, 1854, Kansas territory was organized, and a territorial government put in operation. By this Act, Congress repealed that portion of the Act of March 6th, 1820, which prohibited slavery north of 36° 30', north latitude, commonly called the Missouri compromise line, and provided that the people of Kansas might establish or prohibit slavery, as they might determine in their constitution. This opened the territory to the colonization schemes of the friends and enemies of slavery, and both parties commenced organizing and arming companies, and sending them to Kansas. The people of Missouri being near at hand, at the time of the first election, went into Kansas, took forcible possession of the ballot-boxes at several important precincts, and voted so liberally that the first election was carried for the pro-slavery party. The free State men claimed that the election was carried by fraud, and refused to obey the laws passed by the territorial legislature. They also appealed to President Buchanan, but he turned a deaf ear, and finally took the pro-slavery side. The result that followed was a semi-civil war for nearly three years, in which mobs, resistance to officers, and midnight assassinations, filled the country with violence and murders, and the military of the United States were often used to preserve peace. The principal leader on the part of the pro-slavery men was Mr. Atchison, United States senator from Missouri, while James H. Lane and John Brown were the leaders of the free State men. During this time, armed emigrants came flocking in by regiments from north and south, making claims on government lands, and joining in the melee.

In 1857 the pro-slavery legislature provided for the election of delegates to form a constitution, but with such test oaths to the electors that the free State men refused to vote. The free State men also called a constitutional convention, and both parties adopted separate constitutions. The pro-slavery party, in their constitution adopted in November, 1857, expressly sanctioned slavery, and the other constitution abolished it. The two went before Congress. President Buchanan gave the whole force of his administration for the admission of the State under the pro-slavery, or Lecompton constitution, while Hon. S. A. Douglas, senator from Illinois, the acknowledged author of the Act making Kansas a territory, and of the doctrine of " Squatter sovereignty," opposed the admission of the State under any constitution, until that constitution had been submitted to a fair vote of the people of the territory, and ratified by a majority. Senator Douglas and his associates beat the administration in Congress; and the pro-slavery, or what was called the Lecompton constitution, was submitted to a vote of the people of Kansas, and rejected by a large majority.

The free State men thus learning their strength, rallied at the next election for members of the legislature, and secured a majority of that body. The next summer a new convention was called, and, July 29, 1859, adopted a constitution which they submitted to a vote of the people of the territory, October 4th of the same year, who ratified it by a large majority. This constitution for ever prohibited slavery. It was submitted to Congress in December of the same year; but Kansas was not admitted into the Union until January 29th, 1861.

The repeal of the Missouri compromise line, and the adoption of the "Squatter sovereignty" doctrine, by which the people of the new territory were to determine for themselves, in their constitution, whether they would have slavery or not, was a compromise between the northern and southern democrats; but the South having been finally beaten in the first experiment under the new doctrine, repudiated the whole compromise, and denounced Senator Douglas as an abolitionist. When he was nominated for President in 1860, they brought forward Mr. Breckenridge, thereby dividing the democratic party, and throwing the election into the hands of Mr. Lincoln. Mr. Buchanan gave the whole force of his administration against Mr. Douglas' election, thus joining hands with the South. The rebellion which followed in the spring of 1861, was the inevitable result of the previous combinations, and Mr. Douglas and his political friends could do nothing less than join Mr. Lincoln and the republicans to put down the rebellion. The northern supporters of Mr. Breckenridge having denounced Mr. Douglas and his political friends as abolitionists, were now alarmed at their position, and many of them overleaped the democratic party and landed in the ranks of the abolitionists; while another portion became southern sympathizers, called "copperheads." A few returned to the democratic party, and joined against the rebellion. The close of the civil war was the evidence of the final death of slavery.

Kansas, by the Act of January 29th, 1861, received the usual grants from Congress, of sections sixteen and thirty-six in each township, for common schools; seventy-two sections for a university; ten sections for public buildings; twelve salt springs, with seventy-two sections of land; and five per cent. of the net proceeds of the sale of the public lands in the State. The State is so new that the educational interests are not fully developed; and the breaking out of the rebellion so soon after the admission of the State, required all the energies of its inhabitants to protect their lives and property. They suffered to a considerable extent from rebel raids.

The progress of the State in population was very rapid, in part owing to the excitement on the slavery question; and, by the census of 1860, while still a territory, it was reported as having 107,206 inhabitants, of which only *two* were slaves.

Kansas also showed a rapid advance in newspapers, having, in 1860: *Political*, 3 daily and 21 weekly; and, *Miscellaneous*, 3 weekly; total 27, with an aggregate annual circulation of 1,565,540 copies.

NEBRASKA.

This State derives its name from one of its rivers, which, in the Omaha dialect of the Winnebago, is said to mean "spreading water," or "wide, shallow water."

It was organized as a territory by the "Nebraska Act,"

passed by Congress May 30th, 1854, as a part of the great "Squatter Sovereignty Compromise;" but as the slaveholders did not attempt to colonize it, the territory was suffered to settle according to the ordinary laws of emigration, and, in 1860, had only 28,841 inhabitants, while the sister territory of Kansas numbered 107,206. The population in 1867 was only estimated at 40,000.

The question of the admission of Nebraska as a State was seriously agitated in 1863, and April 19th, the following year, Congress passed an enabling Act. Under this Act a convention was held, and a constitution framed, which was ratified by the people by only 100 majority on a vote polled of 7,776, June 2nd, 1866. This constitution was presented to Congress, and on the 8th and 9th of February, 1867, an Act was passed, under which the territory became a State, March 1st, 1867, as recited in the following proclamation:

"*The Admission of Nebraska — Proclamation of the President.*

"WASHINGTON, March 1st, 1867.

"Whereas the Congress of the United States did, by an Act approved on the 19th day of April, 1864, authorize the people of the territory of Nebraska to form a constitution and State government, and for the admission of such State into the Union on an equal footing with the original States upon certain conditions in said Act specified; and whereas said people did adopt a constitution conforming to the provisions and conditions of said Act, and ask admission into the Union; and whereas the Congress of the United States did, on the 8th and 9th days of February, 1867, in the mode prescribed by the constitution, pass a further Act for the admission of the State of Nebraska into the Union, in which last named Act it was provided that it should not take effect except upon like fundamental conditions that within the State of Nebraska there should be no denial of the elective franchise, or of any other right to any person by reason of race or color, except Indians not taxed; and upon the further fundamental condition that the legislature of said State, by a solemn public Act, should declare the assent of said State to the said fundamental condition, and should transmit to the President of the United States an authenticated copy of said Act of the legislature of said State, upon receipt whereof the President, by proclamation, should forthwith announce the fact, whereupon said fundamental condition should be held as a part of the organic law of the State, and thereupon, and without any further proceedings on the part of Congress, the admission of said State into the Union should be considered as complete; and whereas, within the time prescribed by said Act of Congress of the 8th and 9th of February, 1867, the legislature of the State of Nebraska did pass an Act ratifying the said Act of Congress of the 8th and 9th of February, 1867, and declaring that the aforenamed provisions of the third section of said last named Act of Congress should be a part of the organic law of the State of Nebraska; and whereas a duly authenticated copy of said Act of the legislature of the State of Nebraska has been received by me,

"Now, therefore, I, Andrew Johnson, President of the United States of America, do, in accordance with the provisions of the Act of Congress last herein named, declare and proclaim the fact that the fundamental conditions imposed by Congress on the State of Nebraska to entitle that State to admission to the Union have been ratified and accepted, and that the admission of the said State into the Union is now complete.

"In testimony whereof, I have hereto set my hand and caused the seal of the United States to be affixed.

"Done at the city of Washington, this first day of March, in the year of our Lord 1867, and of the independence of the United States of America the ninety-first.

"By the President: "ANDREW JOHNSON.
"WILLIAM H. SEWARD, Secretary of State."

COLORADO TERRITORY.

The discovery of gold near "Pike's Peak," of the Rocky mountains, attracted great numbers of miners to that region, and Congress, February 28, 1861, granted them a territorial government with the following boundaries: "Commencing on the thirty-seventh parallel of north latitude, where the twenty-fifth meridian of longitude west from Washington crosses the same; thence, north on said meridian to the forty-first parallel of north latitude; thence, along said parallel, west to the thirty-second meridian of longitude west from Washington; thence, south on said meridian, to the north line of New Mexico; thence, along the thirty-seventh parallel of north latitude, to the place of beginning."

The organic act for Colorado contained the usual provisions made for other territories, and the government was speedily put in operation.

The rapid settlement of the territory soon established the necessity of a more permanent organization; and, therefore, March 21, 1864, Congress passed an act authorizing the people of the territory to form a constitution preparatory to their admission into the Union. A constitution was adopted, but by so small a majority of the people, and the census of the people being considerably less than was anticipated, the new State had not been admitted up to June, 1867.

Population of the territory in 1860, 34,197.

DAKOTA TERRITORY.

The Indian traders, having been pressed back to the upper Missouri by the advancing civilization, Congress decided to give them a territorial government; and March 2, 1861, the territory of Dakota was organized, with the following boundaries:

"Commencing at a point in the main channel of the Red

river of the north, where the forty-ninth degree of north latitude crosses the same; thence, up the main channel of the same, and along the boundary of the State of Minnesota to Big Stone Lake; thence, along the boundary line of the said State of Minnesota, to the Iowa line; thence, along the boundary line of the State of Iowa to the point of intersection between the Big Sioux and Missouri rivers; thence, up the Missouri river, and along the boundary line of the territory of Nebraska, to the mouth of the Niobrara or Running Water river; thence, following up the same, in the middle of the main channel thereof, to the mouth of the Keha Paha or Turtle Hill river; thence, up said river, to the forty-third parallel of north latitude; thence, due west, to the present boundary of the territory of Washington; thence, along the boundary line of Washington territory, to the forty-ninth degree of north latitude; thence, east, along said forty-ninth degree of north latitude, to the place of beginning."

By another act of Congress, passed May 26, 1864, the following additional territory was attached to Dakota:

"Commencing at a point formed by the intersection of the thirty-third degree of longitude west from Washington with the forty-first degree of north latitude; thence, along said thirty-third degree of longitude, to the crest of the Rocky mountains; thence, northward along said crest of the Rocky mountains, to its intersection with the forty-fourth degree and thirty minutes of north latitude; thence, eastward, along said forty-fourth degree thirty minutes north latitude, to the thirty-fourth degree of longitude west from Washington; thence, northward, along said thirty-fourth degree of longitude, to its intersection with the forty-fifth degree north latitude; thence, eastward, along said forty-fifth degree of north latitude, to its intersection with the twenty-seventh degree of longitude west from Washington; thence, south, along said twenty-seventh degree of longitude west from Washington, to the forty-first degree north latitude; thence, west, along said forty-first degree of latitude, to the place of beginning, shall be, and is hereby, incorporated temporarily into and made part of the territory of Dakota."

The Sioux war, which broke out in 1862, has stopped the settlement of the country, and up to the present time (June, 1867), the few white inhabitants are confined to the military posts.

MONTANA TERRITORY.

A new "gold fever" having taken possession of the miners, a rush was made to the Rocky mountains, at the head-waters of the Missouri, and the usual consequence of the organization of a new territory followed. This act was passed by Congress May 26, 1864, and gave the following boundaries to the new territory of Montana:

"Commencing at a point formed by the intersection of the twenty-seventh degree of longitude west from Washington with the forty-fifth degree of north latitude; thence, due west, on said forty-fifth degree of latitude, to a point formed by its intersection with the thirty-fourth degree of longitude west from Washington; thence, due south, along said thirty-fourth degree of longitude, to its intersection with the forty-fourth degree and thirty minutes of north latitude; thence, due west, along said forty-fourth degree and thirty minutes of north latitude, to a point formed by its intersection with the crest of the Rocky mountains; thence, following the crest of the Rocky mountains northward, till its intersection with the Bitter Root mountains; thence, northward, along the crest of said Bitter Root mountains, to its intersection with the thirty-ninth degree of longitude west from Washington; thence, along said thirty-ninth degree of longitude, northward to the boundary line of the British possessions; thence, eastward, along said boundary line, to the twenty-seventh degree of longitude west from Washington; thence, southward, along said twenty-seventh degree of longitude, to the place of beginning."

This new region has received a considerable population, but the Sioux war has greatly retarded its progress. It is said, however, that the miners have been somewhat successful in the collection of the precious metals.

CHAPTER XVIII.

THE MISSISSIPPI, AND ITS NAVIGATION.

THE original discovery of the Mississippi was claimed by nearly every new traveler who visited its shores at different periods, for nearly one hundred and fifty years, each of whom sought to immortalize some personal friend, or honor some spiritual patron, by bestowing his or her name upon this magnificent river. But who is entitled to the credit of its discovery has been left in some doubt; and in tracing back the claims of La Salle, Hennepin, Marquette, De Soto, and others, we are inclined to award the honor to Alvarez Alonzo De Pineda, who, with four vessels, appears, in Spanish history, to have sailed along the north coast of the Gulf of Mexico, from Florida to Mexico, in 1519, and who marked on the map of the expedition the mouth of a large river from the north, which he named Rio Del Espiritu Santo, or river of the Holy Ghost. Spanish history also relates, that Pamphilo De Narvaez, with his adventurers from Florida, having been abandoned by his fleet, attempted to escape to Mexico in hastily constructed boats, and on the way entered the mouth of a "very great river of sweet water" from the north, in October, 1528.

But the history of the expedition of De Soto settles the fact beyond a doubt, that that adventurer struck the Mississippi in latitude about 34° north, on the 25th of April, 1541. The historians of that expedition applied to the river the names of *Saint Esprit*, and *Rio Grande*, but De La Vega stated, on the authority of Juan Coles, one of De Soto's followers, that the Indian name was *Chu-ca-gua*, and marked the river on the map of the expedition by that name. The meaning of the Indian name was not given by De La Vega, but the reader will discover a great similarity between that word and *Che-o-kah*, the present Choctaw word for "great water." Chu-ca-gua was the name applied to the river on the French map of Sanson in 1674, following the Spanish authority.

In the north, the Algonquin nations heard of "the great river" from the *O-chunk-o-raws*, of Green Bay, but understanding it as "the great water," which, according to their knowledge, was salt; they therefore named that tribe the *Winnebagoec*, or "people of the sea." The early French made the same mistake; hence Nicolet, in 1639, called the same tribe the Gens De Mer, and the Rev. Father Le Mercier, Jesuit Superior at Quebec, in a letter dated September 21, 1654, wrote that he had learned by "letters, that it is only nine days' journey from this great lake (Green Bay) to the sea that separates America from China."

In tracing the French explorations and discoveries, we find the Rev. Father Claude Allouez, the Wisconsin Jesuit missionary, near the head of Lake Superior, writing in his journal, in 1665, of the Illinois Indians, whose "country is more than sixty leagues from here, towards the south, and beyond, a great river that discharges itself, as near as I can conjecture, into the sea towards Virginia." In speaking of the *Nadouesioux*, the same authority says: "This is a tribe that dwells to the west of this, towards the great river called *Messipi*."

After this, the Jesuit missionaries in the north-west often wrote of the "Great river," and the "Missisipi," until they induced the Governor of Canada to fit out an expedition specially for its exploration. This expedition was placed in the charge of Sieur Jollyet, with the Rev. Father James Marquette, then stationed at Mackinaw, as missionary and interpreter. It was organized early in 1673, at Mackinaw, with bark canoes and five *voyageurs*, and passed by way of Green Bay and the Wisconsin river, and reached the great river at Prairie Du Chien, June 17th, of the same year. From that point they floated down this magnificent river, visiting the several tribes on its banks, until they arrived at the Arkansas river, when they turned back and reached Mackinaw the same season, by way of the Illinois river and Lake Michigan. Marquette was the historian of the expedition, and named the great river "*De la Conception*," and in explanation said: "Above all, I put our voyage under the protection of the Blessed Virgin Immaculate, promising her, that if she did us the grace to discover the great river, I would give it the name of Conception."

Our next French explorer was the Rev. Father Louis Hennepin, a Recollect missionary belonging to the party of La Salle. He was dispatched by that officer from the fort on the Illinois river with two companions in bark canoes, and reached the great river, at the mouth of the Illinois, March 8th, 1680. From thence they journeyed up the Mississippi a few days, were then made prisoners by a war party of the Sioux, and taken to Mille Lac, at the head of Rum river. During the summer they were redeemed by Sieur De Lut, who had reached the great river from Lake Superior with a small guard of soldiers, and Hennepin and companions were taken back to Mackinaw. Father Hennepin, in his published journal, called the great river "Colbert," in honor of Jean Baptiste Colbert, the Marquis De Seignelai, who was then the French Secretary of Marine and the Colonies.

The main expedition of the Cavalier Robert De La Salle, which had been gotten up with great cost and labor to thoroughly explore the great river, was long delayed by the wreck of the supply ship, the "Griffin," and the revival of the war between the Iroquois and the Illinois Indians; and that indomitable officer and his party only reached the great river on the 6th of February, 1682. On the 13th of the same month they launched their canoes on the mighty river, and the 7th of the following month found La Salle reconnoitering the shore of the Gulf of Mexico. On the 9th day of April, 1682, La Salle took formal possession of the country and rivers "in the name of the most high, mighty, invincible, and victorious Prince, Louis the Great, by the grace of God, king of France and Navarre, fourth of that name," etc. He called the country "Louisiana," in honor of his prince, and the great river "River Colbert, or Mississippi."

As the name "Mississippi," of French orthography, became finally established as the name of the great river, and as that word has often been interpreted as meaning the "Father of waters," we in this connection say that the word is composed, in the Illinois dialect, of *Michau*, great, and *Sippi*, river; which the Chippeways contracted for euphony to "Mississippi" of French, or "Mee-zee-see-bee" of English orthography. Mr. Schoolcraft constructed the word from the duplication of *Miss*, great, — meaning great-great. In this construction, Mr. Schoolcraft forgets that in another place in his history of the Indian tribes, he says that the Chippeways use *Michau*, for great, when applied to land or water. But if that tribe do sometimes use the word *Miss*, for great, and *Sippi*, for river, the Chippeway rules which he gives for euphony, — viz.: when two consonants come together, a vowel must be inserted between the syllables, — will explain the combination and make the word *Mis-si-sippi*, or, in English orthography, *Mee-zee-see-bee*.

That the word simply means "great river," is strengthened by the fact that the same name has been given to it by the other tribes; for we find the river called *Kee-che-se-be* by the Ottawas, *Me-chaw-se-poo* by the Sacs, Foxes, and Potowatomies, *Pah-kah-poo-se-bee* by the Menomonies, *Ne-coos-hut-ta-raw*, by the Winnebagoes, and *Wat-pah-tan-kah* by the Sioux. But we will pass from this subject to the physical character of the great river.

The Mississippi has its source in the numerous springs that burst forth from the *hauteurs de terre*, or dividing ridge between the Itasca lake and Red river, and flow into that lake, where they become united, and start on their tortuous course for the ocean. The Itasca lake is in latitude 47° 13′ N., and longitude 95° 2′ west of Greenwich.

Table of Distances and Altitudes on the Mississippi, compiled by Nicolet and Fremont.

FROM THE GULF TO	Distance, miles.	Altitude, feet.
New Orleans	104	‡
Red River	340	76
Natchez light-house	406	86
Yazoo	534	
Montgomery Landing	755	202
New Madrid	1,115	
Ohio river	1,216	324
Cape Girardeau	1,257	
St. Genevieve	1,330	
Cathedral, St. Louis	1,390	384
Illinois river	1,426	
Des Moines river	1,594	444
Montrose	1,609	
Burlington	1,639	
Rock Island	1,722	526
Head Upper rapids	1,737	554
Dunleith	1,861	
Prairie Du Chien	1,932	642
La Crosse	2,014	
Hammand's, Black river	2,035	683
Mt. Trempealeau	2,042	
Roque's, Wabashaw	2,084	
Head Lake Pepin	2,115	714
St. Croix river	2,150	723
St. Paul	2,186	
Minnesota river	2,192	744
U. S. Cottage, St. Anthony	2,200	856
Rum river	2,219	
Crow river	2,229	
Watab river	2,305	
Crow-wing river	2,381	1,130
Pine river	2,429	1,176
Sandy Lake river	2,526	1,253
Leach Lake river	2,675	1,356
Old trading house, Cass lake	2,755	1,402
Schoolcraft I., Itasca lake	2,890	1,575
Dividing ridge	2,896	1,680

By the foregoing table, it will be observed that the distance from Prairie Du Chien to Minnesota river is given at two hundred and sixty miles, but on many steam-boat cards it is put at three hundred and eight miles, a difference of forty-eight miles. As great a discrepancy will probably be found between other points.

The increase of the altitude on the river is too gentle to impede the navigation, except at certain points, as follows: The lower, or Des Moines rapids, are about eleven miles long, with a fall of twenty-four feet; the upper, or Rock river rapids are about fourteen miles long, with a fall, according to Captain Lee, of about twenty-six feet. These rapids are made by ledges of lime-rock passing under the river, and are very difficult to pass at low water, even with light steamers. The rapids from the mouth of St. Peter's, or Minnesota river, to St. Anthony's falls are about eight miles in length, and steamers can seldom go nearer than within four miles of the falls. St. Anthony's falls are about twenty feet perpendicular height. Above the falls, steamers run to Sauk rapids, about seventy miles, in a good stage of water, where steam navigation practically stops; although, in 1859, a small steamer passed the Sauk rapids and Little falls, and reached nearly to the Falls of Pokegoma, a distance of three hundred and fifty miles above St. Anthony. Canoe navigation reaches the Itasca lake by making portages past the several falls.

The Mississippi, from Cairo to St. Anthony's falls, appears to have scooped out itself a channel, averaging perhaps two miles wide, and from one to four hundred feet deep, in the otherwise comparatively level country; thereby creating the impression on the mind of the traveler that the Falls of St. Anthony might have originally been below St. Louis, but rapidly receding by the disintegration of the sand rocks until it reached its present site. Indeed, the falls are known to be still traveling up stream, but as the strata of sandstone has nearly run out, it is supposed that its locomotion will nearly, if not quite, cease at the end of the next mile.

But the great river, being unable to hold the position which it had assumed in its rampant days, finally subsided into a main channel, about half a mile wide, with other smaller channels, called sloughs, leaving much of the two miles or more in width, to emerge from the water, and the higher portions to form sandy prairies for town sites and cultivated fields, while the lower portions form timbered bottoms and islands. At Lake Pepin, however, the rampant river, being pressed nearer together by two opposite flinty promontories, ploughed deeper in the earth, and scooped out a beautiful lake about twenty-two miles long, which still holds its own, and has become classical with Indian legends. Indeed, we believe the Roman calendar of saints might be doubled, if proper research were made among the Indian legends of the north-west.

Below the mouth of the Ohio river, the main channel does not much exceed half a mile in width, but increases in depth, and the timbered bottoms often extend thirty miles before the higher table land is reached.

The rise and fall of the water of the Mississippi, above the Missouri, is generally periodical. The first high water of the year is in the spring, soon after the clearing out of the ice, and usually commences about the second week in April, and subsides by the middle of May. The second high water is called the "June rise," and commences about the first of June, and extends into July. The first rise of water is caused by the melting of the snow and ice in the first warm weather in the spring; while the "June rise" is caused in the same manner, when the warm weather of summer penetrates into the cold, swampy, timbered country on the head-waters of the Mississippi, Rum, St. Croix, Chippeway, Black, and Wisconsin rivers, where the snow falls deep in winter, and remains until the heat of the summer is somewhat advanced. There are exceptions to the general rule, as in 1852, when the month of April being unusually warm, the heat penetrated the icy swamps of the hyperborean regions, creating in May the highest flood for several years. The consequence was, that we failed to get the "June Rise." Seasons like 1863 sometimes occur when but little snow falls in the winter, and the spring and summer floods both fail. Local floods may occur from heavy rains, but these seldom extend far enough to much affect the Mississippi.

In the annals of the country, we find notices of great floods, the first of which, in April, 1728, flooded the French Fort Beauharnais, on the north side of Lake Pepin, which the Sioux said was the highest water they ever knew. Mr. Nicolet, speaking of the flood of 1785, said:

"This year is called *l'annee de grands eaux*—the year of the great flood. In the month of April, the waters of the Mississippi rose fifteen or twenty feet above the highest mark they had ever been known to reach at St. Louis, and at some narrow parts of the river, as high as thirty feet. The whole region of country drained by the Mississippi, to its mouth, presented the aspect of an immense sheet of water studded with islands. The village of St. Genevieve, Fort Chartres, Kaskaskia, St. Phillippe, Cahokia, etc., were totally submerged; and the inhabitants, who had fled to the hills that overlooked the rich bottoms, interchanged visits by water from the rocky bluffs of the right side of the river to the hills that border the Kaskaskia."

The great flood of 1826 was the highest of more modern times in the upper country; the water at Prairie Du Chien reaching twenty-six feet above low water. The flood of 1832 was eighteen feet at the same place, and in 1852 the water rose sixteen feet at La Crosse. In 1835 the flood reached fifty-two feet at Natchez. But the height to which a flood may reach in any given place, of course depends on the width of the river bottoms at such place, and the same flood will reach different heights at different localities.

The depth of the river at low water, except on the bars, between Dunleith and St. Paul, is about twelve feet, and on the bars often less than three feet. In passing below Dunleith, the water does not increase much in depth until it receives the accession of the Missouri, when it seems to take new impetus, and rushes on boldly to the ocean. At New Orleans, the river, at low water, is about one hundred and thirteen feet deep. We can not give the depth of water at Memphis, but there is nothing visible of the confederate fleet of war steamers sunk there June 6, 1862, by the United States gun-boats, but majestic steamers now sweep along, meeting with no obstructions from the bristling gun-boats, or tall smoke chimneys, silent as death in the depths below.

First among the tributaries of the Mississippi, for its usefulness and beauty, stands the Ohio. As the warlike Iroquois floated down its gentle current, watching for spoils along its flowery banks, and seeking enemies on whom he might revenge a lost relative, he became absorbed in the magnificent scenery, and shouted his ecstatic O-ee-o, O-ee-o. The French took up the word, clothed it in its modern orthography, and translated it "La Belle." The English have retained the French orthography, and render the word, "The Beautiful;" and beautiful, indeed, it is in song and story; and beautiful will it remain until the iron hoof of time shall wear out its earthy cradle, or its mountain sources shall be dried up.

This river was first visited at its mouth by Marquette, in 1673; but he mistook it for the Wabash, and probably his Illinois interpreter only knew of the Wabash, and not of the Ohio.

"The Beautiful" river has its western source in Chatauque lake, not distant seven miles from Lake Erie, with an altitude above the latter lake of about seven hundred feet, and above tide water of thirteen hundred feet. The eastern, or Alleghany mountain source, is near Coudersport, Pennsylvania. According to C. Ellet, Jr., Esq., civil engineer, the distances and fall of the river to the Gulf of Mexico are as follows:

Distances and Altitudes on the Ohio River.

	Distance in miles.	Fall in feet.
Coudersport to Olean Point	40	246
Olean Point to Warren	50	216
Warren to Franklin	70	227
Franklin to Pittsburg	130	261
Pittsburg to Beaver	26	30
Beaver to Wheeling	62	49
Wheeling to Marietta	90	49
Marietta to Le Tart's Shoals	31	16
Le Tart's Shoals to Kanawha	55	33
Kanawha to Portsmouth	94	48
Portsmouth to Cincinnati	105	42
Cincinnati to Evansville	328	112
Evansville to Gulf	1,365	320
Coudersport to Gulf—Total	2,446	1,649

By an examination of this table, it will be seen that the fall from Olean Point to Pittsburg, in low water, is on an average, about two feet ten inches per mile; from Pittsburg to Evansville, about five and two-tenths inches per mile, and from Evansville to Gulf, about two and eight-tenths inches per mile. As steamboats, in high water, have been as high as Olean Point, it will be observed that they are capable of overcoming a fall of four feet and four inches per mile, as that is the average fall between that point and Warren.

Itasca lake, the source of the Mississippi, having an altitude above the Gulf of 1,575 feet, and Olean Point of 1,403 feet, it will be observed that steam navigation on the Ohio has already reached an altitude within 172 feet of the main source of the Mississippi.

The greatest flood of the Ohio known, occurred in February, 1832, when the river attained a height of thirty-one feet at Pittsburg, forty-four and one-half at Wheeling, and sixty-three at Cincinnati, above its summer level. This flood reached its highest mark along the river, at the following dates: Pittsburg, February 10; Wheeling, 88 miles, February 11, in evening; Marietta, 176 miles, February 13, at noon; Maysville, 405 miles, February 16, at night; Cincinnati, 460 miles, February 17, at midnight; and Louisville, 613 miles, February 21, in morning. By this statement, it appears that the flood moved from Pittsburg to Cincinnati at the rate of about two and one-half miles an hour, a velocity much less than the center current of the river at high water.

The Missouri river, called by the Algonquins, *Pekitanoui*, or Muddy water, and by Father Membre, the "Ozage river," is next to the Ohio in its present commerce, but as its valley settles up with emigrants, it will increase with great rapidity, and possibly rival the Mississippi itself.

The following are the distances from the Gulf of Mexico, and altitudes above tide water, of the several points hereafter named, as given by Mr. Nicolet and others:

Distances and Altitudes on the Missouri river.

FROM GULF TO	Distance in miles.	Altitude in feet.
Mouth Missouri	1,408	388
Boonville	1,604	530
Fort Leavenworth	1,820	746
Platt River	2,026	
Council Bluffs	2,084	1,024
Fort Pierre	2,664	1,456
Fort Union	3,277	2,019
Fort Benton	3,805	2,780
Highwood Creek	3,820	
Great Falls	3,835	
Cadott's Pass, Rocky mountains	3,903	6,044
Sources Missouri	4,300	

These facts show that the Missouri is nearly 1,410 miles longer than the Mississippi, and that it is already navigated to an altitude about 1,225 feet above Itasca lake, the main source of the latter river.

The late Governor Stevens said, in his report on the Pacific Railroad route, that the Missouri had been navigated to Fort Union for the last thirty years, by steamers carrying five hundred to six hundred tons freight, and drawing from three to four feet of water; that such steamers had often ascended as high as Milk river; and that steamers of two hundred tons burthen can easily go as high as Highwood creek, within fifteen miles of the Great falls.

The Great falls extend eleven and a half miles, with five principal cascades, with rapids between, with a total descent of one hundred and sixty feet. The principal cascades descend successively twenty-five, five, forty-two, twelve, and seventy-six feet. The three principal forks of the Missouri above the falls are called Gallatin, Madison, and Jefferson, and have their several sources in the Rocky mountains far to the south of the Great falls.

The clay mud that colors the Missouri, as well as the Mississippi after the junction of the two, is mainly derived from the Yellow Stone, a tributary that forms a junction with the Missouri at Fort Union. It is a stream of some importance, and is reported navigable for two hundred miles.

The other principal tributaries of the Mississippi are the Red, Arkansas, Illinois, Des Moines, Rock, Wisconsin, Iowa, Black, Chippeway, St. Croix, and Minnesota. The first two named are each understood to be navigable over 1,000 miles by steamers. The number of miles the Mississippi and its tributaries are navigable by steamboats has been variously estimated at from 10,000 to 15,000 miles, while the keel-boat navigation is much more extensive.

The late Hon. Thomas H. Benton, in his letter to the Chicago convention, dated June 10th, 1847, on this subject remarked: "Many years ago the late Governor Clark and myself undertook to calculate the extent of the boatable water in the valley of the Mississippi; we made it about

50,000 miles, of which 30,000 were computed to unite above St. Louis, and 20,000 below. Of course, we counted all the infant streams on which a flat, a keel, or a batteau could be floated, and justly; for every tributary of the humblest boatable character helps to swell not only the volume of the central waters but of the commerce upon them."

The original canoe of the Indian was superseded by the *batteaux* of the early French *voyageurs*. The Spanish often used galleys of forty oars each in navigating the Mississippi, ten of which came from New Orleans to St. Louis with troops in 1797. The early settlers of the Mississippi valley for many years carried their produce and stock to market, at New Orleans, in large, flat-bottom boats and arks, that floated down the river with no other propelling power than the ordinary current. The batteaux are now commonly called the Mackinaw boats, and carry from three-quarters to three tons. The flat bottoms are often called barges, and carry from thirty to one hundred tons. The writer has no data from which he can tell the number of tons burthen of the flat-bottom boat originally navigated by our illustrious late President of the United States, Abraham Lincoln.

At the period of the introduction of steamers on the Mississippi, in 1812, the whole commerce from New Orleans to the upper country was transported in about twenty barges, making but one trip each year. The number of keel boats on the Ohio was about one hundred and sixty. The total tonnage, from 6,000 to 7,000 tons.

The first steamboat in the Mississippi valley was built at Pittsburg, and launched in October, 1811, called the "New Orleans." It was run to Louisville, where it was detained by low water for some three weeks, and in the mean time made several trips to Cincinnati. The last week in November it resumed its trip down the river, was nearly overwhelmed by an earthquake, but finally reached Natchez at the close of the first week in January, 1812. Having been built to run between Natchez and New Orleans, it probably run on that line, and was said to have been of service to General Jackson at the great battle at New Orleans, January 8th, 1815, but evidently did not attract much attention, as some have doubted its ever reaching the Mississippi, and have dated the commencement of steam navigation on the Mississippi in 1817.

Eleven other steamers were built on the Ohio in the five years following 1811, with a total tonnage of 2,235.

The first steamboat which arrived at St. Louis was in 1819. The first steamer to St. Peter's river was the "Virginia," one hundred and eighteen feet long, and drawing six feet of water, which arrived in May, 1823, with Major Taliafero, our Indian agent, and Count Beltrami, as passengers. From this period they began to increase rapidly. In 1834 the number of steamers on the Mississippi and tributaries was two hundred and thirty, with a tonnage of 39,000. In 1840, two hundred and eighty-five, with a tonnage of 49,800. In 1845, the tonnage had increased to 159,713.

According to the report of the Treasury department of the United States for the year ending June 30th, 1859, the enrolled tonnage in steam navigation in the several districts in the Mississippi valley was as follows:

	Tonnage.
New Orleans	57,790
Nashville	5,120
Memphis	7,926
Louisville	29,627
St. Louis	54,515
Galena	5,362
Cincinnati	25,683
Wheeling	13,480
Pittsburg	40,550
Total tonnage of steamers	258,053

When we add the tonnage of other vessels, the total at each point is as follows:

	Tonnage.
New Orleans	215,417
Nashville	5,120
Memphis	7,926
Louisville	29,627
St. Louis	60,760
Galena	5,362
Cincinnati	29,515
Wheeling	13,480
Pittsburg	55,576
Total of tonnage	422,783

From this it appears that the most of the ship and canal-boat building is confined to Pittsburg, Cincinnati, St. Louis, and New Orleans. This latter city being connected with the commerce of the ocean, does nearly twice the amount of ship building that it does of steamboat building.

The report of the Treasurer does not give the number of steamers enrolled; but it is estimated in the report of 1851, on the colonial and lake trade, that the Ohio boats average about $206\frac{1}{4}$ tons; and those on the Mississippi and Missouri, $273\frac{2}{3}$ tons. If we average them at 240 tons, we have 1,075 steamboats running on the Mississippi and its tributaries, with a total tonnage of 258,053 for the year 1859.

The boats manufactured the same year are given as follows:

	Schooners.	Sloops, or canal boats.	Steamers.	Tonnage.
Pittsburg		8	29	4,588
Wheeling			14	1,511
Cincinnati	1	20	15	6,999
Louisville			19	3,702
Paducah			1	114
Galena			1	153
St. Louis			2	154
New Orleans	10	2	2	795
Total	11	30	83	18,016

By this statement it appears that all the schooners but one were built at New Orleans, and that nearly one-third of the steamers were manufactured at Pittsburg, one-sixth at Wheeling, over one-sixth at Cincinnati, over one-fourth at Louisville, and only one fortieth at either St. Louis or New Orleans. Also, that most of the steamers were built on the Ohio, and of a much less tonnage than the previous average.

The progress of steam navigation on the upper Mississippi was extremely slow at first. From 1823 to 1844, only one or two trips a year were made to Fort Snelling, to carry supplies to the troops, and for the Indian trade. In 1844, the number of arrivals at the fort were forty-one. From 1844 to 1847, the little steamers Otter, Rock River, and Lynx, were the principal boats in this trade.

In 1847, on the 8th day of July, the Galena and Minnesota Packet Company was organized at Galena by the following persons, who became the company:

Captain Orrin Smith, Galena; Henry Corwith, Galena; B. H. Campbell, Galena; Captain M. W. Lodwick, Galena; Captain R. Blakesly, Galena; Colonel H. L. Dousman, Prairie Du Chien; B. W. Brisbois, Prairie Du Chien; Hon. H. H. Sibley, St. Paul; Hon. H. M. Rice, St. Paul.

The first boat purchased by this company was the "Argo," of only sixty tons burthen, which was run in the St. Paul trade until October of the same year, when it ran against a snag, and sunk a little above Winona.

The next boat was the "Dr. Franklin," purchased the winter of 1847–48 for $13,500, and put into the trade in the spring of 1848. In 1849 the "Senator" was added to the line, but in the fall was sold, and replaced by the "Nomenee," which was run by Captain O. Smith, the late president of the company. It was not run as a Sunday boat. At twelve o'clock Saturday night, Captain Smith would tie up his boat to an island, or whatever place he was near, and remain until twelve o'clock Sunday night. When the boat stopped at a little village, the Captain would invite any clergyman that might be found, to preach, on the Sabbath, on the boat. Rev. Mr. Chester, of the Methodist church, once enjoyed the Captain's hospitality at La Crosse, in the fall of 1851, and held morning service. The "Noménee," however, suffered the fate of its more unchristian brothers, and was snagged and sunk in the fall of 1854, forty miles below La Crosse.

The "Ben Campbell" was built in the winter of 1851-52, and put in the trade in the spring, but drew too much water, and was sold in the fall of 1852. During the season of 1852, an opposition boat, called the "West Newton," was put into the trade from Galena to St. Paul, by the Harrises of Galena, and run against the Noménee. The "West Newton" was a gallant little boat, and about an equal match for the Noménee. During this opposition, on the 10th of May, 1852, the Noménee, Captain Smith, prepared for a race to St. Paul, and although the "West Newton" did not run, yet Captain Smith run on time, and made the trip to St. Paul and back to Galena in two days, seven hours and forty-nine minutes — a round trip of eight hundred miles. In the fall of the same year, the Harrises were permitted to join the Galena company, and their boat afterwards run in the line.

In the spring of 1854, the "War Eagle," "Galena," and "Royal Arch," were added to the line, and in 1855, the "Golden Era," "Alhambra," "Lady Franklin," and "City Bell," were added.

In June, 1856, the opening of the Galena and Chicago Union Railroad gave a great impetus to the business, and the packet company added to their line of boats the "Northern Bell," "Ocean Wave," "Granite State," "Greek Slave," and "Black Hawk."

Several boats besides the "Noménee" were sunk during this time: namely, "West Newton," in the fall of 1853, near Alma; "Dr. Franklin," seven miles above Dubuque, by colliding with the "Galena," in June, 1854. In 1856, the "Galena" was burned.

Trade fell off considerably in 1858, and subsequently, but in 1861 the packet company increased its number of incorporators to about one hundred, and its capital to $400,000, and run the following boats in the upper trade:

"War Eagle," "Alhambra," "City Bell," "Fanny Harris," "Northern Light," "Key City," "Northern Bell," "Golden Era," "Ocean Wave," "Flora," "Grey Eagle," "Milwaukee," "Itasca."

Some of these boats were of the first class, and might well have been called "floating palaces."

The "Milwaukee" cost the company $39,000; "Grey Eagle," $43,000; and the "Key City," and "Northern Light," each about the same.

The "Key City" was built at Cincinnati, in 1857, was 250 feet long, 35 feet wide, $359\frac{8\frac{1}{2}}{1}$ tons burthen, 51 state-rooms, and four high-pressure boilers, 17 feet long, 38 inches in diameter, and have been subject to a pressure of 200 pounds to the square inch. The "War Eagle" and "Galena," were of a smaller class of boats, the former being but $296\frac{1}{4}$ tons burthen, with 46 state-rooms, and 3 high-pressure boilers, 14 feet long each. It is 219 feet long, and 29 feet wide, and was built at Cincinnati, in the winter of 1853–54.

The Galena Packet Company finally reorganized in February, 1864, under the laws of the State of Iowa, with a cash capital of $400,000, under the name of "The Northwestern Packet Company," with general powers to run steamers, and do a passenger and freight business between Dubuque and St. Paul. The company was bound by contract with the Milwaukee and Prairie Du Chien Railroad Company, to carry freight and passengers for that company between the latter place and St. Paul.

In the fall of 1865, the North-western Company were running the following steamers in the trade: "Milwaukee," "Itasca," "Northern Light," "Key City," "War

Eagle;" all first-class passenger steamers. They also run three light-draught boats for low water, and three additional steamers for freight and towing barges.

The officers of the new company for 1865 were: John Lawler, President; George A. Blanchard, Secretary and Treasurer; and William E. Wellington, Superintendent. The central office was located at Dubuque, where the two latter gentlemen resided.

On the first day of October, 1858, the La Crosse and Milwaukee Railroad was completed, and opened through to the Mississippi at La Crosse, and much of the business of the boats passed over this road.

In 1860, an independent, or opposition, line of steamboats was run from La Crosse to St. Paul, by Mr. Davidson and others, which the Galena Packet Company made a spirited but unsuccessful effort to run off; failing in this, they compromised, by forming with Davidson and others, a combination, on the 17th of August, 1861, which has since done a large business.

In 1863, the La Crosse and St. Paul line ran in connection with the La Crosse and Milwaukee Railroad, the following boats:

"McLellan," Captain P. S. Davidson; "Keokuk," Captain J. R. Hatcher; "Northern Bell," Captain John Cochran; "Frank Steele," Captain Martin; "Clara Hine," Captain J. Newton; "G. H. Wilson," Captain William Butler; "Æolian," Captain Sencerbox.

Running above the Falls of St. Anthony, "Anne Cutler," "Enterprise," and "Gray Cloud."

Running on the Chippewa river: "John Rumsey," Captain Nathaniel Harris; "Chippewa Falls," Captain L. Fulton.

Running on the St. Croix: "Wenona," Captain L. Brown.

Running on the Minnesota: "Pomeroy," Captain Bell;

"Stella Whipple," Captain Haycock; "Albany," Captain Norris; — in all, 16.

These boats were all light-draught, and were seldom stopped by low water, although the low water of 1863 was extremely embarrassing. Nearly the same steamers were running in 1865.

The combination of the steamboat interest proving unsatisfactory, the new North-western Packet company and the La Crosse line, generally called "Davidson's Line," on the 1st of May, 1866, consolidated into a new company, under the general laws of the State of Iowa, at Dubuque, and organized a company which they called the "North-western Union Packet Company," and elected the following officers: William F. Davidson, of St. Paul, president; John Lawler, of Prairie Du Chien, general manager; Geo. A. Blanchard, of Dubuque, secretary; William Rhodes, of St. Paul, treasurer; and William E. Wellington, of Dubuque, and P. S. Davidson, La Crosse, superintendents.

The general office of the company is located at Dubuque, Iowa; and the company organized with a capital of $1,500,000, and put immediately into the trade thirty steamers and seventy-three barges. The officers are men of character and great energy, and the company will be a power that will be felt for good or evil.

The following table will show the time of the opening and closing of navigation at St. Paul, Minnesota, the number of arrivals at that point per year, and the length of the season of navigation:

Date of Opening and Closing Navigation at St. Paul.

First Boat.	River Closed.	No. of Arrivals.	Length of Season.	No. of Boats.	Tonnage.
1844, April 6	Nov. 23	41	231		
1845, " 6	" 26	48	234		
1846, March 31	Dec. 5	24	245		
1847, April 7	Nov. 29	47	236		
1848, " 7	Dec. 4	63	241	2	240
1849, " 9	" 7	95	242		
1850, " 19	" 4	194	229		
1851, " 4	Nov. 8	119	218		
1852, " 16	" 18	171	216		
1853, " 11	" 30	200	233		
1854, " 8	" 27	256	223		
1855, " 17	" 20	560	217		
1856, " 18	" 10	857	212		
1857, May 1	" 14	1,026	198		
1858, March 25	" 15	1,068	236	62	12,703
1859, April 19	" 27	808	222	55	
1860, March 28	" 23	775	240		18,279
1861, April 8	" 26	937	231		

From this table, compiled from the "Statistics of Minnesota," it appears that from 1844 to 1861, inclusive, the shortest season was in 1857, from May 1st to November 14th, of one hundred and ninety-eight days; and that the longest season was in 1846, from March 31st to December 5th, of two hundred and forty-five days' navigation; and that the average tonnage of the boats, in 1858, was nearly two hundred and five tons.

The steamboat business at St. Paul was divided with different points, as indicated by the arrivals for 1861, as follows:

From Pittsburg	-	-	-	-	4 arrivals.
" St. Louis	-	-	-	-	99 "
" Dunleith	-	-	-	-	236 "
" La Crosse	-	-	-	-	273 "
" Fox lake	-	-	-	-	3 "
" Minnesota river	-	-	-	318 "
" Stillwater	-	-	-	-	4 "

According to the census return for 1850, the total population of the United States was 23,191,876, and was divided as follows:

Pacific slope	117,271
Mississippi valley	8,641,754
Atlantic slope	12,729,859
Gulf slope	1,702,992

The full returns of the census of 1860 have not yet been published according to the geographical divisions; but if we take the ratio from 1840 to 1850, we shall find that the Mississippi valley in 1860 had a population of about 13,000,000.

In the compendium of the census for 1850, published by the United States, the States and territories are put down at 2,936,166 square miles, and are divided as follows:

Pacific slope	766,002
Atlantic slope,	514,416
Northern lake and Red R. region	112,649
Gulf region	325,537
Mississippi valley	1,217,562
Total	2,936,166

From this statement it will be seen that over two-fifths of the whole territory of the United States is drained by the waters of the Mississippi and its tributaries; and if we add to this the Gulf region, and the Lake and Red River region, we shall have nearly three-fifths of the entire territory of the United States. By comparing this central region with Europe, we find that it exceeds all the balance of Europe after taking out Russia and Portugal.

The acclivity of the surface, east, west, and north of the Mississippi, is so gentle, as neither to affect the navigation of the tributaries, nor impede the cultivation of the soil; while the southern portion is not too warm, or the northern too cold, to effect more than to give a variety to the vegetable productions. Upon its varied soil may be grown nearly every article necessary for the comfort of man, and its inexhaustible grain fields have become almost the granary of the world.

In its mineral productions it is on quite as grand a scale. Gold and silver are abundant along a large part of the eastern slope of the Rocky mountains; iron rises into hills in Missouri, Michigan, and Wisconsin; lead underlies large districts in Iowa, Illinois, Wisconsin, and Missouri; copper and zinc are abundant, and gypsum is generally disseminated in every State and territory; and in the south-west, on the head waters of the Red and Arkansas rivers, it occupies a region of more than 2,000 square miles.

Salt is found in springs in most of the valleys, and as rock salt in Missouri, and at the bottom of the salt wells in Ohio.

Coal exists in vast quantities in every State and territory except Wisconsin and Minnesota. Along the head waters of the Missouri and its western tributaries, nearly to the Gulf, it is believed to exist in greater quantities than at any other locality on the globe.

Coal oil, which is now attracting so much attention, is found in south-eastern Ohio, western Pennsylvania, and north-western Virginia. The most extensive and productive deposit now known is on the Little Kanawha, about thirty miles above Parkersburg. In this locality, four hundred barrels are said to have run out of one well in five hours.

But the writer need not enlarge upon the natural advantages which the great Creator has congregated in this lovely valley of the Mississippi for the benefit of man. However, as numerous as they are, but few of them can be enjoyed to advantage unless the navigation of the Mississippi and its tributaries are free from the control of the enemies of the people who inhabit the valley. No divided authority can control the great interest here involved for any length of time. It must and will be under one government.

The great southern statesman, Hon. John C. Calhoun,

speaking on this subject in his report to the United States Senate, on the 26th of January, 1846, on the subject of the resolutions of the Memphis convention, remarked: " So urgent, indeed, is the necessity of a common power to regulate its commerce, that it may be safely affirmed that it would require a confederation among the States on its borders for that purpose, as the only means of preserving peace, and preventing the most deadly conflicts among them; destructive alike of their commerce and prosperity, had not the constitution divested the States of the power, and delegated it to the federal government."

The free navigation of the Mississippi early attracted the attention of the government of the United States. By the ordinance of 1787, Congress declared that " the navigable waters leading into the Mississippi and St. Lawrence, and the carrying places between the same, shall be common highways and for ever free, as well to the inhabitants of the said territory as to the citizens of the United States, and those of any other State that may be admitted into the confederacy, without any tax, duty, or impost therefor."

Again, in 1788, Congress " Resolved that the free navigation of the river Mississippi is a clear and essential right of the United States."

The constitution, also, virtually declares that the navigation of this river shall be free, when it says, " Vessels bound to or from one State shall not be obliged to enter, clear, or pay duties in another."

By a treaty with Spain of the 27th of October, 1795, during Washington's administration, Spain finally granted to the United States the free navigation of the river.

October 1st, 1800, Spain ceded Louisiana to France, and, October 16th, 1802, the intendant, Morales, closed the port of New Orleans to our commerce. Finally, April 30th, 1803, the United States, being aware of the difficulties existing if the lower portion of the Mississippi continued under the control of a foreign government, by a treaty at

Paris, purchased Louisiana for $15,000,000, and thereby secured the undisputed navigation of the Mississippi and all its tributaries, from their sources to the Gulf of Mexico; and Governor Clairborne, of Mississippi, and General Wilkinson, of the United States army, took possession of New Orleans December 20th of the same year, and upper Louisiana was surrendered to Major Amos Stoddard, at St. Louis, March 10th, 1804.

The Memphis convention, before alluded to, which was held the 12th of November, 1845, and composed of five hundred and eighty-three delegates, "*Resolved*, That safe communication between the Gulf of Mexico and the interior, afforded by the navigation of the Mississippi and Ohio rivers, and their principal tributaries, is indispensable to the defence of the country in time of war, and essential also to its commerce."

The following remarks from "De Bow's Review," on this subject, are also very pertinent: "The free and uninterrupted navigation of these great inland waters must, of course, be a matter of prime interest to the country. They are to the populous nations on their banks, as the ocean itself, over which commerce, not kings, presides. No construction of State powers as contradistinguished from Federal, can exclude these arteries of trade from the pale of government regard and protection."

To those who have their homes located in the upper Mississippi valley, the free navigation of the Mississippi to the Gulf becomes of paramount importance. They think that no flag save that of our Union should be permitted to wave over 1,200 miles of this great highway between them and the ocean, demanding tribute of our commerce, much less should that tribute be paid to a fraction of the Union, inasmuch as the free navigation was purchased with the joint funds of the whole nation; and the late pressure from the north-west upon the great southern rebellion, has demonstrated that they do not intend to be misunderstood on this question.*

Since the close of the war, the subject of the improvement of the navigation of the Mississippi and its tributaries has again revived, and an important convention was held at St. Louis, February 13th, 1867, to consider that subject. The committee on resolutions were the following prominent gentlemen: Indiana, Charles H. Mekin, A. F. Wemple; Pennsylvania, R. C. Gray, Joseph Knapp; Minnesota, E. D. Williams, W. D. Washburn; Illinois, William Eggleston, O. C. Skinner; Tennessee, W. B. Grau, H. Hiner; Ohio, Theo. Cook, A. D. Geshern; Wisconsin, R. C. Libby, Major E. Paine; Missouri, Judge Samuel Treat, James B. Earls; Louisiana, W. Jeff. Thompson, E. B. Briggs; Kentucky, R. H. Walford, B. C. Live; Michigan, J. C. Joy, A. W. Copeland; Iowa, General H. L. Reed, H. W. Starr.

This committee reported the following, which were adopted by the convention:

"*Resolved*, That the interests of the whole Mississippi valley require the immediate improvement by the national government of the Mississippi river from the Belize to the Falls of St. Anthony, including especially the bar at the Belize, the upper and lower rapids, and the removal of the obstructions above these rapids; and also the Ohio river, from Cairo to Pittsburg, and especially the work at the falls of the Ohio; said improvements to secure the navigation of said rivers free from all tolls or tribute.

"*Resolved*, That the vast importance of such action as will secure the needed improvements at an early day of the following rivers is commended to the favorable and earnest consideration of Congress, viz.: The Missouri river, from

---

* NOTE.—The north-western States furnished the following number of soldiers for the Union army of the great rebellion:

Ohio 317,133	Kansas 0,097	Iowa........ 75,860
Indiana.............195,147	Illinois........ ...258,217	
Wisconsin.......... 96,118	Michigan 90,119	Total........ 1,186,498
Minnesota.......... 25,034	Missouri 108,773	

the mouth of Fort Benton, the Illinois river, the Red river, the Tennessee river to Chattanooga, the Wisconsin river to the Fox river, the Arkansas river to Fort Smith, and the Cumberland river to Nashville.

"*Resolved*, That when the financial condition of the country may justify, Congress be requested to cause proper investigations to be made as to the necessity of improving hereafter all the other rivers of the Mississippi valley.

"*Resolved*, That Congress should so legislate on the subject of bridging the Mississippi and other navigable rivers of the United States as will, while recognizing the equal importance of railroad and river transportation, harmonize the interests by securing proper facilities for both."

CHAPTER XIX.

THE GREAT LAKES, AND THEIR NAVIGATION.

WHEN we contemplate the magnificent proportions of the north-western lakes, we are struck with the grandeur which they exhibit to the human mind; and we become absorbed in the questions whether the Creator really shaped them for the convenience of commerce, or whether it was a pure accident or freak of mother earth, when its crust was cooled down to a temperature fit for the habitation of man. Whichever way we decide the question, we are still bound to admire their peculiar adaptation to the wants of civilization, and often thank God that we are permitted to have them for our enjoyment. These lakes are not only distinguished from those of other countries by their magnitude and depth, but in the purity of their waters, which is not exceeded by the bubbling fountain gushing fresh from the mountain base.

The following table will show at a glance the physical character of these lakes, with their height above tide water:

	Greatest length, miles.	Greatest breadth, miles.	Mean depth, feet.	Elevation, feet.	Area, square miles.
Ontario	180	35	500	332	6,800
Erie	240	80	84	565	9,600
Huron	260	160	900	574	20,400
Michigan	320	100	900	578	22,000
Superior	355	160	900	627	32,000

These lakes are all connected with each other by rivers, and with the ocean by the St. Lawrence river; and the obstruction to navigation by the Niagara Falls, having been surmounted by the Welland canal, and St. Mary's Falls by Sault St. Mary canal, vessels not exceeding 130 feet keel, 26 beam, and 10 feet draught, can now load at any of the lake ports, and pass down to the ocean without transhipment of freight. These lakes are estimated to drain a region of country containing an area of 335,515 square miles.

In tracing the effects of civilization on the commerce of the north-west, the historian ought to be possessed of the data of the commerce which had been carried on by the barbarian nations, long before they were visited by the white race; but this data can not be reached with any degree of certainty at the present day, and can only be approximated from the knowledge we may gain of their manners and customs. We know that the ancient Mound-Builders, on the Ohio river, had sea-shells which must have come from the ocean, and copper and silver, which probably came from Lake Superior; and while these metals might have been found in the drift deposits of Illinois and Wisconsin, there is no conceivable way that the other articles could have been obtained short of the ocean or Gulf of Mexico. The evidence is also regarded as conclusive, that the ancient Mound-Builders were an agricultural people, and by the ordinary laws of production and human wants, it is reasonable to suppose that crops might have failed by drouth and frosts in one locality, and been supplied by another; and so investigating from cause to effect, we come to the conclusion that the Mound-Builders carried on a considerable commerce throughout all the north-west. Their successors, being a far more warlike people, paid little attention to agriculture, and therefore had no great necessity for commerce, except what might gratify their fancy or superstition. The modern Indians, however, were known to have been great travelers, and with their bark canoes fearlessly undertook a journey of one thousand miles.

When Sieur Champlain visited Lake Huron in 1615, he opened a commerce with the north-western tribes, and, except when blockaded by the Iroquois, these north-western tribes annually visited Quebec and the "Three Rivers," with large fleets of canoes loaded with furs and skins, which they exchanged for guns, powder, lead, blankets, and trinkets. Thus we find incidentally mentioned in the Jesuit Relations, that in 1656, three hundred Indians arrived in bark canoes; 1660, a fleet of sixty canoes; 1663, thirty-five canoes of Outaouaks; 1665, there "arrived at Three Rivers a hundred canoes of Outaouaks, and some other savages of our allies, who came from the region of Lake Superior, about four or five hundred leagues from here, to carry on their ordinary commerce, and to supply themselves with what they need, giving us in exchange their beaver skins, which are very abundant with them."

The beaver trade in Canada was granted by the king in 1628 to a company which failed to protect itself and the country from the Indians, and consequently surrendered their monopoly to the people in 1664, for one thousand beaver annually, as "Seigniorage," and then further surrendered their right to one thousand beaver to the king; and the king then granted the trade to the West India Company, with power to nominate all officers of the colony. This company demanded one-fourth of the beavers, and the tenth of the moose skins of all persons engaged in the fur trade, which demand was declared to be legal by the king in 1666; and in 1676, the king expressly prohibited all persons "invested with ecclesiastical or secular dignity" to engage in it.

The value of the fur trade can not easily be ascertained, but M. Talon wrote the King of France, in 1670, that the English of New York, Albany, and Boston, obtained over twelve thousand livres worth of beaver annually, "trapped by the Iroquois in countries subject to the king." The English obtained large quantities, annually, through the Iroquois, who carried on their trade with the western Indians through the valley of the Ohio to the Mississippi.

Although the French of Canada had greatly the advantage in this trade with the Indians, yet, as the English paid fifty per cent. more for the furs, the French were troubled with a contraband trade, constantly carried on with the French and English traders, by which the authorities of Canada were cheated out of their one-fourth of the furs. For instance, in 1689, the prices were stated as follows:

The Indian pays for	At Albany,	At Montreal,
Eight pounds of powder	one beaver	four.
A gun	two beavers	five.
Forty pounds of lead	one beaver	three.
A blanket of red cloth	one beaver	two.
A white blanket	one beaver	two.
Four shirts	one beaver	two.
Six pair of stockings	one beaver	two.
Six quarts rum	one beaver	
One pint to one quart brandy		one.

In 1703, the fur trade in Canada was estimated, in a French document, as being worth two million livres annually.

The English made an attempt to establish trading-posts at Detroit and Mackinaw in 1686, and the following year, Major McGregory and his party of sixty English and some Indians, with thirty-two canoes and Indian goods, on their way to Detroit, were plundered by the French on Lake Erie, and the prisoners sent to Montreal. From this time, the French took possession, and established trading-posts through the whole north-west, which they held until the surrender of Canada in 1760. When the English came in possession of Canada, they took possession of these trading-posts, and held them until 1796, when they were finally surrendered to the United States.

At the close of the war of the revolution in 1783, several of the merchants of Montreal formed a partnership for the fur trade, and in 1787 united with another company, and formed the "North-west Company." The Mackinaw Company was subsequently formed, with head-quarters at Mackinaw. In 1809, John Jacob Astor organized *himself* into the "American Fur Company," and in 1811, with some others, bought out the Mackinaw Company, and organized another, called the "South-west Company." The war of 1812 suspended its operations, and at the close of the war it was effectually dissolved by an act of Congress, prohibiting British fur traders from prosecuting their business in the United States. Mr. Astor then purchased the property of the South-west Company, and reorganized the "American Fur Company," which monopolized the fur trade in the north-west for many years subsequently.

For this company, Mackinaw was made the general depot for Indian goods in the north-west, from which place goods were transported to central points between Mackinaw and the Rocky mountains. The country west of the Rocky mountains was supplied from Astoria, on the Columbia river. Prairie Du Chien had a sub-depot, and supplied the traders along the Mississippi river, and was superintended by Mr. Lockwood for several years, until 1827, when it was put in charge of Colonel H. L. Dousman. The manner of conducting the trade was to fit out a clerk as trader, with from $1,000 to $1,500 worth of goods, in the fall of the year. The clerk was provided with canoes, and two or three *voyageurs*, or boatmen. The goods were carefully loaded in the boats, when the clerk and boatmen paddled the canoes along the water-courses, to the location of some band or tribe of Indians where it was designed to spend the winter to trade. Here a log cabin was erected, which constituted the kitchen, bed-room and store. Where trade was carried on by the same persons for several winters at the same point, additions were generally made to the cabin of a kitchen and bed-rooms.

Here, far from civilization or moral restraint, the clerk and his *voyageurs* spent the winter, in trading with the Indians, hunting, and drinking more or less whisky. The clerk generally secured some influential Indian's daughter as his mistress, and took her into his cabin, while the *voyageurs* contented themselves with running loose among the wigwams.

After the winter had passed, the ice in the streams having disappeared, and the fur of newly-killed beaver became worthless, the clerk and his *voyageurs* loaded up their canoes with their furs and skins, and returned to their employers. Here the summer was generally spent in drinking, dancing, and parties made by the congregated traders from different points, until the time arrived for a new expedition. Thus years would pass, and when clerks and *voyageurs* became too infirm to continue their regular business, they settled down upon a small piece of land at these central points, with a squaw for a wife, and there ended their days. On the death of the husband, if the wife survived, she often returned to her tribe with the children, and these children would grow up and often become the most savage of the tribe.

White blood never improves the Indian, morally, mentally, or physically, but if it changes him at all, it adds to his natural barbarity. Indeed, the contact of the whites with the Indians, from the "landing of the pilgrims" to the present day, has been deleterious to the latter race, except the very limited efforts at times of benevolent individuals to Christianize them. We have *almost* uniformly cheated them in trade, crazed them with brandy, rum, and whisky, debauched their daughters, and robbed them of their lands. Who can blame them if they are distrustful of our Christianity, and cling to the religion of their fathers, as the only thing left to them which has not been polluted by the whites?

The commerce with the Indian tribes was carried on at first in bark canoes, but as business and freight increased, the French introduced the *batteau*, a long, light boat, which proved very effectual in navigating the rivers.

In 1679, Sieur De La Salle, the explorer of the lower Mississippi, impatient of the custom of transporting freight to the upper lakes in canoes and batteaux, built, above Niagara Falls, the "Griffin," a small sail vessel, on which he embarked, with his goods and about thirty men, for Mackinaw, August 7, 1679, arriving at the latter place on the 27th of the same month. Here he remained until September 2nd, when he weighed anchor and sailed forty leagues, to the mouth of Green Bay, where he and most of the party took the freight into canoes, to perform the balance of the journey; the "Griffin" was sent back to Niagara, but was never heard of after it passed beyond Mackinaw. The published account does not name the locality at which the "Griffin" was sent back, but the Rev. Father St. Cosme, who passed over the route in 1699, remarked that forty leagues from Mackinaw, they "cabined in an isle of the detour, (so called) because there the lake begins to turn southerly," and then crossed Green Bay "from ile to ile," leaving the bay of Noquet's "on the right."

The point between Lake Michigan and Noquet bay (Bay De Nock), is still called "Point Detour," and the "Griffin" probably stopped at Sumner island, a trifle south of the point. Many modern writers do not speak of the "Griffin" passing south-west of Mackinaw. The writer does not find any mention of the tonnage of the "Griffin," but Rev. Father Membré, who sailed in it, called it a "barque," and La Salle, in 1684, in a memorial to the king, speaking of his losses by shipwreck in 1678 and 1679, said that "no time had been lost in building, at Fort Frontenac, two new vessels since, one of thirty-five to forty, and the other of twenty-five tons," and that those two cost "nine thousand livres."

La Salle evidently introduced sail vessels on Lake Ontario, as Father Membré says that La Salle, who had previously built Fort Frontenac, "sent off his troops in a brigantine for Niagara, with Father Louis Hennepin, on the 18th of November," 1678, and that La Salle "made frequent voyages from Fort Frontenac to Niagara, during the winter, on the ice, and in the spring, with vessels loaded with provisions," and that "the pilot who directed one of his well-loaded barques, lost it on Lake Frontenac (Ontario). These statements establish the point that La Salle owned these vessels, and that two were lost in 1679, one on Lake Ontario, and the "Griffin" between Mackinaw and Niagara. These vessels on Lake Ontario were probably built between the spring of 1676, when La Salle took possession of Fort Frontenac to rebuild it, and 1677, when he sailed for France to obtain a patent to explore the Mississippi; or it is possible, though not probable, that they were built during his absence to France.

The advent of the enterprising La Salle upon the lakes, with a supposed monopoly of the fur trade, raised up against him the opposition of the whole trading interests, and every appliance possible was arranged to circumvent his operations and defeat his plans; and as La Salle had first introduced sail vessels on the lakes, this fact was resorted to by the traders to arouse the superstitions of the savages, and array them against him. Hence, Father Membré, on this subject, writes that " an enterprise which should have been sustained by all well-meaning persons, for the glory of God and the service of the king, had produced precisely the opposite feelings and effects, which had been already communicated to the Hurons, the Outaoüats of the island, and the neighboring nations, to make them ill-affected." Thus, through the malice of traders against La Salle, the proud little "barques" were driven from the boisterous lakes, never to reappear above Niagara falls while the French held possession of the country, and never to reappear on

Lake Ontario until about the commencement of the great war of 1755, when all superstitions sank into insignificance, in view of the portentous struggle for the sovereignty of all Canada.

The next mention we have of sail vessels is of two at a new French mission and fort at the present site of Ogdensburg, New York, "loaded with hay and the stockades of the fort," which were burned by a party of Mohawks, October 26th, 1749.

Again, in July, 1755, the French Governor of Canada notices the fact that the English at Oswego were building some sloops carrying ten guns; and, the last of the same month, that the English "have actually two, and perhaps three, flat-bottomed sloops with sweeps, armed for war, cruising on Lake Ontario." The French also prepared four small armed vessels, to protect their batteaux when carrying supplies to Niagara. Finally, on the 11th August, 1756, the French, under Montcalm, laid siege to Oswego, and captured it the 14th of the same month, with the English fleet, then consisting of seven vessels of war, one of eighteen guns, one of fourteen guns, one of ten, one of eight, three mounted with swivels, and two hundred barges or batteaux. These vessels, with the most of those belonging to the French, were recaptured by the colonial troops under Colonel Bradstreet, when they took Fort Frontenac, now called Kingston, August 27th, 1758. All but two of the vessels were burned, probably as worthless, and those two were loaded with the trophies of the victory, and taken back to Oswego. This virtually terminated the French navy on the lakes.

The surrender of Canada in 1760 to Great Britain, threw into the hands of the British the then important fur trade of the north-west, and that government early took possession of the different military posts, and prepared to supervise the Indian tribes, then still in a state of semi-hostility. To this end, they constructed two armed schooners, and put them on Lake Erie, probably in the fall of 1762; but the first notice of them to be found is that they were lying before the fort at Detroit, May 8th, 1763, at the commencement of the siege of that fort by Pontiac. One of these, named the "Gladwin," made a trip to Fort Erie, and returned with supplies and a reinforcement for the fort, in June, which saved the fort from being surrendered to the Indians. The "Gladwin" made several trips during the season to Fort Erie. On the 13th of August, 1763, she left Detroit with her consort, called the "Beaver," but the latter was wrecked on her return towards Detroit, on the 28th of the same month, at Catfish creek, fourteen miles from Buffalo. The "Gladwin" only saved from the wreck one hundred and eighty-five barrels of provisions, which she took to Detroit. About this time additional vessels were put on the lake; and the arrivals at Detroit for 1764 showed the names of the "Gladwin," "Victory," "Boston," and "Royal Charlotte." This year the "Gladwin" made one trip to Mackinaw.

From this time up to the commencement of the war of 1812, the commerce of the lakes was mainly confined to the interests of the fur trade, and the sail vessels made a few trips annually to Mackinaw and Sault St. Mary.

Previous to 1800, the North-western Fur Company placed a schooner on Lake Superior, to run from Sault St. Mary to La Point, near the head of the lake. The first American vessel, called the "Washington," was launched at Erie, Pennsylvania, in 1797, after the surrender of the north-western posts to the United States by Great Britain. In 1812 the whole number of vessels on the upper lakes above Niagara falls was only twelve, belonging to both governments. To these were added, in 1813, the armed squadrons of the two nations, which finally became the property of the United States, by "Perry's victory," September 10th, 1813.

The discovery of steam navigation, which has worked a revolution, particularly on the great rivers of the world, was early transferred from the Atlantic to the lakes; and in 1818 was first heard the snorting "Walk-in-the-Water," the first steamer on Lake Erie.

The following table, compiled and published by the editor of the "Buffalo Commercial Advertiser" in 1843, will show the progress of steam navigation for the first twenty-five years, on the lakes above Niagara falls:

List of Steamers on the Upper Lakes to 1843.

Name.	Tôns.	Class.	Where built.	When built.
Walk-in-the-Water	340	Low	Black Rock	1818
Superior	300	"	Buffalo	1822
Chippewa	109	"	"	1824
H. Clay	348	"	Black Rock	1825
Pioneer	230	High	"	"
Niagara	180	Low	"	1826
William Penn	275	"	Erie	"
Enterprise	250	High	Cleveland	"
Peacock	120	"	Barcelona	1829
Newburyport	75	"	Erie	"
Thompson	242	Low	Huron	1830
Ohio	187	High	I. Sandusky	"
Adelaide	230	Low	Chippewa	"
Gratiot	60	High	Charleston	1832
Pennsylvania	395	"	Erie	"
New York	325	"	Black Rock	"
Brady	100	"	Detroit	"
Uncle Sam	280	Low	Gross Isle	"
Perseverance	50	High	Erie	"
Washington (first)	600	Low	Huron	1833
Michigan	472	"	Detroit	"
Webster	358	"	Black Rock	"
Detroit	240	High	Toledo	"
Lady of the Lake	26	"	Mt. Clemens	"
Marcy	151	Low	Black Rock	"
North America	362	High	Conneaut	"
Newberry	170	"	Palmer	"
Delaware	170	"	Huron	"
Victory	77	Low	Buffalo	1834
Porter	342	"	Black Rock	"
Jefferson	428	"	Erie	"
Perry	352	High	Perrysburgh	"
Monroe	341	"	Monroe	"
Mazeppa	130	"	Buffalo	"
Sandusky	377	Low	Sandusky	"
Minnessetuk	250	"	Goderich	"
Jackson	50	High	Mt. Clemens	"
J. Downing	80	"	Sandusky	"
L. Western	60	"	Chatham	"
Fulton	368	"	Cleveland	1835
Columbus	391	"	Huron	"
Townsend	312	Low	Buffalo	"
United States	366	High	Huron	"
Chicago	186	"	St. Josephs	"
Taylor	95	"	Silver Creek	"
Thames	160	"	Chatham	"
Clinton	413	"	Huron	1836

List of Steamers—continued.

Name.	Tons.	Class.	Where built.	When built.
J. Palmer	300	Low	Buffalo	"
L. Erie	149	"	Detroit	"
Barcelona	102	"	Dunnville	"
United	87	High	Detroit	"
St. Clair	250	"	Sandusky	"
Don Quixote	80	"	Toledo	"
Crocket	18	"	Brunersburg	"
Cincinnati	116	"	Sandusky	"
Illinois	755	Low	Detroit	1837
Rochester	472	High	Richmond	"
Madison	630	"	Erie	"
Cleveland	580	Low	Huron	"
Wisconsin	700	"	Conneaut	"
Erie	497	"	Erie	"
Constellation	288	"	Charleston	"
B. Hill	457	High	"	"
Constitution	443	"	Conneaut	"
New England	416	Low	Black Rock	"
Milwaukee	401	"	Grand Island	"
Wayne	390	High	Perrysburgh	"
Macomb	101	"	Mt. Clemens	"
Star	128	"	Belvidere	"
Commerce	80	"	Sandusky	"
Mason	53	"	Grand Rapids	"
Great Western	780	"	Huron	1838
Buffalo	613	Low	Buffalo	"
Chesapeake	412	"	Maumee City	"
Vermillion	385	High	Vermillion	"
Lexington	363	Low	Charleston	"
Fairport	259	High	Fairport	"
Red Jacket	148	Low	Grand Island	"
Vance	75	High	Perrysburgh	"
J. Allen	250	Low	Chicago	"
Washington (second)	880	High	Ashtabula	"
Dole	162	"	Chicago	"
Trowbridge	52	"	Kalamazoo	"
Marshall	51	"	Perrysburgh	"
Owassenonk	45	"	Grand Haven	"
Patronage	56	"	St. Joseph	"
Scott	240	"	Huron	1839
Chautauque	161	Low	Buffalo	"
Brothers	150	High	Chatham	"
Kent	180	"	"	"
Huron	149	"	Newport	"
Harrison (first)	63	"	Erie	"
Missouri	612	"	Vermillion	1840
Harrison (second)	826	"	Maumee City	"
Waterloo	98	Low	Black Rock	"
Minos	400	"	Chippewa	"
Indiana	534	"	Toledo	1841
Franklin	231	High	Algonac	1842
Nile	600	Low	Detroit	1843
Union	64	High	Black Rock	"

Besides the above list, there are a few small boats of which nothing is known other than their names. Among these are the "Pantanguishane," "Cynthia," "Pontiac," and "Phenomenon," making with those above given an aggregate of 27,000 tons, at a total cost of $3,510,000,—one hundred and thirty dollars a ton being what we deem true data for building and fitting out this description of vessels.

The number of boats yet remaining of the whole once in commission on Lake Erie and the other upper lakes is about sixty, with an aggregate of 17,000 tons. Of these, some thirty-five only are used when the consolidation is in existence.

Of the whole number of boats put in commission during the above period, only ten were built and owned in Canada.

The first steamer on Lake Michigan was the Henry Clay, which visited Green Bay with a pleasure party in August, 1827. The first steamer visited Chicago in 1832, and carried there General Scott and troops for the "Black Hawk war," and with them the cholera.

In 1843 a new era in steam navigation was established, by the introduction of the " propeller," by Messrs. Hollisters, of Buffalo. During that season they launched one at Buffalo, one at Cleveland, one at Perrysburg, and one at Chicago. The first was called the "Hercules," and was one hundred and thirty-five feet long, twenty-five feet beam, eight feet hold, and two hundred and seventy-five tons. The engine was one of the Ericsson patent, of fifty horse-power, filled only about six feet square, and weighed only fifteen tons. This left almost the entire hull for storage. It cost about $20,000, and was rigged with sails as well as engine. This class of steamers became popular in lake navigation, and was afterwards greatly multiplied.

In 1825, the whole licensed tonnage of all the lakes above the Falls of Niagara consisted of three steamers of seven hundred and seventy-two tons, and fifty-four sailing craft of 1,677 tons, being an aggregate of only 2,449 tons.

From 1825 to 1851 the aggregate tonnage was as follows: 1830, 16,300; 1835, 30,602; 1841, 55,181; 1846, 90,000; 1851, 153,426.

The Chicago Board of Trade, in 1862, made up the following table, showing the number, class, tonnage, and valuation of vessels, American and Canadian, engaged in the commerce of the lakes from 1858 to 1862:

Class and Tonnage of Vessels.

	AMERICAN.			CANADIAN.		
1858.	No.	Tonnage	Valuation.	No.	Tonnage	Valuation.
Steamers	72	48,031	....	67	24,784	....
Propellers	113	56,994	....	14	4,197	....
Tugs	69	6,366	....	5	415	....
Barques and brigs	129	42,592	....	37	10,793	....
Schooners	830	177,170	....	212	32,959	....
Total	1,213	331,153	....	335	73,148	....
1860.						
Steamers	75	47,333	$2,439,840	77	25,939	$1,499,680
Propellers	190	57,210	3,250,390	27	7,289	407,290
Barques	44	17,929	584,540	23	7,832	246,480
Brigs	76	21,505	484,250	16	3,815	94,380
Schooners	831	172,526	5,233,085	217	31,792	895,560
Total	1,216	316,503	$11,992,105	360	76,717	$3,146,890
1862.						
Steamers	66	43,683	$1,403,800	64	28,104	$1,020,200
Propellers	122	52,932	2,344,300	16	5,154	181,000
Tugs	132	17,280	922,200	22	8,482	202,300
Barques	60	26,555	786,500	22	7,871	224,500
Brigs	75	22,124	466,700	14	4,223	107,000
Schooners	908	199,423	5,439,800	229	35,062	872,500
Total	1,363	361,997	$11,864,100	367	88,896	$2,607,500

The following are the different kinds of vessels built during the year ending June 30th, 1864, with their tonnage and place of construction—American:

	Ships and barques.	Schooners.	Sloops and canal boats.	Steamers.	Total No.	Tonnage.
NEW YORK—						
Oswego		5	78	1	84	12,024
Genesee		1			1	20
Niagara			1		1	150
Buffalo Creek		2	23	26	51	4,757
Cape Vincent		3			3	1,023
OHIO—						
Sandusky		4	2	6	12	1,814
Cuyahoga	1	6	9	11	27	7,351
Toledo		1			1	81
MICHIGAN—						
Detroit	4	7	14	9	34	6,669
Mackinaw	1	4			5	1,446
WISCONSIN—						
Milwaukee		9		1	10	2,346
ILLINOIS—						
Chicago		1	91	4	96	11,468
Total	6	43	218	58	325	49,149
Total for 1863	16	58	329	71	475	68,337

The miscellaneous points between the east and west, to which this large fleet of vessels ran, may be gathered as an approximation from the Report of the Milwaukee Chamber of Commerce for 1863, on the lines of propellers running from that city. The following were the several lines for 1863:

1. The People's Line and Western Transportation Company: Twelve propellers to Buffalo, Erie railroad and Erie canal.

2. The New York Central Line: Ten propellers to Buffalo, New York Central railroad and Erie canal.

3. The Grand Trunk Line: Eight propellers to Sarnia, Canada, Grand Trunk railroad.

4. Evans' Line: Seven propellers to Buffalo, New York Central and Erie canal.

5. Northern Transportation Citizens' Line: Eight propellers to Oswego and New York canals.

6. Great Western Railway Line: Seven propellers to Sarnia, Canada, Great Western railroad.

7. Detroit and Milwaukee Railroad Line: Two steamships to Grand Haven, Michigan.

8. Montreal Propeller Line: Five propellers weekly, to Montreal, Canada.

These lines of propellers were mostly an addition to the shipping of Milwaukee for 1863, as is indicated by the following table:

Shipping of Milwaukee, 1862 *and* 1863.

	1862.		1863.	
	No.	Tonnage.	No.	Tonnage.
Steamers	7	2,546	8	5,353
Propellers			69	38,541
Barques	8	3,487	70	28,883
Brigs	8	2,481	20	6,225
Schooners	107	19,330	405	81,769
Total	130	27,844	572	160,771

This addition to the shipping of Milwaukee, was made necessary mainly by the large surplus of grain raised in north-western Wisconsin, northern Iowa, and Minnesota, nearly all of which was sent to the Milwaukee market, by which that city was made to exceed Chicago in the amount of wheat sent to the eastern market. Another fact has contributed in a measure to this result: namely, the fact that the spring wheat of Wisconsin, Minnesota, and northern Iowa, is a superior article to that raised farther south, and is more sought after for flouring by eastern mill-owners.

CHAPTER XX.

CANALS, RAILROADS, TELEGRAPH LINES, AND COMMERCE.

PREVIOUS to our revolutionary war, the subject of commerce with the North-west attracted the attention of General Washington, of Virginia, and he submitted a scheme to the House of Burgesses, of that State, for the construction of a canal to the head waters of the Ohio river, for which he received a vote of thanks from that body. The scheme, however, was thought to be chimerical by some, and premature by others, and was not commenced by the State.

New York had for nearly two centuries struggled with Canada in the competition for the fur trade of the Northwest, but witnessed with disappointment that the most of that trade had continued to follow the water courses to Montreal and Quebec; hence they early planned schemes for connecting the Hudson river with Lake Erie by water communication. Finally, in 1816, Governor Clinton, of New York, recommended to the legislature of that State the building of a canal from Albany to Buffalo. That year a preliminary survey was made of the route, and, July 4th, 1817, the work was formally commenced, and prosecuted with energy from year to year until its completion, May 26th, 1825.

The progress of the work was watched with great solicitude by statesmen of other States, and its triumphant success was the signal for the commencement of other similar improvements.

The State of Pennsylvania formally inaugurated her works July 4th, 1826, which were completed to Pittsburgh in March, 1834. These were made up of the Columbia railroad, from Philadelphia to Columbia, 82 miles; the eastern and Juniata division of the Pennsylvania canal, from Columbia to Hollidaysburg, at the base of the Alleghany mountains, 172 miles; the Portage railroad, from Hollidaysburg to Johnston, 36 miles, passing over the mountain; and the western division of the Pennsylvania canal, from Johnstown to Pittsburgh, 104 miles;—making the total distance, from Philadelphia to Pittsburgh, 394 miles.

Previous to the completion of the New York canal, the people of Maryland had monopolized the eastern travel to the Ohio river, by the shortness of the route from the Chesapeake bay; but, on the completion of the New York canal, they saw the most of this travel deflected to the New York route; hence we find Maryland early competing for the prize of the commerce of the Ohio valley. Receiving assistance from the cities of Washington, Georgetown, and Alexandria, and from the United States government, Maryland chartered the Chesapeake and Ohio canal, extending from Alexandria up the Potomac river. This work was commenced under favorable auspices in 1828, but was only completed to Cumberland, a distance of 191 miles, in 1851.

The State of Ohio was earlier in the field with her canals than either Pennsylvania or Maryland; and in 1825 that State commenced the Ohio canal, which extended from Portsmouth, on the Ohio river, to Cleveland, on Lake Erie, a distance of 307 miles. The Miami canal was also commenced in 1825, and extended from Cincinnati to Manhattan, on Lake Erie, near Toledo, a distance of 270 miles. Both of these canals were completed in 1832.

The following is a list of the Ohio canals, with their several lengths:

Ohio canal and branches	340 miles.
Walhonding canal	25 "
Miami canal and branches	315 "
Hocking Valley canal	56 "
Muskingham improvement	91 "
Sandy and Beaver canal	76 "
Mahoning canal	77 "
Total length of all,	980 miles.

These works cost over $19,000,000, and have contributed greatly to the prosperity of the State and the commerce of the lakes.

In the financial expansion of 1836, the legislature of the State of Indiana planned an extensive system of works for internal improvements, and the Wabash and Erie canal was constructed from the State line of Ohio up the Maumee river and down the Wabash to Lafayette; but the crisis of 1837-8 caused the State to suspend operations, and the canal passed into the hands of the bondholders, by whom it was subsequently completed to Evansville, on the Ohio river. It extends 379 miles through the State of Indiana, and is of the total length, to Lake Erie, of 467 miles. Indiana has also the White Water canal, extending from Lawrenceville, on the Ohio river, to Hagerstown, a distance of 75 miles.

The State of Michigan also, in 1836, planned extension lines of canals, but the bankruptcy of 1838 suspended operations before they were scarcely commenced. The St. Mary's ship canal, however, several years after, received a grant of land from the United States, and was completed May 19th, 1855. It is cut through solid rock, ten feet deep, one hundred feet wide, and surmounts the falls, which were twenty-two feet perpendicular height.

The State of Illinois followed nearly in the path of Indiana. It commenced the Illinois and Michigan canal in 1836, suspended operations in 1838, and turned the work over to the bondholders, who completed the canal from Chicago to Peru in 1848, a distance of 100 miles.

In June, 1838, the territory of Wisconsin obtained a grant of land from the United States, to aid in the construction of the Milwaukee and Rock River canal, and the work was commenced; but subsequently the work was abandoned, and most of the proceeds of the sales of the grant reverted to the United States, and was deducted from the five per cent. fund due the new State.

Congress made another grant of land to the territory of Wisconsin, August 8th, 1846, " to aid in the improvement of the Fox and Wisconsin rivers, and to connect the same by a canal." This grant was accepted by Wisconsin, by an act of the legislature of the State, approved June 29th, 1848, and the work was soon after commenced, and is still (1867) in progress.

No other north-western State has made any serious attempt to construct canals.

The construction of railroads began to attract the attention of the people of the North-west in 1836, and that year the State of Ohio commenced the Lake Erie and Kalamazoo railroad, which was finished in 1845, thirty-three miles. The Mansfield and Sandusky was also commenced in 1836, and completed in 1847; the Mud River and Lake Erie was commenced in 1836, and completed in 1846, one hundred and thirty-four miles; and the little Miami was commenced in 1837, and finished in 1846, eighty-four miles.

The States of Indiana, Illinois, and Michigan also inaugurated a system of railroads in 1836, but little progress was made until long after the financial crisis of 1837-8 had passed. In fact, the construction of railroads in the North-west progressed very slowly until after 1850.

The building of railroads received a great impetus from the government of the United States. As one of the pacifying measures of the government in the great anti-slavery excitement of 1850, Congress passed a law, the 20th of

September of that year, (the same date as the law suppressing the slave trade in the District of Columbia,) providing " that the right of way through the public lands be, and the same is hereby granted to the State of Illinois, for the construction of a railroad from the southern terminus of the Illinois and Michigan canal [Peru] to a point at or near the junction of the Ohio and Mississippi rivers, with a branch of the same to Chicago, on Lake Michigan, and another *via* the town of Galena, in said State, to Dubuque, in the State of Iowa, with the right also to take necessary materials of earth, stones, timber, etc., for the construction thereof: *Provided*, That the right of way shall not exceed one hundred feet on each side of the length thereof," etc. By the second section of the same act, it was further provided, "That there be, and is hereby, granted to the State of Illinois, for the purpose of aiding in making the railroad and branches aforesaid, every alternate section of land designated by even numbers, for six sections in width on each side of said road and branches," etc.; and if any of the even numbers of sections within six miles had then been sold, or preëmpted, an equivalent number might be selected within fifteen miles of the road.

Section four provided that the State might sell the lands, and that " the said road and branches shall be and remain a public highway, for the use of the government of the United States, free from toll or other charges upon the transportation of any property or troops of the United States. By the fifth section the grant was to be forfeited unless the road was completed in ten years; and by the sixth section the mails were to be carried on the road at such price as should be fixed by law.

By the seventh section of the same act a grant with like provisions was made to the States of Mississippi and Alabama, for the extension of the road from the mouth of the Ohio river to Mobile.

The leading spirit in Congress who urged and procured

this magnificent grant of land, and thus initiated the system of granting lands for railroads, was the late Senator Douglas, of Illinois, a leading champion in north-western civilization.

Hon. S. A. Douglas, late U. S. Senator for Illinois.

The principal grants of land by the United States afterwards made for railroads to other north-western States, were as follows: To Missouri, June 10th, 1852, (1,) from Hannibal to St. Joseph; and, (2,) from St. Louis to the west line of the State, as might be determined by the State legislature. To Missouri and Arkansas, February 9th, 1853, " from a point on the Mississippi river, opposite the mouth of the Ohio, *via* Little Rock, to Texas boundary line, near Fulton in Arkansas, with branches from Little Rock in Arkansas, to the Mississippi river, and to Fort Smith, in said State."

To the State of Iowa, May 15th, 1856, (1,) "from Burlington, on the Mississippi river, to a point on the Missouri river near the mouth of the Platte river; (2,) from the city of Davenport, *via* Iowa City and Fort Des Moines, to Council Bluffs; (3,) from Lyons City north-westerly to a point of intersection with the main line of the Iowa Central Air-Line railroad near Maquoketa, thence on said main line, running as near as practicable to the forty-second parallel, across the said State to the Missouri river; (4,) from the City of Dubuque to a point on the Missouri river near Sioux City, with a branch from the mouth of the Tete Des Morts to the nearest point on said road."

To the State of Michigan, June 3rd, 1856, (1,) "from Little Bay de Noquet to Marquette, and thence to Ontonagon, and from the two last-named places to the Wisconsin State line; and, (2,) also, from Amboy, by Hillsdale and Lansing, and from Grand Rapids, to some point on or near Traverse bay; also, (3,) from Grand Haven and Pere Marquette to Flint, and thence to Port Huron."

By the act of March 3rd, 1865, a further grant was made, "for the purpose of aiding in the construction of a railroad from Marquette on Lake Superior, to the Wisconsin State line at or near the mouth of the Menomonee river, for the benefit and use of the Chicago and North-western Railway Company, a corporation of the States of Michigan, Illinois, and Wisconsin; and from Marquette to Ontonagon, for the use and benefit of the Marquette and Ontonagon Railroad Company, a corporation of the State of Michigan; and for twenty miles westerly from Marquette, of the Bay de Noquet and Marquette railroad, for the benefit and use of the Bay de Noquet and Marquette Railroad Company, four additional alternate sections of land, per mile, to that already granted." The same act extended the time for the completion of the road from Marquette to the mouth of the Menomonee river, and thence to Lake Winnebago in Wisconsin, five years from June 3rd, 1866.

To the State of Wisconsin, June 3rd, 1856, (1,) "from Madison, or Columbus, by the way of Portage City to St. Croix river or lake, between townships twenty-five and thirty-one, and from thence to the west end of Lake Superior, and to Bayfield; and, (2,) from Fond du Lac, on Lake Winnebago, northerly to the State line."

By the act of May 5th, 1864, further grants to Wisconsin were made as follows: (1,) "From a point on the St. Croix river or lake, between townships twenty-five and thirty-one, to the west end of Lake Superior, and from some point on the line of said railroad, to be selected by said State, to Bayfield, every alternate section of public land designated by odd numbers, for ten sections in width, on each side of said road, deducting any and all lands that may have been granted to the State of Wisconsin by the act of Congress of June 3rd, 1856; (2,) from the town of Tomah to St. Croix river or lake, between townships twenty-five and thirty-one," the same number of sections with like conditions as the above. The two foregoing grants only covered that portion of the grant of 1856 extending from Tomah to Lake Superior, and was supplementary thereto, leaving the balance of the grant of 1856, from Tomah to Madison, to still rest on the law of 1856. (3,) "From Portage City, Berlin, Doty's island, or Fond du Lac, as said State may determine, in a north-western direction to Bayfield, and thence to Superior, on Lake Superior," giving the odd numbered alternate sections for ten miles on each side of the road.

To the State of Minnesota, March 3rd, 1857, (1,) "from Stillwater, by way of St. Paul and St. Anthony, to a point between the foot of Big Stone lake and the mouth of Sioux Wood river, with a branch, *via* St. Cloud and Crow Wing, to the navigable waters of the Red river of the north, at such point as the legislature of said territory may determine; (2,) from St. Paul and from St. Anthony, *via* Minneapolis, to a convenient point of junction west of the Mississippi, to the southern boundary of the territory in the direction of the mouth of the Big Sioux river, with a branch, *via* Faribault, to the north line of the State of Iowa, west of range sixteen; (3,) from Winona, *via* Saint Peters, to a point on the Big Sioux river, south of the forty-fifth parallel of north latitude; (4,) also from La Crescent, *via* Target Lake, up the valley of Root river to a point of junction with the last mentioned road, east of range seventeen." By the act of July 12th, 1862, the first route mentioned above was slightly modified, and an additional branch granted from said line, (5,) "from between the Falls of St. Anthony and Crow Wing, and extending in a north-easterly direction to Lake Superior."

To the State of Kansas, March 3rd, 1863, (1,) " from the city of Leavenworth, by the way of the town of Lawrence, and *via* the Ohio City crossing of the Osage river, to the southern line of the State, in the direction of Galveston bay, in Texas, with a branch from Lawrence, by the valley of the Wakarusa river, to the point on the Atchison, Topeka and Santa Fé railroad, where said road intersects the Neosho river; (2,) from the city of Atchison, *via* Topeka, the capital of said State, to the western line of the State, in the direction of Fort Union and Santa Fé, New Mexico, with a branch from where this last-named road crosses the Neosho, down said Neosho valley to the point where the said first-named road entered the said Neosho valley."

By the act of July 1st, 1864, another route was granted, "from Emporia, *via* Council Grove, to a point near Fort Riley, on the branch Union Pacific Railroad;" and the grant in the act of 1863, "from Lawrence, by the valley of the Wakarusa river, to a point on the Atchison, Topeka and Santa Fé Railroad where said road intersects the Neosho river, shall be so changed as to run from Lawrence to Emporia."

The great scheme for a railroad to the Pacific ocean was advocated by Mr. Whitney and others, long before such a measure had become practicable by the advancement of civilization; but the agitation of the subject had prepared the public mind for the early adoption of the enterprise, and Congress, March 3rd, 1853, appropriated $150,000 to the Secretary of War, and authorized him "to employ such portion of the corps of topographical engineers, and such other persons as he may deem necessary, to make such explorations and surveys as he may deem advisable, to ascertain the most practicable and economical route for a railroad from the Mississippi river to the Pacific ocean." Further appropriations were made of $190,000 for the same purpose.

Under this act, the Secretary of War organized several corps for the survey of different routes. The northern route, near the 47° of north latitude, was put under the superintendence of Governor Isaac J. Stevens, who passed up the Mississippi on the steamer "Nominee," May 27th, 1853, and immediately commenced operations at St. Paul. Brevet-Captain George B. McClellan (late Major-General) was put in charge of a similar corps at Puget Sound, on the Pacific, to meet Governor Stevens. Similar parties were organized to survey near the 35°, 38°, and 41° parallels of north latitude, while all previous surveys by Colonel Fremont and others, were brought in requisition for the information they contained. The final result of these surveys, with extensive maps, illustrations, and geographical and scientific discoveries, were published in 1861, in thirteen quarto volumes, by government, at a large expense.

The scheme was then taken up by Congress, and, on the 1st day of July, 1862, the act was approved by the President, organizing "The Union Pacific Railroad Company," which was fully "empowered to lay out, locate, construct, furnish, maintain and enjoy a continuous railroad and telegraph, with the appurtenances, from a point on the one hundredth meridian of longitude west from Greenwich, between the south margin of the valley of the Republican river and the north margin of the valley of the Platte river, in the territory of Nebraska, to the western boundary of Nevada territory," with a branch to the mouth of the Kansas river, and another to Omaha. The capital stock was put at 100,000 shares, of $1,000 each, and the company received a grant of five alternate odd numbered sections on each side of the road, and a loan of the bonds of the United States at the rate of $16,000 per mile, which bonds were to constitute the first mortgage on the road.

By the act of July 2nd, 1864, the shares were reduced to $100 each, and the capital stock was put at 1,000,000 shares, and some other changes made in the original charter for the road.

The Union Pacific Railroad Company was duly organized, and the road located and put under contract, and 305 miles were completed west of Omaha, January 1st, 1867, and 517 miles in September, the same year, with a fair prospect of completing the balance to California in 1870; a distance of nearly 1,565 miles to the west line of Nevada, and, adding the California branch, 1,900 miles to the Pacific. The general route from Omaha is up the North Platte river, thence to the Great Salt lake, and, by the way of Humboldt river, to connect with the Central Pacific road in California, which had 150 miles of the western division from Sacramento completed in September, 1867, which had pierced the Sierra Nevada mountains. The Kansas branch, called the eastern division, had about 300 miles completed in September, 1867, and a contract for 95 miles more, to be completed December 31st of the same year. The eastern division is pointing for Denver City, by the Smoky Fork route.

The other roads west of the Mississippi have been making commendable efforts to connect with the Omaha and Kansas branches; and the Chicago and Northwestern Railroad finally reached Council Bluffs, and brought themselves in connection at Omaha, a distance from Chicago of 492 miles, January 22nd, 1867.

The "Northern Pacific Railroad Company" was chartered by Congress, July 2nd, 1864, and were "empowered to lay out, locate, construct, furnish, maintain and enjoy a continuous railroad and telegraph line, with the appurtenances, namely: beginning at a point on Lake Superior, in the State of Minnesota or Wisconsin; thence westerly by the most eligible railroad route, as shall be determined by said company, within the territory of the United States, on a line north of the forty-fifth degree of latitude, to some point on Puget's Sound, with a branch, *via* the valley of the Columbia river, to a point at or near Portland, in the State of Oregon, leaving the main trunk line at the most suitable place, not more than three hundred miles from its western terminus."

The capital stock of the company was put at 1,000,000 of shares, of $100 each, and the company received a grant of twenty of the odd numbered alternate sections per mile on each side of said railroad where it passes through the territories, and only ten sections per mile each side where it passes through States. The company were required to commence the work in two years from the date of the charter, and after the second year build fifty miles a year of the road, and complete the whole by July 4th, 1876.

The following will show the number of miles of railroads in operation at the periods named, in the northwest:

Table of Railroads.

	1850.	1855.	1860.	1867.
Ohio	575	2,453	2,990	
Indiana	228	1,406	2,125	
Illinois	110	887	2,868	
Michigan	342	474	799	919
Wisconsin	20	187	923	1,136
Iowa		68	680	1,136
Missouri			139	817	962
Minnesota				332
Kansas				357
Nebraska				517

By reference to the foregoing table, it will be observed that Iowa and Missouri had no railroads in 1850, and that Minnesota, Kansas and Nebraska had none until after 1860, the most of which were built after the close of the war in 1865. Some progress has been made since 1860 in Ohio, Indiana, and Illinois, but the writer has not the data to put in the table. In 1867, roads were being extended in all the north-western States; but with the greatest rapidity in Minnesota, Kansas, Nebraska, and Iowa, and in a short period of time several routes will be completed to the Pacific ocean.

The magnetic telegraph has been of great importance to the North-west, by bringing this distant region within speaking distance of the Atlantic cities. Although the first line of telegraph was only put in operation between Washington and Baltimore in May, 1844, yet in about four years it had reached Milwaukee, St. Louis, and other prominent cities in the North-west. It was subsequently extended north-west from Milwaukee, and reached La Crosse in October, 1858, and St. Paul, August 29th, 1860. The telegraph has been extended on the line of every railroad, and to all the principal villages in the North-west; and so perfect is its arrangements, that the President's messages reach the extreme boundaries of the American Union in a few minutes after the last words are pronounced at Washington.

By the act of Congress passed June 16th, 1860, the Secretary of the Treasury was authorized to advertise for proposals " for the use by the government of a line or lines of magnetic telegraph, to be constructed within two years from the 31st day of July, 1860, from some point or points on the west line of the State of Missouri to the city of San Francisco, for a period of ten years," and " provided such proffer does not require a larger amount per year from the United States than $40,000." Under this encouragement, the line was completed to San Francisco, October 22nd, 1861.

By the act of July 1st, 1862, the Pacific Telegraph Company, the Overland Telegraph Company, and the California State Telegraph Company, were authorized to make arrangements with the Union Pacific Railroad Company, to remove said telegraph lines on to the route of the said railroad as fast as the road was completed.

By the act of Congress of July 1st, 1864, Perry MacDonough Collins, of California, and his associates, were authorized to construct branches from the line of the Pacific telegraph through any of the territories of the United States to British America. Collins and Company had previously obtained grants from the Russian and British governments to build a telegraph line from the mouth of Amoor river, in Asia, *via* Behring's Straits, to the United States. This enterprise has been prosecuted with great labor and cost, and in December, 1866, eight hundred and fifty miles had been put in operation north of Westminster, British Columbia, and the balance of the material delivered at convenient points to Behring's Straits and the sub-marine cable at Victoria, Vancouver island, when the company suspended operations in January, 1867.

The limits of this work will not allow us to give the various agricultural statistics of the North-west, but we take the liberty to give a table of the productions of wheat and corn, as given by the United States census of 1850 and 1860.

Production of Wheat and Corn in the North-west.

	WHEAT.		CORN.	
	1849.	1859.	1849.	1859.
	Bushels.	Bushels.	Bushels.	Bushels.
Dakota..........		945		20,296
Illinois..........	9,414,575	24,159,500	57,646,984	115,296,779
Indiana.........	6,214,458	15,219,120	52,964,363	69,641,591
Iowa............	1,530,581	8,433,215	8,656,799	41,116,994
Kansas..........		168,527		5,678,834
Michigan........	4,925,889	8,313,185	5,641,420	12,152,110
Minnesota.......	1,401	2,195,812	16,725	2,987,570
Missouri	2,981,652	4,227,586	36,214,537	72,892,157
Nebraska........		72,268		1,846,785
Ohio............	14,487,351	14,532,570	59,078,695	70,637,140
Wisconsin.......	4,286,131	15,812,625	1,988,979	7,565,290
Total	43,832,038	93,134,353	222,208,502	399,935,546

By an examination of the same census reports, it will be observed that all the States and territories in the United States, produced, in 1849: wheat, 100,485,944 bushels, and in 1859, 171,183,381 bushels; of corn, in 1849, 592,071,104 bushels, and in 1859, 830,451,707 bushels.

By comparing these statistics, it will be seen that in 1849 the north-western States and territories of Dakota and Nebraska, produced nearly forty-four per cent. of all the wheat and corn in the United States and territories, and in 1859, nearly sixty per cent. of the wheat, and nearly forty-seven per cent. of the corn.

In the subsequent years the productions of the North-west in wheat and corn has largely increased, notwithstanding the war of the great rebellion; and according to the report of the Commissioner of Agriculture, there were raised in 1864, in the north-western States, including Nebraska territory, 123,128,416 bushels of wheat, and 404,602,276 bushels of corn.

While wheat and corn are regarded as the staple productions, yet the North-west exports a large surplus of rye, barley, oats, whisky, wool, horses, fat cattle, hogs, and other productions of a temperate climate. Some idea of this surplus may be gathered from the tables made up by the Buffalo Board of Trade, from which it appears that there were shipped to an eastern market, from the North-west, in 1860, 4,106,057 barrels of flour, 32,334,391 bushels of wheat, 18,075,778 bushels of corn, and 7,712,032 bushels of *other grain*. This statement does not include Missouri, Kansas, nor Nebraska, nor the shipments sent South. In 1862, and after the commencement of the war, the same authority gives the eastern shipments as 8,359,910 barrels of flour, 50,609,130 bushels of wheat, 32,985,923 bushels of corn, and 10,844,939 bushels of other grain. These amounts of course did not include the large shipments for the support of the vast armies of the Cumberland, the Tennessee, and of the Mississippi.

According to the same authority, there were received in 1862, at Buffalo, from the North-west: 171,552 barrels of pork, 123,301 barrels of beef, 25,687,657 pounds of bacon, 22,471,204 pounds of lard, 113,253 barrels of whisky, 30,410,252 of staves, 125,289,971 feet of lumber, 129,433 cattle, 524,916 hogs, 105,671 sheep, 4,119,173 pounds of butter, 1,313,030 pounds of cheese, 36,812 bushels of flax seed, 268,685 hides, 8,329,811 pounds of iron, 8,535,992 pounds of lead, 2,624,932 bushels of oats, 1,075,650 pounds of oil-cake, 4,363,884 pounds of tallow, 51,278 bushels of timothy seed, 5,047 bushels of clover seed, and vast quantities of other materials. These items do not include large quantities of the surplus productions sent to an eastern market by railroads, and by the Welland canal; but these show that the productions of the North-west are not confined to wheat and corn.

Manufactures are also receiving considerable attention in the North-west. Large quantities of agricultural implements, pig iron, bar and rolled iron, steam engines, stoves, lead, copper, cloths, boots and shoes, and other articles, are being manufactured. Cotton and woolen factories have been established, to a limited extent, in most of the States, and the public attention is waking up to the importance of their increase.

CONCLUSION.

It has been the writer's endeavor, in this work, to collect and present to the reader those leading facts in the history of the North-west, which are necessary to enable the well-informed citizen to speak intelligently on the growth and prosperity of his country, leaving the more detailed account to be gathered from the thousands of original documents. This subject is doubly interesting to the statesman and philosopher, owing to the wonderful rapidity of the settlement of the country after the close of the war of 1812, being unparalleled, it is believed, in the history of the world. It demonstrates, by facts, many of the peculiarities of human nature, and shows, on an extensive scale, the workings of Divine Providence. Its growth has not been an ephemeral growth, for the institutions have been laid on broad and deep foundations, and the superstructure is of imperishable materials. Neither has the work been planned and executed under the compressing power of bigotry, superstition, or the theories of infidelity; but human nature and Christianity have been allowed to expand themselves to their fullest extent, and spread their more generally approved qualities and principles over the primeval soil. Hence common schools and colleges are endowed in perpetuity, religion has been allowed its greatest latitude, suffrage is not even limited to the white race, while agriculture, manufactures, internal improvements, and commerce, have no limitation nor circumscribed bounds.

But the North-west is yet only partially developed. Large

quantities of land still exists in the older States in a state of nature, being owned by speculators; and in the newer States there are vast quantities of land that are yet in the hands of government, awaiting the arrival of emigrants to occupy it. When all this unoccupied land is converted into cultivated fields, it must necessarily contribute largely to the commerce of the country.

The question is here naturally suggested, will this prosperity be perpetual? Will not the North-west become over-jealous of their rights, and reënact the southern rebellion? We reply, that no embryo element of discord and disaffection to the Union has yet shown itself in any part of the country. Of course its great danger will be from the demagogues, common to all free countries, who seek to alarm the people with imaginary dangers, for the purpose of getting themselves elected to office. These imaginary dangers are often the most potent to drive an honest people into a murderous rebellion. Local jealousies are often made the weapons of the demagogues to cajole the people to gratify their ambitious designs. Bigotry in religion, in the old days of superstition, was often made the foundation of rebellion; but the toleration allowed by the constitution of our Union will probably preserve us from any such rebellion while that instrument is suffered to stand. A general system of education has been regarded by many as the most plausible theory to establish a proper political conservatism, but that theory has never been fully successful. Wars will probably always continue so long as our human depravity exists, and no protection has yet been discovered by man, except the arm of the Almighty.

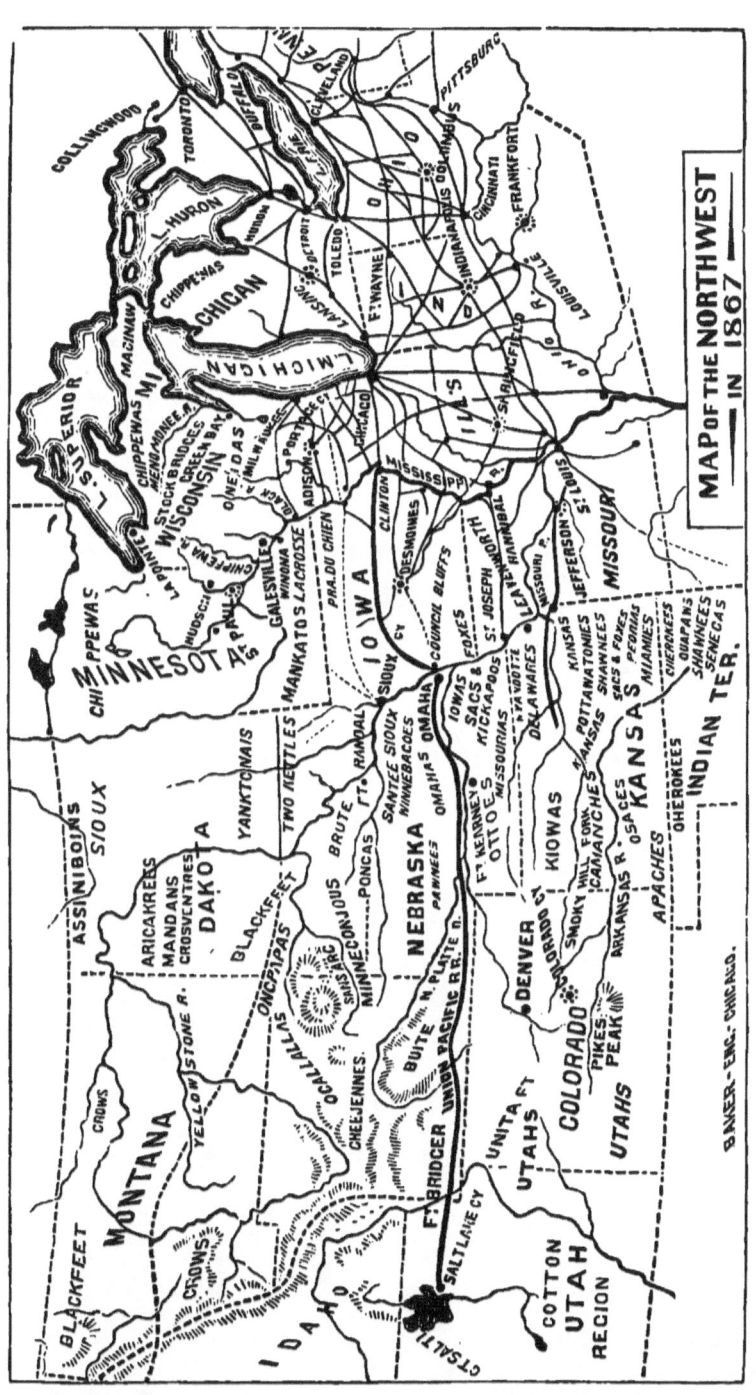

INDEX.

A.

Agricultural productions, 447-448.
Algonquin Confederacy, 42-43.
Allouez, Rev. Claude, 123-125, 131, 344.
Akansea; see Quapaws, 201.
Assiniboins, 59, 224.

B.

Braddock's defeat, 71.
Brebeuf, Rev. John De, 116, 120, 131.
Brandy War, 126-130.
Brunson, Rev. Alfred, 143, 144.
Brothertowns, 170.

C.

Canals, 430.
    Completed in New York, 433.
    "   Pennsylvania, 434.
    "   Maryland, 434.
    "   Ohio, 435.
    "   Indiana, 435.
    "   Illinois, 436.
    "   Michigan, 436.
    "   Wisconsin, 436.
Cayugas; see Iroquois, 159.
Catholic Missions, 114-134, 161, 163, 176, 198, 203, 208, 290, 312.
    Religious bigotry and persecutions, 114.
    First mission in Canada, 115.
    First mission to the Hurons, 115, 116.
    Destroyed by the Iroquois war, 120.
    Mission to Lake Superior, 121, 123, 124.
    Mission to Wisconsin, 123, 124.
    Mission to Illinois, 125, 126, 132.
    List of missionaries, 131, 132.
    Struggles against the sale of brandy, 126, 130.

Champlain's 150 years' war, 43-45.
Chicago, 125, 334, 429, 430.
Chippeways, 265, 290.
    Missions among, 143-145, 149.
Cincinnati organized, 325.
Clarke, Colonel G. R., captures Illinois, 97.
Colorado Territory, 384.
Conclusion, 449.
Corn raised in 1849, 1859, 1864, 447.

D.

Dakotas, 224-264.
Dakotas attacked by the Christinaux, 52.
    War with Sacs and Foxes, 56.
    War with the Chippeways, 59.
    Bands of, in 1867, 226.
Dakota Territory, 384-386.
De Carry, chiefs, 81, 82, 189.
Delawares, 159, 166-169.
    War against the Iroquois, 49, 50.
    Made squaws by treaty, 50.
    Massacre of Christians, 137, 138.
Detroit, 338.
Dickson, Colonel Robert, British Agent, 107.
    Captures Mackinaw, 107
    Arms North-western Indians under Black Hawk, 108.
    Defeats Major Holmes at Mackinaw, 111.
    Sends expedition to Prairie Du Chien, 111.
Dieskaw, Baron De, 72.

E.

Education and schools.
    Ohio, 325.
    Indiana, 328.
    Illinois, 334.
    Michigan, 339.
    Wisconsin, 362-365.
    Missouri, 370, 371.
    Iowa, 372.
    Minnesota, 377, 378.
    Kansas, 381.
    Nebraska, 382.
English attack St. Louis, 368, 369.
Eries, or Kah-kwah, exterminated, 46-49.

F.

Flint Bluffs, 24.
Floods of the Mississippi, 392.
Floods of the Ohio river, 397, 398.
Foxes: see Sacs and Foxes, 291-306.

INDEX.

Fort Chartres, 90, 97, 332, 333.
Fort William Henry Massacre, 76.
French traders, 82.
French and Indian war with English, 68, 79.
    Change of policy with Indians, 68.
    Defeat of General Braddock, 71.
    Defeat of Baron De Dieskaw, 72.
    War declared against England, 73.
    Montcalm captures Fort William Henry, 74, 76.
    Fort Niagara captured by English, 78, 79
    Canada surrendered to English, 79.
    Disasters of the war to the French, 81, 82.
    English alliance with Indians, 79, 80.

G.

Galena and Minnesota Packet Company, 403.
Galesville, 14, 34.
Green Bay, 67, 341, 345-353, 354.

H.

Hennepin, Rev. Father, 224.
Henry Clay, first steamer on Lake Michigan, 429.
Hurons, 159, 164-166.

I.

Illinois, 330-337.
Illinois Confederacy, 172.
Indian Confederacies by languages, 42.
Indian warfare, 112, 113.
Indian tribes in 1866, 315-318.
Indiana, 327-330.
Iowa, 372-373.
Iowas, 199-201.
Iroquois, 159-164.
    War with the French commenced, 43-45.
    War against the Hurons, 44-46.
    War against the Eries, or Kah-kwah, 46.
    War against the Illinois, 49, 53, 54.
    War against the Delawares and Mohegans, 49-50.
    War continued againt the French, 50, 55, 56.
    Treachery of the French, 55.
    Massacre of French at La Chine, 56.
    Treaty of peace in 1700, 57.
    Service in French war, 72, 78.
    Services in the Revolution, 93-98.

J.

Jogues, Rev. Isaac, 119, 120.
Johnson, Sir William, 79.
    Made Indian Agent by English, 79.
    Remonstrates against abuse of Indians, 80.
    Defeats Baron De Dieskaw, 72.
    Captures Fort Niagara, 78.
    Makes peace with Pontiac, 88–90.
    Complains of the pioneers, 91.
    Died in 1774, 93.
Johnson, Guy, appointed Indian Agent, 93.
    Arms the Indians against the Americans, 94.
    Plans the Wyoming massacre, 96.
    His "petite guerre" warfare, 98.
    Defeated by General Sullivan, 97.
Jollyet, 124.

K.

Kansas State, 378, 381.
Kansas, 182, 212–217.
Kaokias, 172, 173.
Kaskaskias, 172, 173, 174.
Kaws: see Kansas, 212.
Kickapoos, 172, 175, 176, 177.
Kieft's, Governor, massacre of Indians, 170.
King Phillips' war, 170.

L.

La Salle, 126, 424.
Lakes, Great, and their navigation, 415.
    Physical character, 415.
    Commerce of the lakes, 416, 421.
    First sail vessel, the "Griffin," 423.
    Steam navigation, 426.
La Crosse, 15.
Lappam, LL.D., Increase A., 15.
La Point, 345.
Langlade, Lieutenant Charles De, 82, 97.
Lead discoveries, 356, 357.
Lenapees: see Delawares, 166.
Little Turtle's Confederacy, 98.
    A scheme of the British, 98.
    They defeat General St. Clair, 99.
    Are defeated by General Wayne, 101.
    Conclude a peace with United States, 102, 105.
Logan's revenge and speech, 92, 93.

M.

Mackinaw Island, 46, 124, 337, 421.
Mandans, 182, 221-223.
Marquette, James, 123-125, 131.
Mascotens, 172, 175, 176.
Marietta settled, 325.
Ménard, Rev. Rene, 121, 122, 165, 343.
Methodists, 139.
Menominies, 182, 194—199, 171.
Miamies, 172, 175, 176, 177.
Michigamias, 172, 173.
Michigan, 337-340.
Milwaukee, 359, 361.
Milwaukee wheat shipments, 432.
Minnesota, 373-378.
Missourias, 182, 209-212.
Missions, 114, 135.
Missouri, 367-371.
Missouri Compromise, 370, 380.
Mississippi and its navigation, 388.
    First discovery of the river, 388-391.
    Origin of its name, 391.
    Physical character, 392-394.
    Floods of the river, 394-396.
    Ohio river, 396-398.
    Missouri river, 398-399.
    Navigation of the river, 399, 400.
    Steam navigation, 400-408.
    Mississippi valley, 409-411.
    Navigation of the river free, 411, 413.
    Navigation to be improved, 413, 414.
Missions to Indians, 114.
Mohawks: see Iroquois, 159.
    Mohegans, 159, 169-171.
Morand, Captain, 66, 67.
Montana Territory, 386-387.
Mound-Builders, 11-40.
    Extent of Territory, 12.
    Intellectual capacity, 13.
    Population and extent of works, 14-18.
    Agriculture and Commerce, 17-20.
    Manufactures and Science, 21-24.
    Religion, 21-31.
    Effigies of animals, 31-35.
    Speculations of Dr. Morton, 36.
    Traditions of Indians, 37.
    Concluding speculations, 39-40.
Munsees, 171.
Musquakies: see Sacs and Foxes, 291.

N.

Nadouessioux: see Dakota, 224.
Nebraska, 381-383.
Newspapers in States, 326, 330, 337, 340, 365, 366, 371, 372, 378, 381.
Niagara captured, 78, 79.
Nicolet, Sieur Jean, 182, 184, 389.
Nicolet and Fremont, 392, 398.
Noquets, 194.
Nomenee packet, 404.
North-western Packet Company, 405.
North-western Union Packet Company, 407.

O.

O-chunk-o-raws: see Winnebagoes, 182.
Ohio, 319-327.
Ojibway Confederacy, 265-290.
Omahas, 182, 217-219.
Ongwe-honwe: see Iroquois, 159.
Oneidas: see Iroquois, 159, 162.
Onondagas: see Iroquois, 159.
Osages, 182, 203-208.
Ottoes, 182, 209-212.
Outagamies: see Sacs and Foxes, 291.

P.

Peorias, 172, 173, 174.
Pequod war, 170.
Pontiac war, 85-90.
Pontiac assassinated, 90.
Poncas, 182, 219-221.
Population of Indian Tribes in 1866, 315-318.
Population of States, 325, 329, 333, 340, 362, 371, 372, 377, 387, 329.
Potowatomies, 306-314.
Prairie Du Chien, 111, 20, 346-352.
Propeller "Hercules" built, 429.
Propellers in Milwaukee lines, 431, 432.
Protestant missions, 135-158.
    Eliot, of Massachusetts, 135.
    Brainard, 136.
    Moravian, 136-138.
    Methodist, 139-149, 162, 163, 171, 180, 288, 306.
    Friends, 180, 216.
    American Board, 149-151, 163, 253, 263, 289.
    Presbyterian Board, 151, 211, 218.
    Cumberland Presbyterian, 151.
    American Baptist, 152, 153, 163, 169, 178, 313.
    Protestant Episcopal, 153, 263.
    American M. Association, 153.
    Struggles against whisky-sellers, 154-158.

INDEX.

Q.

Quapaws, 201-203.

R.

Railroads, 436.
    Land grants to, by Congress, 436-441.
    Pacific Railroad, survey of, 441-442.
    Union Pacific Railroad Company organized, 442, 443.
    Northern Pacific Railroad Company chartered, 443-444.
    Miles completed in North-west, 444.

S.

Sacs and Foxes, 291-306.
    War against the Sioux, 56.
    Massacre by the French at Detroit, 57-63.
    Make peace with the Sioux, 59.
    War against the Chippeways, 59.
    War of the French against, 63-67.
Saulteurs: see Ojibways, 265.
Senecas: see Iroquois, 159, 166.
Shawnees, 178, 179, 180.
    Attacked by the Iroquois, 49.
    Settle near the Iroquois, 168.
Shipping on the lakes in 1858, 1860, 1862, 430.
Shipping built in 1864, 431.
Shipping of Milwaukee in 1862, 1863, 432.
Sioux: see Dakota, 224-264.
Sioux massacre, 245-260.
Steamers on upper lakes to 1843, 427.
St. Clair, General Arthur, 99-101.
St. Louis settled, 368.
    St. Regis, 161.
St. Tammany, 167.
Stockbridges, 170.
St. Paul, 373, 374, 408.

T.

Tamarois, 172.
Tecumseh and the Prophet, 106.
    Make a new religion, 106.
    Are defeated at Tippecanoe, 106, 107.
    Tecumseh killed, 108.
    Indians sue for peace, 108.
Telegraph, 445, 446.
Tonnage of the upper lakes, 429.
Tuscaroras, 159, 160.

W.

Walk-in-the-Water, first steamer on lake, 427.
Wa-saw-sees: see Osages, 203.
Wheat, amount raised in 1849-1864, 447.
Whisky war, 154, 158.
Williams, Rev. Eleazer, 162.
Winnebagoes, 182-193.
Wisconsin, 341-366.
Wyandots: see Hurons, 164-166.
Wyoming massacre, 96.

www.ingramcontent.com/pod-product-compliance
Lightning Source LLC
Chambersburg PA
CBHW031958300426
44117CB00008B/815